The Spotsylvania Campaign

The
SPOTSYLVANIA

MILITARY CAMPAIGNS

OF THE CIVIL WAR

The University of North Carolina Press

Chapel Hill & London

Edited by Gary W. Gallagher

CAMPAIGN

© 1998
The University of North Carolina Press
All rights reserved
Set in Minion type by
Tseng Information Systems, Inc.
Manufactured in the United States of America
The paper in this book meets the guidelines for
permanence and durability of the Committee on
Production Guidelines for Book Longevity of the
Council on Library Resources.
Library of Congress
Cataloging-in-Publication Data
The Spotsylvania campaign / edited by Gary W.
Gallagher.
    p.   cm. — (Military campaigns of the Civil
War)
Includes bibliographical references and index.
ISBN 0-8078-2402-X (alk. paper)
1. Spotsylvania Court House, Battle of, Va., 1864.
I. Gallagher, Gary W.   II. Series.
E476.52.S66   1998
973.7′36 — dc21   97-36876
                        CIP
02   01   00   99   98   5   4   3   2   1

For MATTHEW HODGSON,

friend and mentor

Contents

Introduction

The battles of Spotsylvania formed the second phase of the memorable campaign that had commenced when Ulysses S. Grant and Robert E. Lee first took each other's measure in fighting at the Wilderness on May 5–6, 1864. For two weeks in mid-May, the most famous armies of the Union and Confederate republics maneuvered and fought around the hamlet of Spotsylvania Court House, shedding blood in prodigious quantity as their commanders sought to gain tactical and strategic advantage. Moments of exhilarating success and brutal failure marked each side's efforts. The Army of Northern Virginia twice avoided apparent disaster — initially on May 8 when it seemed the Federal army might reach the Court House first and thus control the direct route to Richmond, and again when a spectacular northern attack on May 12 shattered the Confederate center. Lee's soldiers survived this pair of crises and repelled a number of other Federal assaults, the last of which took place on May 18. Union infantrymen at Spotsylvania learned a bitter lesson about the power of defenders sheltered by formidable field entrenchments, and soldiers on both sides realized that henceforth the spade incontrovertibly would rival the musket and the cannon as critical variables on all their battlefields.

As at the Wilderness, neither army could claim a tactical victory at Spotsylvania. More than 18,000 Federals and 12,000 Confederates had been killed, wounded, or captured in the course of reaching this impasse on the blasted landscape surrounding Spotsylvania Court House.[1] Grant resumed his southward movement on May 21, thereby maintaining strategic momentum and forcing Lee into the unaccustomed position of reacting rather than dictating the action. The ensuing three weeks witnessed fighting along the North Anna River, at Cold Harbor, and in front of Petersburg. Skirmishing preceded and followed each of the larger clashes in this gigantic operation, and soon the entire campaign from Grant's crossing of the Rapidan River in early May through his investment of Petersburg in mid-June took on the character of a single, seamless, and enormously costly confrontation. In a letter to his wife, Julia, on May 13, for example, Grant fused action in the Wilderness and at Spotsylvania in reporting that the "ninth day of battle is just closing with victory so far on our side." The Union general-in-chief suggested that the "world has never seen so bloody or so protracted a battle as the one being fought and I hope never will again."[2] Observers behind the lines — as well as many participants — often struggled to determine who had won and lost on each battlefield. Because they tended to blend together and defied easy categorization as victories or defeats, the Wilderness and Spotsylvania were not seared into the popular consciousness as discrete events in the way Antietam, Chancellorsville, Gettysburg, and other battles had been earlier in the conflict.

One or two striking episodes typically defined popular understanding of Spotsylvania and other individual battles of the Overland campaign. Although the armies of Grant and Lee maneuvered and fought near Spotsylvania for a fortnight, this period often has been distilled into a few images associated with the struggle for several hundred yards of Confederate earthworks at the "Bloody Angle" on May 12, 1864. Winfield Scott Hancock's massive Union assault against the Confederate "Mule Shoe" salient that day gained temporary success, after which a series of determined counterattacks pushed the Federals back across the works they had captured. Subsequent fighting along those works, especially at the point later known as the Bloody Angle, continued for hours and impressed even hardened veterans as uniquely hellish.

Contemporary newspaper reporters seized on the gruesome action at the Bloody Angle as their focal point. Writing for the *New York Times*, William Swinton claimed that "[n]othing during the war has equaled the savage desperation of this struggle. . . . The angle of the works at which Hancock entered, and for the possession of which the savage fight of the day was made, is a perfect Golgotha. . . . The one exclamation of every man who looks on the spectacle is, 'God forbid that I should ever gaze upon such a sight again.'" Confederate correspondent Peter W. Alexander, who had covered important military events in both the Eastern and Western theaters, similarly wrote: "The battle was soon fully joined, and for nine hours it roared and hissed and dashed over the bloody angle and along the bristling entrenchments like an angry sea beating and chafing against a rock bound coast." The artillery fire at the angle, added the experienced Alexander, "was the most sustained and continuous I have ever heard for so long a time."[3]

Richmond bureaucrat John B. Jones, whose diary provides many insights into how Confederate civilians interpreted news from the military fronts, also singled out the action on May 12 along the northern arc of the Mule Shoe as the only element of the operations at Spotsylvania worthy of extensive comment. On May 14, Jones recorded word of "a most terrific battle in Spottsylvania County day before yesterday. . . . Our men (with extra muskets) fought behind their breastworks." Unwilling to concede gallantry to the enemy, the rebel diarist attributed the steadfastness of northern attackers to liquor: "The host of assailants came on, stimulated by whiskey rations, ten deep, and fearful was the slaughter." Jones estimated that 20,000 northern soldiers had fallen on the

12th, yet the enemy had not retreated. "Grant says he will not recross the Rappahannock as long as he has a man left," concluded Jones, adding defiantly that "Lee seems determined to kill his last man."[4]

Most modern readers almost certainly would echo these earlier writers in pointing to the contest for the Bloody Angle as the key to understanding military operations around Spotsylvania. Fortunately, they have at hand two superior studies that give the rest of the campaign full attention. William D. Matter's well-researched *If It Takes All Summer: The Battle of Spotsylvania* offers an excellent tactical treatment in one volume. Gordon C. Rhea, whose earlier work includes the best monograph on the battle of the Wilderness, has completed the first of a projected two-volume study of Spotsylvania. Based on extensive research in unpublished materials and titled *The Battles for Spotsylvania Court House and the Road to Yellow Tavern: May 7–12, 1864*, it carries the tactical story through the fight for the Mule Shoe.[5]

The essays in this volume are not intended to provide a full narrative of the military action at Spotsylvania. Their authors approach the campaign from a variety of perspectives, exploring questions relating to high command, tactics and strategy, the impact of the fighting on officers and soldiers in both armies, and the ways in which some of the participants chose to remember and interpret the battle. As a group, the authors consulted previously untapped sources and reinterpreted more familiar ones, sometimes focusing closely on Spotsylvania and sometimes using it as a point of departure from which to consider broader issues.

The opening essay evaluates Robert E. Lee's handling of problems relating to corps-level command in his army during the middle of May 1864. No period in the history of the Army of Northern Virginia presented Lee with more challenges of this type. In the two weeks beginning on May 6, James Longstreet received a debilitating wound, A. P. Hill collapsed physically, and Richard S. Ewell performed in a manner Lee deemed utterly unacceptable. The Confederate commander found himself in the position of fending off Grant's powerful offensive blows at Spotsylvania while also struggling to ensure competent leadership in his army's three infantry corps. The essay argues that Lee's response to this crisis not only reveals his superior skills as an administrator and judge of men, but also that it contradicts common assumptions that Lee gave top subordinates too much leeway on the battlefield and was too much of a gentleman to make hard decisions concerning personnel.

William D. Matter shifts attention to the Federal high command in the second essay. He considers some of the difficulties that grew out of an awkward arrangement by which Ambrose E. Burnside, who headed the Ninth Corps and held rank senior to Army of the Potomac commander George G. Meade, received orders directly from Grant. Tensions between Meade and Cavalry Corps chief Philip H. Sheridan, a below par performance by Winfield Scott Hancock, and Horatio G. Wright's difficult initiation into Sixth Corps leadership after John Sedgwick was killed on May 9 also figure in Matter's analysis. Throughout the middle of May, Grant assumed increasing control of Federal tactical decisions, relegating Meade and Burnside to decidedly secondary roles. Matter credits Grant with steadfastly retaining the initiative as he continued his army's southward movement after Spotsylvania, but he emphasizes that confusion, poor decisions, and lost opportunities plagued Union leadership at Spotsylvania.

Among the North's top generals at Spotsylvania, Fifth Corps chief Gouverneur Kemble Warren's performance raised the most troubling doubts. A brilliant officer who had been one of the Union heroes at Gettysburg, Warren displayed in mid-May characteristics that earlier had caused concern in the Wilderness. Gordon C. Rhea's essay portrays Warren as consistently out of step with his superior officers, holding back when they wanted aggressive leadership and rashly attacking when restraint better suited their plans. Perhaps most damaging, Warren seemed incapable of executing orders without first seeking to adjust them to suit his own tactical ideas, behavior that alienated both Meade and Grant. Deliberate, headstrong, and lacking the offensive spirit preferred by Grant, the New Yorker contributed almost nothing positive to the northern effort at Spotsylvania. In light of behavior such as that he exhibited at the Wilderness and Spotsylvania, suggests Rhea, Warren's eventual removal from corps command at Five Forks should come as no surprise. The interesting question is why superiors tolerated him for so long.

Robert K. Krick undertakes in the fourth essay to add something new to the enormous existing literature on the fight for the Bloody Angle. His account of the Confederate response to Hancock's assault on May 12 and the resulting day-long struggle along the northwest corner of the Mule Shoe proves that diligent research can uncover a range of fresh material about even intensively studied topics. Krick's meticulous weighing of often conflicting sources yields the most detailed and persuasive account to date of this famous episode — and shows as well why almost any historical event can benefit from the attention of a careful historian willing to dig deep for evidence.

As Robert E. Lee strove to compensate for the loss of James Longstreet and the failures of A. P. Hill and Richard S. Ewell, he received the bitter news that "Jeb" Stuart had been mortally wounded on May 11 at Yellow Tavern. In the fifth essay, Robert E. L. Krick examines the Confederate cavalry commander's reaction to Philip Sheridan's raid against Richmond, the battle of Yellow Tavern and subsequent skirmishes associated with the raid, and the effect this action had on the larger campaign. He notes that fighting between Union and Confederate horsemen in mid-May 1864 underscored how dramatically cavalry tactics had changed since the beginning of the war. Mounted charges almost always failed, most of the action occurred between troopers fighting on foot, and artillery played a much larger supporting role. Krick acknowledges Stuart's death as a major blow to Lee, but adds that it had no long-term deleterious effect on the southern cavalry's efficiency because Wade Hampton maintained a high degree of competency in the mounted arm. Hampton's availability to step in as a successful replacement for Stuart stood in sharp contrast to the paucity of capable officers at hand to fill the top positions in Lee's three infantry corps.

The unremitting quality of fighting during the Overland campaign introduced soldiers in both armies to new patterns of psychological and physical stress. Carol Reardon's essay uses the concept of "military effectiveness" to search for insights into how men performed under such conditions. Employing a comparative framework, Reardon explores such factors as quality of leadership, weather, personal hygiene, infusion of replacement troops, lack of sleep, construction of earthworks, and the nature of combat that ranged from all-out assaults to sniping and skirmishing. She finds remarkable resiliency within the ranks of both armies as soldiers came to terms with changing styles of warfare. In the context of May 1864, however, she concludes that the Army of Northern Virginia maintained a somewhat higher degree of military effectiveness than the Army of the Potomac.

The 15th New Jersey Infantry suffered the second highest percentage of casualties among Union regiments at Spotsylvania. An assault against Confederates at the Bloody Angle on May 12 proved especially devastating, claiming more than 50 percent of the attacking Jerseymen. In the seventh essay, Peter S. Carmichael discusses this regiment's role at Spotsylvania, the ways its members reacted to their awful trial, and efforts early in the twentieth century to commemorate their service. Time inevitably wrought major changes in the men's attitudes about their experience at Spotsylvania. In 1864, many soldiers in the 15th questioned their leaders, expressed hatred for their Confederate foes, and lamented their inability to give dead comrades proper burials. In dedicating a monument opposite the Bloody Angle in 1909, they dwelled on their manly courage in 1864, the need for future generations to learn lessons of patriotic sacrifice from the 15th's example, and the fact that all who fought — on either side — on May 12 had been brave Americans. Veterans at the dedication hoped to shape future understanding of what had transpired at Spotsylvania — to help ensure that all who saw their monument and walked the fields around the Bloody Angle would remember that northern and southern soldiers alike had exemplified a type of American manhood that made the nation great.

William A. Blair's concluding essay demonstrates that Ulysses S. Grant also labored diligently to influence the historical memory of his role in the war. Concentrating on the general's published memoirs, Blair challenges the notion that they avoided the bias so evident in most Civil War military reminiscences. By the time Grant wrote in the mid-1880s, former Confederates had mounted an extensive campaign to cast him as a commander of limited skill whose generalship amounted to nothing more than pouring in northern manpower to overwhelm southern resistance. These Lost Cause partisans, who used the Overland campaign as the centerpiece of their critique, labeled the Union hero a "butcher" whose talents paled in comparison to Lee's. Grant responded through the writings of his former military secretary Adam Badeau, in a newspaper interview he knew would gain wide circulation, and finally in his own *Personal Memoirs*. In each case, he denied Lee's brilliance and overestimated Confederate strength during the Overland campaign to make the point that northern numbers alone had not guaranteed Union victory. *Personal Memoirs* received generally laudatory reviews that masked Grant's sometimes questionable use of evidence and overlooked his deft special pleading, and most later critics, both historical and literary, wrote enthusiastically about Grant's achievement as an author. The memoirs deserve their high place in Civil War literature, concludes Blair, but an appreciation of their flaws enhances understanding of both Grant and the circumstances under which he wrote his famous personal account.

Readers of previous titles in the Military Campaigns of the Civil War series will recognize that this book completes a four-volume cycle devoted to the major battles waged in and around Fredericksburg, Virginia. Future titles will move away from the Rappahannock-Rapidan river lines to explore other campaigns that should offer essayists equally fruitful subjects.

The annual task of preparing books for publication in this series rarely has become burdensome. The reason lies in the professional and cooperative spirit exhibited by scholars such as Bill Blair, Pete Carmichael, Bob Krick, Robert E. L. Krick, Bill Matter, Carol Reardon, and Gordon Rhea. The expert cartographic work of George Skoch, which invariably arrives before its deadline, also eases editorial burdens. I cheerfully express my debt to all these friends. I acknowledge as well support from the College of the Liberal Arts at Penn State University, which assisted with the preparation of maps and illustrations.

NOTES
1. Until fairly recently, writers typically placed Lee's casualties at about 7,500 and Grant's at about 17,500. Researchers using a variety of sources, including manuscript records in the

National Archives and reports in Civil War newspapers, have raised the estimates to a minimum of 12,000 for Lee and 18,400 for Grant. See Noah Andre Trudeau, *Bloody Roads South: The Wilderness to Cold Harbor, May–June 1864* (Boston: Little, Brown, 1989), 213, 341.

2. Ulysses S. Grant, *The Papers of Ulysses S. Grant*, ed. John Y. Simon, 20 vols. to date (Carbondale: Southern Illinois University Press, 1967–), 10:443–44.

3. J. Cutler Andrews, *The North Reports the Civil War* (Pittsburgh: University of Pittsburgh Press, 1955), 538–39 (quoting the *New York Times* of May 18, 1864); J. Cutler Andrews, *The South Reports the Civil War* (Princeton, N.J.: Princeton University Press, 1970), 394 (quoting the Richmond *Daily Dispatch* of May 16, 18, 1864). Andrews's treatment of Spotsylvania's coverage in the North and the South underscores the centrality of the fighting at the Bloody Angle.

4. J. B. Jones, *A Rebel War Clerk's Diary at the Confederate States Capital*, 2 vols. (1866; reprint, Alexandria, Va.: Time-Life, 1982), 2:210.

5. Matter's book was published by the University of North Carolina Press in 1989, Rhea's by Louisiana State University Press in 1997. Rhea's *The Battle of the Wilderness: May 5–6, 1864*, also published by Louisiana State University Press, appeared in 1994.

The Spotsylvania Campaign

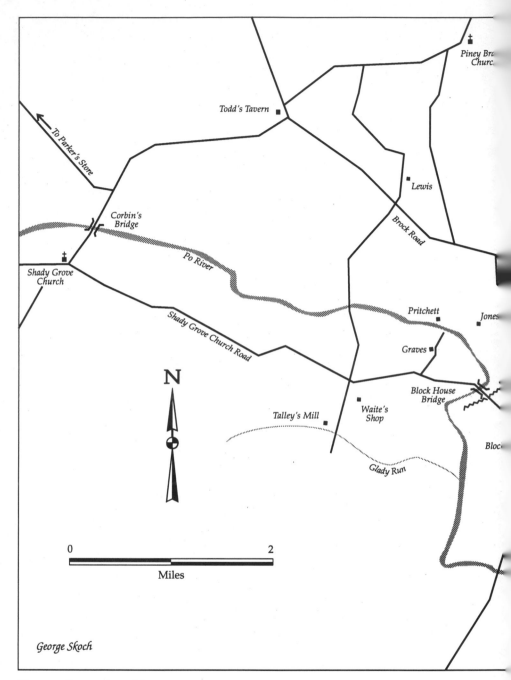

To Parker's Store

Todd's Tavern ■

Piney Br
Churc †

Lewis ■

Corbin's
Bridge

Brock Road

Po River

Shady Grove
Church †

Shady Grove Church Road

Pritchett ■

Jones

Graves ■

Block House
Bridge

N

Talley's Mill ■

Waite's
Shop ■

Bloc

Glady Run

0   2
Miles

George Skoch

Theater of operations, May 1864

I Have to Make the Best of What I Have
Robert E. Lee at Spotsylvania

The Spotsylvania campaign marked a crossroads for Robert E. Lee in his handling of senior subordinates in the Army of Northern Virginia. From an ominous beginning on May 8, when Third Corps chief A. P. Hill collapsed physically, to a disappointing coda at the Harris farm on May 19, when Richard S. Ewell waged an ineffective fight with his battered Second Corps, Lee confronted problems that taxed his abilities as both military administrator and combat leader. Consummate skill as a field commander enabled him to juggle personnel while staving off U. S. Grant's powerful offensive blows, but only at the cost of taking an increasing burden on his already overtaxed shoulders. As the armies marched southward from Spotsylvania on May 21, Lee knew he lacked corps commanders on whom he could rely with the confidence he once had exhibited in "Stonewall" Jackson and James Longstreet.

Lee's actions at Spotsylvania shed considerable light on his style of generalship. He possessed unusual gifts as a military politician, an attribute much in evidence as he addressed crises arising at the level of corps leadership. His behavior at Spotsylvania and in its immediate aftermath also offers a revealing test of two commonly held assumptions about his generalship. Was he too much of a gentleman to make hard decisions concerning personnel? And did he follow a hands-off style in directing corps commanders that sometimes compromised his strategic and tactical plans?

Lee's conduct of the Overland campaign has generated a good deal of analysis. Most historians have praised his broad management of the operations, including his effort at Spotsylvania.[1] It is beyond the scope of this essay to critique Lee's tactical and strategic decisions at Spotsylvania, but a few words about his handling of the "Mule Shoe" salient in Ewell's sector of the battlefield are in order because it was controversial and illuminates a key element of his leadership. A pair of questions arise from any consideration of Lee and the Mule Shoe. First, why did he allow the hastily drawn line to remain in such a vulnerable configuration? And second, aware that artillery would provide firepower essential to defending the salient, why did he order southern guns to be withdrawn on the night of May 11?

Edward Porter Alexander, whose perceptive critiques of Lee's campaigns are without equal among writings by participants, commented after the war about the Mule Shoe. "[B]y all the rules of military science," wrote Alexander, "we must pronounce these lines a great mistake although they were consented to, if they were not adopted by Gen. Lee's chief engineer Gen. M. L. Smith, who was a West Pointer & an ex-officer of the U.S. Engineers . . . & recently distinguished in the defence of Vicksburg." Lee probably accepted Smith's opinion that the salient could be defended if Ewell deployed his infantry behind well-prepared breastworks and supported it by adequate artillery. But Jedediah Hotchkiss later suggested that Lee, although acquiescing in the placement of the works, harbored significant doubts: "On the morning of [May] the 9th, Lee rode along the line that had been occupied, but was not favorably impressed with it." [2]

Lee's misgivings loom larger when considering his orders to withdraw artillery from the salient on the night of May 11. At 4:30 P.M. on that day, W. H. F. "Rooney" Lee, the commander's son and a major general of cavalry, reported a worrisome Federal march. "There is evidently a general move going on," stated the young cavalryman. "Their trains are moving down the Fredericksburg road, and their columns are in motion." Lee inferred from his son's information that Grant might be shifting away from Spotsylvania. If placed somewhere outside the wooded salient, he reasoned, the guns supporting Ewell's infantry could be moved rapidly toward the next point of danger. Winfield Scott Hancock's massive assault against the northern curve of the salient on the morning of May 12 succeeded in part because Confederate infantry fought without supporting artillery.[3]

Lee willingly took full responsibility for the consequences of his decisions concerning the Mule Shoe. Whatever his private thoughts about culpability, he publicly trained the spotlight directly on himself. William W. Old, a member of Edward "Allegheny" Johnson's staff who witnessed the debacle in the salient, recounted a discussion between Lee and Ewell on this point: "After the

General Robert E. Lee.
This portrait—an engraving
based on a photograph by Minnis and
Cowell—reached a wide audience
shortly after the battles at Spotsyl-
vania Court House, appearing in *The
Illustrated London News* on June 4,
1864, and in *Harper's Weekly* on
July 2, 1864.
Harper's Weekly, July 2, 1864

disaster of the 12th," wrote Old, "General Lee said to General Ewell, in my presence, that he had been misled in regard to the enemy in our front, by his scouts,
and that the fatal mistake was in removing the artillery on our line." The army
commander also approved an official report from William Nelson Pendleton,
his chief of artillery, that attributed to Lee the decision to remove the artillery
and alluded to "the unfortunate withdrawal of our guns" as a principal cause
of the Union breakthrough.[4] Lee's unhesitating assumption of responsibility
for events in the Mule Shoe graphically underscored his habit of leading by example—an element of his generalship that promoted trust and loyalty among
his subordinates.

May 1864 brought the third great watershed in the development of the Army
of Northern Virginia's high command. The first had come in the wake of the

Seven Days, when Lee reorganized the army into right and left wings commanded by Longstreet and Jackson, respectively. During this period, division commanders Theophilus H. Holmes, Benjamin Huger, W. H. C. Whiting, and John Bankhead Magruder — all of whom had been Longstreet's and Jackson's peers — left the eastern army. When Congress approved the grade of lieutenant general in the fall of 1862, Longstreet and Jackson were promoted to that rank and their commands designated the First and Second Corps. The structure that divided the army's strength between Longstreet and Jackson functioned effectively for nearly a year, a period that witnessed a string of notable victories from Second Manassas through Chancellorsville. During this period, Lee granted wide discretion to Longstreet and Jackson — the only practical arrangement by which the commander of a large army distributed over a wide area could exercise effective control — and the practice yielded excellent results.

Jackson's death in early May 1863 prompted Lee to reorganize a second time, reducing the size of the two existing corps and creating a new Third Corps. Longstreet retained the First Corps, Richard S. Ewell succeeded Jackson in command of the revamped Second, and A. P. Hill took charge of the Third. The triumvirate of Longstreet, Ewell, and Hill served as Lee's corps commanders for roughly a year, from the Gettysburg campaign through the battle of the Wilderness. Lee initially employed the same method of dealing with his corps leaders under this organization that he had used with Longstreet and Jackson, but episodes at Gettysburg and during the autumn of 1863 raised doubts in his mind about Ewell's and Hill's competence in their new positions.[5]

Events on May 6–7, 1864, triggered a third major reshuffling and inaugurated eleven months of relative flux among Lee's corps commanders.[6] Lee had begun the Overland campaign with problems at the corps level that reached crisis stage on the eve of fighting at Spotsylvania. The first harsh blow came at the battle of the Wilderness on May 6 when James Longstreet suffered a crippling wound while riding along the Plank Road. Although Longstreet had sulked at Gettysburg and failed ignominiously as an independent commander in East Tennessee during the fall and winter of 1863–64, his return with the First Corps to the Army of Northern Virginia in the spring of 1864 undoubtedly had cheered Lee. Justifiable concern that Longstreet's pouting behavior at Gettysburg might reappear probably gave way to relief at having his proven lieutenant back. Walter Taylor of Lee's staff likely mirrored his chief's feelings when he wrote in late April, "A portion of *our family* has been returned to us. Old Pete Longstreet is with us and all seems propitious." Longstreet's superior performance in blunting Hancock's assaults on the morning of the 6th and then mounting a telling counterattack highlighted his value to Lee. Upon hearing that his "Old War Horse" had been wounded, Lee manifested visible distress. Francis W. Dawson of Longstreet's staff described "the sadness in [Lee's] face, and the almost despairing movement of his hands, when he was told that Longstreet had fallen."[7]

Longstreet's loss proved doubly pernicious because both A. P. Hill and Richard S. Ewell had fallen short of Lee's expectations. Hill had been the obvious choice for promotion to lieutenant general after Jackson's death. Long the head of the Light Division, which counted as many bayonets in its ranks as most Federal infantry corps, Hill had earned Lee's respect in the summer and fall of 1862. Lee had confided to Jefferson Davis in October 1862 that except for Jackson and Longstreet, "I consider A. P. Hill the best commander with me. He fights troops well, and takes good care of them." Ten days after Jackson's death, Lee reiterated his belief that Hill, "upon the whole, is the best soldier of his grade with me" and recommended his advancement to command the new Third Corps.[8]

Unfortunately for Lee, Hill never equaled at the corps level his previous record. On July 1 at Gettysburg, he allowed Henry Heth to stumble into battle with one Third Corps division (though Hill scrupulously kept Lee informed of his actions that day), then nearly disappeared during the next two tumultuous days of fighting. Lee's decision on July 3 to give Longstreet control over thousands of Hill's soldiers for the Pickett-Pettigrew assault implied a lack of confidence in Hill as well as demonstrating an awareness that "Little Powell" was suffering one of his numerous bouts of illness.[9] Lee's confidence almost certainly eroded further after the fiasco in October 1863 at Bristoe Station, where Hill rashly launched unsupported and costly assaults. Following the battle, Hill and Lee shared a tense ride over the field. According to Jedediah Hotchkiss, "Lee met Hill with stern rebuke for his imprudence, then sadly directed him to gather his wounded and bury his dead." Armistead L. Long of Lee's staff recalled that Hill, "mortified by his mishap, endeavored to explain the causes of his failure." Lee rode along in silence before answering "with sad gravity": "Well, well, general, bury these poor men and let us say no more about it."[10]

The battle of the Wilderness brought scant evidence that Hill had grown as a corps commander. Following heavy fighting on May 5, he chose to leave the divisions of Henry Heth and Cadmus M. Wilcox in vulnerable disarray astride the Orange Plank Road. Hill had been informed that James Longstreet's divisions would relieve his corps about 1:00 A.M. on May 6 and elected to permit his tired men a night's rest rather than have them entrench. Federal attacks just after daylight on the 6th smashed the two divisions and threatened to divide Lee's army. Longstreet's soldiers arrived literally at the decisive moment to stave off disaster.

Both of Hill's division leaders wrote about the uneasy night of May 5–6.

Heth claimed in his memoirs that he repeatedly requested Hill's permission to straighten his lines and dig in, provoking his superior, who once again had fallen ill, at length to lose his temper: "D[amn] it Heth, I don't want to hear any more about it; the men shall not be disturbed." Heth also stated that he and Wilcox went together to Hill's headquarters, although nothing from the latter's pen confirmed such a joint visit. Wilcox's official wartime account did note that he "reported to the Lieut. Gen. commanding and gave him a resume of affairs, and was informed that the Division would be relieved at day break by Gen. Longstreet's troops." After the war, Wilcox described seeking out Lee that night to express concern about the condition of his lines. Before the division chief could explain the reason for his visit to army headquarters, Lee told him that Longstreet's corps and Richard H. Anderson's division of Hill's corps were nearby, and that "the two divisions that have been so actively engaged will be relieved before day." In light of Lee's comments, Wilcox ventured no suggestion about improving his division's position. But his postwar comments included the observation that "failure to rearrange his line" contributed to the calamitous Confederate rout on the morning of May 6. A correspondent for the London *Herald*, whose account appeared shortly after the battle, confirmed that Lee's assurances had not laid to rest Wilcox's doubts. According to this journalist, a still uneasy Wilcox "looked anxiously throughout the night for the coming of the divisions of Anderson and Field, and disappointed in the delay of their arrival, began at daybreak to cover his front by an abatis of felled trees."[11]

Most historians have accepted Heth's especially damning testimony as evidence that Hill erred in taking no precautions during the night of May 5–6. Whatever his division commanders and Lee thought, these scholars have argued, normal vigilance dictated that Hill prepare for the possibility that Longstreet might reach the field later than anticipated. A few historians have defended Hill by placing responsibility either above or below him in the chain of command.[12]

What did Lee think? A message to the secretary of war dated 8:00 P.M. on May 6 employed the blandest of language: "Early this morning as the divisions of General Hill, engaged yesterday, were being relieved, the enemy advanced and created some confusion." Elsewhere, Lee's wartime correspondence is silent on the subject; however, in postwar conversations with William Preston Johnston, who had served during the war as an aide-de-camp to Jefferson Davis, Lee implicitly criticized Hill. He observed that when Hancock attacked, Hill's "men received a blow that injured their morale." Lee stated that he "always felt afraid when going to attack after that"—a serious disappointment for a soldier with his strong predilection for the offensive. The depth of his distress at the spectacle of Hill's veterans sprinting away from the fight-

Lieutenant General
Ambrose Powell Hill.
Francis Trevelyan Miller, ed., *The
Photographic History of the Civil War*,
10 vols. (New York: Review of
Reviews, 1911), 10:143

ing, which obviously remained vivid during his conversation with Johnston six years later, had stood out starkly on the morning of May 6. "My God! Gen. McGowan," he had shouted to one of Hill's brigadiers, "is this splendid brigade of yours running like a flock of geese?"[13]

Ill health probably compromised Hill's effort to rally Heth's and Wilcox's broken divisions. For the second time in as many major battles since he became a lieutenant general, he collapsed physically at a critical juncture. On May 8, Special Orders No. 123 announced that "Lieut. Gen. A. P. Hill is relieved from duty on account of sickness." Jubal A. Early transferred from his division in the Second Corps as a temporary replacement at Third Corps headquarters.[14]

Hill's incapacity persisted throughout the fighting around Spotsylvania Court House. Charles S. Venable of Lee's staff charitably noted in the 1870s that "General Hill, though unable to sit up, in these days of Spotsylvania would have himself drawn up in his ambulance immediately in rear of the lines. Such was his anxiety to be near his troops." In a similar vein, a second witness noted that during the entire Overland campaign, Hill "was dragged from field to field, yet unwilling to be absent from the post of duty and danger." His brothers implored Hill's physicians to insist that he take a rest away from the army, but the lieutenant general refused. On May 12, Hill ordered his ambulance almost to the firing line, whence he offered "the aid of his personality to Gen. Early" (Early's reaction to this assistance went unrecorded).[15]

On the 18th, Hill tried to resume command but lost his temper in Lee's pres-

Brigadier General
Ambrose Ransom Wright.
Francis Trevelyan Miller, ed., *The
Photographic History of the Civil War*,
10 vols. (New York: Review of
Reviews, 1911), 10:115

ence. Furious that Brig. Gen. Ambrose R. Wright had mishandled his troops
during an attack at Myer's Hill on the Confederate right, Hill vowed to con-
vene a court of inquiry. "These men are not an army," Lee told the sputtering
Hill, "they are citizens defending their country." Wright was not a professional
soldier but a civilian fighting for his people's independence. "I have to make
the best of what I have and lose much time in making dispositions," explained
Lee, adding that Hill surely understood this. If Hill humiliated Wright by calling for an official inquiry, he might offend the people of Georgia. "Besides,"
asked Lee pointedly, "whom would you put in his place? You'll have to do what
I do: When a man makes a mistake, I call him to my tent, talk to him, and use
the authority of my position to make him do the right thing the next time."
Hill's most recent biographer concluded that this episode convinced Lee that
the Third Corps chief, who had been very ill as recently as May 16, "was not
mentally up to the task" of resuming field command.[16]

A week later, while back in charge of his corps at Jericho Mills on the North
Anna, Hill learned to his discomfort that Lee also tried to persuade corps commanders who had attended West Point to "do the right thing." After a wasteful
assault by Cadmus Wilcox's division against the Federal Fifth Corps on May 23,
Lee contemplated the hundreds of casualties while examining the ground early
the next morning. Jedediah Hotchkiss later wrote that Lee "sharply rebuked
his lieutenant" for the action, closing with a stinging rhetorical question: "Why

did you not do as Jackson would have done—thrown your whole force upon those people and driven them back?" Douglas Southall Freeman, who attributed Lee's hurtful words to ill humor arising from an "intestinal ailment," characterized the episode as perhaps "the stiffest rebuke ever administered to any of his general officers during the war." In his biography of Hill, James I. Robertson Jr. echoed Freeman's assessment: "Lee's outburst was more an expression of his own weakened condition than a judgment of what Hill did or did not do."[17]

Lee's dressing down of Hill at the North Anna also might have reflected exasperation with a corps commander who had exhibited rash behavior on two battlefields within eight months. That behavior, together with Hill's unfortunate habit of falling ill at times when Lee most needed stalwart corps leadership, likely persuaded him that his subordinate simply lacked the qualities requisite to succeed in his current position. Because no obvious replacement lay at hand, Lee kept Hill at his post. Just as corps commanders would have to do what they could with nonprofessional soldiers such as Ambrose Wright, Lee had "to make the best" of what he had in the way of potential lieutenant generals.

With Longstreet lost for the foreseeable future and Hill consistently unreliable, Lee might have turned to Richard S. Ewell, the third of the triumvirate that had headed corps since before Gettysburg. Unfortunately, Lee already had determined to ease Ewell out of his post on the grounds of incompetence. He had known Ewell far less well than Hill as a Confederate officer before both were promoted to lieutenant general after Chancellorsville. Only during the Seven Days had Ewell served directly under Lee's eye; in the 1862 Valley campaign and during the preliminary stages of the Second Manassas campaign, he had been part of Jackson's semi-independent forces. Wounded at Groveton on August 28, 1862, Ewell lost a leg and endured a long convalescence. Lee believed him sufficiently recovered to resume field command in May 1863. Aware that the soldiers and officers of the Second Corps respected Ewell, he also might have heard rumors that Jackson, while lying near death at Guiney's Station, had remarked that "Old Bald Head" should be his successor.[18] On May 20, he recommended Ewell as Jackson's replacement in the Second Corps. Lee described the nominee to Davis as "an honest, brave soldier, who has always done his duty well"—tepid praise when compared to that touting Hill in the same letter.[19]

Lee confessed after the war that he had experienced doubts from the outset about Ewell's capacity for corps command. In talks with William Allan, who had served as Ewell's chief of ordnance in the Second Corps, Lee indicated that on the basis of prewar familiarity with Ewell "he had long known his faults as a military leader—his quick alternations from elation to despondency his want of decision & c." At the time of Ewell's appointment to corps command,

Lee hoped the forty-seven-year-old Virginian had gotten over his tendency to vacillate and "talked long & earnestly" with him on this subject. Ewell's subsequent conduct at Gettysburg generated considerable debate, especially his failure to attack Cemetery Hill and East Cemetery Hill late on the afternoon of July 1. Critics often have relied too heavily on postwar narratives that minimize the obstacles Ewell faced that day, but there is no doubt that Lee considered his performance less than distinguished. He complained to Allan of the "*imperfect, halting way in which his corps commanders* (especially Ewell) *fought the battle*." Even Ewell's conduct during June 1863 — a period for which most historians have given him high marks — disappointed Lee. At Second Winchester, Ewell first sent encouraging messages about his prospects for trapping the Federal defenders, then "suddenly sent a dispatch stating that upon closer inspection he found the works too strong to be attacked, and asking his (Lee's) instructions!" Such indecision from an officer on the ground deeply troubled Lee.[20]

The winter of 1863–64 added questions about Ewell's health to Lee's worries about his competence. Complications with the stump of his amputated leg caused Ewell to take sick leave more than once. In January, Ewell insisted to the secretary of war that he was strong enough to return to the field and sent a copy of his letter to Lee. Lee somewhat tersely expressed pleasure that Ewell believed he had recovered but emphasized that a lieutenant should not expect his army commander "to take upon myself to decide in this matter. You are the proper person, on consultation with your medical advisers." "I do not know how much ought to be attributed to long absence from the field, general debility, or the result of your injury," continued Lee bluntly, "but I was in constant fear during the last campaign that you would sink under your duties or destroy yourself." Turning his eye toward the spring campaigning, Lee closed with words that left no room for misunderstanding: "I last spring asked for your appointment provided you were able to take the field. You now know from experience what you have to undergo, and can best judge of your ability to endure it. I fear we cannot anticipate less labor than formerly." Ewell's own chief of staff had expressed similar concerns the preceding fall. In November, Sandie Pendleton somewhat cruelly complained about "our superannuated chieftain, worn out as he is by the prostration incident, in a man of his age, upon the amputation and doting so foolishly on his unattractive wife."[21]

The battle of the Wilderness deepened Lee's unhappiness with Ewell. As with his actions on July 1 at Gettysburg, Ewell's decision to delay an assault against the Federal right flank on May 6 inspired lively debate in which his critics too often have quoted John B. Gordon's self-serving reminiscences. Again as with Gettysburg, there can be no doubt that Lee found his subordinate wanting. Lee told William Allan that he had "urged Ewell to make the flank attack,

Lieutenant General
Richard Stoddert Ewell.
Based on a photograph and published
three months before the battles at
Spotsylvania Court House, this
woodcut provided northerners with
a portrait of an important rebel
commander.
Frank Leslie's Illustrated Newspaper,
February 13, 1864

made later in the day by Gordon, several times before it was done. He (Lee) intended it to be a full attack in flank, & intended to support it with all Ewell's corps and others if necessary, and to rout the enemy." Lee surmised that Jubal Early persuaded Ewell to defer the assault, but he clearly held Ewell, as corps commander, rather than Early ultimately responsible. The belated attack, Lee concluded, commenced "too late in the day, and . . . was not supported with sufficient force to accomplish anything decisive."[22]

Events at Spotsylvania on May 12 and during the following week sealed Ewell's fate with the Army of Northern Virginia. From Lee's perspective, Ewell twice exhibited thoroughly unsatisfactory behavior. The first instance occurred on the morning of May 12, as both Ewell and Lee sought to direct reinforcements toward the broken Confederate line at the apex of the Mule Shoe. Lee's later acceptance of responsibility for what happened on the 12th should not obscure his initial unhappiness with the position of the Second Corps. During an inspection of the salient on May 9, he had observed, "This is a wretched line. I do not see how it can be held." Ewell shared that opinion but thought his corps should remain where it already had dug in. If relinquished, argued Ewell, the high ground in the salient could be used by Federal artillerists to threaten other parts of the Confederate position. Assurances from his engineers that sufficient artillery would make the line safe persuaded a reluctant Lee to go along with Ewell. On the night of May 11, Lee first ordered Ewell to pull his entire corps out of the Mule Shoe in anticipation of shifting to thwart Grant's next movement; however, Ewell persuaded him to remove only the guns and allow the infantry a good night's sleep in their somewhat sheltered lines.[23]

The stressful morning of the 12th likely summoned thoughts of Lee's initial estimate of Ewell as a man given to dramatic fluctuations of emotion. William J. Seymour of Harry Hays's Louisiana brigade described the "strong contrast in the demeanor" of Ewell and Lee during the initial phase of the effort to restore the Confederate line. "Gen. Ewell was greatly excited and, in a towering passion, hurled a terrible volley of oaths at the stragglers from the front, stigmatizing them as cowards, etc.," wrote Seymour. "Gen. Lee was calm, collected and dignified, he quietly exhorted the men not to forget their manhood and their duty, but to return to the field and strike one more blow for the glorious cause in which they were enlisted." Seymour closed with a slight to Ewell: "It is hardly necessary to say that Gen. Lee's course was by far the more effective of the two." Another witness similarly wrote that Lee, "in the calmest and kindest manner," sought to rally the soldiers, whereas an agitated Ewell bellowed "Yes, G[o]d d[am]n you, run, run; the Yankees will catch you; that's right; go as fast as you can." This man emphasized that the soldiers "Gen. Lee addressed at once halted and returned . . . all that Gen. Ewell so angrily reproached continued their flight to the rear."[24]

Lee agreed with these judgments about Ewell's ineffectiveness during this critical moment. Eyewitness Walter A. Montgomery of the 12th North Carolina sketched a memorable confrontation between the two generals. "General Ewell, who was on the spot, personally engaged in trying to rally the men, lost his head, and with loud curses was using his sword on the backs of some of the flying soldiers," remembered Montgomery. "Just then General Lee rode up and said: 'General Ewell, you must restrain yourself; how can you expect to control these men if you have lost control of yourself? If you cannot repress your excitement, you had better retire.'" For Lee, who prized self-control above almost all other virtues, Ewell had crossed a line. He later spoke of Ewell's "being perfectly prostrated by the misfortune of the morning, and too much overwhelmed to be efficient."[25]

The second incident involving Ewell's self-control occurred on May 19. Instructed on the evening of the 18th to locate the Federal right flank, Ewell received permission to conduct a reconnaissance-in-force with his corps (which numbered just 6,000 men after the hard fighting of the previous two weeks). On the 19th, his soldiers slogged along roads made nearly impassable by heavy rains over the preceding days. Fighting flared late in the afternoon at the Harris farm, northeast of Spotsylvania Court House near the Fredericksburg Road. Following an indecisive engagement, Ewell, who had taken a hard fall when his horse was killed, experienced some difficulty in extricating his soldiers. A newspaper correspondent reported shortly after the battle that because some Second Corps troops behaved poorly, Ewell "did not press his advantages, nor bring off some forty-five wagons which he captured. . . . [H]e returned late at night to his former position, leaving his dead and a portion of his wounded behind." William Allan's postwar memoir succinctly summed up the day's action: "Ewell moved out to the front across the ——— river & tried Meade's right, had a severe fight and was glad to get back at night fall. I rode that march. The roads bad, wood & swamps. . . . Ewell had his horse killed this afternoon & at one time lost his head in the severity of the fight. . . ." [26]

William Allan's notes of Lee's postwar comments include a very harsh appraisal of Ewell on May 19. Ewell "lost all presence of mind, and Lee found him prostrate on the ground, and declaring he cd not get Rodes div. out. (Rodes being very heavily engaged with the enemy.) He (Lee) told him to order Rodes back and that if he could not get him out, he (Lee) could." Ewell's most careful biographer suggests that the general's fall from his horse may have prompted Lee's comment about finding him "prostrate on the ground"; however, it seems at least as likely that Lee used the phrase not to mean Ewell lay literally collapsed on the ground but that, to quote the *Oxford English Dictionary*, he had been "laid low in mind or spirit; submissive; overcome; overthrown; powerless." [27]

Whatever the truth about Ewell's actions on the 19th, Lee decided to remove him from command of the Second Corps. The availability of Jubal Early, in whom Lee had great confidence, made this decision possible. A welcome pretext came late in May when Ewell fell ill. Lee replaced him on May 29 with Early, who had left his temporary post at Third Corps headquarters after A. P. Hill recovered from his latest malady. Informed by Lee that he could "retire from the field that he may have the benefit of rest and medical treatment," Ewell responded that he would be fit for duty in two days and — guessing Lee's real intention — "sent a certificate of Staff Surgeon [Hunter H.] McGuire to the same effect." Determined not to step aside quietly, Ewell reported for duty on the 31st and, as he explained, "remained over a week with the army, wishing to place the question of health beyond a doubt, but the change of commanders was made permanent, and on June 14 I was placed in command of the Defenses of Richmond." He followed up on June 1 with another note affirming his good health. [28]

Lee's official explanation stressed concern for Ewell's physical condition as the reason for his removal. In early June, he wrote about Ewell to Adj. and Insp. Gen. Samuel Cooper: "Although now restored to his usual health, I think the labor and exposure to which he would be inevitably exposed would at this time again incapacitate him for field service. The general, who has all the feelings of a good soldier, differs from me in this opinion," admitted Lee, "and is not only willing but anxious to resume his command. I, however, think in the present emergency it would jeopardize his life, and should his strength fail, it would prove disadvantageous to the service." In the midst of this sad drama, recalled Lee after the war, Maj. Gen. Robert E. Rodes, who led a division in the Second Corps, *"protested against E[well]'s being again placed in command."* But friends of Ewell also went to work to counter such sentiments. An anonymous letter reached army headquarters urging Ewell's reinstatement on the grounds of Lee's long friendship with him, and others let Lee know that Ewell "thought hardly of his treatment." In retrospect, Lee affirmed that he was "very reluctant to displace him, but felt compelled to do so." [29]

Ewell eventually forced his chief to tell him the truth. After first pleading his case with Jefferson Davis, he went to see Lee on the morning of June 8. His wife, Lizinka, reported on the meeting in a long letter written that night to Ewell's brother Benjamin. Ewell told Lizinka that he assured Lee of his physical strength and asked if Early seemed preferable for other reasons. Lee replied that he chose Early solely because of the health issue. Ewell confessed to Lee his great anxiety during the days he had been denied restoration to command, to which Lee responded, "It is due Early and the Corps that he receive the appointment just as Anderson has." Somewhat pathetically, Ewell said he would "go somewhere to be out of the way." "You are not in the way," answered Lee without giving any ground, "but you had better take care of yourself." Lee offered a version of the meeting that suggests Ewell shielded his wife from its most unpleasant moments. When the Second Corps was about to depart for the Shenandoah Valley under Early, stated Lee in 1868 referring to the meeting of June 8, Ewell asked to be reinstated as its commander. Lee "tried to put him off by sickness, but when E. insisted, he told him plainly he could not send him in command." [30]

Most observers at the time and subsequent historians accepted Lee's official explanation, which made for the smoothest possible resolution of a vexing problem.[31] Members of Ewell's inner circle better understood what had happened. Second Corps ordnance chief William Allan later recalled that "everybody was uncomfortable . . . yet we all felt that his removal was inevitable & indeed was proper." Campbell Brown, Ewell's stepson and staff officer, did not share this attitude and seethed at what he considered a gross injustice. The previous November, when Ewell's physical problems had obliged Lee to replace him temporarily with Early, one of Early's staff officers noted that Ewell believed "there had been a conspiracy to get rid of him." Remaining at corps headquarters after Early took over in May 1864, Brown fueled Ewell's suspicion that "Old Jube" and perhaps others had conspired to influence Lee. On June 13, Brown informed his stepfather that "Old Early did not ask me how you were, but I made my speech so that he will hear it." Brown vowed to avoid Early as much as possible, adding bitterly, "He looks at me like a sheep-stealing dog, out of the corner of his eye. . . ." For his part, Early sought to reassure Ewell in a conciliatory letter that gave no hint of his long-standing ambition for promotion: "I wish to say to you General that in the arrangement which has been made by which I am given the temporary command of the Corps I have had no agency directly or indirectly either by procurement or suggestion. . . . I assure you, General, I should regret excessively if any misunderstanding between ourselves should result. . . ."[32] Ewell undoubtedly declined to accept Early's letter at face value. The two never communicated after early June 1864.

Ewell's reassignment constituted the final act in a three-week drama that had fractured the army's high command. In addition to the problems besetting each of his infantry corps, Lee faced the cruel loss of "Jeb" Stuart, who had led the Cavalry Corps with distinction until mortally wounded on May 11 at Yellow Tavern. Longstreet's wounding and Hill's and Ewell's various shortcomings presented the most vexing problems, and Lee displayed an array of skills in dealing with them. The ramifications of assigning Early to head the Third Corps on May 8 offer an excellent case in point. Lee had long since marked Jubal Early as a man capable of larger responsibility, and Hill's illness presented Old Jube with a trial run in corps command.[33] Early's departure from his division provided a similar opportunity for John Brown Gordon, a capable brigadier whom Lee wished to advance. Because Harry Hays ranked Gordon among Early's brigadiers, Lee shifted Hays's Louisiana brigade to Edward Johnson's division, where it was consolidated with the depleted Louisiana regiments formerly commanded by Leroy Stafford. Hays's removal not only cleared the way for Gordon to move up, but it also supplied adequate leadership for the Louisianians who had lost Stafford to a mortal wound during the first day's fight in the Wilderness. The loss of Hays's command left Early's division one brigade short: "In order to equalize your divisions," Lee wrote Ewell, "you will . . . transfer R. D. Johnston's brigade, or some other of Rodes's [five] brigades, whose command is junior to General Gordon, to General Early's division, so that General Gordon may take command of the latter."[34]

This shuffling underscored Lee's grasp of the command resources in his army, as well as his ability to focus on organization in the midst of taxing strategic and tactical circumstances. The process left each of the Second Corps divisions with four brigades, placed Early and Gordon where Lee wanted them, and neatly sidestepped potential acrimony about date of rank.

The lecture to A. P. Hill on May 18, during which Lee schooled his lieutenant about how to handle subordinates, revealed another facet of his leadership. Sensitive to the special problems of running an army whose officers predominantly were volunteers representing proud states of a republic, he understood the need to balance military and political needs and to gauge how decisions relating to command would affect morale behind the lines. Lee's grasp of the special needs of citizen soldiers eluded many — if not most — of his West Point-

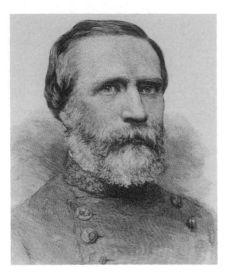

Major General
Richard Heron Anderson.
Robert Underwood Johnson and
Clarence Clough Buel, eds., *Battles
and Leaders of the Civil War*, 4 vols.
(New York: Century, 1887–88), 4:717

trained peers, and helped to explain the unparalleled bond he forged with his officers and men. His decision to name Richard H. Anderson as Longstreet's temporary successor, for example, likely stemmed at least in part from a belief that Longstreet's soldiers would welcome the South Carolinian (whose division had been in the First Corps before being transferred to the Third in May 1863). Lee surely had greater respect for Jubal Early's soldierly qualities, but First Corps staff officer Moxley Sorrel, speaking about the relative merits of Early and Anderson on the morning of May 7, addressed the matter of reaction with the corps. He conceded that Early probably was the ablest available man but thought he would "be objectionable to both officers and men" in the First Corps. Of Anderson, in contrast, Sorrel stated, "We *know him* and shall be satisfied with him." Sorrel believed Lee would select the best soldier; Lee took a broader view.[35]

Spotsylvania also demonstrated that Lee could exhibit a hard side concerning subordinates. This element of his generalship often has been obscured by contemporaries and historians who pronounced him too much of a gentleman to make difficult personnel decisions. British observer A. J. L. Fremantle stated in his famous diary that Lee's "only faults, so far as I can learn, arise from his excessive amiability." Walter H. Taylor, who spent more time with Lee than any other officer during the war, noted in his widely cited first memoir: "If it shall be the verdict of posterity that General Lee in any respect fell short of perfection as a military leader, it may perhaps be claimed . . . that he was too careful of the personal feelings of his subordinate commanders, too fearful of wounding their pride, and too solicitous for their reputation." Taylor believed this tendency prompted Lee to retain in command men "of whose fitness for their position he was not convinced, and often led him, either avowedly or tacitly, to assume responsibility for mishaps clearly attributable to the inefficiency, neglect, or carelessness, of others." Jefferson Davis similarly wrote that Lee's "habitual avoidance of any seeming harshness, which caused him sometimes, instead of giving a command, to make a suggestion, was probably a defect."[36]

Many historians have seconded Taylor's and Davis's thoughts. Two examples will convey the tenor of their analysis. Most influential has been Douglas Southall Freeman, who echoed Fremantle's language when he wrote of the deep "defect of Lee's excessive amiability." In a chapter weighing Lee's strong and weak points as a soldier, Freeman concluded that "His consideration for others, the virtue of the gentleman, had been his vice as a soldier." British historian J. F. C. Fuller delivered a less gentle verdict in claiming that it was Lee's "inexhaustible tact which ruined his army."[37]

Perhaps inevitably, a psychological dimension has been added to this long-standing interpretation. A psychiatrist and journalist recently coauthored an article that claimed to locate in Lee's boyhood the reason for his later habit of never confronting anyone. They maintained (without benefit of substantial historical evidence) that the young Lee grew up watching his father's "likely abuse of alcohol, his intense pain, volatile temperament, and narcissistic character disorder; and the inevitable eruption of abuse in such circumstances." Having seen "Light Horse Harry" Lee shame his mother repeatedly, "Robert E. Lee would grow up, not to repeat the act of shaming, but to take the only other alternative — never to shame anyone at almost any cost." This trait carried over into his style of command. "Shame witnessed and shame felt were the source of his inability to control his subordinates," wrote these authors in a strikingly unsupported generalization. "Lee could not confront his wayward lieutenants for fear of shaming them. He was determined never, if at all possible, to let them feel humiliated as he had painfully watched his mother be mortified."[38]

Even a cursory look at the Spotsylvania campaign and its immediate aftermath should dispel the idea that Lee habitually shied away from confrontations with his lieutenants. He spoke plainly to both Hill and Ewell when he thought it necessary. With Hill, the exchange at the North Anna on May 23 could have left no doubt about Lee's displeasure; neither could his insistence that Ewell gain control of himself in the Mule Shoe on May 12 have been misinterpreted by his raging lieutenant. Lee's unhappiness with Ewell on the 19th and later refusal to reinstate him as commander of the Second Corps similarly indicated a willingness to take a stand. It no doubt pained Lee in early June to have to tell Ewell, about whom he "expressed the kindest of personal feelings,"[39] precisely why he would not return him to his old corps. For the good of the army and Ewell's reputation, Lee publicly hewed to the rationale based on physical condition, but to his old acquaintance in person he admitted doubts about his capacity to command.

This is not to say Lee relished such unhappy episodes. He dealt with failures among subordinates in a variety of ways and almost always sought to discipline or transfer officers with the least possible acrimony. Reassignment of such men as Benjamin Huger, Theophilus H. Holmes, and Daniel Harvey Hill left scarcely a ripple within the Army of Northern Virginia — a testament to Lee's ability to avoid the poisonous infighting that wracked the high command of the Army of Tennessee. But did he seek accommodation even if it hurt the army? Certainly Richard S. Ewell would say he did not.[40]

Closely related to the idea that Lee shunned confrontations is the argument that he allowed his corps commanders too much latitude. According to Justus Scheibert, a Prussian observer who campaigned with the Army of Northern Virginia at Chancellorsville and Gettysburg, Lee explained: "I strive to make my plans as good as my human skill allows, but on the day of battle I lay the fate of my army in the hands of God; it is my generals' turn to perform their duty." Citing Scheibert, Douglas Southall Freeman described this as "mistaken theory of the function of the high command," adding that it may have resulted from Lee's gentlemanly concern for others. Conceding that this method might work on the wooded battlefields of Virginia, Freeman thought it returned disastrous dividends at Gettysburg on July 2–3.[41]

Down to the time Lee spoke with Scheibert, his method had worked beautifully, with Jackson and Longstreet executing their commander's broad orders. When Hill and Ewell failed to operate equally well under a light rein at Gettysburg and — in Lee's opinion — in the Wilderness, he took a more active role. In other words, he adapted his style of command to suit changing personnel.

At Spotsylvania, this showed especially at the tactical level. On May 6 at the Wilderness, Lee had withdrawn from danger at Widow Tapp's farm once Longstreet arrived because he trusted his senior corps chief's ability to manage the fighting along the Plank Road. Just six days later, Lee's prolonged involvement in the Mule Shoe — amid a crisis no greater than that his army had confronted at dawn on May 6 — betrayed doubts that Ewell could orchestrate the Confederate defense. Ewell's erratic behavior on the 12th doubtless contributed to Lee's decision to remain under fire longer than was prudent. In effect, he functioned as both corps commander and army commander for much of that trying day, a circumstance that would have been unthinkable on battlefields where he had trusted Jackson and Longstreet to oversee their troops. Nor did A. P. Hill likely inspire much greater confidence in this respect. He had proved unable to rally his shattered troops on May 6 and had exercised little control over the action at the North Anna on the 23rd. As for Richard H. Anderson, Lee took special care to direct his movements with the First Corps.[42]

Events along the North Anna on May 24–26 revealed the crippling legacy of Spotsylvania. U. S. Grant carelessly placed his army in an extremely vulnerable position, with three large bodies of troops separated by the curving river. Here was the tactical opportunity Lee had awaited since the opening of the Overland campaign. According to his physician, Lafayette Guild, "Genl. Lee all though sick had not from the 5th to the 25th had two hours consecutive sleep." The commanding general succumbed to a severe intestinal malady on the 24th. For two days he tried to work through the pain, unwilling to entrust a tactical offensive to any of his corps commanders. Anderson had done well enough at Spotsylvania under close supervision but had yet to demonstrate that he could do more. Hill's latest failure lay only one day in the past, and Ewell's recent record fell below even that of Hill. A year earlier, Lee unhesitatingly would have directed Jackson or Longstreet to smite the exposed enemy; later in 1864, he probably would have called on Jubal Early. No such alternative existed on the 24th and 25th, rendering him unable to do more than deplore his misfortune. "We must strike them a blow," Charles Venable quoted the prostrate Lee's saying from his tent, " — we must never let them pass us again — we must strike them a blow!" Perhaps unintentionally, Venable obliquely damned the lieutenant generals on whom the stricken army commander believed he could not rely: "But though he still had reports of the operations in the field constantly brought to him, and gave orders to his officers, Lee confined to his tent was not Lee on the battlefield."[43] Had Lee believed a disciplined and effective presence prevailed at any corps headquarters, one of those orders would have instructed a lieutenant general to strike the blow he desired.

A month after fighting ended at Spotsylvania the armies settled into siege lines at Richmond and Petersburg. The relatively static nature of the last nine months of the war in eastern Virginia reduced the likelihood that poor corps leadership would initiate a strategic or tactical crisis. The brightest opportunities came to Jubal Early, whom Lee deployed to the Shenandoah Valley with the Second Corps in June 1864. Early achieved heartening success during his first eight weeks of detached duty before suffering utter defeat in a trio of battles between September 19 and October 19. Neither Longstreet, who returned to the First Corps before his wounds from the Wilderness had healed properly, nor Hill, whose infirmities continued until his death in early April 1865, added any laurels to his earlier record. Richard Anderson presided quietly over a one-division demi-corps for much of the last period of the conflict, and youthful John B. Gordon, who succeeded Early as head of the Second Corps, made the most of limited opportunities to demonstrate promise in 1865.

Ironically, the siege Lee had dreaded from the moment Grant crossed the Rapidan River cushioned the effect of his disintegrating high command. The post-Spotsylvania version of the Army of Northern Virginia likely would have experienced major lapses of corps leadership if engaged in a war of maneuver comparable to that it had waged with Jackson and Longstreet at the height of their powers in 1862–63. Because Lee and his army sustained their nation's morale throughout the last year of the war, battlefield defeats arising from those lapses probably would have shortened the life of the Confederacy.

NOTES

1. Even critics of Lee's overall generalship during the Civil War usually have given him high marks for the Overland campaign. For example, Alan T. Nolan, who argued that Lee's strategic and tactical aggressiveness in 1862–63 hurt the Confederacy by rapidly depleting its manpower, praised his conduct of the Overland campaign. (Nolan *Lee Considered: General Robert E. Lee and Civil War History* [Chapel Hill: University of North Carolina Press, 1991], 100–101). Similarly, Grady McWhiney and Perry D. Jamieson, who also criticized Lee's penchant for the offensive, wrote glowingly about his "brilliant defensive campaign against Grant in 1864" (McWhiney and Jamieson, *Attack and Die: Civil War Military Tactics and the Southern Heritage* (Tuscaloosa: University of Alabama Press, 1982], 164).

2. Edward Porter Alexander, *Fighting for the Confederacy: The Personal Recollections of General Edward Porter Alexander*, ed. Gary W. Gallagher (Chapel Hill: University of North Carolina Press, 1989), 372; Douglas Southall Freeman, *R. E. Lee: A Biography*, 4 vols. (New York: Charles Scribner's Sons, 1934–35), 3:315; Jedediah Hotchkiss, *Virginia*, vol. 4 of *Confederate Military History*, ed. Clement A. Evans, 12 vols. (Atlanta: Confederate Publishing Company, 1899), 447.

3. U.S. War Department, *The War of the Rebellion: A Compilation of the Official Records of the Union and Confederate Armies*, 127 vols., index, and atlas (Washington, D.C.: GPO, 1880–1901), ser. 1, 51(2):916–17, 36(1): 1044 (hereafter cited as *OR*; all references to ser. 1).

4. William W. Old, "Trees Whittled Down at Horseshoe," in *Southern Historical Society Papers*, ed. J. William Jones and others, 52 vols. and 3-vol. index (1877–1959; reprint, Wilmington, N.C.: Broadfoot Publishing Co., 1990–92), 33:24 (hereafter cited as *SHSP*); *OR* 36(1):1044.

5. For details of the various reorganizations, see Douglas Southall Freeman, *Lee's Lieutenants: A Study in Command* (New York: Charles Scribner's Sons, 1942–44), 1:605–19, 670–75, 2:236–68, 683–714.

6. During the period May 7, 1864, to April 9, 1865, Richard S. Ewell, Jubal A. Early, and John Brown Gordon commanded the Second Corps; A. P. Hill and Early the Third; and James Longstreet and Richard H. Anderson the First. Lee also created a two-division corps for Anderson in October 1864 (sometimes referred to as the Fourth Corps and other times as Anderson's Corps; this command was reduced to one division in late 1864). Thus, although Jackson and Longstreet provided continuity at corps (and wing) headquarters for nearly a year between July 1862 and May 1863, corps leadership changed comparatively rapidly during the last phase of the war. On Anderson's corps, see Joseph Cantey Elliott, *Lieutenant*

General Richard Heron Anderson: Lee's Noble Soldier (Dayton, Ohio: Morningside, 1985), 121–26; *OR* 42(3):1280–86.

7. Walter H. Taylor to Bettie Saunders, April 24, 1864, in Walter H. Taylor, *Lee's Adjutant: The Wartime Letters of Colonel Walter Herron Taylor, 1862–1865*, ed. R. Lockwood Tower (Columbia: University of South Carolina Press, 1995), 155; Francis W. Dawson, *Reminiscences of Confederate Service, 1861–1865*, ed. Bell I. Wiley (1882; reprint, Baton Rouge: Louisiana State University Press, 1980), 116.

8. R. E. Lee to Jefferson Davis, October 2, 1862, in *OR* 19(2):643; Lee to Davis, May 20, 1863, in *OR* 25(2):810.

9. On Hill's performance at Gettysburg, see Gary W. Gallagher, "Confederate Corps Leadership on the First Day at Gettysburg: A. P. Hill and Richard S. Ewell in a Difficult Debut," in *The First Day at Gettysburg: Essays on Confederate and Union Leadership*, ed. Gary W. Gallagher (Kent, Ohio: Kent State University Press, 1992).

10. Hotchkiss, *Virginia*, 426; A. L. Long, *Memoirs of Robert E. Lee: His Military and Personal History, Embracing a Large Amount of Information Hitherto Unpublished* (Philadelphia: J. M. Stoddart & Company, 1886), 311.

11. Henry Heth, *The Memoirs of Henry Heth*, ed. James L. Morrison (Westport, Conn.: Greenwood Press, 1974), 184; Cadmus M. Wilcox's report for the period May 4–December 7, 1864, typescript, bound vol. 178, Fredericksburg and Spotsylvania National Military Park, Fredericksburg, Virginia; Cadmus M. Wilcox, "Lee and Grant in the Wilderness," in *The Annals of the War Written by Leading Participants North and South*, ed. [Alexander K. McClure] (1879; reprint, Dayton, Ohio: Morningside, 1988), 495; article by a correspondent for the London *Herald* dated May 18, 1864, reprinted in W. S. Dunlop, *Lee's Sharpshooters; or, the Forefront of Battle* (1899; reprint, Dayton, Ohio: Morningside Bookshop, 1982), 400–401.

12. For accounts critical of Hill, see Freeman, *Lee's Lieutenants*, 3:353–55; Gordon C. Rhea, *The Battle of the Wilderness: May 5–6, 1864* (Baton Rouge: Louisiana State University Press, 1994), 276–82; Gary W. Gallagher, "The Army of Northern Virginia in May 1864: A Crisis of High Command," *Civil War History* 36 (June 1990):115. For a defense of Hill, see Peter S. Carmichael, "Escaping the Shadow of Gettysburg: Richard S. Ewell and Ambrose Powell Hill at the Wilderness," in *The Wilderness Campaign*, ed. Gary W. Gallagher (Chapel Hill: University of North Carolina Press, 1997).

13. *OR* 36(1):1028; William Preston Johnston, "Memoranda of Conversations with General R. E. Lee," in *Lee the Soldier*, ed. Gary W. Gallagher (Lincoln: University of Nebraska Press, 1996), 29; Edward Porter Alexander, *Military Memoirs of a Confederate: A Critical Narrative* (New York: Charles Scribner's Sons, 1907), 503.

14. *OR* 36(2):974–75. Scholars have offered different explanations for Hill's recurring illnesses. William W. Hassler's *A. P. Hill: Lee's Forgotten General* (Richmond, Va.: Garrett and Massie, 1957), 237–38, suggested that he "suffered from chronic malaria." James I. Robertson Jr.'s *General A. P. Hill: The Story of a Confederate Warrior* (New York: Random House, 1987), 11–12, 250, attributed the general's problems to complications from chronic prostatitis arising from a case of gonorrhea contracted while a cadet at West Point. Douglas Southall Freeman, in *Lee's Lieutenants*, 3:442, postulated that "a psychosomatic malady" struck Hill down in the Wilderness. Russell P. Green, a physician, argued that Hill "suffered from depression" (Green, "A. P. Hill's Manic Depression: 'Bury These Poor Men, and Let's Say No

More About It,'" *Virginia Country's Civil War* [Middleburg, Va.: Country Publishers, 1986], 4:65–69).

15. Charles S. Venable, "The Campaign from the Wilderness to Petersburg," in *SHSP* 14:532; "Sketch of Gen. A. P. Hill," *Land We Love* 2 (February 1867):288–89; Robertson, *A. P. Hill*, 270.

16. Freeman, *Lee*, 3:330–31; Robertson, *A. P. Hill*, 272. Freeman's source for this anecdote was a letter dated June 25, 1920, from Col. William H. Palmer, who had served on Hill's staff and "on whose memory Lee's words were indelibly imprinted." Freeman also noted that another individual "had the same story from Colonel Palmer and made a detailed memorandum of it, which he generously gave the writer." Palmer stated that the episode took place on May 18; Freeman cited a telegraphic message from Lee to Jefferson Davis on the night of May 15 that "makes it almost certain that the incident occurred on the 15th" (331 n. 12). In this instance, Freeman was confused; the incident involving Hill and Wright at Myer's Hill could not have taken place on May 15. Testimony from members of Wright's brigade indicates that their commander was ill on May 14–15 and that Lt. Col. M. R. Hall commanded the brigade in his absence (unsigned letter dated May 18, 1864, in Macon *Daily Telegraph*, May 31, 1864; James P. Verdery [Co. I, 48th Georgia Infantry] to sister, May 17, 1864 [excerpts from both letters supplied to the author by Keith S. Bohannon of East Ridge, Tenn.]). Hill also was temporarily out of command because of illness on the 15th. Finally, although the Confederates had launched a successful assault at Myer's Hill on May 14, they mounted no attack there the next day. On the 18th, there was a small southern assault in the vicinity of Myer's Hill, which the Federals repulsed easily. Wright's brigade held a position in that part of the Confederate line on the 18th, and both Wright and Hill could have been present (Hill resumed command of his corps on the 21st and might have been back in the field on the 18th as an observer). In sum, the nature of the action at Myer's Hill on the 18th and the likelihood that Wright and Hill both were present support Palmer's account.

17. Hotchkiss, *Virginia*, 460; Freeman, *Lee's Lieutenants*, 3:496–97; Robertson, *A. P. Hill*, 276.

18. On rumors of Jackson's supposed deathbed statement about Ewell, see William Dorsey Pender to Fanny Pender, May 14, 1863, in Pender, *The General to His Lady: The Civil War Letters of William Dorsey Pender to Fanny Pender*, ed. William W. Hassler (Chapel Hill: University of North Carolina Press, 1965), 237. "Do not believe all you see about the last words of Jackson," stated Pender, who had served as a brigadier under A. P. Hill, "for some designing person is trying to injure Gen. Hill by saying that he frequently said that he wanted Ewell to have his Corps."

19. Robert E. Lee to Jefferson Davis, May 20, 1863, in *OR* 25(2):810.

20. William Allan, "Memoranda of Conversations with General Robert E. Lee," in Gallagher, *Lee the Soldier*, 11, 14.

21. Robert E. Lee to Richard S. Ewell, January 18, 1864, in *OR* 33:1095–96; W. G. Bean, *Stonewall's Man: Sandie Pendleton* (Chapel Hill: University of North Carolina Press, 1959), 151.

22. Allan, "Memoranda of Conversations with Lee," 11. Gordon's influential account is in his *Reminiscences of the Civil War* (New York: Charles Scribner's Sons, 1903), 243–61. For an able defense of Ewell, see Carmichael, "Ewell and Hill at the Wilderness."

23. Donald C. Pfanz, *Richard S. Ewell: A Soldier's Life* (Chapel Hill: University of North Carolina Press, 1998), 378, 382.

24. William J. Seymour, *The Civil War Memoirs of Captain William J. Seymour: Reminiscences of a Louisiana Tiger*, ed. Terry L. Jones (Baton Rouge: Louisiana State University Press, 1991), 125; Columbus (Ga.) *Daily Sun*, December 22, 1865.

25. Walter A. Montgomery, *The Days of Old and the Years That Are Past* (Raleigh, N.C.: n.p., n.d.), 28; Allan, "Memoranda of Conversations with Lee," 11.

26. *OR* 36(1):1073; Pfanz, *Ewell*, 392–93; Richmond *Daily Dispatch*, May 25, 1864; typescript (prepared by R. E. L. Krick) of William Allan memoir, May–June 1864, folder 11, William Allan Papers, Southern Historical Collection, Wilson Library, University of North Carolina, Chapel Hill (repository hereafter cited as SHC).

27. Allan, "Memoranda of Conversations with Lee," 11; Pfanz, *Ewell*, 393. Pfanz found "no credible evidence" suggesting that Lee was near the Harris farm on May 19 or that Ewell ever suffered any mental collapse during the action. Allan's memoir (quoted in the preceding note), which probably was written after the ordnance officer's conversations with Lee, does mention one episode of loss of control.

28. *OR* 36(3):846; (1):1074; (3):863.

29. Robert E. Lee to Samuel Cooper, in Robert E. Lee, *The Wartime Papers of R. E. Lee*, ed. Clifford Dowdey and Louis H. Manarin (Boston: Little, Brown, 1961), 776; Allan, "Memoranda of Conversations with Lee," 11–12.

30. Lizinka C. Ewell to Benjamin Ewell, June 8, 1864, in Richard S. Ewell, *The Making of a Soldier: Letters of General R. S. Ewell*, ed. Percy Gatling Hamlin (Richmond, Va.: Whittet & Shepperson, 1935), 127–30; Allan, "Memoranda of Conversations with Lee," 11.

31. See, for example, Walter H. Taylor, *General Lee: His Campaigns in Virginia 1861–1865, with Personal Reminiscences* (1906; reprint, Dayton, Ohio: Morningside House, 1975), 249; Alexander, *Military Memoirs*, 534; Shelby Foote, *The Civil War: A Narrative, Red River to Appomattox* (New York: Random House, 1974), 277.

32. Everard H. Smith, ed., "The Civil War Diary of Peter W. Hairston, Volunteer Aide to Major General Jubal A. Early, November 7–December 4, 1863," *North Carolina Historical Review* 67 (January 1990):76 (entry for November 16); William Allan memoir, folder 11, William Allan Papers, SHC; Campbell Brown to Richard S. Ewell, June 13, 1864, and Jubal A. Early to Richard S. Ewell, June 5, 1864, box 1, folder 11, Polk, Brown, Ewell Papers, No. 605, SHC.

33. For more than eighteen months, Lee's assignments of responsibility to Early had demonstrated his confidence in Old Jube's potential for advancement. As a brigadier during the fall of 1862, Early often had commanded Ewell's division. Lee also had selected him over senior major generals to hold the Confederate position at Fredericksburg during the Chancellorsville campaign, and during the fall and winter of 1863–64 Early had stood in for the ailing Ewell at Second Corps headquarters.

34. *OR* 51(2):902–3; 36(2):974–75.

35. G. Moxley Sorrel, *Recollections of a Confederate Staff Officer* (1905; reprint, Jackson, Tenn.: McCowat Mercer Press, 1959), 238–39. Lee's belief that Early might soon replace Ewell or the frail Hill also likely entered into his decision to name Anderson as Longstreet's replacement.

36. Arthur James Lyon Fremantle, *Three Months in the Southern States: April–June, 1863* (1863; reprint, Lincoln: University of Nebraska Press, 1991), 249; Walter Taylor, *Four Years with General Lee* (1877; reprint, Bloomington: Indiana University Press, 1962), 146–47; Jefferson Davis, "Robert E. Lee," in *SHSP* 17:371.

37. Freeman, *Lee*, 4:168; J. F. C. Fuller, *Grant and Lee: A Study in Personality and Generalship* (1932; reprint, Bloomington: Indiana University Press, 1957), 119.

38. J. Anderson Thomson Jr. and Carlos Michael Santos, "The Mystery in the Coffin: Another View of Lee's Visit to His Father's Grave," *Virginia Magazine of History and Biography* 103 (January 1995):87–88, 93–94.

39. Allan, "Memoranda of Conversations with Lee," 12.

40. For discussions of Lee's skill at removing unwanted officers from his army, see Freeman, *Lee's Lieutenants*, 1:605–32, and Robert K. Krick, "The Army of Northern Virginia in September 1862: Its Circumstances, Its Opportunities, and Why It Should Not Have Been at Sharpsburg," in *Antietam: Essays on the 1862 Maryland Campaign*, ed. Gary W. Gallagher (Kent, Ohio: Kent State University Press, 1989), 196–97.

41. Freeman, *Lee*, 2:347, 4:168–69.

42. Freeman discussed Lee's oversight of Anderson in *Lee's Lieutenants*, 3:509.

43. William McWillie notebooks (typescript supplied by Robert K. Krick), Mississippi Department of Archives and History, Jackson; Venable, "Wilderness to Petersburg," 535. In *Lee*, 3:358, Freeman offered Ewell's health as the reason Lee believed he could not call on the Second Corps. He also mentioned P. G. T. Beauregard, who commanded below Richmond at Bermuda Hundred, as a potential candidate whose "hands were full" with his own duties.

The Federal High Command at Spotsylvania

n a letter to his wife written near the end of the Spotsylvania campaign, Maj. Gen. George G. Meade, head of the Army of the Potomac, discussed the command situation in that army. Two U.S. senators had visited him on the previous day and praised his performance to date, stating that it was well understood in Washington that all of the fighting so far in the Overland campaign had been his battles. The general immediately corrected the visitors, explaining that he initially had maneuvered the army but that Lt. Gen. Ulysses S. Grant gradually had taken control and that it would be injurious to the army to have two heads. Meade also mentioned to his wife that a newspaperman, in attempting to understand the command arrangement within the army, had decided that Grant performed the grand strategy and Meade the grand tactics. Then the general quoted another viewpoint from the *Army Magazine*, which described "The Army of the Potomac, directed by Grant, commanded by Meade, and led by [Winfield Scott] Hancock, [John] Sedgwick and [Gouverneur K.] Warren." Meade thought that this last distinction "about hits the nail on the head."[1]

This spectrum of interpretations concerning responsibilities for the strategic and tactical operations of the Army of the Potomac grew out of Grant's decision to accompany the army during the spring campaign of 1864. The presence of Maj. Gen. Ambrose E. Burnside's independent Union Ninth Corps

Lieutenant General Ulysses S. Grant: a heroic image from the spring of 1864.
Frank Leslie's Illustrated Magazine, March 19, 1864

complicated the situation. Because Burnside ranked Meade, Grant's presence was necessary to coordinate the operations of the Ninth Corps with those of Meade's troops. This cumbersome arrangement boded ill for the command and control of the Federal force and inevitably would foster delays, confusion, and frustration. Problems would arise, for example, when Grant issued orders directly to Meade's subordinates and when Meade hesitated to take an unplanned action without first obtaining Grant's approval.

Four men served as Meade's principal subordinates when the campaign opened. Maj. Gen. Winfield Scott Hancock headed the Second Corps, Maj. Gen. John Sedgwick the Sixth Corps, Maj. Gen. Gouverneur K. Warren the Fifth Corps, and Maj. Gen. Philip H. Sheridan the Cavalry Corps. Although the most competent of the four, Hancock remained in relatively poor physical condition because a wound sustained at Gettysburg had healed very slowly and continued to cause him pain. A few days before the campaign commenced he requested permission from army headquarters to ride in a spring wagon if necessary until his troops were about to become engaged with the enemy; once fighting began he would revert to horseback. Although his request was granted, Hancock's performance would be affected by this constant annoyance.[2]

The first week of campaigning yielded clear evidence that Grant would wield the guiding hand on the Union side. Failure to gain a decisive victory in the battle of the Wilderness on May 5-6 convinced the general-in-chief that he must exercise more direct control over Meade's and Burnside's commands. He decided to march them south to Spotsylvania Court House and practically dictated the details of the movement to Meade.[3]

Meade and Sheridan soon found themselves in an antagonistic relationship because they disagreed about the proper role for the Cavalry Corps. Meade maintained that the horsemen should guard the army's front and flanks while it was in a static position or on the march. Moreover, he wanted the cavalry to escort and guard the huge trains that followed the Army of the Potomac. Sheridan, on the other hand, believed that his command should seek out the enemy's cavalry to harass and destroy it. In this situation, insisted the cavalry commander, the army's trains would not be endangered by enemy horsemen. The fiery Irishman further believed that marching infantry columns should be able to protect their own front and flanks. The noneffectiveness of the Union cavalry in the battle of the Wilderness, where it performed according to Meade's model, stemmed partially from the role assigned it by army headquarters and contributed to the Federal failure to gain a clear victory.[4]

During the night of May 7-8, the cavalry provided little support for the army's march from the Wilderness toward Spotsylvania Court House. Because of poor work from his staff, orders concerning the movement (dated midafternoon of the 7th) did not reach Sheridan, who was at the front near Todd's Tavern. Only upon returning to his headquarters at approximately 9:30 P.M. did Sheridan learn of the army's movement already in progress and of his assigned responsibilities for supporting it. The Confederates consequently won the so-called race to Spotsylvania Court House and stopped the advancing

Major General George Gordon Meade (fourth from right) and Major General John Sedgwick (second from right) several weeks before the battles at Spotsylvania Court House. Francis Trevelyan Miller, ed., *The Photographic History of the Civil War*, 10 vols. (New York: Review of Reviews, 1911), 3:55

Federals a mile and a half short of their goal. While at lunch on May 8, Sheridan and Meade engaged in a hot discussion that escalated into a shouting match. Before stalking off, Sheridan declared, among other things, that if Meade would only turn him loose he could whip Maj. Gen. James E. B. Stuart and all of the cavalry with Gen. Robert E. Lee's army. Meade reported the altercation, including Sheridan's boast, to Grant, who decided to allow the cavalryman to make good on his prediction. The following morning Sheridan led practically the entire Cavalry Corps on a southward march that eventually would result in the mortal wounding of Stuart two days later at the battle of Yellow Tavern.[5]

Although removal of the talented Stuart from the Army of Northern Virginia assisted the Federal cause, Sheridan's stripping all but one regiment of the Cavalry Corps from Meade's army also caused Union delays and otherwise hampered the Army of the Potomac during its operations in the vicinity of Spotsylvania Court House.

On the morning of May 7, the 5th New York Cavalry of Sheridan's Third Division had been detached from its parent brigade and assigned temporarily to the cavalry brigade of the Ninth Corps. When Sheridan and his corps departed on the morning of May 9, the New Yorkers and Burnside's four cavalry units—the 3rd New Jersey, 22nd New York, 2nd Ohio, and 13th Pennsylvania—faced the stern prospect of carrying out all the tasks Grant and Meade might assign cavalry with the main body of the army. The 22nd New York, an inexperienced unit with only two months' service, soon rode to protect Union wounded from the Wilderness fighting being treated in makeshift hospitals at Fredericksburg. The remaining regiments were assigned to Brig. Gen. Edward Ferrero, who commanded two brigades of United States Colored Troops in Burnside's Fourth Division. These horsemen spent the critical next ten days of the campaign guarding the rear of the army and sending patrols as far north as the Rapidan River. In essence, the Army of the Potomac and Burnside's three divisions confronted the Army of Northern Virginia without cavalry support from May 9 onward.[6]

Grant and Meade consequently experienced a significant decline in their ability to acquire intelligence. Robert E. Lee avoided a similar handicap because Stuart, upon departing to pursue Sheridan, left two cavalry brigades to watch and operate from either flank of the Army of Northern Virginia. Responsibility for this Federal disadvantage must be assigned primarily to Grant. He had approved Sheridan's raid in part to solve, at least in the short term, the problem of inharmonious relations between his army and cavalry commanders. Meade should have requested and Grant should have ordered that at least one reliable brigade of horsemen be retained with the army. Both men had time to make this arrangement, as Sheridan's orders were dated 10:00 P.M. on May 8.[7]

Hindsight reveals that the absence of a mounted force began to affect the Union army even before Sheridan's troopers were out of sight. On the morning of May 9, Hancock's Second Corps was located at Todd's Tavern beyond the right of the army's position. At daylight, Hancock sent forward infantry skirmishers who discovered the departure of a Confederate corps that had

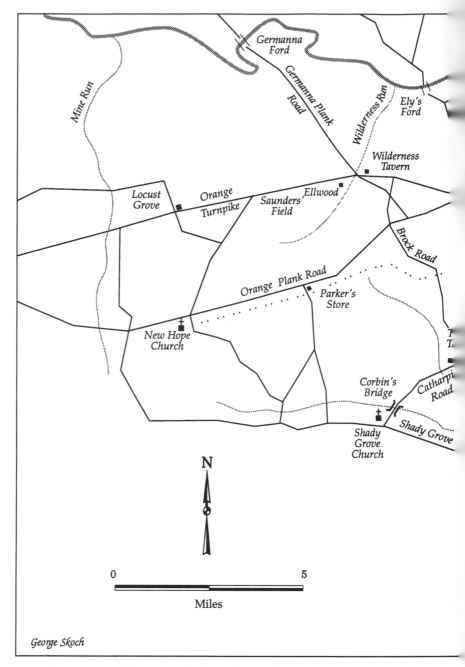

Area of action around Spotsylvania Court House, May 8–21, 1864

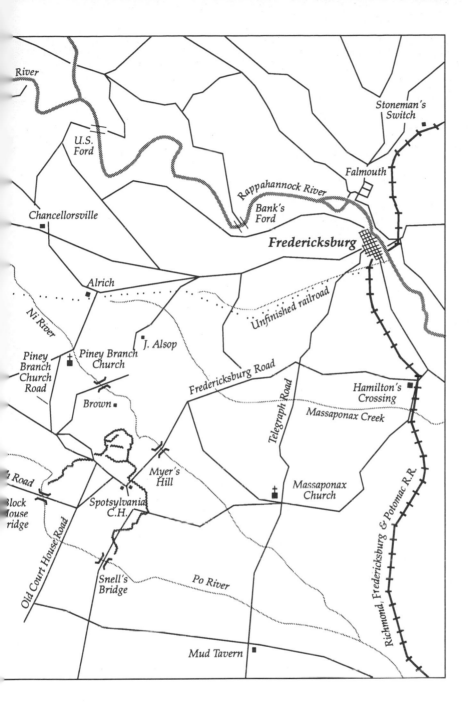

River

Stoneman's
Switch

U.S.
Ford

Rappahannock River

Falmouth

Bank's
Ford

Chancellorsville

Fredericksburg

Alrich

Unfinished railroad

Ni River

J. Alsop

Piney Branch
Church

Piney
Branch
Church
Road

Fredericksburg Road

Telegraph Road

Hamilton's
Crossing

Massaponax Creek

Brown

Myer's
Hill

Spotsylvania
C.H.

Massaponax
Church

Richmond, Fredericksburg & Potomac R.R.

Road

Block
House
ridge

Old Court House Road

Snell's
Bridge

Po River

Mud Tavern

Site of Sedgwick's death on May 9, 1864 (sketch by Alfred A. Waud). Sedgwick was standing near these cannons on the Brock Road when he was hit by a musket round. Library of Congress

been opposite their lines the previous day. Hancock relayed word of this to headquarters but soon thereafter announced that he expected to be attacked. Meade directed a division to support Hancock, then heard from the Second Corps chief that the rumored attack had been a false alarm generated by infantry pickets. Meade recalled the supporting division, and at noon Hancock received instructions to march three of his divisions to join the army's right flank. These troops crossed the Po River later in the afternoon and reached an unoccupied road that led to Lee's left rear; however, the advent of darkness precluded the Federals from taking advantage of the situation. During the night, Lee took measures to meet Hancock's threat, obliging the Unionists to recross the river the following day. Had Union cavalry been on the scene early on May 9, they almost certainly would have detected the withdrawal of the Confederate corps from Hancock's front west of Todd's Tavern. Meade and Grant likely would have known by 8:00 A.M. at the latest that the Union right was free of threat. The Second Corps then might have crossed the Po River during mid-morning and perhaps generated some trouble for Lee.[8]

The Union army also lost John Sedgwick on the morning of May 9. While overseeing some minor adjustments to his front line, the popular Sixth Corps

Major General
Horatio Gouverneur Wright.
Robert Underwood Johnson and
Clarence Clough Buel, eds., *Battles
and Leaders of the Civil War*, 4 vols.
(New York: Century, 1887–88), 4:228

commander jovially chided some of his men for ducking whenever an occasional Confederate minié ball whistled by from long range. One such missile suddenly struck the general in the face, and he crumpled to the ground dead. Brig. Gen. James B. Ricketts, the ranking division leader in the corps, declined to assume command because he knew Sedgwick had desired that Brig. Gen. Horatio G. Wright be given the position should a change become necessary. Thus Wright, whose only previous experience at this level had been when put in charge while Sedgwick was absent from the army during quiet periods, assumed the command. He would be severely tested in the days just ahead.[9]

During the next three days, Meade experienced difficulty in coordinating the actions of his three corps. Some of this resulted from the inadequacy — one officer preferred the word "uselessness" — of the Federals' maps. Grant's efforts to direct Burnside similarly suffered because the Ninth Corps was stationed far from army headquarters, on the left of the Union line and separated somewhat from the left of the Army of the Potomac. Both Grant and Meade worried about Burnside's isolated position. They knew the Ninth Corps stood near the Fredericksburg–Spotsylvania Court House Road but, because that area on their maps was blank, lacked knowledge about the distance between Burnside's troops and the left flank of the Army of the Potomac. Again, cavalry scouting in this area could have provided valuable information.[10]

Lee reacted on the night of May 9 to the danger of Hancock's presence west of the Court House. He dispatched two of the three divisions of his Third Corps in that direction, retaining on May 10 just one division opposite two Ninth Corps divisions east of the village. Neither Burnside nor Grant became aware of this until too late to react to the opportunity. When informed on the morning of the 10th about Lee's attempt to counter Hancock, Grant erroneously presumed that these troops had been extracted from the enemy line opposite the position of the Army of the Potomac rather than from Burnside's sector east of the Court House. The Union commander determined to conduct simultaneous attacks with Meade's three corps against the supposedly weakened force to their front, with the attacks to begin at 5:00 P.M. Meade sent the necessary orders to his corps commanders at 10:00 A.M.

According to the Union plan, Hancock would move his command to the north side of the Po River and commit two of his divisions to a joint attack with Warren's Fifth Corps. Late in Hancock's withdrawal across the Po, Confederates attacked his rear division. The Second Corps chief personally recrossed the stream to supervise the retirement of his troops, which concluded successfully after some hard fighting. Warren, meanwhile, had been apprised that two of Hancock's divisions would be on the Fifth Corps's right during the attack and that Hancock, by seniority, would exercise command of the combined assault.[11]

The alignment of Meade's three corps from right to left consisted of Hancock's Second and Warren's Fifth as far as the Brock Road fronting generally south. Across the road, Wright's Sixth Corps continued the line in a northeasterly then northerly direction facing east. Hancock's Fourth Division under Brig. Gen. Gershom Mott lay nearly three-quarters of a mile to the northeast of the left of Wright's line. Mott's soldiers had been kept at Todd's Tavern the previous day and ordered early on May 10 to their new location on the Brown farm. For the time being, Mott would be under the direction of Wright, which gave more responsibility to that officer on his first full day of corps command.

The Federals ran a great risk in placing Mott's two-brigade (seventeen-regiment) division in such an isolated location. Moreover, the vicinity had not been scouted for enemy troops. Mott's initial mission was to send out parties in all directions to locate the right of Burnside's line, which lay somewhere to the south approximately one and one-half to two miles through uncharted terrain. Shortly after midday, Burnside added four regiments to the right of his picket line, which scouted to their right up the left bank of the Ni River. At 3:00 P.M., some of Burnside's soldiers finally made contact with some of Mott's men. Although this connection by no means constituted a battle line (the Confederate position was one-half to three-quarters of a mile in front of the Federals), both army headquarters and Burnside could now comprehend more clearly the relative position of the other's command.[12]

Grant sent Burnside his orders at 10:30 A.M. After mentioning the proposed attack at 5:00, they read: "Reconnoiter the enemy's position in the mean time,

Brigadier General Gershom Mott.
Francis Trevelyan Miller, ed., *The
Photographic History of the Civil War*,
10 vols. (New York: Review of
Reviews, 1911), 10:219

and if you have any possible chance of attacking their right do it with vigor
and with all the force you can bring to bear. Do not neglect to make all the
show you can as the best co-operative effort." Grant probably assumed that
Burnside, in his isolated position, would be wary of conducting a large attack with little knowledge of the locations and strengths of other Confederate
and Union forces. A separate message informed the Ninth Corps commander
about Mott's new position and that some of the latter's troops were working
their way toward Burnside's right.[13]

Hancock returned to the north bank of the Po River at 5:30 P.M. to discover, to his surprise, the Fifth Corps and Brig. Gen. John Gibbon's division of
the Second Corps engaged in the final stage of an unsuccessful assault against
Confederates opposite Warren's position. Skirmishers from the three corps of
Meade's army had been probing the enemy's positions since daylight in generally fruitless attempts to discover the location and strength of the Confederate
main line. In mid-afternoon, however, some of Warren's pickets drove the
occupants of an advanced enemy picket post back out of sight. Warren decided an offensive in that area might yield victory and requested permission
from Meade to attack immediately. The army commander told him to proceed with his corps and Gibbon's division. Meade also ordered Wright to be
prepared either to attack immediately or to send Warren support, but the new
corps commander moved sluggishly. The attack began at 4:00–4:30 P.M. and
resulted in heavy casualties. Acting solely on Warren's expectation of success,

Meade had permitted assaults that removed any chance for a combined offensive along the army's line at 5:00 P.M. As a result, the time for a broader series of attacks was delayed until 6:00.[14]

Meade stipulated that Hancock would still direct the operations of his own and Warren's corps. This arrangement was questionable in view of the fact that the Second Corps commander, who had spent most of his time since mid-afternoon of the previous day south of the Po River, possessed little if any knowledge of Warren's troop positions or the characteristics of the enemy front to be attacked.

The attack force consisted of five brigades from the Fifth Corps and two from the Second. Most if not all of these troops had participated in Warren's earlier failed assault and lacked enthusiasm about the prospects for another effort. A report of an enemy force sighted just beyond the right flank of the army's line delayed the attack until shortly after 7:00 P.M. (this proved to be a small Confederate scouting party that Union cavalry could have identified in minutes). In the assault, many Federals merely moved forward a certain distance, halted, fired a round or two, and returned to or beyond their starting points. A few small groups fought their way close to the Confederate line before falling back. Near the right of the line, two regiments from one of the Second Corps brigades overran a small segment of the Confederate line, briefly fought hand-to-hand, and then were driven back because they lacked support. This round of attacks thus accomplished nothing substantive. To the left beyond the Brock Road, another Federal assault had resulted in a modest temporary success.[15]

The ten o'clock order to General Wright announcing the proposed attack at 5:00 P.M. instructed him to commit Mott's division in cooperation with Warren and Hancock. Wright immediately notified his three division commanders and directed them to examine the terrain in front of their respective positions to determine the practicality of an attack.[16]

During the morning, Lt. Ranald S. Mackenzie of the U.S. Corps of Engineers had been reconnoitering beyond the position occupied by Brig. Gen. David A. Russell's First Division of Wright's corps. Earlier that morning, northern artillery had compelled enemy pickets in this vicinity to fall back to sheltered ground. Mackenzie followed a woods path to reach the edge of a field, approximately two hundred yards across which he sighted the main Confederate line. No southern pickets stood in advance of the main enemy position, and Mackenzie could see only one artillery battery positioned on the line off to his right. The lieutenant summoned Russell to his observation point, some three-quarters of a mile in advance of the Sixth Corps works, and the latter concluded that a force concealed in the woods probably could cross the field

Colonel Emory Upton
(in a photograph taken after his
promotion to major general).
Library of Congress

quickly enough to reach the enemy works with few casualties. He explained
the situation to Wright, who approved an attack.[17]

The generals decided to use twelve regiments drawn from Wright's First
and Second Divisions. Col. Emory Upton, an ambitious brigade commander
in the First Division with a reputation as a stout fighter, would lead the attack.
In preparing for this assault, Upton enjoyed two luxuries denied Hancock and
Warren on the right of the line: time and a concealed position relatively close
to the enemy line.

After being shown the area for the attack, Upton gathered the twelve regimental commanders to view the field so that, in his words, "they might understand the work before them." He then explained that the attack formation
would consist of a near solid mass of three regiments across and four deep.
Each of the four lines of three regiments would have a separate role to play.
Finally, Upton ordered all officers to repeat the command "Forward" continually from the beginning of the advance until the works were carried.[18]

Instructed to include Mott's division in the attack, Horatio Wright sent
Capt. George H. Mendell of the U.S. Engineers to relate his views about general dispositions and to help Mott select the point to be attacked. The only
known portion of Wright's instructions responded to a query from Mott about
whether he should call in his extensive line of pickets for the attack. That process might take until after 5:00 P.M., believed Mott. Wright answered that the
pickets could advance from their present positions, adding somewhat oddly

that Mott should "Use your artillery [one battery] whenever there is a chance, as it serves to inspirit our men and demoralize the enemy, even if it does not hurt them very much."[19]

Wright wrestled with the problem of coordinating the movements for two separate bodies of attackers separated by more than three-quarters of a mile in an unmapped area. Upton's regiments would have to march 200 to 250 yards to reach the enemy works; Mott's soldiers would negotiate at least five times that distance, the initial portion of which would be through woods. While advancing, Mott's force would constantly narrow the lateral distance between the two columns but still would strike the enemy approximately one-quarter mile to the left of Upton's target.

Wright received no known assistance from army headquarters, and Mott's assigned role remains unclear. One logical mission would be to engage enemy troops to the right of Upton's target to prevent them from reinforcing comrades at the primary point of contact. Some of Upton's troops heard before the attack that they would be supported on their left by Mott's division. Their regimental historians later claimed that Mott's orders directed him to move forward through any breakthrough and exploit the success, a view Upton's official report, submitted in September 1864, strongly intimated to have been the case. The relative positions of the two forces renders this scenario unlikely. Any exploiting force more likely would have been drawn from the Sixth Corps, although it appears that Wright planned no such action. His orders obliged him to maintain the remainder of his line and stand prepared to send reinforcements to Warren. The new corps commander's first full day on the job was proving to be interesting indeed.

An order changing the time for the combined attack from 5:00 to 6:00 P.M. probably reached Wright's headquarters between 4:45 and 5:00. The final plan stipulated that three Sixth Corps artillery batteries bombard the target area for ten minutes prior to the attack. The battery situated on the left of this artillery line and closest to Mott at the Brown house (one mile distant) did not receive the delay order in time and opened fire early. The revised order arrived at the battery a few minutes later, but firing continued sporadically during the hour delay so as not to alert the enemy of the impending attack. This lapse in the delivery of orders raises the possibility that Mott's revised orders also arrived late. The few regimental reports from his division place the starting time for their assault at 5:00 P.M.[20]

At their commander's order, Mott's 1,200 to 1,500 infantrymen stepped off southward through the trees behind a line of skirmishers. The area through which they moved had not been reconnoitered, most likely because of Mott's apparently lackadaisical manner of performing when not guided by specific orders. A Sixth Corps staff officer who visited him in the morning claimed that the division commander "seemed somewhat stupid and flurried."[21]

The Yankees approached the southern edge of the woods after covering approximately one-quarter mile. Confederate pickets stationed there fired a volley before retiring across a large field. Upon reaching the clearing, the Federals looked across about six hundred yards to Confederate works located along the northern face of a large bulge in Lee's line that would become known as the salient or "Mule Shoe." Troops from Lt. Gen. Richard S. Ewell's Second Corps manned these works and enjoyed ample artillery support.

Confederate artillerists waited until the Federals entered long canister range before opening fire. After a few rounds, the entire Federal attacking column retired in confusion into the woods, and most of the soldiers continued all the way back to their starting point. This poor performance by Mott's troops, which would constitute the extent of their contribution to the so-called joint attack, seemingly confirmed a poor reputation they had earned in the Wilderness fighting.[22]

The tense wait from 5:00 to 6:00 must have seemed endless to the men of Upton's twelve regiments concealed in woods opposite the west face of the salient. At 5:50 P.M., two Union batteries added their fire to that of the one that had been firing during the hour-long delay. The guns ceased firing after ten minutes, and 4,500 to 5,000 infantrymen rose to their feet. They were sent forward with orders not to fire their weapons until reaching the enemy works. The attackers sustained few casualties while crossing the field and overran the enemy works after brief hand-to-hand combat. Perhaps an hour later, they had been driven back to the outside of these works by Confederate reserves. During that hour, the Yankees attained some successes, including the capture of more than nine hundred enemy troops. They also overran a second line of works situated a short distance behind the main one, fired into the left rear of two regiments in the next Confederate brigade up the line, causing them to abandon their positions, and temporarily captured the battery that Lieutenant Mackenzie had spotted during his morning reconnaissance. Because no infantry supported either of their flanks and no force had been assigned to exploit their breakthrough, however, Upton's men eventually relinquished the ground they had gained. From outside the works, they fought stubbornly until dark against increasing numbers of enemy reinforcements, whereupon Russell, realizing that no Union reinforcements were forthcoming, ordered Upton to retire his troops to the main line three-quarters of a mile to the rear.[23]

On the far left of the northern line, Burnside's soldiers provided no support because they lay too distant to exert any effect. Burnside had remained on the Orange Plank Road until mid-afternoon on May 9, then moved for-

Major General Ambrose E. Burnside.
Robert Underwood Johnson and
Clarence Clough Buel, eds., *Battles
and Leaders of the Civil War*, 4 vols.
(New York: Century, 1887–88), 3:109

ward only as far as the J. Alsop dwelling, still three miles to the rear of his
frontline troops who had been skirmishing with the enemy since noon along
the Fredericksburg–Spotsylvania Court House Road. At 1:15 P.M., Grant had
strongly suggested that the corps commander move up to take overall charge
of his troops in person, but Burnside halted at the Alsop house and spent the
night there. Not until mid-afternoon of the 10th did he join his forward troops
to oversee the advance.[24]

Burnside remained unsure about his role during the combined attack. He
apparently considered his proposed advance to be merely a reconnaissance-
in-force and reported it as such. At 6:00 P.M., three of his divisions moved
forward slowly for one-half mile before halting to dig in as darkness arrived.
Some of these Yankees were now within one-quarter mile of the Court House.
The enemy to their immediate front consisted of only four infantry brigades
supported by artillery, a force that had constituted the only Confederate military presence east of the village since the previous night.[25]

The operations of May 10 thus ended in frustration for the Federals. Meade
had been unable to mount a coordinated attack with his three corps. Burnside's position on the left was too distant for his troops to support Meade's
offensive. Meade's decision to allow Warren's premature attack appears almost
foolhardy; perhaps it can be explained by the army chief's being pleasantly
surprised by — and wishing to take advantage of — Warren's aggressive enthusiasm. It is also possible that Meade may have overreacted because of his own
growing concern that Grant was forming an unfavorable opinion of the Army
of the Potomac's offensive prowess.

The responsibilities with which Wright struggled on May 10 would have
taxed the abilities of an experienced corps commander. He probably believed

that he could not spare more troops from his line to help exploit any break-through Upton achieved. Mott's troops lay too far to Wright's left and rear to permit any timed coordination with Upton's effort. Unfortunately, Wright's specific instructions to Mott for the assault, other than those already quoted, remain unknown.[26]

Upton's temporary success provided the single bright spot for the Federals on May 10. Grant immediately promoted Upton to the rank of brigadier general (an action later confirmed by the Senate). Mott's performance placed him at the opposite end of the scale. Wright, Russell, and Upton all expressed anger about Mott's lack of support — wherever it was supposed to have been applied. Later that night, Wright informed Meade quietly but firmly: "General, I don't want Mott's men on my left; they are not a support; I would rather have no troops there."[27]

Amid this Federal anger, frustration, and gloom, Upton's attack probably did provide a positive contribution to the Federal cause. During the night, Wright, possibly accompanied by Russell and Upton, described the mechanics and initial success of the Sixth Corps assault to Grant and Meade. The general-in-chief appreciated the relative ease with which Upton's twelve massed regiments had penetrated the enemy's works and soon decided that a much larger but similarly organized attack might work. He would employ Hancock's entire corps and most of Burnside's in a combined assault to begin at 4:00 on the morning of May 12. Located on the army's right, Hancock's three divisions would move after dark on May 11, shifting to their left behind Warren's and Wright's troops to join Mott's command near the Brown house. From there they would initiate an attack to the south across roughly the same ground traversed by Mott's troops in their brief sally on May 10.

The Second Corps would advance against Confederate works along the north face of the salient. Because of the great size of the attacking force, its left element would strike the tip or apex of the salient where the enemy's works veered from an easterly to a southerly direction. The Federal high command probably did not know the precise location of the apex (a potential weak spot of the defensive line). Federals had not reconnoitered that area or the ground extending down the east face of the salient in the direction of Burnside's position. The relative directions in which the lines of the Army of the Potomac and the Ninth Corps faced did confirm that a gigantic bulge in Lee's line existed somewhere between the Brock Road on the west and the Fredericksburg Road to the east.

Grant's order to Meade specified the functions of the Second and Ninth Corps in the attack and directed that "Warren and Wright should hold their corps as close to the enemy as possible to take advantage of any diversion caused by this attack, and to push in if the opportunity presents itself." The commanding general also disclosed that he would send one or two staff officers to Ninth Corps headquarters that night to remain with Burnside and "impress him with the importance of a prompt and vigorous attack." This order bore a time of 3:00 P.M., but Meade, advised of the attack earlier, had been engaged in preparations since morning.[28]

At 7:30 A.M. on May 11, Grant asked his corps chiefs to report what force would be necessary to maintain their present positions and how many troops would thus be available for an attack or to extend the front of the army. Just before noon he ordered Hancock to send scouting parties south of the Po River and back to Todd's Tavern to confirm the security of the army's right flank before the Second Corps pulled out after dark. Infantry regiments performed these missions because no cavalrymen were available.

That afternoon a regiment and some pickets from Mott's division retraced the route of their previous day's advance. Attempting to locate and occupy a position overlooking the approaches to the target area for the upcoming attack, these Yankees were driven back by Confederate pickets before gleaning much information. Lee probably regarded this small clash as insignificant (if he heard about it at all), but it represented the one Federal operation before dark that provided a reliable clue as to Grant's intentions.[29]

Typical of Union practice early in the Overland campaign, Meade conveyed instructions to his corps commanders but not to Burnside. He instructed Hancock to move only his First and Third Divisions to Mott's position at the Brown farm. Because Gibbon's Second Division was situated within the lines of the Fifth Corps, which lay closer to the enemy, its withdrawal could alert the Confederates. The army commander assured Hancock that, if at all possible, Gibbon would be withdrawn before daylight and reunited with the Second Corps for the attack. Warren learned that his corps must occupy the segment of the line occupied by the Second Corps after Hancock's troops departed. The New Yorker was granted authorization to shorten his new line from the right should that become absolutely necessary. Meade also advised Warren that a Sixth Corps division would be posted a short distance up the Brock Road from the Fifth Corps line as support should the army's right be attacked. One of Wright's two remaining divisions would withdraw from its position in the Sixth Corps line and stand by to support Hancock as needed.[30]

Grant's orders to Burnside for the attack, timed at 4:00 P.M., probably did not reach Ninth Corps headquarters until nearly dark. Why these (as well as Meade's orders to his subordinates) went out relatively late in the day is not known. Between 8:00 and 9:00 that morning, Grant composed a message to Maj. Gen. Henry H. Halleck, the Union chief of staff, concerning primarily losses, supplies, and reinforcements. He also sent messages to Meade and Burnside about retrieving these supplies at Belle Plain and delivering them to the army. What other duties Grant may have performed from mid-morning to mid-afternoon are not recorded. The late arrival of Burnside's order, together with its misleading wording due to possibly being composed hurriedly, would adversely affect the Ninth Corps's contribution to the Union effort on May 12.[31]

The initial portion of Grant's order to Burnside read: "Major-General Hancock has been ordered to move his entire corps under cover of night to join you in a vigorous attack against the enemy at 4:00 a.m. to-morrow, the 12th instant. You will move against the enemy with your entire force promptly and with all possible vigor at precisely 4 o'clock to-morrow morning. Let your preparations for this attack be conducted with the utmost secrecy, and veiled entirely from the enemy." The remainder of the message explained that Cyrus B. Comstock and Orville B. Babcock of Grant's staff would be sent to acquaint Burnside with the direction of Hancock's attack and to render other assistance. The message closed with an explanation of Warren's and Wright's roles in the operation.[32]

Burnside assumed from these instructions that he should attack in the direction of the Court House to his front. He also understood Hancock would be moving his entire Second Corps that night to join the Ninth Corps in this attack. From what position the Second Corps would launch its assault, whether to Burnside's immediate right or from some other location, would be revealed when Comstock and Babcock arrived. As darkness fell, Burnside awaited Grant's staff officers. He also looked for the return of most of his troops from across the Ni River, where they had been sent in mid-afternoon to establish a new line connecting on the right with Mott. These soldiers marched and waited through a long afternoon made miserable by rain and thunderstorms. The last of them were not back in their entrenchments until 10:00 p.m.[33]

Comstock and Babcock arrived after dark and briefed Burnside concerning the location and direction of Hancock's proposed attack. According to Burnside's report, "[I]t was decided to assault farther to the right at points nearer to the salient of the enemy's works, with a view to establishing and keeping up, if possible, a connection with the Second Corps."[34]

The ideal position from which to initiate such an attack was three-quarters of a mile or more beyond the Ninth Corps's present right flank. It is doubtful whether Burnside or the two staff officers considered moving the troops in the darkness or even reconnoitering a route to the area. The steady rain had initiated the formation of a ground fog, and an afternoon of useless marching had exhausted the troops. Moreover, the attack was intended to surprise the enemy. If Grant's order had arrived earlier in the day, specified the location of Hancock's point of attack, and clearly indicated that Burnside should connect with the left of the Second Corps, there would have been time before dark to lay out the route to the jump-off point for the Ninth Corps. Instead, that task would wait until 4:00 A.M.[35]

Late in the afternoon, Meade summoned his three corps commanders to discuss the proposed attack. Hancock soon discovered that no one at army headquarters had any knowledge about the appearance of the point to be attacked or about the approaches to it. Comstock, who earlier in the day had been in the vicinity of the Brown house, accompanied two of Hancock's staff officers to reconnoiter the area. The trio lost their way in the rain, turned up in Burnside's lines, and, after retracing their steps, arrived at the Brown house just before dark. Mott provided little assistance beyond pointing in the general direction of the Confederate position. The staff officers crept forward to Mott's picket line and discovered their view blocked by an intervening ridge. They decided to recommend that the van of the assault column be formed here in the general area of the picket line. They then separated in the darkness, Hancock's officers returning to report to him and Comstock proceeding to Burnside's headquarters as instructed by Grant.[36]

Hancock convened a meeting with three of his division commanders (Mott being detached) at 7:00 P.M. Brig. Gen. Francis C. Barlow, whose First Division would lead the march and the attack, later recalled that Hancock had no information concerning any aspect of the planned operation. Barlow was ordered to report with his division at 10:00 P.M. to corps headquarters, where staff and engineering officers would lead his troops to the proper position and provide all necessary information. The division and its commander arrived punctually, followed by Maj. Gen. David Bell Birney's Third Division. Lt. Col. Charles H. Morgan — Hancock's chief of staff — and Captain Mendell joined Barlow at the head of the column as the two corps moved off. Hancock did not accompany his command on what would be a miserable three-mile march through rain and mud.

As the column made its way through the darkness, Barlow queried Morgan and Mendell for additional information concerning the proposed attack, only to learn that they had nothing to offer. The column slogged along with the officers at its head profanely voicing anger at the absurdity of their situation. They were moving into position for a supposedly important attack with no knowledge of the position or strength of the enemy. Exhausted infantrymen plodding along to their rear remained silent.

Arriving in the vicinity of the Brown house shortly after midnight, Barlow ordered his brigade commanders to permit their men to attempt to get some sleep in the rain. He then went into the house seeking information, but again Mott provided no assistance. One of Mott's subordinates, however, did try to

Major General Winfield Scott Hancock (seated), with (left to right) Brigadier
Generals Francis Channing Barlow, David Bell Birney, and John Gibbon.
Francis Trevelyan Miller, ed., *The Photographic History of the Civil War*, 10 vols.
(New York: Review of Reviews, 1911), 2:237

help. As Mott's field officer of the day on May 11, Lt. Col. Waldo Merriam had
participated in that afternoon's unsuccessful reconnaissance. He also had been
present during the short advance on May 10. Consequently, he had gained
glimpses of the terrain leading to the Confederate works. Merriam drew a map
on a wall of the house for Barlow that indicated his division initially would
move through a wide clearing between two stands of trees. If Barlow maintained the same course after entering the open field of the Landrum farm, his
division should strike the enemy's works at the desired point. Barlow later

claimed that the information derived from Merriam's rough sketch was the sole basis on which he determined the formation of his division for the advance.[37]

Hancock arrived at the Brown house sometime after midnight. Birney's troops sloshed in after 2:00 A.M. At another meeting, the frustrated Barlow announced that because he lacked information concerning the enemy's dispositions and strength, he would form his division in a near solid mass for the attack—this despite the fact that Mott's troops had been repulsed solely by artillery fire on May 10. After some discussion, Hancock approved this formation. Birney would form on Barlow's right in the standard two-line formation. Mott would march behind Birney, and Gibbon, who arrived after 3:00 A.M., was positioned in the rear as a reserve. The attacking force would total nearly 19,000 troops. Ground fog had by now reduced visibility to fifty yards or less.[38]

At 4:00 A.M. Hancock notified Meade, who had relocated army headquarters to a point a half-mile north of the Brown house, that reduced visibility required a brief delay of the advance. First light would permit the troops to see where they were going. Also at 4:00, approximately one and three-quarter miles to the southeast, two divisions of the Ninth Corps began to plod north in the murky rain along a woods road. They tramped into unmapped, unreconnoitered territory.[39]

Hancock ordered his divisions to advance at 4:35 A.M. The Federals sustained few casualties in crossing three-quarters of a mile to the Confederate position. Pouring over the rebel works on a line extending from just to the left of the apex to a point approximately three hundred yards to the right, they overwhelmed 4,000 Confederate defenders after brief hand-to-hand combat. Their effort netted 3,000 prisoners and eventually twenty artillery pieces.

Plain luck largely explained their initial success. Visibility was no more than 150 to 200 yards when the Federals started across the Landrum field. Posted 400 yards away, Confederate infantrymen could hear them coming but could not fire until the Federals came into view. When finally ordered to shoot their weapons, southerners found that many malfunctioned because of wet powder. In addition, the artillery pieces that had repulsed Mott's troops so easily on May 10 were not fully in position. They had been sent to the rear the previous evening by Lee, who acted on the erroneous assumption that the Federals were preparing to move east to Fredericksburg. Confederate gunners got off only a few rounds before Federals overran most of their pieces.[40]

All of Hancock's officers, including the division commanders, advanced on foot, and when the assault swept over the southern works they lost control of their men. Some Yankees began to herd prisoners across the field to the rear, while others stopped to collect booty. Still others moved to the left or right behind the Confederate traverses collecting more prisoners. Most of the rest continued straight ahead down the inside of the salient in disorganized masses. By 8:00, all of the Federals still on their feet inside the Mule Shoe were driven back to the outside of the captured works by five reinforcing Confederate brigades.

Hancock called on Meade for support on his flanks from Wright and Burnside. By noon, Wright had forwarded the ten brigades of his three divisions to positions on Hancock's right and right rear. To counter this threat, Lee during the morning advanced three brigades to man the inside of the works astride a bend in the line that became known as the "Bloody Angle."[41]

Although Burnside's troops enjoyed a thirty-five-minute head start over Hancock's, they failed to strike the eastern side of the salient simultaneously with the Second Corps's attack along its northern arc. By the time Ninth Corps soldiers engaged a line of enemy pickets, Hancock's men had achieved their breakthrough and were moving down the salient. Elements of Burnside's corps occupied some advanced rifle pits, and a number of them captured a small segment of the Confederate main line. But the reinforcing Confederate brigades that drove Hancock's troops out of the eastern part of the salient also threatened the left of Burnside's advanced contingent, obliging these Federals to relinquish their farthest gains and retire a short distance to establish a defensive line. The two Union corps had established a tenuous link, only to see it broken as the connecting troops withdrew or were driven back, the Ninth Corps to the east and the Second to the north.

Throughout the morning, Grant and, to a lesser extent, Hancock urged Burnside to reconnect with Hancock's left at all costs. The commanding general still did not appreciate the length of Burnside's front. The distance from Burnside's left on the Fredericksburg Road to his right opposite the east face of the salient exceeded a mile. Because his corps constituted the left element of the entire Union force, Burnside prudently retained one of his three divisions to guard that flank. A dubiously efficient Provisional Brigade of infantry composed of dismounted cavalrymen and heavy artillerymen occupied the road.[42]

When Hancock's men were driven back across the works near the apex, he reestablished them in lines located along the outside of these works and farther to the rear (north). The left of the Second Corps line was located at or a short distance east of the apex for the rest of the morning. Burnside would have to sidle his two already overextended divisions another quarter mile to their right to link up with Hancock's left. By 10:00 A.M., Burnside covered a one-mile front with three divisions; in contrast, Hancock and Wright occupied a front approximately one-quarter mile long with six divisions. Burnside nonetheless informed Grant at 9:30 A.M. that a connection with Hancock had been reestablished. A half hour later, Grant ordered Comstock to urge the Ninth Corps commander to push hard with everything he had, including the Provisional Brigade. In another twenty minutes Burnside was peremptorily ordered to move one of his divisions to the right to assist Hancock. He started the one nearest to the Fredericksburg Road but recalled it after the men had marched a half mile. Finally realizing Burnside's situation by early afternoon, Grant informed the harried corps commander that if he was unable to hold his present line he could shorten it to the right and give up the Fredericksburg Road. All three Ninth Corps divisions and the Provisional Brigade must be used in the attacks. Burnside wisely retained the last-named unit on the road.[43]

Burnside was not the only Union corps commander whose performance troubled Grant on May 12. Warren's Fifth Corps manned the line to the right of the Brock Road. There they faced a five-brigade Confederate division that since May 8 had repulsed several Federal attacks. On the morning of the 12th, the troops of one of Lee's reinforcing brigades reached the works at 7:30 to 7:45 A.M. and drove some of Wright's men away from this line. Wright requested support. At 8:00 Meade, assuming erroneously that these Confederates had been drawn from in front of the Fifth Corps position, ordered Warren to attack in his front. Warren replied with a number of excuses for not doing so, including the presence of a heavy enfilading fire from his left. Army chief of staff Humphreys informed him at 9:15 A.M. that the order to attack was peremptory. A few minutes later a sympathetic Humphreys advised Warren not to hesitate because Meade had assumed responsibility and would shoulder the consequences. But Warren's despondent messages to headquarters had raised doubts about how well he might do. He was told that should his assaults fail, he must prepare to withdraw his troops and send them quickly to the support of Wright and Hancock. Warren queried at least one of his division commanders, who reported that his men were losing heavily and that he could not get them to advance to the enemy works.[44]

At about this time, Meade informed Grant that Warren seemed reluctant to attack despite having received positive orders to do so. Grant replied that if the corps commander refused to attack promptly Meade should send Humphreys to command the Fifth Corps and relieve Warren. Although Meade did not take this drastic step, he sent his chief of staff to monitor the withdrawal of two of Warren's divisions and expedite their move to the left.[45]

Grant and Meade decided that the Army of the Potomac's major effort in the afternoon should hit the northern line of the salient. The situation there had evolved into a bloody stalemate, with Hancock's and Wright's troops packed several ranks deep behind slight undulations in the ground 15 to 40 yards out from the works. Most of the Yankees in the front rank sought to discourage enemy troops from sallying forth by maintaining a steady volume of fire directed toward the top of the rebel entrenchments (few Confederates had demonstrated an inclination to leave their sheltered position after 8:00 A.M.). Similarly, the southerners fired back to dissuade these Federals from attempting to rush the works. Groups of 50 to 100 Federals occasionally sprinted forward, scaled the works, and dropped down into a traverse or two to engage the defenders in bloody combat. Inevitably, those assailants who escaped death, wounds, or capture scampered back to their original positions. There was no coordination between the two Federal corps and little between their divisions. The Federal situation fairly screamed for the presence of a designated overall commander.

Meade had personally visited Warren in mid-morning and at 10:20 A.M. moved to Hancock's headquarters at the Landrum house.[46] From there he could view the Federal line opposite the tip of the salient. But Meade either did not recognize or dismissed as insignificant a peculiar situation that existed along the left segment of this line. Hancock's troops, lying in some places forty ranks deep, manned the stretch of the line beginning to the left of the apex and extending right approximately two-thirds of the distance to the West or Bloody Angle. These Yankees were firing very little and receiving no return fire from the works to their front. To their right, however, fighting raged in the vicinity of the Bloody Angle.

The explanation for the relative quiet at the apex of the salient was simple. Confederates who had driven the Yankees out of the Mule Shoe earlier in the morning lacked the numbers to reoccupy the lines at the apex. Instead, they assumed position along the eastern face of the salient in a line that began 200 yards or so south of the apex and continued in that direction along the works for perhaps 600 yards. The works running west for the initial 250 to 300 yards from the apex similarly were unoccupied.

Hancock must have recognized the lack of southern infantry fire against his troops. But from the time his soldiers retreated from the salient he appears to have thought primarily in defensive terms. He and his men had endured an exhausting night and ensuing morning. His nagging wound probably bothered him. Above all, in this advanced position he worried about his left flank. The connection with Burnside's troops was shaky at best. Hancock knew little about what the Ninth Corps had accomplished along the eastern face of the salient, and because of inadequate maps and lack of reconnaissance also remained unaware of the location of Burnside's troops relative to his own. Shortly after midday he ordered some of his idle men to erect works extending to the Federal left from the apex. Hancock may have been thinking about an unhappy episode from six days earlier in the Wilderness. On May 6 along the Plank Road, an advanced component of his corps had been surprised by a vicious enemy attack on their left flank that drove thousands of troops in confusion back to their former position. Here at Spotsylvania he would exercise caution and erect works from which to defend his position against attack. He would not reconnoiter the quiet area to his immediate front.[47]

While Hancock worried about his left, Horatio Wright continued his severe indoctrination to corps command. Early in the action he had been nicked by a piece of shrapnel. By noon he had advanced all ten of his brigades from the main line to positions opposite the West Angle; some of the units had executed unsuccessful assaults against the Confederates there before withdrawing one hundred yards or more to the relative safety of tree cover. Wright kept two of his brigades fairly close to the works on Hancock's immediate right while retaining the other eight farther to the rear. When Humphreys inquired just after midday whether an attack augmented by a part or all of the Fifth Corps along his front might succeed, Wright, despite the presence of ten brigades near at hand, replied, "I think a large force might carry the line at this point. I have not the force to do it."[48]

Sometime after midday, Wright relocated his field headquarters to the Landrum house. No longer able to see his firing line, he necessarily relied on dispatches from his division commanders for information. In messages to Meade he described his frontline troops as hard pressed to maintain their positions. This misleading phraseology probably led both Meade and Grant to believe the enemy opposite Wright's position was attacking out over the works in attempts to drive the Yankees away. In reality, the Confederates had no intention of conducting such action in that sector.

The first of Warren's two reinforcing divisions reported to Wright between 2:00 and 2:30 P.M. Wright immediately ordered most of these troops forward to relieve some of his Sixth Corps men, many of whom had been in position on the firing line for eight hours. This concern for his troops ordinarily would have been laudable, but by early afternoon on May 12 everyone in the Union army was approaching a state of exhaustion. Wright's action in this instance doomed any chance that a major assault could be executed before dark. Increasingly pessimistic about the chances for a successful northern assault as the afternoon wore on, Wright joined Hancock in worrying about the possibility of an enemy counterattack if such an assault failed. Both began to entrench in the rear of their positions. Finally, at 5:10 P.M., with Hancock's concurrence, Wright decided not to conduct the attack and so informed Meade. The army commander reluctantly approved the decision.[49]

The Federals experienced no greater success on Burnside's end of the line. At Grant's urging, Burnside at 2:00 P.M. ordered his reserve division to attack straight ahead from its position north of the Fredericksburg Road. Grant hoped this would prevent Lee's shifting any troops from that area to assist those fighting Wright and Hancock. The Federal attackers collided in the woods with two advancing Confederate brigades; the antagonists fought bitterly for a time, then returned to their respective lines.[50]

The intense drama inaugurated by Hancock's massive assault at dawn on May 12 finally drew to a close about 4:00 A.M. on May 13. After nearly twenty-four hours of combat between combatants inside and along the outer rim of the Mule Shoe, the last Confederates abandoned their positions in the salient and withdrew to a newly constructed line of works across its base.

Although thousands of additional soldiers would be killed and maimed, the remaining nine days of the Spotsylvania campaign served as an anticlimax to the horror of May 12. By May 15, the Army of the Potomac had moved behind the Ninth Corps and aligned on the left of Burnside's troops facing to the west. Lee reacted by transferring the division that had opposed Warren west of the Brock Road to a position south of the village.

As the Federals waited for the roads to dry reinforcements made their way southward from Washington. Grant had assured his government on May 10, via a message to Chief of Staff Halleck, that he would not retreat and that he believed his army eventually could defeat the Army of Northern Virginia. He requested supplies of forage, provisions, ammunition, and men. Grant believed the positions of the opposing armies were such that 10,000 troops could be stripped from the defenses of Washington and forwarded to him without placing the capital at risk. In a radical reversal of previous policy, the administration approved Grant's request. The president obviously trusted his general-in-chief.[51]

The final Federal offensive at Spotsylvania took place on May 18. Upon the recommendation of Wright and Chief of Staff Humphreys, the Second and Sixth Corps returned to the vicinity of the Landrum farm and advanced against the enemy line across the base of the former salient. The enemy's position was strong and the attack failed.[52]

With reinforcements arriving and the roads drying, Grant planned the next move south. Hancock received orders to put his corps on the march at 2:00 A.M. on May 20 along the railroad that ran between Fredericksburg and Richmond. If Lee pursued Hancock directly, the remainder of the Union army would follow and attempt to catch the Army of Northern Virginia at a disadvantage. Should Lee not pursue directly, the rest of Grant's troops would follow Hancock and seek to engage the enemy somewhere in the open farther to the south.

An unanticipated Confederate movement on May 19 delayed execution of the Federal plan for nearly twenty-four hours. Richard S. Ewell's Second Corps mounted a reconnaissance-in-force that afternoon, striking Meade's right flank at the Harris farm near the Fredericksburg Road. Many of the newly arrived Federal reinforcements, heavy artillerymen serving as infantry, received their baptism of fire in this engagement. The firing ceased shortly after dark, and Grant hoped to continue with Hancock's scheduled departure at 2:00 the next morning. He reluctantly agreed to wait, however, because many of Hancock's troops, as well as other Federal units, were now out of position. Not until 11:00 on the night of May 20 did Hancock lead his troops to the railroad, where they turned south. Lee did not pursue directly. The two armies would next meet along the North Anna River.[53]

The Spotsylvania campaign thus terminated with the Union army moving south and the Confederates following. The Federals had failed to defeat or destroy the Army of Northern Virginia, but, as after the battle of the Wilderness, they moved deeper into the Confederacy rather than retiring to lick their wounds. Unable to prevent Grant's movement, Lee tacitly acknowledged that his opponent had seized the strategic initiative (the Federals would hold the tactical initiative for most of the rest of the war in Virginia as well).

Ulysses S. Grant's presence with the Army of the Potomac largely explains this development. He had begun to dictate tactical movements in the battle of the Wilderness, leaving Meade and Burnside to implement them. Outwardly stoic about his reduced role in the army, Meade concealed his mortification from most of his military colleagues. In a letter of May 23, however, he informed his wife that if there were an honorable way to retire from his false position he would certainly adopt it. As there seemed to be no such remedy, he would patiently submit and bear the humiliation God had seen fit to inflict on him.[54]

Shortly after the fighting of May 12, Grant recommended Meade and Sherman for promotion to the rank of major general in the Regular Army. In calling for their advancement, the general-in-chief remarked that Meade and Sherman were the most qualified officers for large commands that he had yet encountered. He also reported that Meade had far exceeded his expectations. Some members of Grant's staff did not share their commander's opinions, complaining in a sometimes heated discussion that Meade merely implemented Grant's tactical decisions and should receive neither praise nor blame for the results. In addition, the Pennsylvanian's violent temper made him difficult to work with. Grant acknowledged that the situation had produced embarrassments but said he would not change it. He could not assume the many duties of an army commander while still acting as general-in-chief of all Union forces. Moreover, he insisted that Meade was perfectly subordinate and, equally important, knew far better than did Grant the strengths and weaknesses of higher ranking officers in the Army of the Potomac.[55]

Grant's decision concerning the use of Sheridan's Cavalry Corps had hurt the army at Spotsylvania. In allowing Sheridan to take nearly all his troopers southward on May 9, Grant rendered Union infantry commanders practically blind regarding the army's flanks. Not until approximately May 17 was the 5th New York Cavalry released from its patrolling role under Ferrero. On May 17– 18, the 5th New York and Burnside's 13th Pennsylvania Cavalry scouted the routes leading south for the movement that began on the night of the 20th.[56]

The strain imposed upon Hancock (and almost everybody else) in the Wilderness fighting apparently carried over to Spotsylvania. Together with persisting problems associated with his Gettysburg wound, this strain ap- pears gradually to have blunted Hancock's aggressive qualities. The corps commander opposite the Mule Shoe lines after 9:00 A.M. on May 12 scarcely resembled the man who had defended Cemetery Hill and Cemetery Ridge on July 1–3, 1863, at Gettysburg. Hancock took no initiative in reconnoitering his front after mid-morning on the 12th; left in the dark about the enemy in his front, he mistakenly feared an attack from an area cleared of Confeder- ate troops. In a postwar letter, Hancock recognized the need for a designated commander to coordinate the operations of his and the Sixth Corps along the north face of the salient, but on May 12 he never suggested this to Meade.[57]

Gouverneur K. Warren created frustration for the army's high command throughout the campaign. His one great fault, according to Meade, was a con- stitutional inability to obey a direct order without first thoroughly analyzing it to determine whether it coincided with his own military judgment. This nearly cost him his command May 12. One of Meade's aides, who possessed little mili- tary experience, believed Warren incapable of effective corps command be- cause he could not spread himself over three divisions. This opinion probably stemmed from Warren's proclivity to attempt to oversee every operation of his vast command. During the army's departure from the Wilderness, for example, Warren remained behind to oversee the safe extraction of his last infantry and artillery units from the line when he should have been leading the Fifth Corps down the Brock Road. In June, an exasperated Meade composed a nine-page letter requesting that Warren be relieved from duty with the Army of the Poto- mac. Although the army commander decided not to forward the request, he continued to lecture Warren about what Meade considered his shortcomings.[58]

John Sedgwick's death on May 9 delivered a severe blow to the Army of the Potomac and thrust Horatio G. Wright into a daunting position. On May 10, Wright received the nearly impossible assignment of coordinating simulta- neous advances by two forces (Upton's and Mott's) separated by nearly a mile. On the 12th, his troops fought the enemy from positions in front of the Bloody Angle — in some instances for nearly twenty-four hours. Wright's concern for his exhausted men led him to squander the services of initial reinforcements from Warren, an action that doomed hopes for a late afternoon combined attack and effectively ended Union offensive operations on the 12th. The new Sixth Corps chief did show promise as a fighter, however, when a few days later he joined Humphreys in suggesting that his corps conduct an attack rather than remaining idle while the army waited for roads to dry and reinforcements to arrive.

Ambrose E. Burnside and the Ninth Corps provided additional infantry and artillery but promoted administrative inefficiency during the Union effort at Spotsylvania. Meade wielded no control over Burnside, who was subject only to Grant's orders. During the critical first five days of the campaign, the Ninth Corps was located a minimum of two miles from Grant's headquarters. Because no telegraph line connected army and Ninth Corps headquarters, mounted couriers had to carry messages back and forth across unmapped and unreconnoitered ground. Grant expected Burnside to support to the left of Meade's attacking forces on both the 10th and 12th of May. The length of his assigned line made such support difficult if not impossible for Burnside. His three divisions were inadequate to defend such a long line, let alone to participate in all-out attacks. Thus, Lee on the morning of May 12 could shift three infantry brigades from Burnside's front in the vicinity of Spotsylvania to the top of the salient, where they stymied the efforts of Hancock and Wright for the remainder of the day. Burnside attempted to comply with his orders and accomplished as much as could be expected under the circumstances.

As the Union army marched away from Spotsylvania, Grant, Meade, and the four corps commanders probably reflected occasionally on the events of the past two weeks. Fighting had been severe and bloody, coordination between major units ineffective at times. But they were moving south again, which may have instilled in them the first fluttering of hope for final victory. Only three of the six generals would still hold commands with the Army of the Potomac eleven months later at Appomattox. Grant would be entering the McLean house to await the arrival of Lee. Meade and Wright would be with their troops.

NOTES

1. George G. Meade [Jr.], ed., *The Life and Letters of George Gordon Meade*, 2 vols. (New York: Charles Scribner's Sons, 1913), 2:197–98.

2. U.S. War Department, *The War of the Rebellion: A Compilation of the Official Records of the Union and Confederate Armies*, 127 vols., index, and atlas (Washington: GPO, 1880–1901), ser. 1, vol. 36, pt. 2:320 (hereafter cited as *OR*; all references are to ser. 1); David R. Jordan, *Winfield Scott Hancock: A Soldier's Story* (Bloomington: Indiana University Press, 1988), 111.

3. Gordon C. Rhea, *The Battle of the Wilderness: May 5–6, 1864* (Baton Rouge: Louisiana

State University Press, 1994), 431–34; Andrew A. Humphreys, *The Virginia Campaign of '64 and '65* (New York: Charles Scribner's Sons, 1883), 425.

4. Rhea, *Battle of the Wilderness*, 72–74, 91–92, 253–60.

5. Theodore Lyman, *Meade's Headquarters, 1863–1865: Letters of Colonel Theodore Lyman from the Wilderness to Appomattox*, ed. George R. Agassiz (Boston: Atlantic Monthly Press, 1922), 105–6; Horace Porter, *Campaigning with Grant* (1897; reprint, Bloomington: Indiana University Press, 1965), 83–84; *OR* 36(2):553.

6. *OR* 36(1):891, 893, (2):586. Ferrero's infantrymen served as a rear guard for the army's trains. Burnside took the 13th Pennsylvania with his Ninth Corps to its position on the army's left.

7. *OR* 36(2)552.

8. *OR* 36(2):564–66.

9. Martin T. McMahon, "The Death of General John Sedgwick," in *Battles and Leaders of the Civil War*, eds., Robert Underwood Johnson and Clarence Clough Buel, 4 vols. (New York: Century, 1887–88), 4:175; *OR* 36(2):577.

10. Theodore Lyman, "Uselessness of the Maps Furnished to the Staff of the Army of the Potomac Previous to the Campaign of May 1864," in *Papers of the Military Historical Society of Massachusetts*, 14 vols. (1895–1918; reprint with a general index, Wilmington, N.C.: Broadfoot Publishing, 1989–90), 4:79–80 (hereafter cited as *PMHSM*); *OR* 36(1):293.

11. *OR* 36(2):600, 604.

12. *OR* 36(2):602–3; (1):954.

13. *OR* 36(2):610.

14. *OR* 36(1):334; (2):596, 600.

15. *OR* 36(1):334.

16. *OR* 36(2):609.

17. *OR* 36(1):297.

18. *OR* 36(1):667.

19. *OR* 36(2):603.

20. *OR* 36(1):765, 490, 494, 499, 502.

21. Oliver Wendell Holmes, *Touched with Fire: Civil War Letters and Diary of Oliver Wendell Holmes, Jr., 1861–1864*, ed. Mark De Wolfe Howe (Cambridge, Mass.: Harvard University Press, 1946), 111.

22. *OR* 36(1):490, 494.

23. Marsena R. Patrick, *Inside Lincoln's Army: The Diary of Marsena Rudolph Patrick, Provost Marshal General, Army of the Potomac*, ed. David S. Sparks (New York: Thomas Yoseloff, 1964), 371; *OR* 36(1):688–89.

24. *OR* 36(1):908–9; (2):582.

25. Porter, *Campaigning with Grant*, 94–95; *OR* 36(1):908–9.

26. *OR* 36(2):603.

27. Ulysses S. Grant, *Personal Memoirs of U. S. Grant*, 2 vols. (New York: Charles L. Webster & Company, 1885), 2:224–25; Lyman, *Meade's Headquarters*, 105–6, 100 n. 1.

28. *OR* 36(2):629.

29. *OR* 36(2):630; (1):334.

30. *OR* 36(2):635, 637–38.

31. William Marvel, *Burnside* (Chapel Hill: University of North Carolina Press, 1991), 362; *OR* 36(2):595–96, 627–28.

32. *OR* 36(2):643.

33. Marvel, *Burnside*, 362; *OR* 36(1):909, 928.

34. *OR* 36(1):909.

35. Marvel, *Burnside*, 362.

36. Humphreys, *Virginia Campaign*, 90; Francis A. Walker, *A History of the Second Army Corps* (New York: Charles Scribner's Sons, 1886), 468.

37. Francis C. Barlow, "Capture of the Salient, May 12, 1864," in *PMHSM* 4:245–49.

38. John D. Black, "Reminiscences of the Bloody Angle," in Minnesota Commandery of the Military Order of the Loyal Legion of the United States, *Glimpses of the Nation's Struggle. Fourth Series* (St. Paul: H. L. Collins Company, 1898), 423.

39. *OR* 36(1):335; (2):638.

40. *OR* 36(1):335.

41. *OR* 36(1):336; (2):656.

42. Marvel, *Burnside*, 363.

43. *OR* 36(2):679.

44. *OR* 36(2):662–63, 671.

45. *OR* 36(2):654–55.

46. *OR* 36(2):655.

47. Rhea, *Battle of the Wilderness*, 358–66.

48. *OR* 36(2):673.

49. *OR* 36(1):611–12, 685; (2):674–75.

50. *OR* 36(1):941.

51. *OR* 36(2):595–96.

52. *OR* 36(1):337–38.

53. *OR* 36(1):340–41.

54. George G. Meade to wife, May 23, 1864, George G. Meade Papers, Historical Society of Pennsylvania, Philadelphia (repository hereafter cited as HSP).

55. Porter, *Campaigning with Grant*, 114–15; *OR* 36(2):695.

56. *OR* 36(1):892, 803; (2):848.

57. Winfield Scott Hancock to Francis A. Walker, January 25, 1886, folder titled "Maine Commandery 1865–1896," Military Order of the Loyal Legion of the United States War Library and Museum, Philadelphia.

58. Lyman, *Meade's Headquarters*, 110 n. 1; Grant, *Memoirs*, 2:214–15; George G. Meade to Brig. Gen. John A. Rawlins, June 21, 1864, Meade Papers, HSP.

The Testing of a Corps Commander
Gouverneur Kemble Warren at the Wilderness and Spotsylvania

I n 1864, at thirty-four years of age, Gouverneur Kemble Warren became the Army of the Potomac's youngest and most promising corps commander, proudly sporting the yellow sash of a major general. Lt. Gen. Ulysses S. Grant, the new Federal general-in-chief, considered him the most likely replacement for the Potomac army's head, Maj. Gen. George G. Meade, should Meade become incapacitated. Warren felt "light hearted and confident," he wrote his wife, Emily. "We are going to have a magnificent campaign; and I have a situation commensurate with it."[1]

But by the eighth day of fighting, Grant was contemplating Warren's dismissal. Grant's aggressive mode of warfare had no place for Warren's deliberate style. As the campaign unfolded, Grant fumed through frustrating delays and missed opportunities, and Union casualty returns lengthened. The story of Warren's dramatic change in fortune provides a fascinating glimpse into the Union army's fractious leadership during the war's final year. It also underscores the scarcity of Civil War corps commanders who proved able to conduct successfully large-scale offensive operations with little or no personal supervision from their commanding generals.

Warren was born on January 8, 1830, the eighth of twelve children of Sylvanus Warren, a prominent citizen of Cold Spring, New York. He was an intelligent but sickly child, sensitive to criticism and, judging from surviving letters, sometimes arrogant and self-assured. He entered the nearby United States

Military Academy at sixteen, graduated second in the class of 1850, and received a coveted appointment as second lieutenant in the prestigious Corps of Topographical Engineers. His first assignment was to assist Capt. Andrew A. Humphreys surveying the lower Mississippi River. The two men became fast friends, forming an association that proved valuable to Warren in the years ahead.[2]

The New Yorker's life crackled with adventure. He surveyed the upper Mississippi, charting treacherous shoals and opening the river to navigation, and helped select the route for a transcontinental railway. He went west as chief engineer of the Sioux expedition, tasting combat and mapping the Nebraska Territory. He ascended the Yellowstone River, traversed the Black Hills, and parlayed with the suspicious Sioux. His father died in early 1859, and he returned east as assistant professor of mathematics at West Point to be near his family.

The outbreak of hostilities in 1861 thrust Warren back into active service. He began the war as lieutenant colonel in the 5th New York Infantry and was appointed the unit's colonel three months later. He commanded two regiments at Gaines's Mill, where a spent ball severely bruised his knee, waged a disastrous defense at Second Manassas, and was commissioned brigadier general to date from his "distinguished conduct" at Gaines's Mill. At Fredericksburg, he acquired a healthy respect for earthworks that remained with him throughout the war. "Fortifications must be turned or besieged," he wrote in a letter to his brother. "The bravery of our men is quailing before these things."[3]

In February 1863, Maj. Gen. Joseph Hooker appointed Warren chief topographical engineer of the Army of the Potomac. The position eminently suited his talents and disposition, and he reveled in the details of staff work. On May 12 he was promoted again, to the position of chief engineer. His private life also flourished. Early in the war, while stationed in Baltimore, he had met Emily Chase, a cultured and wealthy former sweetheart of Confederate general Ambrose P. Hill. On June 17, 1863, Warren and Emily were married.

Two days after his wedding, the groom rushed back to the army. On July 2 at Gettysburg, he recognized the importance of Little Round Top and hurried troops there. His decisive action saved the day for the Federals and made him the toast of the North. A fellow officer observed that without Warren's "coup d'oeil and prompt acceptance of responsibility, Gettysburg might have been noted as the grave of the Union."[4]

As commander of the Army of the Potomac, Meade selected Warren as temporary head of the Second Corps. The tangled maneuvers during 1863's summer and fall brought Warren new laurels. In October, he defeated Hill's veterans at Bristoe Station and sent his opponent a boastful message: "Hill, I have not only whipped you, but married your old sweetheart." In November,

Meade assigned Warren to assault a Confederate position at Mine Run, this time with his own corps and part of another. Once again Hill was his adversary, but this time the Confederates were firmly entrenched. Warren canceled the attack and was roundly criticized. Although several of the army's generals delighted in Warren's humiliation, the army's rank and file viewed his decision as a refreshing demonstration of moral courage.[5]

Warren's relationship with Meade suffered significantly as a result of Mine Run. Angered over Meade's failure to support fully his decision to abort the attack, Warren wrote Humphreys, now the army's chief of staff, that Meade's "manner towards me should have saved me from that seeming public censure which everyone is spared till sentenced by a Genl. Court Martial." He privately complained to his brother that his fellow corps commanders were "not fit to be generals," suggesting that if Meade had removed them after Gettysburg as he had urged, "we should have succeeded." He added, "I do not feel very kindly toward Genl. Meade under all the circumstances." Warren further strained the relationship in March 1864 by testifying before the Joint Committee on the Conduct of the War. Hesitancy and indecision by the Potomac army's senior generals, he asserted, had forfeited victory at Gettysburg.[6]

On March 23, 1864, the Army of the Potomac was reorganized into three infantry corps. Warren received permanent command of the Fifth Corps, numbering some 28,000 men. The young New Yorker had emerged as one of the army's most influential generals. His future depended on how he managed his corps in the crucial campaign ahead.

Lt. Col. Theodore Lyman, aide to General Meade, described Warren as a "small, slender man, with a sun-burnt face, two piercing black eyes, and withal bearing a most ludicrous resemblance to cousin Mary Pratt!" His "striking characteristic," another aide observed, was his "habitual and noticeably grave expression which harbored in his dusky, sallow face." The general impressed one officer as a "most kind man," but his artillery chief, Col. Charles S. Wainwright, discerned a darker side. "I used to think the Charleston hackmen the most profane in the world," Wainwright wrote his family. "But I never heard anything which could begin to equal [Warren's] awful oaths poured out tonight; they fairly made my hair stand on end with their profaneness, while I was filled with wonder at the ingenuity of invention and desperate blackguardism they displayed." A fellow New Yorker termed Warren generally unpopular and viewed as "dull and uninteresting." He could be unmerciful to subordinate officers and brazenly confronted his superiors, which cost him their good will. He soon would discover that friends in high places were important commodities, particularly in the Army of the Potomac.[7]

On May 4, 1864, Grant initiated a campaign designed to bring Gen. Robert

Major General Gouverneur Kemble Warren (fifth from left), with members of his staff. *Harper's Weekly*, August 13, 1864

E. Lee's Army of Northern Virginia to its knees. His first step was to flank Lee from his fortifications below the Rapidan River. Warren led the Fifth Corps across Germanna Ford, followed by Maj. Gen. John Sedgwick's Sixth Corps, while Maj. Gen. Winfield Scott Hancock's Second Corps crossed a few miles downstream at Ely's Ford. Warren camped four miles below the river at Ellwood, a two-story home perched nobly on high ground above Wilderness Run. He extended Brig. Gen. James S. Wadsworth's division east along the Orange Turnpike, thrust Maj. Gen. Samuel W. Crawford's Pennsylvania Reserves a short distance southwest along a wagon trail toward Parker's Store, halted Brig. Gen. John R. Robinson's division along the Germanna Plank Road, and had Brig. Gen. Charles Griffin's division spread its blankets beside the Orange Turnpike, west of Ellwood. Griffin's position was critical. If Lee attacked, he would likely do so on the Turnpike, which meant that Griffin had to keep the road well posted. Warren, however, had been misinformed that Union cavalry was prowling the countryside toward the rebels, so he discounted any need to fortify. "Pickets were thrown out," an officer observed, "but not with such care as should be exercised in the presence of the enemy."[8]

Warren resumed his corps's movement shortly after daylight on May 5. Resplendent in dress uniform and yellow sash, he supervised the exercise from his large dapple gray horse. Crawford continued southwest along the wagon trail toward Parker's Store; Wadsworth fell into line behind Crawford; Robinson pulled up, prepared to follow Wadsworth; and Griffin started withdrawing from the Turnpike to bring up the column's rear. Warren's instructions were to march "well closed and held well in hand, ready to meet an attack any moment." Lee was somewhere west, but he appeared to pose no immediate threat.[9]

Shortly before 6:00 A.M., Griffin's outpost spotted dust boiling up from the west. Rebel cavalry, followed by infantry, was approaching at a steady pace. Col. David T. Jenkins of the 146th New York hastily scribbled a dispatch. "The rebel infantry have appeared on the Orange Court House turnpike and are forming a line of battle, three quarters of a mile in front of General Griffin's line of battle," he warned. "I have my skirmishers out, and preparations are being made to meet them. There is a large cloud of dust in that direction."[10]

A courier pounded up to Warren with Jenkins's note. The general read it quickly. "I do not believe that Warren ever had a greater surprise in his life," a witness related, "but his thin, solemn, darkly sallow face was nowhere lighted even by a transitory flare." Turning to a young ordnance officer, Warren commanded, "Tell Griffin to get ready to attack at once." As the staffer started to go, Warren thought better of his choice and directed a more experienced officer to deliver the message. Then he notified Meade that he intended to continue the morning's maneuver. Seizing the opportunity to lecture his superiors, Warren added, "Such demonstrations are to be expected, and show the necessity for keeping well closed and prepared to face toward Mine Run and meet an attack at a moment's notice."[11]

An hour later, Meade reached Warren's headquarters at Ellwood. "If there is to be any fighting this side of Mine Run, let us do it right off!" he directed. Suspicious that the rebel force might be larger than initially thought, Meade ordered the army to halt until he could determine the state of affairs. "I have directed General Warren to attack them at once with his whole force," Meade reported to Grant. "I think the enemy is trying to delay our movement, and will not give battle, but of this we shall soon see." Grant fired back his approval: "If any opportunity presents itself for pitching into a part of Lee's army, do so without giving time for disposition."[12]

Lt. Gen. Richard S. Ewell's Confederates were deploying across the western edge of a clearing known as Saunders's field. Shovels flew and axes rang as the rebels raised formidable entrenchments across high ground on the far side of the field. Warren's deep-seated respect for earthworks, born of his experience at Fredericksburg and Mine Run, governed his actions. He concentrated Griffin along the eastern edge of Saunders's field, facing the rebels. To support Griffin, he halted the rest of his corps, which had started along the Parker's Store trail, and began facing it west, so as to connect to Griffin's left. Griffin's right flank was unprotected, but Sedgwick's Sixth Corps began cutting over from the Germanna Plank Road to fill that void. Once Sedgwick was in place, Warren would be ready to proceed.

Progress was agonizingly slow. Wadsworth's division had to claw its way through a mile of tangled thickets. Many regiments used compasses to find their way. Then more Confederates — Hill's men — appeared on Warren's left, near Crawford. Warren's aide, Washington A. Roebling, urged the corps commander to reinforce Crawford to counter this new threat. Meade, however, insisted that Warren concentrate his efforts against Ewell's burgeoning rebel line on the Turnpike.

Noon came. Wadsworth had arrived on Griffin's left, but the troops were thoroughly jumbled and needed rest. Sedgwick had not appeared, so Griffin's right-most brigade — an outfit under Brig. Gen. Romeyn B. Ayres — was unsupported and exceedingly vulnerable. With Confederates extending well past Ayres's right flank, charging across Saunders's field would be suicide. Warren urged Grant and Meade to wait, but they insisted that he faced only an "observing brigade." If Warren delayed his assault, the rebels might escape. "It would do well to move only with matters well in hand," Warren pleaded, emphasizing that the "repulse of my force would make a bad beginning." His superiors would have none of it. "We are waiting for you," Meade snapped.[13]

Against his better judgment, Warren directed Griffin to begin. Ayres protested, and Griffin, who shared Ayres's concern, asked Warren to postpone the attack. Warren appealed to his superiors and was again rebuffed. Apparently Grant questioned the bravery of Meade's army, and Meade in no uncertain terms ordered Warren to begin the assault.[14]

At 1:00 P.M., Griffin's division stepped into Saunders's field. The outcome was as Warren and his subordinates had predicted. Ayres came under withering frontal and flanking fire and sustained massive losses. Griffin retreated, uncovering Wadsworth's right, and Robinson was swamped by Wadsworth's fugitives streaming back from the front. Crawford, separated from the rest of the corps, retraced his path to Ellwood. Within two hours, the offensive was over. Ewell's Confederates commanded the field.[15]

Warren and his subordinates roundly condemned the ill-conceived assault, which had cost the Fifth Corps some 2,000 men. In his battle report, Warren implicitly criticized his superiors for forcing him to charge before Sedgwick arrived. Writing candidly after the war, he termed the precipitate attack the "most fatal blunder of the campaign." In his view, "If we had waited until the Sixth Corps or two divisions of it got up with the enemy on the road the Sixth Corps was taking, we should have begun the attack on Ewell's flank." Pounded simultaneously by two Union corps, Ewell would have collapsed, opening the way for victory over Lee's army. Warren correctly observed that waiting for Sedgwick would have cost the Federals nothing, as Ewell had no reinforcements to summon during the interval.[16]

The action at Saunders's field starkly dramatized Grant's and Warren's different approaches to warfare. Warren saw the slaughter as vindicating the views he had expressed at Mine Run. Assaulting well-appointed earthworks without sufficient preparation was madness, and he did not intend to rush into combat again, whatever the inducements. Grant was of a different mind. His key to beating Lee involved rapid assaults that afforded the rebels no opportunity to respond or to initiate their own offensives. Some assaults, such as the Saunders's field foray, might fail, but under Grant's program tactical reverses were acceptable so long as the army hewed to his overall strategy. Warren and many of his compatriots found Grant's military philosophy unpalatable. The aide Swan later remarked that Saunders's field marked the "beginning of a reckless (brutal it used to be muttered in those days) way of fighting battles by a hurrying into action one division, one brigade, or even a single regiment at a time, which characterized every contest from the crossing of the Rapidan to the battle at Cold Harbor."[17] The lesson was clear. Unless Warren adapted to Grant's style of fighting, his days in the Army of the Potomac were numbered.

The reverse at Saunders's field stunned Warren. During the afternoon of May 5, Sedgwick attacked, but Warren did not participate. As fighting escalated, Grant detached four of Warren's brigades to help Hancock. The battle's focus remained in Hancock's sector the following day, with Warren relegated to keeping the Confederates in front of him occupied. For May 7, however, Grant assigned the Fifth Corps an important role. Having reached a tactical impasse in the Wilderness, Grant decided to interpose part of his army between Lee and Richmond and force the Confederates to fight him on more favorable ground. Warren would lead the way.

At 8:00 P.M. on May 7, the Fifth Corps evacuated its trenches and started along the Brock Road toward the crossroads hamlet of Spotsylvania Court House. Progress was slow, and not until 3:00 A.M. on the 8th did the head of Warren's column reach Todd's Tavern, halfway to its objective. Confederate cavalry barred the route. Maj. Gen. Philip H. Sheridan's Union horsemen tried unsuccessfully to pound through, and around 6:30 in the morning, the assignment went to Warren. His dust-caked soldiers pried themselves from

Union soldiers on the march from the Wilderness to Spotsylvania Court House, May 8, 1864. Robert Underwood Johnson and Clarence Clough Buel, eds., *Battles and Leaders of the Civil War*, 4 vols. (New York: Century, 1887–88), 4:164

their roadside bivouac and formed in column, Robinson leading, Griffin immediately behind.

Pressed by the Fifth Corps, the Confederate cavalrymen retired, waging heated delaying actions behind makeshift breastworks of timber and fence rails. A few miles below Todd's Tavern, the rebels reached their final position. A field on the Spindle farm lay ahead, and on the clearing's south side, along a shallow ridge, Confederates could be seen throwing up another defensive line. A mood of "positive exhilaration" animated Warren's men. "The impression gained ground that Lee's army was in full retreat toward Richmond," related a Union colonel, "and that we had in our immediate front only his rear guard of cavalry and horse artillery, maneuvering to cover his retreat."[18]

Warren saw an inviting opportunity to redeem his fortunes. In the Wilderness, he had been criticized for moving too deliberately. This time, he would adapt to Grant's style and ruthlessly press ahead, wasting no time for dispositions, to paraphrase Grant's instructions in the Wilderness. Robinson, riding with Warren at the head of the column, suggested waiting until more of the corps arrived. But caution did not fit Warren's plan. "We must drive them from there, or they will get some artillery in position," he answered, striking a dramatic pose on his mount. "Never mind cannon! Never mind bullets!" he shouted, pointing at the far rise and gesturing emphatically at the end of each sentence. "Press on and clear this road!" Appealing to his men's immediate needs, he added, "It's the only way to get to your rations."[19]

The hands on Warren's watch pointed to 8:30 A.M. Three of his brigades were up. From Robinson's division, Col. Peter Lyle's brigade deployed east of the Brock Road. Col. Andrew A. Denison's Maryland brigade formed on the road's west side. Bunched behind Denison and slightly to his right came Brig. Gen. Joseph R. Bartlett's brigade of Griffin's division. "Hurry up, or you won't get a shot at them!" Bartlett chided his men. "Up to this point we thought we were fighting cavalry," Warren's aide Roebling later confirmed.[20]

The Federals pressed into the clearing, dressing their lines as they moved, all eyes on the far ridge. With a powerful roar, a withering volley tore into their ranks. Warren had been mistaken. The slouch-hatted forms along the crest were not cavalrymen. They were veteran infantry from Lee's vaunted First Corps, under Maj. Gen. Richard H. Anderson. The Confederates had won the race to Spotsylvania Court House and were transforming Laurel Hill, as the ridge was called, into an imposing bastion.

The Spindle farm rivaled Saunders's field as a graveyard for the Fifth Corps. Lyle's brigade lay pinned in front of the rebel entrenchments. Robinson was shot, as was Denison, and the Maryland brigade was decimated. Some of Bartlett's men made it to the Confederate works only to be killed or captured. Warren rode into the clearing and tried to rally the fugitives by waving a shattered flagstaff. He also pumped three more brigades — the remainder of Robinson's and Griffin's commands — into the fracas, but they could accomplish nothing against the rebel stronghold. Around 10:15 A.M., after a short breathing spell, Warren sent the rest of his corps into battle. East of the Brock Road, Crawford floundered in swampy low ground. Across the road, Brig. Gen. Lysander Cutler, who had succeeded the mortally wounded Wadsworth as division commander, followed Griffin's path and was repulsed. By noon, the attack was finished. The Fifth Corps, horribly battered, retired to the northern edge of the Spindle field and began digging earthworks. Fifteen hundred of its soldiers were dead or wounded.[21]

Writing Meade at 12:30 P.M., Warren conceded that he had been defeated. "I have done my best, but with the force I now have I cannot attack again unless I see very great weakness on the enemy's left flank," he informed headquarters. He was low on ammunition, his staff was "all tired out," and, he added pathetically, he had "lost the old white horse." He could hold his line if attacked, but he had no stomach for more fighting. "I incline to think," he observed, "that if I let the enemy alone he will me."[22]

Grant and Meade were determined to renew the offensive. Sedgwick's Sixth Corps was arriving on Warren's left. Once those troops were in place, Grant reasoned, the two corps could fashion a joint assault. Warren responded gamely that the Confederates must be as tired as his soldiers, which gave some hope for success. Meade, whose job it was to command the attack, suggested that Warren and Sedgwick simply cooperate. "I'll be damned if I'll cooperate with Sedgwick or anybody else," Warren retorted. "You are the commander of this army and can give your orders and I will obey them; or you can put Sedgwick in command and he can give the orders and I will obey them; or you can put me in command and I will give the orders and Sedgwick will obey them; but I'll be God damned if I'll cooperate with General Sedgwick or anybody else." Meade's aide Lyman observed that "never were officers and men more jaded and prostrated."[23]

At 6:30 P.M., elements from the Fifth and Sixth Corps charged the Confederate line. The delays had enabled Lee to bring up Ewell's troops, who shifted next to Anderson and repulsed the Federal attack. That evening, Meade called a meeting of his corps commanders. Sedgwick and Hancock came in person, but Warren remained at his headquarters and sent a rambling narrative that concluded: "I am so sleepy I can hardly write intelligently." Meade accused Sedgwick of being "constitutionally slow" and unnecessarily deferential to Warren, whom the army commander considered a bitter disappointment. "I told Warren today that he lost his nerve, at which he professed to be very indignant," Meade told Theodore Lyman. After the meeting, Warren wrote Sedgwick inviting him to spend the night at Fifth Corps headquarters, but Sedgwick declined, preferring to curl up next to a haystack.[24]

May 5 had been bad for Warren, but May 8 had proven to be even worse. In an attempt to please Grant, he had sent his brigades against Laurel Hill as soon as they arrived. Misled by the belief that only cavalry opposed him, he certainly hoped that acting decisively would dispel the cloud that had darkened his reputation after his cautious performances at Mine Run and in the Wilderness. He was ill suited, however, to wage the style of warfare that Grant expected of him and suffered another tragic failure.

The next morning, Warren vented his frustration in a note to Humphreys. The army's chief failing seemed to be that no one was in charge. "If we yesterday had moved according to the program of the General Order for the day, General Sedgwick would have been so close to me that we should undoubtedly have whipped [Anderson], and all of Ewell that came to his support," he complained. "As it was, the delays in halting General Sedgwick made his arrival here too late." Warren insisted that he had "fought yesterday with all the rapidity possible, and know I could have kept going on if supports had been close by." He faulted Meade for not taking charge after Sedgwick appeared. "Whether he thinks I am capable or not, my want of rank makes me incompetent when two corps come together, and I don't think our other two corps commanders are capable." He charged that Sedgwick "does nothing of himself," and confessed that he had completely "lost confidence in General Hancock's capability." The note ended abruptly. Apparently news that a Confederate sharpshooter had killed Sedgwick interrupted Warren. He folded the paper and never delivered it.[25]

On May 9, Grant concluded that Lee was shifting east and decided to send Hancock across the Po River against Lee's western flank. Once the rebel line began crumbling, the rest of the Federal army was to pitch in. Early on May 10, Grant revised his scheme. Lee, it developed, had fathomed Grant's purpose and was preparing a nasty reception for Hancock. The Union commander responded by leaving a division near Lee's western flank to encourage the rebels' belief that the Federals intended to strike there. In fact, the Union army was to prepare for a coordinated frontal assault, with all of Grant's soldiers attacking simultaneously across Lee's line. Grant reasoned that the Confederate formation must have weak points that a concerted push would uncover. He scheduled the massive attack for 5:00 P.M. so that everyone would have ample time to prepare.

Warren's corps comprised the Union line's right wing, extending west from the Brock Road. As morning advanced, two of Hancock's divisions deployed on Warren's right. Senior to Warren, Hancock assumed command of his own and Warren's corps for the joint attack. Around 2:00 P.M., Confederates began threatening the lone Union Second Corps division that Grant had dangled as a decoy. Hancock departed to rescue the outfit, leaving Warren in charge of the Union right wing.

Still smarting from his poor showings in the Wilderness and at Laurel Hill, Warren quickly moved to exploit Hancock's absence. He knew that he was not in good standing and tried to act as he presumed Grant would want. He urged Meade to let him attack right away. Warren's arguments were not recorded, but they persuaded Meade, who gave him permission to assault as soon as he was ready. From the scant existing evidence, Warren's motives appear to have been unabashedly selfish. Laurel Hill was stronger than ever, but the New Yorker felt that a show of aggression might impress his superiors. His troops had no stomach for the venture. "Every man in the ranks saw the folly in the attempt," a soldier noted. Maj. Gen. John Gibbon, commanding one of Hancock's divi-

The battlefield on May 9, looking toward the Confederate lines from near the Alsop house. Warren's troops occupied the open ground in the middle distance.
Frank Leslie's Illustrated Newspaper, June 4, 1864

sions, insisted that the Confederate works were too formidable to be taken, but Warren was obdurate. He seemed "bent upon the attack with some idea that the occasion was a crisis in the battle of which some advantage must be taken," Gibbon noted. The crisis that impelled Warren involved his career, not the battle's progress. Gibbon petitioned Meade to cancel the attack, but the army commander supported Warren. "Comrades gave messages to comrades for the loved ones at home," related a Union soldier. "No jest or gay banter now; every face wears a serious but determined look; that strange hush which precedes a battle was over all." [26]

At 4:00, the Fifth Corps, with Gibbon's division in tandem, started toward Laurel Hill. Rebel musketry and artillery tore bloody gaps in the Union line. Warren attempted to ride forward with his troops, but Col. Rufus R. Dawes of the Sixth Wisconsin grabbed his yellow sash and guided the general and his mount to safety behind a hillock. The Fifth Corps retired to its entrenchments, leaving wounded men to perish in flames sparked by the intense musketry.

"This preliminary attack showed that the enemy was all set for us," observed the aide Roebling, "and that the subsequent attack [still set for 5:00 P.M.] would have but little chance."[27]

Warren's assault disrupted Grant's timetable. The Fifth Corps was in no condition to attack at 5:00, and the armywide assault deteriorated into a series of disjointed attacks that the Confederates defeated piecemeal. "I tell you this is sheer madness, and can only end in wanton slaughter and certain repulse," Crawford predicted. At 7:00 P.M., Warren's troops grudgingly advanced a short distance, then came "tumbling and scrambling back in the greatest confusion, a wild panic taking possession of the men and causing them to break to the rear without ceremony." Warren again rode into the field, "mounted on a great tall white horse, in full uniform, sash and all, and with the flag in his hand," wrote the artillerist Wainwright. His efforts went for naught. Assistant Secretary of War Charles Dana, whom President Lincoln had sent to keep him informed of Grant's progress, reported that the attack exhibited "the caution and absence of comprehensive *ensemble* which seem to characterize [Warren]."[28]

That night, Lyman jotted his assessment in his private journal. "Warren is not up to a corps command," he concluded. "As in the Mine Run move, so here, he cannot spread himself over three divisions. He cannot do it, and the result is partial and ill-concerted and dilatory movements."[29]

Grant determined to try again. His new scheme envisioned a massive assault at dawn on May 12. Hancock would thrust his entire corps against a bulge in the rebel works known as the Mule Shoe while Maj. Gen. Ambrose E. Burnside's Ninth Corps plowed into the eastern side of the Confederate formation. Warren's assignment reflected the general's diminished currency. He was to have no part in the charge. Rather, he was to keep the rebels on Laurel Hill occupied and await orders to follow after Hancock and Burnside breached the Confederate line.

Hancock started his troops forward through a foggy drizzle shortly after 4:30 A.M. They overran the Mule Shoe's northern tip, and Burnside attacked on Hancock's left. Lee responded with a determined counterattack, whereupon Grant added the Sixth Corps to the fray. Warren received instructions to maintain as "threatening an attitude as possible" so that the rebels on Laurel Hill could not assist those in the Mule Shoe. By 8:00, both armies had concentrated their efforts at a bend in the Mule Shoe appropriately called the "Bloody Angle." To prevent Lee from reinforcing his troops there, Grant and Meade decided to send Warren forward. The orders left no room for quibbling. "Attack immediately with all the force you can," Meade wrote the Fifth Corps commander, "and be prepared to follow up any success with the rest of your force."[30]

The instructions struck Warren as absurd. His corps was stretched thin, and

General Warren, holding a battle flag and attempting to rally his soldiers on May 10, 1864 (sketch by Alfred A. Waud). Library of Congress

the Confederate works on Laurel Hill appeared as strong as ever. Attacking now would only add to the slaughter of May 8 and 10. Warren's instincts rebelled against obeying Meade's order, and he protested. It would be better, he proposed, to "attack the key points first." He also expressed concern that if he advanced, Confederates on his right might flank him.[31]

Yet Warren sent part of his corps forward to test the rebel works. "It was the fourth or fifth unsuccessful assault made by our men, and it is not a matter of surprise that they had lost all spirit for that kind of work," Roebling noted. "Many of them positively refused to go forward as their previous experience had taught them that to do so was certain death on that front." A few units charged near the Spindle house only to come flying back. Warren canceled the attack, notifying Meade that "my left cannot advance without a most destructive enfilade fire until the Sixth Corps has cleared its front." His position, he observed, was Lee's "point-d'appui if he throws back his right."[32]

Warren's excuses won him no favor at headquarters. Grant and Meade had concluded that Warren must attack. Whether he succeeded was not important. The critical thing in their eyes was that he tie up the Confederates in front of him, and his equivocation while he second-guessed their orders threatened to wreck their plans. An aide noted that Meade seemed "greatly chagrined at this delay, for it was losing all the advantage that Hancock's brilliant achievement had obtained." Seething, the army commander sent another missive to Warren. His order was "peremptory that you attack at once at all hazards with your whole force, if necessary." Humphreys, who was overseeing Warren's efforts as Meade's chief of staff, did his best to persuade the general to comply. "Meade has assumed the responsibility and will take the consequences," he reminded Warren, signing the note, "Your friend." Humphreys also suggested that since the Second and Sixth Corps were hard pressed, the Confederates may have relaxed their hold on Laurel Hill.[33]

Meade, however, had lost his patience. "Warren seems reluctant to assault," he wrote Grant. "I have ordered him at all hazards to do so, and if his attack should be repulsed to draw in his right and send his troops as fast as possible to [the Sixth and Second Corps]." Grant was in no humor to tolerate insubordination. "If Warren fails to attack promptly," he directed Meade, "send Humphreys to command his corps, and relieve him."[34]

Under Humphreys's insistent prodding, Warren bowed to his superiors' will. "General Meade repeats in most peremptory manner the orders to attack at once with your whole force," Warren informed his division commanders. "Do it," he tersely directed in a tone that reflected his disagreement with the instruction. "Don't mind consequences."[35]

Once again, Warren's soldiers stepped from their protective earthworks. "Again and again did our brigade charge, and as often came those terrible sheets of flame in our faces, while solid shot and shell enfiladed our lines," a northerner reported. "To advance was certain death or capture; to remain here, no better," recounted another. Rebel firepower swept away men "even as the coming wind would sweep the leaves from the laurel overhead," wrote a third. The attack had no chance of succeeding. "Gettysburg is a skirmish compared to this fight," observed a soldier in the famed Iron Brigade.[36]

Warren watched the slaughter in horror. Cutler requested permission to withdraw, but, considering the mood at headquarters, Warren was reluctant to retreat. He told Cutler to put the request in writing, which the division commander did, asserting that his command was "losing badly" and that he could not persuade his men to charge. Warren discussed the situation with Humphreys. Convinced that the attack was doomed, Humphreys ordered the Fifth Corps back to its earthworks.[37]

With the fight clearly gone from Warren, Meade decided to temporarily disband the Fifth Corps. He sent two of Warren's divisions—Cutler's and Griffin's—to assist the Sixth Corps. Only Crawford's division remained with Warren, performing the relatively simple task of guarding the Union position across from Laurel Hill. Warren never again commanded the trust of his superiors.

According to Grant's aide, Horace Porter, the Union commander was pleased that Warren had finally attacked because it saved him from the unpleasant task of relieving the general. Porter related that Grant initially had developed a "very high regard" for Warren and was impressed by his "quickness of perception, personal gallantry, and soldierly bearing." But Warren had not lived up to his earlier promise. "I began to feel, after his want of vigor in assaulting on the 8th, that he was not as efficient as I had believed," Grant observed. "His delay in attacking and the feeble character of his assaults today confirm me in my apprehensions." Porter noted that Grant spoke with an air of "serious disappointment," blaming Warren "not so much for not carrying the line in his front as for delays in making the attack." [38]

Warren's performance at the Wilderness and Spotsylvania Court House commanded mixed reviews. On the ledger's positive side, Grant listed Warren's "superior ability, quick perceptions, and personal courage to accomplish anything that could be done with a small command." Warren exhibited a firm grasp of tactical situations. Had he been permitted to defer his attack in the Wilderness until Sedgwick arrived, he likely would have defeated Ewell and perhaps have brought the campaign to a quicker and less costly conclusion. His appraisal of his prospects at Laurel Hill on May 12 was faultless. [39]

But Warren was poorly suited to serve as a corps commander. As Grant expressed it, Warren spent his time plotting "how all the balance of the army should be engaged as to properly cooperate with him" and managed his corps by "forgetting that a division commander could execute an order without his presence." Grant considered Warren's meddlesome nature "constitutional and beyond his control." Meade found his independence exasperating. On May 12, for example, Meade needed Warren to attack quickly to relieve pressure against Hancock, but Warren resisted. By Meade's estimation, Warren had "no right to delay executing his orders under any circumstances." Warren's proper course, Meade wrote, would have been to promptly advise him of his views, stating, "Such is my opinion, but I shall proceed to attack unless otherwise ordered." Grant's aide Adam Badeau summed up the case against Warren: "An excess of caution, a delay in assuming the offensive, even when ordered, an indisposition to take tactical risks, an unwillingness to trust that his superiors would protect, or perhaps even knew how to protect his advance, or his equals support it, destroyed the effect of otherwise brilliant talents, and marred his reputation as a soldier."[40]

Warren's fatal flaw was an inability, shared by many of the Potomac army's commanders, to adapt to Grant's aggressive style. A biographer noted that Warren prided himself as a "scientific soldier," and he might have performed superbly under a general who shared his cautious philosophy. Grant's bludgeoning tactics were repugnant to him, and the carnage deeply affected him. "For thirty days now, it had been one funeral procession, past me; and it is too much!" he remarked to Lyman in June, as the slaughter continued. "Today I saw a man burying a comrade, and, within half an hour, he himself was brought in and buried beside him. The men need some rest."[41]

The Wilderness and Spotsylvania sealed Warren's fate. Grant and Meade lost confidence in him. He quarreled bitterly with Meade, complained openly about Grant's costly methods of fighting, and, after several more months of undistinguished service, was finally unceremoniously relieved of command near the end of the war at the battle of Five Forks. He spent the remainder of his life attempting to restore his reputation. A court of inquiry convened in 1880 and issued findings in November 1882 that exonerated Warren of misconduct at Five Forks. Warren died three months before the findings were released and never knew of this partial vindication.

As for his conduct in the Wilderness and at Spotsylvania, the final verdict remains with history.

NOTES

1. Horace Porter, *Campaigning with Grant* (New York: Century, 1897), 108; Gouverneur K. Warren to Emily Warren, May 3, 1864, Gouverneur K. Warren Collection, New York State Library and Archives, Albany (repository hereafter cited as NYSLA).

2. Emerson Gifford Taylor, *Gouverneur Kemble Warren: Life and Letters of an American Soldier* (Boston: Houghton Mifflin Company, 1932), and Vincent J. Flanagan, "The Life of General Gouverneur Kemble Warren" (Ph.D. diss., City University of New York, 1969), contain excellent sketches of Warren's early life, based largely on Warren's papers at NYSLA.

3. Gouverneur K. Warren to William Warren, January 10, 1863, Warren Collection, NYSLA.

4. Henry L. Abbot, *Gouverneur Kemble Warren — Class of 1850* (West Point, N.Y.: n.p., 1883), 8.

5. Taylor, *Gouverneur Kemble Warren*, 114.

6. Gouverneur K. Warren to William Warren, October 30, December 8, 1863, Warren Collection, NYSLA; Gouverneur K. Warren to Andrew A. Humphreys, December 11, 1863, Andrew A. Humphreys Collection, Historical Society of Pennsylvania, Philadelphia (repository hereafter cited as HSP); *Report of the Joint Committee on the Conduct of the War at the Second Session, Thirty-Eighth Congress* (Washington, D.C.: GPO, 1865), I, 378–79.

7. Theodore Lyman to family, October 1, 1863, in Theodore Lyman, *Meade's Headquarters 1863–1865: Letters of Colonel Theodore Lyman from the Wilderness to Appomattox*, ed. George R. Agassiz (Boston: Atlantic Monthly Press, 1922), 26; Morris Schaff, *The Battle of the Wilderness* (Boston: Houghton Mifflin, 1910), 30; Charles S. Wainwright, *A Diary of Battle: The Personal Journals of Colonel Charles S. Wainwright, 1861–1865*, ed. Allan Nevins (New York: Harcourt, Brace and World, 1962), 405; Josiah M. Favill, *The Diary of a Young Officer Serving with the Armies of the United States during the War of the Rebellion* (Chicago: R. R. Donnelley and Sons, 1909), 274.

8. William W. Swan, "Battle of the Wilderness," *Papers of the Military Historical Society of Massachusetts*, 16 vols. (Boston: Military Historical Society of Massachusetts, 1881–1918), 4:124.

9. Washington A. Roebling's Report of Operations, Warren Collection, NYSLA.

10. U.S. War Department, *The War of the Rebellion: A Compilation of the Official Records of the Union and Confederate Armies*, 127 vols., index, and atlas (Washington, D.C.: GPO, 1880–1901), ser. 1, 36(2):415 (hereafter referred to as *OR*; all references to ser. 1).

11. Schaff, *Battle of the Wilderness*, 125–26; *OR* 36(2):413.

12. *OR* 36(2):403.

13. Gouverneur K. Warren to Charles Porter, November 21, 1875, Warren Collection, NYSLA.

14. Elwell S. Otis to Sartell Prentence, December 26, 1888, Manuscript Division, Library of Congress, Washington, D.C.; Swan, "Battle of the Wilderness," 129.

15. Gordon C. Rhea, *The Battle of the Wilderness: May 5–6, 1864* (Baton Rouge: Louisiana State University Press, 1994), 145–72, relates the details of the attack.

16. *OR* 36(1):539–40; Gouverneur K. Warren to Charles Porter, Warren Collection, NYSLA.

17. Swan, "Battle of the Wilderness," 134.

18. Charles E. Phelps, "Personal Recollections of the Wilderness Campaign," Maryland Historical Society, Baltimore (repository hereafter cited as MHS).

19. Abner R. Small, *The Road to Richmond: The Civil War Memoirs of Major Abner R. Small of the Sixteenth Maine Volunteers*, ed. Harold A. Small (Berkeley: University of California Press, 1939), 126; Phelps, "Personal Recollections of the Wilderness Campaign," MHS.

20. Amos M. Judson, *History of the Eighty-Third Regiment Pennsylvania Volunteers* (Erie, Pa.: B. F. H. Lynn, 1865), 196; Eugene A. Nash, *A History of the Forty-fourth Regiment, New York Volunteer Infantry, in the Civil War, 1861–1865* (Chicago: R. R. Donnelley and Sons, 1911), 188; Roebling's Report of Operations, Warren Collection, NYSLA.

21. Gordon C. Rhea, *The Battles for Spotsylvania Court House and the Road to Yellow Tavern: May 7–12, 1864* (Baton Rouge: Louisiana State University Press, 1997), 45–88, relates the details of the attack.

22. *OR* 36(2):540–41.

23. *OR* 36(2):541; James H. Wilson, *Under the Old Flag*, 2 vols. (New York: D. Appleton and Company, 1912), 1:895–96; Theodore Lyman journal, May 8, 1864, Theodore Lyman Collection, Massachusetts Historical Society, Boston (repository hereafter cited as MASSHS).

24. *OR* 36(2):542; Theodore Lyman journal, May 8, 1864, Lyman Collection, MASSHS; Charles A. Whittier, "Reminiscences of the War, 1861–1865," Boston Public Library, Boston.

25. Gouverneur K. Warren to Andrew A. Humphreys, May 9, 1864, Warren Collection, NYSLA.

26. *OR*: 36(2):600; Judson, *History of the Eighty-Third Regiment Pennsylvania Volunteers*, 202–3; John Gibbon, *Personal Recollections of the Civil War* (New York: G. P. Putnam's Sons, 1928), 218–19; P. S. Potter, "Reminiscences of Spotsylvania," *National Tribune*, April 15, 1882.

27. Rufus R. Dawes, *Service with the Sixth Wisconsin Volunteers* (Marietta, Ohio: E. R. Alderman and Sons, 1890), 265–66; Roebling's Report of Operations, Warren Collection, NYSLA.

28. Charles H. Weygant, *History of the One Hundred and Twenty-Fourth Regiment, N.Y.S.V.* (Newburgh, N.Y.: Journal Printing House, 1877), 310; Wainwright, *Diary of Battle*, 364; *OR* 36 (1):67.

29. Theodore Lyman journal, May 10, 1864, Theodore Lyman Collection, MASSHS.

30. *OR* 36(2):661–62.

31. *OR* 36(2):662.

32. Roebling's Report of Operations, Warren Collection, NYSLA; *OR* 36(2):663.

33. Adam Badeau, *Military History of Ulysses S. Grant, from April, 1861, to April, 1865*, 3 vols. (New York: D. Appleton and Company, 1868–81), 2:177; Andrew A. Humphreys, *The Virginia Campaign of '64 and '65* (New York: Charles Scribner's Sons, 1883), 101; *OR* 36(2):663.

34. *OR* 36(2):654.

35. *OR* 36(2):668, 671.

36. George W. Burchell to "M and M," May 13, 1864, Sullivan Dexter Green Papers, Bentley Library, University of Michigan, Ann Arbor; Orville Thomson, *From Philippi to Appomattox: Narrative of the Services of the Seventh Indiana Infantry in the War for the Union* (n.p.: n.p., n.d.), 187–88.

37. *OR* 36(2):671; Humphreys, *Virginia Campaign*, 101 n. 3.

38. Porter, *Campaigning with Grant*, 108.

39. Ulysses S. Grant, *Personal Memoirs of U. S. Grant*, 2 vols. (New York: Charles S. Webster, 1886), 2:214–15.

40. Ibid.; George G. Meade to John Rawlins, June 21, 1864, George G. Meade Collection, HSP; Badeau, *Military History of Ulysses S. Grant*, 2:184.

41. Taylor, *Gouverneur Kemble Warren*, 173; Lyman, *Meade's Headquarters*, 147.

An Insurmountable Barrier
between the Army and Ruin
The Confederate Experience at
Spotsylvania's Bloody Angle

V eteran soldiers awaiting the renewal of fighting in the spring of 1864 had seen enough of raw courage to believe that nothing could shock them. Pickett's men had charged with unimaginable devotion across the Emmitsburg Pike. Burnside's doomed regiments had bravely done their duty in facing hopeless butchery in front of Marye's Heights. In Sharpsburg's Bloody Lane and the Deep Cut at Second Manassas, men of both armies had fought desperately, often to the death. Events on May 12, however, precisely one week after the inauguration of the 1864 campaign, would establish a new standard for intense, short-range savagery. The twenty-hour hand-to-hand fight at Spotsylvania's "Bloody Angle" was never matched during the Civil War, and rarely if ever anywhere else in the annals of military history.

The chain of events that led to the deadly struggle of May 12 began casually, almost randomly, during the pitch-black night of May 8–9. Federals of Gen. George G. Meade's Army of the Potomac had sought to gain an advantage by marching southeast from the battlefield of the Wilderness on May 7. If they could reach either of two intersections near Spotsylvania Court House ahead of Gen. Robert E. Lee and his Army of Northern Virginia, they would be between the Confederates and Richmond. Despite the array of breathless modern analyses about cities being irrelevant, Lee simply could not leave his nation's industrial, transportation, and political center undefended. He must protect the routes to Richmond via Spotsylvania.

Confederates won the race by the narrowest of margins early on May 8 when they turned back Federals pressing down the Brock Road. Throughout the day, northern reinforcements extended their line west toward the Po River, then northeast away from the Brock Road. Southern troops, who had a longer march (but one uninterrupted by hostile cavalry thanks to Gen. Philip Sheridan's indulgence in army politics at this auspicious moment), spread out in hurried reaction to the various threats.

By the time Gen. Edward Johnson's division of the Second Corps reached the field, darkness had fallen. Both sides had anchored a flank on the Po, so Johnson moved northeast of the Brock Road. He reached the right end of Gen. Robert E. Rodes's division and moved beyond it. With neither guides nor lights, Johnson and his staff led a ragged column through dense woods. Capt. W. W. Old recalled keeping his hands up in front of his eyes, "which were really of no use to me at that time, to protect them." Unseen tree limbs tore at uniforms. As the Confederates emerged from the thickets they saw campfires ahead, "considerably below the plane of our position." Johnson followed the crest of his high ground around to the right, to avoid the enemy camps, and deployed his men. It took all night. By the morning of May 9, Johnson had formed the nose of a projecting salient that would become famous as the "Mule Shoe." Part of the northern face of that salient would become the Bloody Angle three days later.[1]

Dawn revealed the extent to which Rodes and Johnson projected north beyond the axis of their comrades farther west, but their haphazardly chosen position survived review. Lee's chief engineer, Gen. M. L. Smith, considered the line safe if amply supplied with artillery. In the aftermath of the disaster that subsequently struck the nose of the Mule Shoe salient—which was made possible by the mistaken removal of that essential artillery—Lee apparently blamed one of Smith's subordinates for the bad engineering. The army commander, a staff officer wrote, "was very much out with Col. [Walter H.] Stevens . . . for the disposition that had been made of the troops at Spottsylvania C.H." The commander of an artillery battalion situated at the nose called the salient "a wretchedly defective line. . . . only kept because of the work done upon it, and the belief that our troops, entrenched, could never be driven out."[2]

During the three days between establishment of the line and the Bloody Angle fighting, troops labored to make the position more secure. The evolving concept of field fortification, which Lee did much to foster, burgeoned at Spotsylvania. Small trees cut down and laid longwise formed much of the bulk of the strong entrenchments. Men "worked like beavers. . . . Trees were felled

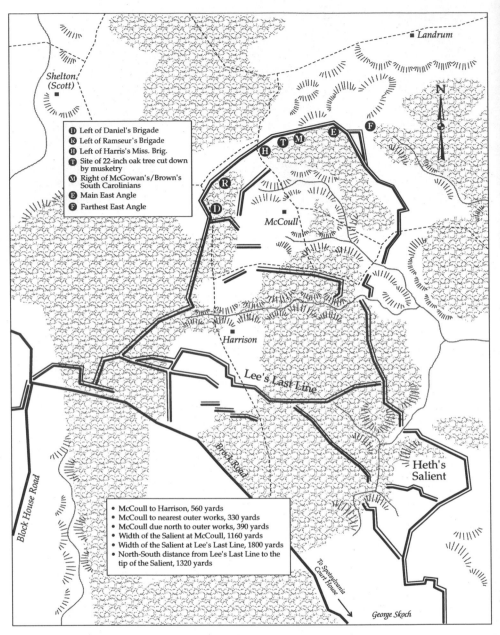

- Left of Daniel's Brigade
- Left of Ramseur's Brigade
- Left of Harris's Miss. Brig.
- Site of 22-inch oak tree cut down by musketry
- Right of McGowan's/Brown's South Carolinians
- Main East Angle
- Farthest East Angle

Landrum

Shelton (Scott)

McCoull

Harrison

Lee's Last Line

Brock Road

Block House Road

Heth's Salient

To Spotsylvania Court House

- McCoull to Harrison, 560 yards
- McCoull to nearest outer works, 330 yards
- McCoull due north to outer works, 390 yards
- Width of the Salient at McCoull, 1160 yards
- Width of the Salient at Lee's Last Line, 1800 yards
- North-South distance from Lee's Last Line to the tip of the Salient, 1320 yards

George Skoch

The Mule Shoe salient, May 12, 1864, with positions for Confederate brigades during the fight for the Bloody Angle (after J. N. Brown)

Confederate field works at the Bloody Angle.
Francis Trevelyan Miller, ed., *The Photographic History of the Civil War*, 10 vols.
(New York: Review of Reviews, 1911), 3:57

and piled upon each other, and a ditch dug behind them with the earth out of it thrown against the logs" (despite engineering dogma that the ditch should be on the enemy side—an uncomfortable concept in actual execution in the presence of a foe). A soldier who fought behind the works described them as having a "double row of stakes like a tomato trellis . . . filled in with poles and dirt. . . ." Initially, the works were four to six feet thick and breast high. Before the climactic fight over them, head logs were added, "laid upon blocks," leaving only a narrow gap for firing through. Between the depth of the ditch and the height of the works, firing steps sometimes had to be cut for soldiers to reach the space below the head log.[3]

After they built the works, the Confederates went beyond them and cut down the small but thickly growing pine shrubs in their front to improve the field of fire. Using those pines and "the limbs and tops of the trees [mostly hardwoods] cut off from the trunks" in building the main works, they then constructed abatis on the enemy side of the fortifications. This work consisted of "making the ends of the limbs sharp" and then "placing them . . . with the sharpened points towards the enemy."[4]

A final refinement—new to field fortifications in Virginia—completed the job. The blunt nose of the Mule Shoe projected so far north that Federal batteries from both sides, especially from the west, easily could deliver enfilading fire into its flanks. The obvious southern response was to throw up more works "right and left," in the words of one of the builders. These "traverses," as military engineers called them, ran back perpendicular to the main line of works and were made primarily of logs rather than earth. The soldiers rapidly protecting themselves from enemy fire did not follow any carefully engineered specifications, so it is hardly surprising that estimates of the distance between the lateral walls vary from twenty feet to forty feet. The originals probably varied that much, on the whim of harried men erecting them. The southward length of the traverses ranged from twenty to thirty feet. One soldier called the resulting three-sided enclosures "regular pens, large enough to hold eight to ten men each." Another described them as "little short works built of poles and earth at right angles to the main line." A Federal who saw the pens likened them to "a row of cellars without drainage." Traces of some traverses can be seen on the ground today, but most, having been built primarily of short-lived wood fiber, have disappeared.[5]

On May 10, a cleverly planned and well-led assault against a point on the northwest shoulder of the salient broke through the Confederate line and created temporary havoc. Hard fighting and hastily summoned reinforcements restored the position. Late on May 11, massive Federal forces concentrated to try the same measure on a larger scale. Confederates in the Mule Shoe became aware that something was afoot. Among the frontline units was the famous old Stonewall Brigade. Col. William Terry of the brigade's 4th Virginia received orders to send a strong detail forward to reconnoiter. He asked for one hundred volunteers, but only a handful of men responded, so Terry had to detail the balance. At the last minute the orders were canceled, to the considerable relief of the colonel and his reluctant detachment.[6]

Unmistakable indications of Federal activity convinced Lee that his foe was up to something. Lee was very good at divining such things, but on May 11 — for one of the few times during his three years in command — he figured wrong. His subordinates agreed with the mistaken analysis (James Longstreet being absent wounded and thus in no position to pretend later that he had known precisely what to do all along). "Enemy reported to be falling back," a Second Corps officer wrote in his diary. "Our commanding officers are under the impression that the enemy will retreat tonight." Lee decided that Meade's army would move eastward, apparently toward a new base of operations at Fredericksburg. News from a succession of scouts and couriers seemed to confirm the notion. In a meeting at the Harrison house that included Ewell and Rodes, the army commander announced his conclusion. As a result, the artillery essential to defense of the vulnerable salient was withdrawn in preparation for whatever countermeasures Lee might take in the morning.[7]

Confederates posted across the tip of the Mule Shoe passed an extraordinarily pensive night. The music of northern bands playing martial airs echoed eerily through the pitch-black, drizzly darkness. A staff officer listened to the indistinct sound of many enemies moving into position. It sounded, he mused, "like distant falling water, or machinery." The worrisome absence of artillery he blamed erroneously on the battalion system that had taken control of that arm away from infantry brigadiers. Battalion commander Robert A. Hardaway resisted the order to remove his guns. When he made no headway by seeking an annulment from Gen. Jubal A. Early, Hardaway solicited support from Gens. Rodes and Stephen Dodson Ramseur. With their connivance, he proposed to disobey his orders. Lee had left the vicinity, however, and no one would override the army commander's directive.[8]

A few pieces of artillery avoided the withdrawal dictum, but unfortunately these were west of the nose and on the fringe of the coming crisis. Maj. Robert W. Hunter of Johnson's staff spent the night striving mightily to have the rest of the artillery returned to face the growing threat. He hunted up Ewell at the Harrison house and made his case in vain. Hunter then awakened Johnson, who had been asleep at the McCoull house, and urged him to try to use his influence with the corps commander. Ewell succumbed to Johnson's blandishments and promised to have the artillery back in the line by 2:00 A.M., but his orders rectifying the mistake ran afoul of fatal delays imposed by darkness, mud, confusion, and inertia.[9]

The blue-clad storm gathering opposite the Mule Shoe enjoyed far less certainty of purpose than its eventual success seemed to suggest. Infantrymen staggering through soggy woods found little rest. "The cold rain continued and we were very uncomfortable in our wet clothes," one of them wrote. Gen. Francis C. Barlow, a bright young New Yorker, was rightfully proud of the important role he played in the assault, but he clearly recognized the good fortune that attended the attempt. The attack that morning, he wrote, though "undoubtedly the most brilliant thing of its kind of the war," was "a lucky accident" for several reasons. Barlow described an "exquisitely ludicrous scene" in which a staff officer sent to lead the troops explained that he had no idea where they were going. "For Heaven's sake," Barlow pleaded, "at least, face us in the right direction, so that we shall not march away from the enemy, and have to go round the world and come up in their rear." That droll transaction seemed to Barlow to typify "the purely haphazard character of this apparently brilliant attack. . . ."[10]

Before sunup, a massive wedge of Federal troops achieved reasonably solid alignment and swept impressively forward, moving southwest toward the northeastern tip of the Mule Shoe — the "East Angle." Confederates in that sector included, from left to right, the famous Stonewall Brigade; a sturdy

Louisiana brigade that had been led by Gen. Leroy A. Stafford until his mortal wounding at the Wilderness; the Virginia brigade of Gen. John M. Jones, who was killed at the Wilderness; and a mixed brigade of Virginians and North Carolinians under Gen. George H. Steuart. The generous allotment of artillery that had made those brigades' positions tenable was scurrying frantically forward to resume its assigned locations.[11]

Some Confederates offered stout resistance; others did not. Jones's old brigade faced the onslaught from the most crucial position, just west of the East Angle. Ben Jones of the 44th Virginia had a typical experience. "We could not see but a few feet from us," he wrote, and in that befogged state thought the approaching troops "were our men until three of them had their guns leveled on me." Jones surrendered, he noted wryly, "as Napoleon would have done if he had been in my place." Capt. E. D. Camden of the 25th Virginia thought the brigade killed many of the foe before being surrounded. He broke his sword rather than surrendering it. Much of the army viewed the resultant breakthrough as reflecting badly on Jones's men. A soldier at Ewell's headquarters wrote in his diary: "Jones's Va. Brigade gave way which compelled the others to fall back." Another officer used almost identical language before concluding: "Some fought as become men and soldiers, whilst others have imprinted a stain upon their character that time cannot erase."[12]

The primary components of the Confederate disaster had to do with their basic armaments: the artillery remained missing, and many muskets had succumbed to the weather. Lt. Horace Hawes of the Orange Artillery described an experience typical for many of Lee's long arm: "As we drove down into the marshy bottom and began to rise the hill to our positions a sharp infantry fire met us, coming we couldnt tell from where, but seemed a cross fire." Soon after Hawes's gun reached the works, a column of enemy materialized out of the mist from a daunting quarter: the left rear. "They were within about 15 or 20 steps of us," Hawes recalled, "when I ordered our Parrott gun turned upon them (inside our works) and gave them Cannister in their faces. . . . The smoke from the gun fell and obscured everything! Before it fairly lifted they were upon us, and we were prisoners."[13]

Most southern artillery did not even manage the single shot that Hawes delivered. Page's battery got the order to dash forward at 3:30 A.M. and wound up in a hand-to-hand fight. One gunner, George W. Tiller, was bayoneted. The battery was destroyed in a military sense, but many of its members slipped away in the smoke-shrouded confusion. Its total losses were 2 killed, 5 wounded, and 18 prisoners. The loss of 25 men from a unit about 100 strong is hardly negligible, but it is not a daunting proportion for a battery surrounded and apparently obliterated. Nevertheless, the guns of Page and his colleagues were not available at the decisive moment. It is hard to quarrel with General Ewell's analysis: "If the artillery had been in position we would have destroyed [the Federal] army." Lee also attributed the result to the missing artillery, remarking to both Ewell and Gen. A. L. Long that he had misread indications of enemy movements. General Barlow agreed. "There was only a scattering and feeble fire from the enemy," he wrote, and "it would have been very difficult to get through under a cool and well-directed fire." [14]

The failure of Confederate musketry in the salient probably cost the defenders at least as much as did the absence of artillery. In the era of flintlock shoulder arms, "Keep your powder dry" had been axiomatic. Percussion rifles, however, did not expose the powder to a spark in an exterior pan. Firearms failures during the Civil War therefore rarely affected battle action. The pervasive humidity invading every rifle barrel and cartridge box on this sopping morning made May 12 an exception to that rule. One brigade commander declared that "if the muskets of our men had been serviceable. . . . one well-directed volley, such as our men knew so well how to give, [would have] made their future movements too slow and dispirited to render success in such a charge possible." The "searching damp," however, "had disarmed them, and instead of the leaping line of fire and the sharp crack of muskets came the pop! pop! pop! of exploding caps. . . . A muzzle-loading musket with damp powder behind the ball is as useless to a soldier . . . as a walking-cane." [15]

Despite the stunning failure of their muskets, men near the East Angle put up sturdy, albeit fruitless, resistance. Some of Steuart's officers forethoughtfully had ordered their men to draw the old, damp loads from their weapons and clean their guns before the attack came. Officers who failed to use that ready means of averting misfires, one soldier wrote, had been guilty of "inexcusable" carelessness. After a sharp fight east of the East Angle, many Confederates there fell into enemy hands, General Steuart among them. The Louisianians next west from Jones's brigade gave a good account of themselves. So did the Stonewall Brigade just to their left. Gen. James A. "Stonewall Jim" Walker was sheltered under a tarpaulin when the attack awakened him from a deep sleep. His men clung stubbornly to the traverses that faced east toward the penetration. Walker inspired them mightily until a bullet shattered his arm. Tom Doyle of the 33rd Virginia remembered a nightmare scene visible through ropes of fog and billows of gunsmoke: "The figures of the men seen dimly through the smoke and fog seemed almost gigantic, while the woods were lighted by the flashing of the guns and the sparkling of the musketry. The din was tremendous and increasing. . . . Men in crowds with bleeding limbs, and pale, pain-stricken faces, were hurrying to the rear. . . ." Despite its best efforts, Walker admitted, the Stonewall Brigade "was annihilated & ceased to exist." [16]

Brigadier General George H. Steuart (left) and Major General Edward Johnson as prisoners guarded by black Union soldiers on the morning of May 12, 1864. The caption that accompanied this engraving misidentified the two officers as "The Rebel Generals Bradley Johnson and E. Stuart." *Frank Leslie's Illustrated Newspaper*, June 4, 1864

The destruction of Johnson's division threw open to the Federal attackers the heart of Lee's line, but they were unable to grasp the opportunity. Millennia earlier, the troops of Scipio Africanus had been "clearly imbued with the principle that a penetration must be promptly widened before it is deepened" — a military precept grudgingly relearned by hard lessons, for instance on the fields of Flanders in the early twentieth century. A British analyst cited ancient armies in commenting on the Spotsylvania breakthrough: "The superiority of Roman tactics over Greek lay in this, that all the troops not actually fighting were kept as far as possible from the turmoil, in small closed bodies, instead of being sent forward at first in one large mass." General Barlow wrote in the same vein of May 12: "[W]hat ought to have been done was plain. . . . The occasion for 'charging,' for rush and confusion, was past, and troops ought to have been soberly and deliberately put in position, and ordered to sweep down the rebel line. . . ."[17] Instead, whatever Federal momentum remained after the initial triumph pressed straight ahead. That allowed Lee and his lieutenants the chance to seal the shoulders of the penetration and then attempt to narrow its breadth.

Most important among those rallying lieutenants was Gen. John B. Gordon, a superb soldier despite having no prewar military education or experience. Gordon's late-life memoir is so compromised by romantic viewpoints and purple prose that historians often do him the disservice of discounting his wartime performance on that basis. In the confusion early on May 12, the citizen-soldier was at his magnificent best, bringing his own troops and others hurriedly into line behind the breach. An onlooker saw Gordon "talking rapidly and literally foaming at the mouth" as he sought to persuade Gen. Abner Perrin to form on his troops. Perrin agreed, and paid with his life.[18]

When Robert E. Lee became involved in the rally, the third "Lee-to-the-Rear" episode within six days resulted. Gordon's coalescing line stretched roughly east to west near the McCoull house. Revisionist scholarship suggests that it formed much farther south, near — even behind — the Harrison house, and that Lee found it there. The frantic Confederate scramble to restore order certainly covered all of the fields of both farms. Capt. Campbell Brown of Ewell's staff, however, wrote soon after the war that he found Gordon's line "near the McCoul house, with its . . . right in the woods, to the right of the house." Gen. Robert D. Johnston, commanding a brigade in the melee, "found General Lee only a few hundred yards in the rear of the lines that had been carried [McCoull was 390 yards south of the works, Harrison about 1,000], and exposed to the fire of the enemy from the entrenchments."[19]

An artillery officer marveled at Lee's composure as the legendary leader traded on his immense popularity among the men to rally them: "perfectly calm and self possessed, he stretched out his right hand toward the retreating men, 'Stop right here men, your comrades need you, we are going to form a new line.'" A colonel could tell that Lee was "deeply moved, as I never saw him before," and reported that at Lee's appeals, "the men went frantic." As he had six days earlier on the Widow Tapp's field in the Wilderness, and again on May 10 not far from his current location, Lee prepared to lead his troops in person, hat in hand. Once again, the men shouted that their commander must go to the rear. "We don't want you killed," a Georgian yelled. Once again, someone grabbed the reins of Lee's mount and led him to the rear. "I never saw a man look so noble," an eyewitness wrote emotionally, "or a spectacle so impressive." [20]

Lee's effective role contrasted sharply with that of General Ewell, who was in his last fortnight with the army before being shuffled off to another arena. That reassignment evidently was based in some part on the events of this crucial day. Ewell responded to the crisis bravely but without much poise. He "was under very great excitement," General Johnston wrote, "pulling his moustache with both hands" and shouting "charge them Gen'l D[am]n em charge em." An eyewitness watched Lee "in the calmest and kindest manner" entreat the men to do their duty while Ewell shouted at them: "Yes, G——d d——n you, run, run; the Yankees will catch you; that's right; go as fast as you can." Not surprisingly, "All that Gen. Lee addressed at once halted and returned . . . all that Gen. Ewell so angrily reproached continued their flight to the rear." Lee pointedly reminded Ewell of his duties: "[Y]ou must restrain yourself; how can you expect to control these men when you have lost control of yourself? If you cannot repress your excitement, you had better retire." William Allan of Ewell's staff recalled with sorrow that his chief "lost his head in the severity of the fight." A few days later, after Ewell had been relieved and was complaining bitterly of his fate, Allan noted that "every body was uncomfortable . . . yet we all felt that his removal was inevitable & indeed was proper." [21]

The stand inspired by Gordon and Lee broke Federal momentum in the center and allowed gradual restoration of some of the lines near the nose of the salient. Because of the configuration of the works and of the ground beyond them, Confederates fighting up the west shoulder faced the sternest challenge and then were swept into the deadly Bloody Angle fighting. Southerners holding the line southeast of the East Angle also faced a trying, if less famous, day of battle. Some of Jones's remnants, especially a regiment that had been on picket duty and escaped by a circuitous path, helped on the right of the salient. They saw enemy troops massed in the traverse pens "as thick as herrings in a barrel" and took a heavy toll of them. Part of Perrin's Alabama brigade fought in the same vicinity after their brigadier bled to death from a severed femoral artery. The Alabamians "huddled up in large pens." Men who put a head above either the traverses or the forward works risked instant death. A lieutenant arranged his men to receive the enemy with bayonets: "Now you stand here, and as you see them come I will run the bayonet through them and pitch them over to you and you catch them." One of Perrin's men summarized the experience succinctly: "I regard this day as the most dismal one I ever passed through." [22]

On the northwest face of the Mule Shoe, three brigades played key initial roles in stabilizing the breakthrough: Junius Daniel's on the left, William T. Wofford's in support of Daniel, and Ramseur's on Daniel's right, immediately adjacent to a bend in the works that soon would become the Bloody Angle. Daniel aligned his troops and had them fire to their front and right against the swarming Federals. He stood erect in front of his line, sword in hand, amid "a perfect hail of Minnie balls." Eventually one of them struck the general, and he fell with a mortal wound "through his bowels." [23] Despite the loss of their leader, Daniel's North Carolinians reached the original outerworks and clung to them all day long.

Wofford's Georgians came from behind Daniel to support that crucial sector. The two brigades soon became intermixed. Much later, during an afternoon lull, a far too sanguine officer decided to hurl some of the Georgians across the works toward the Federals. The move accomplished nothing and quickly piled up needless casualties. [24]

The final, most difficult, piece of the Confederate tactical puzzle that set up the Bloody Angle fight involved a stalwart performance by Ramseur and his brigade. These Tarheels hurried forward to thwart a farther Union advance, moving just northeast of Daniel's right before facing northwest. Ramseur's men went to ground parallel to the outer works, their right near the McCoull road. Near an intermediate line of works, well short of the old front line, they pushed their knapsacks forward as ersatz bulwarks and frantically loosened the earth with bayonets to provide more protection. Around the captured works there swarmed "a living mass of Yankees, in full view." Ramseur personally fired double-shotted canister into that inviting target. The brigade flagstaff was shot in two as the men crouched beneath it. Pvt. Tisdale Stepp of the 14th North Carolina began singing "The Bonnie Blue Flag" in "a stentorian voice" and others picked up that favorite song. After what seemed to one participant like forty minutes of waiting, the brigade leaped up and charged. Stepp did not go along. During his bravura performance, he had been "shot dead by an awkward soldier in our rear rank." [25]

Ramseur's attack went forward under the spur of "the war yell, or whoop" and did not halt until it captured the works. At each step, it seemed, Confederates fell "almost like grass before the scythe." Ramseur and Col. Bryan Grimes led the desperate attack. When a bullet hit the general's right arm, Grimes led on alone. As they closed to hand-to-hand range, the southerners overwhelmed their foe and took scores of prisoners. A man on the brigade's right captured five soldiers from Delaware, "nice clever boys," and told them to go to the rear. All five fell dead in the hail of lead before they had gotten far. Unfortunately, the ground to Ramseur's right remained full of Yankees and was appreciably elevated. The traverses facing that direction were invaluable to the brigade as it held its position all day long; the higher ground around the Bloody Angle, however, meant that the Tarheels had to stay low with the utmost care. [26]

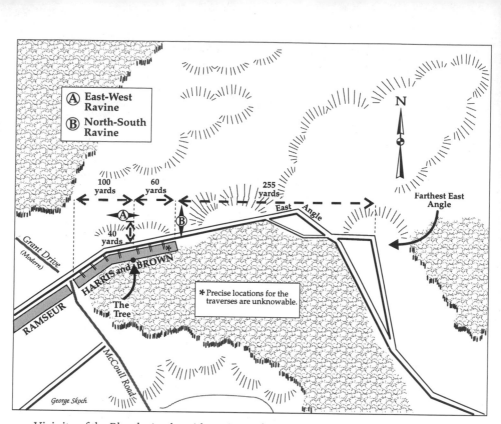

Vicinity of the Bloody Angle, with positions for the principal Confederate brigades

Two brigades from distant sectors of the battlefield were by this time en route to Ramseur's vicinity to extend his line. If they could recapture the tip of the Mule Shoe, they would complete a tourniquet across the dangerous wound to Lee's center. The stage was set. Nathaniel H. Harris's Mississippians and Samuel McGowan's South Carolinians were headed, unaware of their fate, for costly fame at the Bloody Angle.

The regiments of the Mississippi Brigade—the 12th, 16th, 19th, and 48th Infantry—had fought with distinction as a brigade for two years. Harris's men had prepared for the spring campaign with a mixture of bravery and concern characteristic of both armies. In mid-March, John Berryman Crawford of the 16th responded to a discouraged letter from his wife: "wee ant half whip hear." The patriotic soldier mentioned three deserters by name and expressed the hope that they would be hanged within two hours after their capture. Crawford admitted a yearning for home: "I waunt to see you and home mity bad once more in life, my Dear." But he died at the Bloody Angle a few weeks later.[27]

The 19th Mississippi engaged in a pseudo-medieval revel on April 11–12, staging a grand ball and the knightly jousting of a "ring tournament." "Each

Brigadier General
Nathaniel Harrison Harris.
Francis Trevelyan Miller, ed., *The Photographic History of the Civil War*, 10 vols. (New York: Review of Reviews, 1911), 10:277

Successful Knight danced the first set with the Lady he crowned," reported one participant, who boasted that he had euchred Gen. E. A. Perry out of a dance. The unit's camp newspaper celebrated the dance by publishing an essay, "Tactics of Kissing," in broad parody of Hardee's famous tactical manual. One month to the day after the tournament, the 19th was enmired in the Bloody Angle fight.[28]

In a more serious vein, men of both regiments succumbed to the religious promptings of Chaplain Alexander A. Lomax at the beginning of May. Lomax baptized four men of the 16th one week before the Bloody Angle: all four were hit on May 12; one of them was killed and another lost an arm. The four members of the 19th whom Lomax baptized all survived.[29]

Nathaniel Harris had been a brigadier general for only nine weeks. Gen. W. S. Featherston had led the brigade without much distinction in 1862, then Carnot Posey ably commanded it until mortally wounded at Bristoe Station late in 1863. Harris made "a very popular leader," one of his men wrote. A Georgia soldier without any parochial reason for favoring Harris's brigade enthusiastically called it the "grandest body of men that I ever saw (taking the whole war through)."[30]

This "grandest body of men" numbered perhaps 1,200 muskets as it neared the Bloody Angle maelstrom. The 48th was small, really a slightly expanded

Brigadier General Samuel McGowan. Francis Trevelyan Miller, ed., *The Photographic History of the Civil War*, 10 vols. (New York: Review of Reviews, 1911), 10:113

battalion, and the 12th was the strongest. The soldiers stirred awake at dawn as the din of battle far to their right announced the crisis. One of them described the bivouac for the wet night just ending as affording him "about as much comfort as a wet starving steer." Despite sleeping "in a puddle of mud," however, the weary fellow admitted: "we slept like graven images." The brigade was on Lee's extreme left, across the Po River and far from the danger point.[31]

Not long after the grime-caked troops awakened, they heard a running horse splashing toward them through the mud. The bedraggled animal carried a courier from Gen. William Mahone calling for Harris. What one soldier had taken for "a bundle of dirty rags" lying in the pasture stirred at the call and unfolded into the general. One glance at the message and Harris called for his horse and yelled for the men to fall in. "Come on boys," he shouted, "Hell's to pay! Pass the word down the line!"[32]

The column had the 16th Mississippi in front, followed in order by the 19th, 12th, and 48th. Harris was visibly excited, "which was very unusual." Under his prodding the men slogged through the mud at a wearing double-quick for about three miles, "every man in his place and as silent as a tomb." At this range the roar of battle to the north filled the skies. A member of the 16th described the noise somewhat inaptly: "musketry and artillery were rolling in beautiful sublimity." Closer exposure would obliterate the beauty. The Mississippians halted for about thirty minutes and then Lee sent an order for them to advance to the tip of the salient.[33]

As Harris's men closed on the broken nose of Lee's line, a second reinforcing brigade moved toward the same point from the opposite flank of the army. Samuel McGowan's five regiments—1st, 12th, 13th, and 14th South Carolina Infantry and Orr's Rifles—had been brigaded under the brilliant scholar and devoted soldier Maxcy Gregg in 1862. McGowan had led the seasoned regiments capably for a year by the spring of 1864. A rout beyond their power to contain in the Wilderness six days earlier had mortified the Carolinians "in the extreme," the ranking colonel wrote, and they were "well prepared to retrieve it at the next opportunity." The 1,300 men of the brigade would have ample occasion to renew their sterling reputation on this day.[34]

McGowan was north of the Court House at dawn on the 12th, about two miles from the nose of the Mule Shoe. The noise his men heard from the northwest told first of intense fighting and then—as the sound of battle moved—of Confederates in trouble. Sometime after Harris had received his mud-spotted courier, word reached McGowan to move to his left. Part of the brigade's route led through fields with "mud knee deep," and under "a torrent of rain." The Carolinians moved at a double-quick only part of the time. Artillery rounds came nearer and nearer, throwing mud and water high in the air as they struck. When McGowan halted the march near a brick kiln, Lee rode up and told the men that the line had been broken, "but we will have it all right very soon." McGowan reported to Ewell, who told General Rodes to put him into line on Harris's right.[35]

By the time McGowan drew near the nose of the salient, Harris's men had completed a rapid advance to the front. En route they participated in yet another Lee-to-the-Rear episode, the fourth within a week. The army commander's peripatetic efforts to discover the extent of damage to his center already had put him at risk that morning. Near Perrin's Alabamians, Lee sat "perfectly calm" astride Traveller and surveyed the front with his field glasses. A soldier jumped up and "almost in a frenzy" shouted, "Won't some one take that damn fool away from there?" Lee looked at the man calmly without a word, but soon left. Shortly thereafter, as he again examined the front, "very much absorbed" by what he saw through his glasses, two enemy shells burst "right in among Gen. Lee and his staff, enveloping them with thick clouds of smoke." Anxious observers could see two horses and riders down, but soon "Old Mas' Bob rode out of the smoke" to the cheers of onlookers. From that close call the general rode directly to the approaching front of Harris's column, asked its identity and, significantly, inquired how many rounds of cartridges were in the men's boxes.[36]

As Lee and Charles S. Venable of his staff and General Harris conversed near the head of the brigade, a fresh barrage of artillery crashed into the area. Traveller had been through a good bit of that already and fitfully reared up in excitement. As he did so, a 12-pound round solid shot hurtled past just under Lee's stirrups. Lee calmed his frantic mount while the missile caromed barely over the heads of the nearby infantry.[37]

The Mississippians did not know that was the general's third close call in recent minutes, but they all balked at the danger to their legendary chief. Lee's mien convinced them that he intended to go forward with them, a dire expedient they would tolerate no more than had the Texans on May 6 in the Wilderness. A member of the 16th cried, "Can't you trust us?" "Vociferous cries" of "Go back, go back, General Lee, for God's sake, go back" swelled as men down the line took up the chant.[38]

The general used his moment as the cynosure of every eye to challenge the Mississippians. His shouted exhortations, variously reported (as variously delivered), included: "Remember, you strike for Mississippi to-day!"; "Go and may God go with you"; and "promise me to drive those people from our works." Lee's "face was flush and eyes sparkling," a soldier wrote, but, another man reported, he "did not seem to lose his composure." A staff officer was struck by "the homely simplicity" of Lee's demeanor at this dramatic moment.[39]

When there was time for reckoning credit, accounts varied about who grasped Traveller's reins and ushered Lee to the rear. Some Mississippians saw Venable holding the horse's bridle, but the aide's own account does not mention it. Harris and a reliable witness from the 16th identified unnamed members of the 12th (which was the front regiment) as the hostlers of the moment. No doubt many willing hands patted and pulled and pushed and steered as Lee and his familiar mount headed back where they belonged—to organize the restoration of the line from the rear.[40]

Harris's advance soon reached the McCoull farm, with its lane running past the house and north 400 yards to the main line of works. Rodes was near McCoull and so was Ewell, leaning on a crutch and not much protected from enemy fire. Rodes assigned an aide (whose name Harris later sought in vain to learn) to guide the Mississippians to the deadly but crucial point just to the right of Ramseur's position. The troops pressed grimly forward past the left of the house, dropped into the wooded ravine beyond, crossed the McCoull spring branch, and swept up the rise toward the Bloody Angle.[41]

In a day already full of southern mistakes and misfortune, what happened next to Harris, between McCoull and the Bloody Angle, might have proved fatal: Rodes's staff officer, assigned because he knew the ground, lost his nerve

The McCoull house, which stood in the Mule Shoe salient southeast of the Bloody Angle. Francis Trevelyan Miller, ed., *The Photographic History of the Civil War*, 10 vols (New York: Review of Reviews, 1911), 3:57

and fled. Harris's courier, Asbury W. Hancock, chased the craven aide but "failed to overhaul him," Harris reported with evident chagrin. Untutored, Harris pressed straight north in column instead of deploying into a broad line. He was unwittingly heading end-first into a hostile position perpendicular to his own axis. Hundreds of northerners would be able to fire at the Mississippians, almost none of whom could respond. Fortunately, the woods and brush screened the advancing men for a time. So did a dense cloud of misty fog and sulfurous battle smoke that hovered close to the ground.[42]

When Federals swarming around the captured works spotted the approaching Confederates, they unleashed a concentrated fire against them. The Mississippians could not respond until they swung through an arc of ninety degrees to face their foe, nor could they accomplish anything by charging until they made that realignment. Harris mounted some earthworks and, "exposed to a shower of bullets," tried to ascertain what to do. He obviously needed to move right, anchoring his left on the McCoull lane. Harris issued orders to that effect and believed they had been obeyed. He described wheeling first two regiments and then the other two, as resistance heightened. The men doing the shifting, however, were beyond the reach of disciplined commands. Most did what needed doing by reflex: "every man for himself," "without an order," or "with the instinct of veterans...."[43]

Under ordinary circumstances, 1,200 attackers ought not to have been able to get up the slope to the earthworks against the Union troops massed there. The northerners, however, could not defend the works as well as if those defenses had been facing south. They also had lost tactical cohesion in the aftermath of their dawn success. Even so, "a forest of muskets played with awful fury over the ground...." Harris's men advanced "at a run" into that awful fury with formidable elan and determination. "We yelled and dashed head on," one of them wrote. Capt. John M. McAfee of the 48th shouted, "Don't forget your native State and your bravery," one of his men recalled, adding that "our only hope was in one desperate charge . . . with a wild yell." The hollering, of course, was the famous southern battle cry, what Robert Gambrell of the 19th called "that kind of a Rebel yell."[44]

Many of the Mississippi soldiers were riveted by the regimental battle flags moving bravely at the forefront. Alexander Mixon of the 16th waved his flag as he ran and his "clarion-like voice resounded along the line, urging the men to follow." They did, "through a storm of bullets." Mixon planted his flag atop the recaptured works just as he was shot through the head. J. B. Summer and A. M. Swittenberg of his color detachment also were killed as they reached the works. Harris himself was near the front. One of his men spun into the general's arms reeling from a mortal wound. Harris, "in this hail of death, laid him gently on the ground, with the exclamation, 'Oh, my poor fellow!' "[45]

The valor of Mixon and his comrades has received far less attention than the twenty-hour struggle that followed. Without the undaunted assault, however, the Bloody Angle fight would never have developed. Confederates looking on marveled. One of Ramseur's men could see the battle flags jammed into the works. General Rodes declared: "It was the bravest deed I have ever seen performed!" Ewell expressed his "intense admiration for men who could advance so calmly to what seemed and proved almost certain death. I have never seen troops under a hotter fire than was endured on this day by [Harris's] brigade...."[46]

The assault captured nearly 300 prisoners, many of whom were killed by northern bullets as they headed to the rear. More important, it extended Confederate control onto the tip of the salient, denying the enemy unrestricted access to Lee's center. The cost had been staggering. Col. Samuel E. Baker of the 16th, who incredibly had been mounted at the front of the charge, was shot off his horse and then riddled with bullets. His executive officer, Lt. Col. Abram M. "Dode" Feltus, was killed too. So were Col. Thomas J. Hardin of the 19th and Capt. McAfee and dozens more.[47]

Harris's hard-won toehold needed to extend farther east than it did. His left overlapped Ramseur's right — "a portion of the left regiment now tapping the right of Ramseur's brigade," in Harris's words. The essential expansion in that direction, up the slope toward the Bloody Angle crest, was bitter and costly. Harris led the way, calling individuals by name and shouting "Charge!" "The battle at this point," Harris wrote, "became a hand to hand conflict, the bayonet and butt of the musket being freely used; the Union troops contesting the possession of each traverse stubbornly." The Mississippians could not reach all the way over the crest, so some traverses to their east continued to pour fire at them. Hundreds of Harris's men were casualties by this time, and the ordeal had only begun.[48]

Soon after Harris reached his position, McGowan's Carolinians repeated his experience. At about 10:00 A.M., that sturdy brigade arrived around the McCoull house and tried to evaluate the situation. "It was so desperate that staff officers would not go near enough to point out where we must enter," a colonel wrote. McGowan put the 12th on his right and in order to its left the 1st, the 13th, Orr's Rifles, and the 14th. The McCoull lane was crooked and the brigade alignment reflected that. Violent fire from in front made standing still a dreadful ordeal. So McGowan and his men started across the same 400 yards that had faced Harris, but angling a bit more to the east.[49]

General McGowan, astride a striking gray horse, shouted "Forward! my brave boys" and led the way. Down the northern McCoull slope the men hurried, past the spring, and up into "a whirlwind of rifle balls." When they reached an inner line of works, two thirds of the way to the outer line, four of the regiments halted: only the 12th impetuously swept forward. The others soon followed, but without McGowan, whose "portly form" was "too conspicuous a mark for the bullets, now flying fast and furious, to miss." Benjamin T. Brockman of the 13th, the ranking colonel, also fell. Despite the loss of leaders, the Carolinians pressed ahead and reached the outer works — the front line. Scott Allen of the 14th was yelling at the top of his voice when a bullet passed through both cheeks, missing his tongue.[50]

As had the Mississippians — as did most charging Civil War troops — the Carolinians followed battle flags being waved by the most daring men in the units. The 12th's flagstaff "was shot in two twice before reaching the works." Even so, a soldier boasted, "it was the first colors planted on the line." Calvin M. Galloway carried the flag of Orr's Rifles into the attack and was shot in the forehead; his body never was recovered. Charles E. Whilden, flag bearer of the 1st, was too sick to keep up with the advance, so relinquished his banner to an officer, but then found the energy to run forward and reclaim it. A bullet tore off the top of the flag; another hit Whilden's left shoulder. Whilden scrawled an informal last testament to his brother—but forty years later he still had the treasured flag.[51]

Just as Harris's men had done, McGowan's deflected farther left than would have been ideal, away from the highest ground at the Bloody Angle. That put some, perhaps many or even most, of them in amongst the Mississippians, who gestured and shouted, "*go to the right*." To dampen the fire from their right, and to reach the important apex of the works, McGowan's troops now had to attack eastward, traverse by traverse. Tactical identity had largely dissolved by this time, but men of the 12th on the right led the way, "by the flank up the works" in what a colonel aptly called "one of the fiercest and most bloody struggles of the war." Lt. Col. Washington P. Shooter of the 1st, short of stature but long on heart, waved his sword and cheered the men on until a bullet crashed into his chest. He exhorted those who hurried to his aid to keep attacking: "Forward, men, I die with my eyes fixed on victory." Shooter's brother died a few feet away; another brother had been killed in the Wilderness.[52]

Later, as veterans tried to untangle the trying events of that day, some Mississippians concluded that no Carolinians reached any point on their right. Harris declared in various accounts that McGowan's men halted behind his own *left* and Ramseur's right, "gained no ground to the right," and could not be induced to move to the right! He claimed to have assumed command of the Carolinians as well as his own force. An 1866 unit history echoed this view and added the (not unlikely) claim that McGowan's men fired into Harris's rear as they advanced. Other Mississippi histories have repeated those statements.[53]

Some Mississippians, of course, were well situated to see their comrades from South Carolina move to the right, and benefited from their presence there. One such man described how McGowan's "left, which overlapped Harris' right," joined them in the works. A member of the 16th Mississippi saw the Carolinians "breasting the terrible storm . . . with the left . . . over lapping the right of ours." One of McGowan's officers charitably suggested that Harris "was too intent in urging his brigade . . . to notice, through the rain and smoke, McGowan's brigade, in . . . their swift movement to traverses at his right." The newcomers readily admitted that "we partly covered Gen. Harris's Brigade," and that, to the left, "both brigades were crowded several lines deep." McGowan's official report provides a nice summary: "they (Mississippians and Carolinians) mingled together."[54] Events would demonstrate how thoroughly intermingled the men were.

With both brigades at the front, the scene for defending the Bloody Angle was set. No organized reinforcements would reach the scene. The 2,000 or so men from the Deep South now faced nearly twenty hours of unrelieved horror. Fortunately, they had no idea of the duration of the ordeal just beginning. There was, in fact, a brief lull. On the left, the Mississippians hastily collected five or six guns apiece from the ample supply abandoned by captured Confederates or dropped by wounded Yankees. Using multiple rifles, many survivors fired several hundred shots during the day ahead. Officers doubtless did their best, but one Mississippian remarked that "at the point of immediate contact no officer commanded . . . each private was commander-in-chief." Some infantrymen began accumulating hatchets against the ominous prospect of deadly close-in fighting. Confederate quartermasters never delivered such exotic equipment, but many men had captured ones and they found others on Federal prisoners and dead.[55]

Even by the ghastly standards of combat, the Bloody Angle already was a mess. Rain poured in torrents, mixed with blood from the dead and dying, and filled the shoes of defenders obliged to sit or stand on water-covered bodies. Fog and smoke eerily hugged the ground. Through the haze, "an incessant stream of rifle balls" crackled in the air just above the works. Intermittently, Federals wielding bayonets emerged from the smoke. Harris described repeated attacks, but to the frontline soldiers, the onslaughts soon after their arrival seemed the worst. Fortunately, the mud slowed the enemy and the works afforded protection. The flag of the 16th attracted attackers like a magnet. For a time, Yankees kept their national flag and a New York flag waving right next to the 16th's banner. Eight times the Mississippians shot down men with those flags. Federal dead fell off the top of the works into the interior ditch. When the staff of the 16th's colors was completely shattered, bearer Peter Stockett fashioned a new one from a tree limb; then he was hit and another man took over. Hand-to-hand fighting became so savage and primal that desperate Mississippians went from bayonets to clubbed muskets to the hatchets they had collected: "A tall, brawny fellow, was seen to throw down his musket and pick up a hatchet. As a Federal comes at him with a bayonet, he pushed it aside with his left hand, while with the hatchet in his right he brains his opponent. Others, seeing the advantage of the hatchet as a weapon of defense followed his example, while the Federals shrank from the sickening scene, many of them throwing down their guns and surrendering, while the others left the works in haste, scores of them being struck down in the attempt."[56]

Once the heavy initial counterattack subsided, and Confederates could take stock of their position, they discovered that the two brigades held a narrow front only some 500 feet wide. The left lay at the McCoull lane. The right was where a ravine curled up from the north to the outer face of the works. Sixty yards left of the ravine there stood an oak tree of 22-inch diameter that would become a universal landmark when musketry chewed it through some hours later. Beyond the ravine, east of the Confederate right, no one occupied the works for more than 100 yards. A shelf running north from the main Bloody Angle works for 40 yards dropped into an east-west ravine that gave invaluable shelter to approaching Federals. Some Mississippians were as far east as the tree and even the ravine, but the proportion of Carolinians to Mississippians must have increased steadily with each traverse eastward from the McCoull road.[57]

The Carolinians at the Angle at first did not know who was commanding the brigade, although the men at the battle's front cared little about such things. With General McGowan and the senior colonel both casualties, Lt. Col. Isaac F. Hunt of the 13th South Carolina assumed command of troops within his reach on the right. Col. Joseph Newton Brown of the 14th had become senior after the casualties, but his regiment was farthest left and out of easy reach. Hunt heard an erroneous report that Brown had been hit, too, so he retained command until Brown showed up on the brigade's right and took over. Hunt then went to the left and spent the day pushing men and ammunition up to the right with what Brown called "almost superhuman strength." Harris's claim that an unnamed "ranking officer" reported to him "and received orders and instructions" seems obviously in error. The general no doubt shouted at a number of unfamiliar officers, but without ever actually assuming command of the adjacent unit.[58]

Carolinians unaware of the uncertain command situation prepared to fight at close range in circumstances at least as bad as the Mississippians had found. "The sight we encountered was not calculated to encourage us," one wrote. "The trenches . . . were almost filled with water. Dead men lay on the . . . ground and in the pools of water. The wounded bled and groaned, stretched or huddled in every attitude of pain. The water was crimsoned with blood." Near the oak tree, where the two lines were separated only by the width of the works, both sides reached muskets over the top for a quick shot, briefly exposing only a wrist. The head logs afforded some shelter for soldiers facing a "terrific cross current of musket balls, which literally combed the parapets." Men either fatalistic or unimaginably brave actually leaped atop the works to fire a round before falling back down—usually wounded or dead. Some Carolinians admitted that they "merely held the works and did not try to shoot." Most casualties were hit fatally in the head or neck.[59]

Although the major Federal counterattack that hit Harris's troops probably had abated by the time Brown's men reached the front, an endless array of enemies came into focus at short range. The woods north of the Bloody Angle field "seem[ed] to be one moving mass [of] their reenforcements." Northern regiments gathered in such numbers that their "flags crowded together" opposite the works. The most distinct features affecting the Federals at once became obvious: the ravine parallel to the works and 40 yards north of it, and the draw running south into the works 60 yards east of the big oak tree. Using the east-west draw, Yankees "could crawl up without being perceived, and, by lying down just at the crest . . . have almost as secure a place for firing as was afforded by the Confederate works." A Mississippian wrote: "It was only a short distance from the breastworks to the decline of the hill [where] the Federal line was reformed." Yankees looking at the high ground, with its east end curling up to the works, called the position a knoll (an inapt description because the southern and western faces do not decline). Because Federals could not shelter opposite the draw defining the eastern edge, the Bloody Angle fighting did not extend beyond that point.[60]

The extent of the Bloody Angle came into dispute after the war. Federal generals Barlow and Lewis A. Grant waged a warm quarrel in which each was talking about a different location (Bloody Angle versus East Angle). Confederates bewildered by the same confusion debated in a haze—the acute East Angle of course did not resemble the gentle curve at the Bloody Angle. Two things entangled postwar discussions: the broad, shallow "V" of the Federal positions north of the works was based on terrain, not on earthworks; and soon after the battle, some Federal works did go up to reface the salient (especially just northwest of the tree). Ample evidence, tied to the ground, survives from local civilians whose point of reference was the oak tree. Edward Landrum, on whose farm the fight took place, said, "There were not many dead farther eastward, but on the crest on the right and left of the fallen oak tree (pointing out a distance of 30 yards on his right and about 50 on his left), they were so piled upon one another that you could not tell them apart. . . ."[61]

The deadly excitement of the initial attack to the works steadily turned into an even deadlier enervation as close-range fighting continued without ceasing. Most participants had experienced attack and counterattack before. None had participated in an endless slugging match in which neither side had, nor could muster, any momentum. Rain mixed with blood was the most commonly reported defining experience. Continuous rain filled ditches on both sides of the works "half leg deep," and, "from the number of dead and wounded, this water became as bloody as if it flowed from an abattoir." Officers and men crouched in blood stained water. Wounded fell in the ghastly muck and died, some of them by drowning while helpless. The mess begrimed muskets on which defense depended. "We could hardly tell one another apart," Mississippian David Holt recalled. "No Mardi Gras Carnival ever devised such a diabolical looking set of devils as we were. It was no imitation of red paint and burnt cork, but genuine human gore and gun powder smoke. . . ."[62]

The bloody water that so bedeviled the hard-pressed troops stood in stark contrast to the water they yearned for—fresh water from the McCoull spring

One of the most famous depictions of the hand-to-hand fighting at the Bloody Angle. Robert Underwood Johnson and Clarence Clough Buel, eds., *Battles and Leaders of the Civil War*, 4 vols. (New York: Century, 1887–88), 4:170

only 300 yards away: "It was so near and yet so far . . . owing to the terrible fire that swept our rear. . . . Every one that was ever in battle knows what intense thirst is caused by excitement and burnt powder. . . . Men threw their heads back and opened their mouths to catch up the drizzling rain . . . on parched tongue and encrusted lips."[63]

Was there hope of relief? Rumors circulated that Ewell had promised help if the men could hold on just a little longer. The help never came. When Harris asked for assistance, word came back that a diversion to the east should relieve the pressure. It did not. The Bloody Angle was immune to military manipulation. Men fighting in its arc were by now controlled by primal, not tactical, influences. Confederates in the midst of the horror knew "the vital importance" of the spot, and believed "that the safety of Lee's army" depended on them — as in fact it did.[64]

Torrents of lead killed any wounded not under cover, then "riddled beyond recognition" their corpses. The wooden parts of the works fell prey to the storm, "splintered like brush-brooms." Federals hit on the shelf north of the works faced certain death. They were trampled by running men, then shattered by bullets. The "faint, pitiful cries" of enemy wounded haunted southerners who had shot them. Franz Metzel from Massachusetts was hit by twenty-six bullets on May 12, but somehow he survived for eighteen days. The searching balls put one observer "in mind of some musical instrument; some sounded like wounded men crying; some like humming of bees; some like cats in the depth of the night; others cut through the air with only a 'Zip' like noise."[65]

Among the missiles hurled at the Angle were rounds from coehorn mortars, in use against Lee's army for the first time. Confederates could see and time the high-trajectory rounds, so the mortars had little effect. Field artillery from both sides fired across the lines, but some Federals near the Angle thought that friendly artillery did them more harm than it did the rebels.[66]

Artillery rarely ruled infantry affairs during the war, and it certainly did not do so at the Angle. Men like Max Freunthal of the 16th Mississippi determined the outcome. This "little Jew," a comrade wrote, "though insignificant in appearance, had the heart of a lion. For several hours he stood at the immediate point of contact, amid the most ter[r]ific hail of lead, and coolly and deliberately loaded and fired without cringing." Others fought with bayonets. Confederate surgeons reported that the fight on May 12 "presented us with [bayonet] wounds for the first time." Federal surgeons also reported treating bayonet wounds on this day, including two in the knee, which suggests men coming across high works at their foes.[67]

The endless fighting bore no resemblance to anything in the considerable experience of Brown's and Harris's veteran soldiers. By early afternoon most distinctions between the two brigades had dissolved. In the words of a Carolinian, "the breastworks were crowded with Confederates all mixed up, but fighting like demons." "A good part of Harris's Mississippians were with us," the historian of McGowan's brigade wrote. Thus, it was a group of Carolinians who recorded the dying words of a Mississippi boy, "a little, smooth-faced fellow, very out of place in this carnage." The lad lived only a moment after he was hit, crying out to the strangers he had fallen among with a message to his mother.[68]

The need to keep up strength on the right drew some Mississippians all the way to the Bloody Angle's eastern verge. Two of the best accounts of the far right are by veterans of the 16th, showing clearly that they fought in a sector without tactical distinctions. "Again came the appeal for more volunteers for the right," T. T. Roche recalled, "as nearly all the defenders at that point had been cut down." Roche leaped into a pit on the far right with four men from two other regiments. In the traverse-lined pit "men lay four deep . . . limbs interlaced and entwined, sleeping the sleep that knows no waking. Among them were many . . .

Federals." When Roche turned from talking to two Carolinians he found alive in the pit, he saw that all four of his comrades already had been killed. Yankees were firing their guns over the works "without exposing the head or body . . . the bullets striking with a dull, sickening thud into the dead bodies that were piled within it." Roche hurriedly fell back to the next pit westward.[69]

David Holt had a similar experience. He had fought with his 16th Mississippi on the left of the Angle, loading seven guns and firing them when crises erupted: "Many times we could not put the gun to our shoulder by reason of the closeness of the enemy, so we shot from the hip." Holt and his buddies then moved to the far right against intense pressure under which "no man thought at all. That function seemed to be suspended." Finally, so many Yankees crowded close that Maj. Edward C. Councell yelled "Fall back to the left!" Northerners quickly poured into the abandoned spot. In one pit, Confederates escaped by crawling *under* a traverse where it bridged the ditch. Councell's men then fired back into their old position and, "in a remarkably short time, not a man of them was left alive." After the Mississippians returned to the original pit and cleared it of the fresh corpses, another Federal onslaught rolled in. A soldier named Harrison shot one then leaped on the works and knocked down four more with the butt of his musket before "he crumpled up like a bundle of bloody rags and sank down into the ditch."[70]

Carolinians fighting beside Holt and Roche to hold the Angle's right face recognized that "the question became, pretty plainly, whether one was willing to meet death, not merely to run the chances of it." John Landrum of the 14th was one of many who lost the gamble, ironically on the farm of a Virginian named Landrum.[71]

How had all of the momentum of two great armies degenerated into this undirected melee over a narrow stretch of works? The works themselves provide the answer. Although weak in its location, Lee's Mule Shoe line was the strongest yet seen in a field engagement on the continent. No one was ready for the impact of such formidable entrenchments upon tactical matters. Without the works, neither side could have fought long on that short, hot crest — shorter than two football fields in length, and only a few yards in depth.[72]

Every Confederate who fought at the Angle remembered two events: a bizarre surrender episode, and when the oak tree fell, cut down by bullets. The pseudo-surrender developed early in the afternoon, based on widespread mutual misunderstandings. Firing slackened and stopped as rumors spread on both sides that the other wished to give up. Federals approached the works to accept what they fancied to be a capitulation. Confederates awaited them, ready to accept what they too thought would be prisoners of war. Major Councell met a cheerful Federal officer who was astounded when Councell said,

"No, sir; we have not surrendered, but consider yourself a prisoner." Lt. Col. Thomas F. Clyburn of the 12th Mississippi yelled at his men to shoot a Federal officer who leaped atop the works and demanded a surrender. Capt. Cadwallader Jones countered his colonel's orders, "holloaing, 'Don't shoot! don't shoot!' We thought they had surrendered; they thought we had surrendered. It was such a hot place, both sides were about ready to quit."[73]

Colonel Brown met another optimistic enemy officer and was astonished to learn that he expected a surrender. Brown rejected the notion "in a polite but most positive manner," saying that "his men have come to stay," and asked what had spawned the confusion. The Federal said he had seen a white flag flying on the left. Matters instantly degenerated into noisy verbal chaos: "A Babel of tongues succeeded — officers ordering the resumption of the firing; men calling out to the Federal line, questioning each other, imploring for the fire to be held and the enemy allowed to come in." A thoughtful Confederate admitted: "To those who reflected a moment, it should have been plain that we were deceiving ourselves. . . . But a general infatuation prevailed — a silly infatuation, if it had not involved so much. So the two lines stood, bawling, gesticulating, arguing, and what not."[74]

Neither side had engaged in trickery to bring on the curious episode. Each had succumbed to "a silly infatuation." Men of both armies genuinely believed their enemies had raised a white flag. Southern recollections suggest three origins for their confusion. Some clearly saw a pale flag in the Union ranks before firing ceased — "the light-colored flag . . . of Connecticut, I believe" — and mistook it for a symbol of truce. On parts of the line, Confederates saw Federals approach waving hats, not flags, asking to parley ("It is useless. Surrender and save bloodshed."). Once the confusion began, Federals showed handkerchiefs as protection as they went forward to accept the imaginary surrender. Hundreds of Confederates who saw those truce hankies thought they betokened northern capitulation.[75]

No Federal admitted seeking to surrender, although hundreds did so during the day. Many northerners already captured benefited from the cessation of fire to dash south across ground theretofore impassable. Confederates later recognized that somewhere along their lines, men driven beyond their capacity for horror *had* sought to surrender, and that those actions by individuals may have triggered the misunderstanding.[76]

An observant and literate Mississippian took advantage of the momentary truce to examine the Federal ground. He carefully described the shallow "V" of the enemy line, bending away from the works to both east and west, and the carnage around it: "The field presented one vast Golgotha in immensity of the number of the dead. . . . [Behind the Federal front line] the ground was almost covered with the dead and wounded, while between the lines they were literally piled. . . . The writer counted fifteen stand of colors lying between the lines, some of them having fallen against our breastworks—the brave hands which had borne them so gallantly forward now lying cold in death." [77]

The truce did not survive long. As it became clear that no surrender would ensue, Federals who had approached the works asked to be allowed to return to their lines unharmed. In each case their foes readily agreed. In most instances, however, men on either flank, unaware and excited, shot them down. An enemy who had approached David Holt's stretch of the line had hardly turned to leave when someone shot him in the head. Holt slid down behind the works as enraged Yankees "rushed forward in a desperate charge. Many got into the ditch and were killed" with bayonets and musket butts; war to the death resumed its reign.[78]

A horrible component of the surrender incident ensued when Confederates saw some of their fainthearted mates try to give up. Tom Roche saw fifteen or twenty Confederates throw down their arms and head for the Federals as the truce broke down. None reached their goal under a volley from their former friends. In another Mississippi traverse, "a good soldier" who had "allowed himself to be overcome by the horror and terror of the situation" raised his shirt on the muzzle of his gun. A longtime friend grimly shot the man dead as he started for the Federal lines.[79]

One of the best primary accounts of the Bloody Angle summarized the bizarre incident aptly: "There was very absurd blundering . . . a number on each side fancying that the men on the other side wished to surrender. [It was] a sort of parley in which almost everybody talked, and hardly anybody listened. Men are unlike women, who can talk and listen at the same time." [80]

Late in the afternoon, word spread across the front that "if we would hold the place till dark we should be relieved." The sun seemed "hung up" in the sky to men who "wished it was night." Two brigades did arrive in the Mule Shoe near dark, but they went into supporting positions while frantic Confederates struggled to complete a new line behind the Harrison house under the supervision of General Gordon. "Dark came, but no relief." [81]

When the sun set at 7:00 P.M., firing abated as men adjusted to the changed circumstances. Then it resumed "with great fierceness and fury." Confederates heard a new sound: "bull bats" swooping low, "their cries and the swish of their swoops" audible above the din. Some soldiers, incredibly, fell asleep in a sort of nervous swoon. The dominant concern at dusk was a quest for ammunition. Hours of fighting had used up almost every round. Some men fired surplus ramrods at the Federals, saving only a single one to service all of the muskets they had accumulated. Man after man went down while trying to forward ammunition. Ramseur's men absorbed much of the resupply before it could reach the Angle. Harris's courier, Asbury Hancock, finally set up a shuttle system that worked, albeit perilously. Farther east, Holden Pearson of the 16th Mississippi worked out a covered route down the slope behind the Angle and dragged forward tent sections laden with cartridges. Getting the rounds distributed laterally once they reached the front looked like "a real suicidal job" to a Mississippian faced with the task. He hung string-tied, ten-round ammunition packets across a ramrod and reached them carefully across a traverse to men waiting in the next pit.[82]

Federal bullets kept sluicing across the lip of the works in the gathering darkness, sometimes ricocheting onto a new tangent. A South Carolinian still in his teens had been fighting "with great perseverance and coolness. . . . He was a handsome boy, tall and slender, with . . . a smooth, fair cheek, just darkening with the first downy beard. . . . About sunset, he sat down in the cross-trench to rest. He was hardly down, when a ball glanced from a tree and struck him just behind the right ear. He struggled up and shook with a brief convulsion. . . . He raised his eyes, with the sweetest, saddest smile I think I ever saw on earth, and died almost on the instant." The fatal bullet had not broken the youngster's skin.[83]

The leaden storm searching ceaselessly in the darkness completed an astounding process at about midnight: it chipped through, one tiny nip at a time, a towering, 22-inch-thick oak tree. Each man in both brigades heard the giant crash to the ground and located himself relative to that point in recalling the battle. Unfortunately for historical clarity, several smaller specimens went down nearby (most aided by artillery strikes), prompting confusion among soldiers who had dodged falling limbs all day and then full trees in the dark of night. The huge oak, sawn through entirely by whistling bullets, stood sixty yards west of the ravine that marked the east end of the Bloody Angle. The owner of the farm and other civilians kept the site marked with a stake well into the twentieth century, when a cement-based metal marker assumed the duty.[84]

In the next few days, thousands of men from both armies, including General Lee, examined the shattered wooden monument to the power of musketry. A doctor carefully measured the stump's 22-inch thickness. Twenty-four years later the lead-filled wooden relic reached the Smithsonian Institution, where it survives today. Military tourists walking near the Angle also found bullets that had smashed into each other in midair. In the same vein — it must be an exaggeration — a member of the 16th Mississippi claimed that his regiment's flag had about 250 bullet holes in it after the fight![85]

Confederates near the falling tree could not be sure in the "intensely dark" night where the main trunk would land, though toppling away from the works

A portion of the 22-inch-thick oak tree cut down by musket fire at the Bloody Angle on May 12, 1864. Smithsonian Institution

seemed likeliest. Several who guessed wrong were injured, a few of them severely. The noisy crash and southern shouts in reaction triggered a renewed burst of Federal musketry, "the most terrific fire of the whole action." When that abated, soldiers dug their friends out of a mass of wood and bloody mud. A 14th South Carolina private who had been stunned concluded that Yankees had thrown limbs at him.[86]

On past midnight the firing rattled and roared "without ceasing," wrote Newton L. Bennet of the 13th South Carolina, who survived unhit despite having his hat and clothes "riddled with bullets." When Colonel Brown went to the rear in another effort to secure help, he "had no trouble in finding the Brigade" as he started back: "The heavy firing concentrated on one point indicated our position." Brown claimed that, despite the convenient cover of darkness, "not a man was known to have left." Some Federals still charged up to the works at times. More and more Confederates fell asleep despite the danger and the din.[87]

Joseph Brown thought that more of his Carolinians were killed after dark than during daylight hours. Even so, human endurance eventually dictated an abatement in the violence and the firing "sank into the sharp whizzing of skirmish shooting." Brown thought finally "the enemy became discouraged." General Ewell took the opportunity to send a major forward to look for lost cannon. When the mission failed, and the officer admitted that instead of going in person he had sent "a reliable and intelligent sergeant," Ewell rejoined: "Well sir the sergt. had better be made the Major and you the sergeant." With corps commanders sassy again, and artillery retrieval on the agenda, the crisis clearly had passed.[88]

At last, Colonel Brown secured orders to fall back with the remnants of his brigade "at day break." Bratton's brigade was in position behind the Angle to protect the withdrawal, and a new line of works across the base of the salient stood ready to become Lee's front. Most Carolinians said their ordeal ended "about daylight" or "shortly before dawn" (sunrise in Richmond was 5:01). Other participants specified 4:00 A.M.[89]

Some departing Carolinians employed all the stealth they could muster to get away, whispering to one another and moving noiselessly. Others observed the lack of Federal reaction and abandoned the Angle without trying to conceal their movement. Northerners still in the vicinity at dawn noticed nothing; most had fallen back across the field earlier.[90]

Those of Harris's Mississippians still centered on the left of the Bloody Angle may have departed earlier than Brown's men; they certainly had a more difficult time getting away. Harris received orders by 3:00 A.M. to pull out. Pvt. A. W. Hancock, who already had distinguished himself twice around the Angle, volunteered to run the gauntlet to deliver the withdrawal orders. Hancock "sprang upon the breastworks and ran upon the top of the parapet the whole distance and, springing into the ditch among the men, delivered the order." Harris was to retire leftward, through Ramseur's zone. Ramseur's men went out first, on their hands and knees, leaving canteens behind to hold down noise. No accounts from either brigade echo the comments of South Carolinians about an undisputed departure. Federals at vantage points looking into the lower ground west of the Angle delivered "a severe fire of musketry" across the works there.[91]

David Holt of the 16th Mississippi almost got left behind. He had fallen asleep surrounded by corpses. Friends slipping past whispered to one another that poor Dave was dead. After all had left, something startled Holt awake. As he left the Angle, he took in the macabre scene around the fallen tree. "One wounded man was cursing, another praying. . . . Many were crying for water, some begging to have the dead taken off them. I don't expect to go to hell, but if I do, I am sure that Hell can't beat that terrible scene." Dragging his rifle behind him, Holt ducked low and tore southwestward down the trench as fast as he could go.[92]

Hundreds of men sprawled around the Bloody Angle were beyond waking. Some Mississippi companies, which averaged perhaps thirty men on the morning of May 12, had ten men killed and as many more wounded; losses of two-thirds of strength were not unusual in the most heavily engaged units. Despite their proud histories and traditions, Harris's four regiments soon were consolidated into two regimental commands. The brigade's loss totaled at least 344, of whom 73 were killed and 109 missing — many in the latter category being killed also. If Harris carried 1,200 men into battle, his losses came close to 30 percent.[93]

Brown's South Carolinians suffered even more heavily than the Mississippians. The most heavily engaged companies took enormous losses. The 12th South Carolina — which advanced first, alone and farthest right — predictably bled worst, with 118 casualties. Brown's 451 losses equaled more than one-third of his strength; 207 of them were killed or missing. Many of the missing lie today in unknown graves in the Spotsylvania Confederate Cemetery. The identified dead in the South Carolina and Mississippi sections of that burial ground are almost exclusively from Bloody Angle regiments. Only a handful of bodies ever went home. One who did was Clarence J. Pollock of the 1st South Carolina, who is buried in the Columbia Hebrew Benevolent Society Cemetery.[94]

Staggering, hollow-eyed survivors took stock and gave thanks as they fell back. Bill West of the 16th Mississippi had been shot through the cap three times, one ball cutting a groove down his scalp; another round cut off the bottom of one ear; another creased his shoulder; his blanket roll was shredded; bullets had torn his jacket, shirt, and undershirt; but he survived. Another man of the 16th also had his clothing thoroughly perforated and had been hit squarely in the chest — where a pack of playing cards stopped the bullet when it reached the ace of spades. In a company of the 16th, only one man came away without the mark of a bullet on either his body or clothes.[95]

Early on the 13th, the Bloody Angle was in no-man's land. Federals who took horrified looks at the scene left graphic descriptions: "Horses and men chopped into hash by the bullets . . . appearing . . . like piles of jelly." "The . . . logs in the breastworks were shattered into splinters. . . . We had not only shot down an army, but also a forest. . . . Below the mass of fast-decaying corpses, the convulsive twitching of limbs and the writhing of bodies [revealed] wounded men . . . struggling to extricate themselves from their horrid entombment." Gen. Lewis Grant wrote: "It was there . . . that the brush and logs were cut to pieces and whipped into basket-stuff . . . that fallen men's flesh was torn from the bones and the bones shattered . . . that the rebel ditches . . . were filled with dead men several deep." [96]

Some Confederate veterans of the fight returned as early as 11:00 A.M. They gazed upon "a perfect picture of gloom, destruction and death — a very Golgotha of horrors." "The dead are lying in the trenches . . . half filled with water; it is black with powder and streaked with blood." "The awful stillness of the place after such a dreadful fury almost unnerved me." Other men visited the scene of their ordeal two or three days later. By that time heat and humidity had worked on the dead: "[I]f a man wants to see hell upon earth, let him come and look into this black, bloody . . . horrid corruption of rotting corpses, that fill the air with this intolerable stench." [97]

With the resilience of young soldiers in every era, the battered Bloody Angle men soon restored their will. Even the "hell upon earth" fellow admitted that within "a few days, I was 'spoiling for a fight,' and so were the rest." "To days fight must cripple Grant's Army and weaken the confidence of his men in him," a Mississippian wrote in his diary. In a letter not long after, another insisted that Grant had "been badly whipped. . . . Our troops are confidant of success. . . . A great many thinks that this campaign will bring the war to a close." Southerners noticed that Grant was "a real bull-dog," with the result that they "never saw dead Yankees lie so thick on the ground" as at Spotsylvania. [98]

Passing time did nothing to dim the awareness of survivors that the Bloody Angle's horrors had been of unparalleled intensity. "The whole history of warfare . . . cannot give another such instance," wrote a northern veteran. Southern analyses included these earnest declarations: "the bloodiest, the hardest-fought, the most obstinate of the war"; "the most terrible day I have ever lived"; "I had never before imagined such a struggle to be possible"; "the most terrific battle I have ever witnessed . . . the most desperate struggle of the war." A Mississippian enumerated the war's famous battles and concluded, "for grand, terrible, terrific and long sustained fighting, none of these approached the bloody angle." Colonel Brown wrote that despite being in all of the army's battles — he specified Sharpsburg and Gettysburg — he "never saw anything to equal in desperate character that of the Bloody Angle." [99]

The Bloody Angle soon extended its impact to homes in South Carolina and Mississippi. The family of William L. Walters of the 14th South Carolina learned on a Sunday evening that he had gone missing at the Angle. "Never will I forget the sad cry of my aged parents . . . their sad wail," a brother wrote. Unlike most such stories, Walters's had a happy ending. He had been captured alive and survived imprisonment at Fort Delaware. A forlorn tale, clearly without any cheerful conclusion, lies behind a personal advertisement in an 1866 Fredericksburg newspaper. "Information wanted of Oliver H. P. Anderson" of the 48th Mississippi, advertised Mrs. Rebecca Anderson. Oliver — among many others, of course — had "been missing ever since the battle of Spotsylvania Courthouse, May 12th, 1864."[100]

The Angle itself survives as a monument to those who made it forever famous, although at this writing the threat of adjacent development has the potential to dilute the site's awesome impact. The earthworks have shrunken to a modest, but readily discernible, state. Visitors during the 1920s described them as two or three feet high in the open and four or five feet high in the woods, which is about their current condition. A 1930s full-scale reconstruction not far below the East Angle promptly melted back down to the shape of the rest. Once the wood fiber rots, dirt piles achieve a kind of equilibrium.[101]

Postmortems were not part of the survivors' short-term agenda. Once they reached safety, they simply "sat down on the wet ground and wept. Not silently, but vociferously and long." Mud puddles provided a chance to wash their hands and faces, but otherwise they remained "covered with bloody mud from head to foot." Commissaries brought cornbread and bacon, but no one could eat. "May God in his mercy never again permit us to behold such a field of carnage and death!" one veteran exclaimed. He and his comrades had forged "an insurmountable barrier between the Army of Northern Virginia and ruin," but at immense cost.[102] Several hundred Mississippians and South Carolinians had etched their performance on the tablet of great Civil War deeds. Their styluses were bayoneted muskets; the reagent, their own blood.

NOTES

1. William W. Old, "Trees Whittled Down at Horseshoe," in *Southern Historical Society Papers*, ed. J. William Jones and others, 52 vols. (Richmond, Va.: Southern Historical Society, 1876–1959), 33:20–21 (cited hereafter as *SHSP*).

2. In ibid., 21, Old mentioned Smith's visit and approval, albeit somewhat tentatively. The quote about Stevens, framed in the context of the North Anna campaign, is from Jedediah Hotchkiss in the Hotchkiss Papers, roll 49, frames 455–67, Library of Congress, Washington, D.C. (repository cited hereafter as LC). The possibility that Hotchkiss mistook one engineer for the other is suggested by the fact that Stevens nonetheless won promotion to brigadier three months later, whereas Smith soon transferred to the Army of Tennessee in Georgia, where he served as its chief engineer with the special mission of completing and strengthening the fortifications of Atlanta (a mission he carried out successfully). The artillerist quoted was Thomas H. Carter in *SHSP* 21:239. Another officer who blamed the

engineers was Lt. Col. Isaac Hardeman of Rodes's division, who was captured on May 10 within sight of what became the Bloody Angle. The works, he said, "were imperfect owing to the lack of an engineer competent to make a correct alignment." Hardeman reminiscence, drawer 283, box 27, Georgia Department of Archives and History, Atlanta (repository cited hereafter as GDAH).

3. Cadwallader Jones, "Tree Cut Down by Bullets," *Confederate Veteran* 34 (January 1926):8; James A. Walker, "The Bloody Angle," *SHSP* 21:233; W. B. Howell, "Didn't Know They Had Surrendered," *Confederate Veteran* 28 (October 1920):384.

4. John H. Worsham, *One of Jackson's Foot Cavalry* (New York: Neale Publishing Company, 1912), 209; Rufus R. Dawes, *Service with the Sixth Wisconsin Volunteers* (Marietta, Ohio: E. R. Alderman & Sons, 1890), 268; W. P. Snakenberg (14th Louisiana) memoir, 34, in possession of John N. R. Bass of Spring Hope, N.C.; Walker, "Bloody Angle," *SHSP* 21:233.

5. Snakenberg memoir, 34; Worsham, *Jackson's Foot Cavalry*, 209; Randolph Barton, *Recollections* (Baltimore: Press of Thomas & Evans Printing Company, 1913), 55; Howell, "Didn't Know," 384; B. F. Brown (1st South Carolina), in Varina Davis Brown, *A Colonel at Gettysburg and Spotsylvania* (Columbia, S.C.: The State Company, 1931), 135; Mamie Yeary, *Reminiscences of the Boys in Gray* (Dallas: Smith & Lamar, 1912), 149; Dawes, *Sixth Wisconsin*, 268. The Brown book is one of the four best sources on the Bloody Angle fighting. Varina Brown put together a strong selection of the writings of her father (Col. Joseph Newton Brown, who commanded the South Carolina Brigade) and his comrades and added some careful, intelligent commentary of her own based on early visits to the field. The inconclusive evidence about traverse construction supplied by modern remains is very much complicated by alterations to the works made by Federals, who reoriented them through 180 degrees to face southward.

6. The 4th Virginia affair is recounted in an anonymous (apparently by an officer of Garber's battalion), scribbled two-page manuscript, folder "1904–1907 Spotsylvania," box 23, John Warwick Daniel Papers, Alderman Library, University of Virginia, Charlottesville (repository cited hereafter as UVA), and confirmed in Barton, *Recollections*, 54. The first source is cited once below as "Anonymous Garber bn. ms."

7. B. L. Wynn diary, Mississippi Department of Archives and History, Jackson (repository cited hereafter as MDAH); May 11 letter from "P. W. A" [Peter Wellington Alexander], *Daily South Carolinian* (Columbia), May 28, 1864; Robert W. Hunter, "Maj.-Gen. Johnson at Spotsylvania," Richmond *Times-Dispatch*, November 26, 1905; G. Campbell Brown memoir, Brown-Ewell Papers, Tennessee State Library and Archives, Nashville (repository cited hereafter as TSLA). Campbell Brown claimed that the initial intention was to withdraw Ewell's infantry at once that evening, but Ewell interceded in the interest of his men's comfort under shelters from the rain that they already had erected. This seems utterly fantastic, since no new line yet existed.

8. *SHSP* 21:252; McHenry Howard, "Notes and Recollections of the Opening of the Campaign of 1864," in *Papers of the Military Historical Society of Massachusetts*, 14 vols. (Boston: The Military Historical Society of Massachusetts, 1895–1918), 4:112 (cited hereafter as *PMHSM*); Robert A. Hardaway to N. B. Johnston, June 25, 1894, copy in the historical files of Richmond National Battlefield Park, Richmond, Va.

9. Anonymous Garber bn. ms., UVA; Hunter, "Johnson at Spotsylvania"; *SHSP* 21:253. The first source describes how some of Garber's pieces avoided the withdrawal.

10. Anonymous 139th Pennsylvania memoir, Harold C. George Papers, LC; Francis C. Barlow, "The Capture of the Salient, May 12, 1864," *PMHSM* 4:256, 246–48.

11. *SHSP* 14:232. A graphic depiction of the Confederate infantry positions is in McHenry Howard, *Recollections of a Maryland Confederate Soldier and Staff Officer* (Baltimore: Williams & Wilkins Company, 1914), 299. An important manuscript sketch of artillery locations in the salient is at frame 477, roll 39, Jedediah Hotchkiss Papers, LC. For a good description of the plight of the Virginians from Jones's brigade cut off while on picket duty in front of the main line, see Worsham, *Jackson's Foot Cavalry*, 211–13.

12. Benjamin Anderson Jones, "A Brief Sketch of My Relation to the War between the States," typescript in the author's possession; Edward D. Camden diary, typescript in possession of Richard L. Armstrong, Millboro, Va.; B. L. Wynn diary, May 12, 1864, MDAH; C. W. McCrary, "Letter from Virginia," Selma *Morning Reporter*, May 30, 1864.

13. S. H. Hawes to W. E. Cutshaw, October 7, 1905, folder dated 1904–1907 under Spotsylvania heading, box 23, John Warwick Daniel Papers, UVA.

14. Richard C. M. Page, *Sketch of Page's Battery, or Morris Artillery* (New York: Thomas Smeltzer, Printer, 1885), 10, 74 (casualty figures compiled from annotated roster on pp. 12–82); David W. Anderson, "The Bloody Angle," *SHSP* 21:253; Old, "Trees Whittled Down," *SHSP* 33:24; R. H. Fife, "An Incident in Lee's Life," Richmond *Dispatch*, February 8, 1903; *PMHSM* 4:252–53. The accounts of Lee's accepting blame for the artillery mistake are Old (to Ewell) and Fife (to Long). Seven of the eighteen prisoners from Page's battery died in Yankee prisons.

15. Walker, "Bloody Angle," *SHSP* 21:235–36.

16. Howard, "Notes and Recollections," *PMHSM* 4:113; T. J. Watkins memoir, owned by Robert E. Little III of Wadesboro, N.C. (cited hereafter as "Watkins memoir"); Barton, *Recollections*, 54; Thomas S. Doyle memoir, LC; James A. Walker to William P. Hopkins, June 30, 1886, original owned by August Payne, Chicago, Ill. For an obscure but good account of the Stonewall Brigade's experience, see "War Reminiscence," Winchester *Times*, June 6, 1888. A lively account of hand-to-hand fighting by the 23rd Virginia of Steuart's brigade, which degenerated from firing to bayonets to musket butts to fists, is "An Incident of the 'Bloody Angle,' " Fredericksburg *Free Lance*, April 29, 1887.

17. Basil H. Liddell Hart, *A Greater Than Napoleon: Scipio Africanus* (London: W. Blackwood & Sons, Ltd., 1926), 36; C. F. Atkinson, *Grant's Campaigns of 1864 and 1865* (London: Hugh Rees, Ltd., 1908), 303; *PMHSM* 4:253.

18. Alfred Lewis Scott memoir, Virginia Historical Society, Richmond (repository cited hereafter as VHS); Charles S. Venable, "The Campaign from the Wilderness to Petersburg," *SHSP* 14:530. J. S. McNeily, "The Big Fight at Spotsylvania C. H.," Richmond *Times-Dispatch*, March 19, 1905, asks, not unreasonably, "Was there ever another army that would not have been demoralized and forced to retire from such a situation?"

19. Campbell Brown memoir, Brown-Ewell Papers, TSLA; R. D. Johnston, "Fighting under the Eye of the General," *The Wake Forest Student*, January 1907, 308. The much more southerly site for the Lee-Gordon rally is espoused in the careful study by William D. Matter, *If It Takes All Summer: The Battle of Spotsylvania* (Chapel Hill: University of North Carolina Press, 1988), 200–202. In a letter to the author dated July 24, 1986, Matter touted in support *SHSP* 21:247 and 32:201, and especially Gordon's official report in U.S. War Department, *The War of the Rebellion: A Compilation of the Official Records of the Union and Confederate Armies*, 127 vols., index, and atlas (Washington: GPO, 1880–1901), ser. 1, 36(1):1079, which

strews units all across the interior of the Mule Shoe (cited hereafter as *OR*; all references are to ser. 1). A contemporary letter by James Kincheloe of the 49th Virginia (typescript in the author's possession) estimated the Federal penetration as "a quarter of a mile," which would be precisely to McCoull.

20. Willis J. Dance, *Elbert Madison Williamson* (Danville, Va.: Privately printed, 1969), 21; C. B. Christian, "Lee to the Rear," Richmond *Times-Dispatch*, December 25, 1904; W. A. Compton, " 'Lee to the Rear' at Spotsylvania," Richmond *Times-Dispatch*, April 23, 1905; "Gen. Lee and Gordon's Charge," Richmond *Dispatch*, June 2, 1864; Alexander S. Coffman diary, *Augusta Historical Bulletin* 28 (Fall 1992):19; account of John F. Methvin in undated newspaper clipping, drawer 283, box 34, GDAH; David B. Fitzgerald, "Incident in Life of a Stewart County Confederate Veteran," Sara Dixon Genealogical File, Stewart County, Georgia, Miscellany, GDAH. Another eyewitness account, although not quoted or cited in the text, is by Col. J. Catlett Gibson, ". . . The Contest of May 12th at Spotsylvania Courthouse Given in Detail," Richmond *Times-Dispatch*, December 11, 1904. For a detailed summary of the first, most famous Lee-to-the-Rear episode, see Robert K. Krick, " 'Lee to the Rear,' the Texans Cried," in *The Wilderness Campaign*, ed. Gary W. Gallagher (Chapel Hill: University of North Carolina Press, 1997).

21. Johnston, "Fighting under the Eye," 308; ms. note by R. D. Johnston on the verso of letterhead of L. C. Leadbetter, undated file, box 1905–1910, John Warwick Daniel Papers, William R. Perkins Library, Duke University, Durham, N.C. (cited hereafter as DU); Columbus (Ga.) *Daily Sun*, December 22, 1865; Walter A. Montgomery, *The Days of Old and the Years That Are Past* (n.p., n.d.), 28; William Allan memoir, folder 11, William Allan Papers, Southern Historical Collection, Wilson Library, University of North Carolina, Chapel Hill (repository cited hereafter as SHC). Johnston's obscure account also is important for details of the attack made by his brigade back to the works, which is not discussed in this essay.

22. Worsham, *Jackson's Foot Cavalry*, 215; George Clark, *A Glance Backward* (Houston: Press of Rein & Sons, 1914[?]), 51–53. Gordon Rhea, whose *The Battles for Spotsylvania Court House and the Road to Yellow Tavern: May 7–12, 1864* (Baton Rouge: Louisiana State University Press, 1997) and a projected companion volume surely will become the standard authority, believes that part of Perrin's command may have wound up intermingled with Ramseur's brigade, *west* of the Bloody Angle. That is entirely possible, given the confusion endemic on May 12, but an eventual easterly position seems more likely. The fine account by Thomas T. Roche ("The Bloody Angle," Philadelphia *Weekly Times*, September 3, 1881) places part of one of Perrin's regiments in the Bloody Angle itself, east of Harris's brigade and among the South Carolinians.

23. Julius L. Schaub, "Services of Julius L. Schaub in CW"; letter of Schaub to O. C. Whitaker, June 5, 1909; and "History of 14th N.C. Vols." by Julius L. Schaub; all in the Troup County (Ga.) Archives (repository cited hereafter as TCA). Schaub served in Company B, 14th North Carolina, Ramseur's brigade. His three descriptions are cited hereafter as "Schaub accounts."

24. The heretofore unknown role (a frequent late-war phenomenon because surviving Confederate official reports are uncommon) played by Wofford's brigade can be reconstructed from three sources uncovered by nonpareil Georgia historian Keith S. Bohannon: "Wofford's Georgia Brigade," (Atlanta) *Southern Confederacy*, June 15, 1864; letter of Lt. R. J. Wilson, Cobb's Legion, to John White, in Athens (Ga.) *Southern Watchman*, July 13, 1864; and William S. Shockley (18th Georgia) to "Dear Eliza," May 16, 1864, Shockley Papers, DU.

25. Watkins memoir, 35–36; J. A. Stikeleather reminiscence, 64–66, North Carolina Department of Archives and History, Raleigh (repository cited hereafter as NCDAH).

26. W. E. Ardrey diary (30th North Carolina), printed in 23 parts in the Matthews (N.C.) *News*, September 1991–January 1992; Bryan Grimes to wife, May 14, 1864, Bryan Grimes Papers, SHC; Watkins memoir; Schaub accounts, TCA.

27. John Berryman Crawford to "Dear Wife," March 18, 1864, MDAH.

28. Joseph C. Robert, "A Ring Tournament in 1864," *Journal of Mississippi History* 3 (October 1941):289–96.

29. The Alexander A. Lomax diary, MDAH, contains the records of baptism on May 1 and 5. The four 16th Mississippi men were Benjamin F. Brown (arm amputated); Andrew J. Lee (killed); Harrison R. Gibson (absent "with leave"—the 16th's clerk's euphemism for absent wounded); and F. M. Grubbs (wounded). Lomax also baptized two black men associated with the regiment on May 5, a free man named W. Morris and a slave named William. The four 19th Mississippi men were Joseph Lawhorne; James M. Lawrence (wounded by late June, perhaps on May 12); John H. Welch; and Rufus N. Hunt (died, apparently of disease, on August 1). The eight men's records are from "Compiled Service Records of . . . Organizations from the State of Mississippi" (M269), rolls 202, 204, 206, 243–44, and 249, National Archives (repository hereafter cited as NA).

30. John J. Hood, "Reference to the Featherstone-Posey-Harris Brigade," New Orleans *Picayune*, June 8, 1902; C. W. Reynolds, "Comrade's Tribute to Gen. G. M. Sorrell," Atlanta *Journal*, August 17, 1901. Harris's record in M331, NA, shows that he only accepted his commission on March 4, despite a "rank from" date six weeks earlier.

31. General N. H. Harris to Thomas T. Roche, January 31, 1881, in Roche, "Bloody Angle," declared that he began the day with 1,600 men, but that estimate clearly is far too high (Venable, in *SHSP* 14:531, says 800). Roche's invaluable narrative is one of the four essential sources on the Bloody Angle (with Holt, Brown, and Caldwell, cited elsewhere). Other sources for this narrative paragraph are F. H. Foote, "Three Heroes of the Civil War," unidentified (ca. 1900) newspaper clipping in a scrapbook, J. J. Hood Papers, MDAH; *OR* 36(1):1091; Yeary, *Boys in Gray*, 147; David Holt, *A Mississippi Rebel in the Army of Northern Virginia: The Civil War Memoirs of Private David Holt*, ed. Thomas D. Cockrell and Michael B. Ballard (Baton Rouge: Louisiana State University Press, 1995), 252; Nathaniel H. Harris, *The Battle of the Salient, Spottsylvania C. H., Virginia, May 12th, 1864* (n.p., n.d.), 4. The last source cited exists, so far as I know, only in one copy that is headed "Proof Sheet," but nonetheless is paginated. Roche and other accounts make it clear that Harris had been pulled out of line into his muddy bivouac on the night of the 11th, but apparently remained well beyond the Po because his official report mentions crossing that stream on the 12th, and his *Battle of the Salient* describes the march beginning from "the extreme left."

32. Holt, *Mississippi Rebel*, 253; Roche, "Bloody Angle." The timing of the brigade's march varies as widely as usual for such things in Civil War accounts. Roche thought it came "shortly after daylight." Harris's own versions varied dramatically, from an obviously erroneous "near the hour of 8 A.M." in *Battle of the Salient*, to "At 5 o'clock A.M." in his *Movements of the Confederate Army in Virginia and the Part Taken Therein by the Nineteenth Mississippi Regiment* (Duncansby, Miss.: Privately printed, 1901), 27. The latter book is nearly as rare as *Battle of the Salient*, only two complete surviving copies being known. Eugene Matthew Ott Jr., ed., "The Civil War Diary of James J. Kirkpatrick, Sixteenth Mississippi Infantry, C.S.A." (M.A. thesis, Texas A&M University, 1984), 193–94, placed the march

at daybreak (entry for May 12, 1864; all citations hereafter are to this letter and these pages and will be given as Ott, "Diary of Kirkpatrick," without reference to page number).

33. Roche, "Bloody Angle"; Holt, *Mississippi Rebel*, 253; Robert Gambrell, "Fighting at Spottsylvania C. H.," *Confederate Veteran* 17 (May 1909): 225; Ott, "Diary of Kirkpatrick"; Harris, *Movements of the Confederate Army*, 27; *OR* 36(2):1091. In the last two sources cited, Harris estimated the halt at a half hour and "a few minutes."

34. Joseph N. Brown, *An Address Delivered by . . . on the Battle of the "Bloody Angle,"* *May 12th, 1864* (Anderson, S.C.: The Advocate Publishing Co., 1900), 3. The estimated strength of 1,200 is from the reliable James Fitz James Caldwell in his "Reminiscences of the War of Secession," in *History of South Carolina*, ed. Yates Snowden, 5 vols. (Chicago: The Lewis Publishing Company, 1920), 2:829. Charles Scott Venable of Lee's staff put the combined strength of the two brigades at 2,500 (*SHSP* 14:531). That seems accurate. As mentioned above, despite Harris's late estimate of 1,600 men for his brigade, 1,200 for the Mississippians seems more likely. The five-regiment South Carolina brigade certainly was not any smaller than the four-regiment Mississippi unit (especially since the 48th Mississippi was undersized). A convincing case for 1,300 men in the Carolina brigade is in V. D. Brown, *A Colonel*, 273n.

35. J. N. Brown, *An Address*, 3; Harry Hammond letter, May 15, 1864, Hammond-Bryan-Cumming Family Papers, South Caroliniana Library, University of South Carolina (item cited hereafter as Hammond letter; repository cited as USC); Col. Isaac F. Hunt in V. D. Brown, *A Colonel*, 126; James Fitz James Caldwell, *The History of a Brigade of South Carolinians Known First as "Gregg's," and Subsequently as "McGowan's Brigade"* (Philadelphia: King & Baird, Printers, 1866), 140; Charleston *Daily Courier*, May 28, 1864; Robert R. Hemphill, "Gallant Enemies Become Friends in After Years," Spartanburg (S.C.) *Herald*, August 17, 1910; *OR* 36(1):1093. McGowan's march probably started about 9:00 A.M., although the sources offer the usual wide spectrum of options. He marched about half as far as Harris, evidently less rapidly, and arrived later.

36. Clark, *Glance Backward*, 54; Henry R. Berkeley, *Four Years in the Confederate Artillery* (Chapel Hill: University of North Carolina Press, 1961), 75–76; John Ritchey, "General Lee's Readiness to Lead His Men," *Confederate Veteran* 15 (December 1907):546; E. Howard McCaleb, "Featherstone-Posey-Harris Mississippi Brigade," New Orleans *Daily Picayune*, June 1, 1902.

37. *SHSP* 14:531; Yeary, *Boys in Gray*, 147–48; letters written in 1871 by both Harris and Venable in Charles S. Venable, " 'General Lee to the Rear' — The Incident with Harris' Mississippi Brigade," *SHSP* 8:105–7. Both letters are also in "Gen. Lee to the Rear," Richmond *Times-Dispatch*, May 22, 1904.

38. Holt, *Mississippi Rebel*, 255; Nathaniel H. Harris to William Mahone, August 2, 1866, Virginia State Library (item cited hereafter as Harris letter to Mahone; repository cited hereafter as VSL); Harris, *Movements of the Confederate Army*, 27; *SHSP* 14:531. Roche, "Bloody Angle," who is generally highly reliable, came away with the "impression that he did not intend to lead" the infantry in person. It is possible that the reaction to Lee's close call from the shelling triggered the episode, but he clearly used the occasion to encourage the men to go forward in his stead, as in the earlier incidents.

39. McCaleb, "Featherstone . . . Mississippi Brigade"; E. Howard McCaleb, *Address Delivered . . . at the Reunion of the Surviving Veterans, Harris' Mississippi Brigade, Army of Northern Virginia held at Port Gibson . . . November 13th, 1879* (New Orleans: A. W. Hyatt

Printer, [1879]), 10–11; Holt, *Mississippi Rebel*, 255; Harris, *Movements of the Confederate Army*, 27; *SHSP* 8:107, 14:534; Yeary, *Boys in Gray*, 148.

40. Each source cited in the preceding note pertains to this paragraph as well. In addition, Roche, "Bloody Angle," is the second witness for the 12th's soldiers. The source in which Harris cites that regiment is his letter to Charles J. Lewis, March 22, 1899, typescript in the author's possession (cited hereafter as Harris letter to Lewis).

41. Roche, "Bloody Angle"; *OR* 36(1):1091; Harris, *Movements of the Confederate Army*, 27; Harris, *Battle of the Salient*, 5. The last of these four sources is the only one that mentions the McCoull house by name, but each of them unmistakably describes its location or the distances to the main works (Roche: "about four hundred yards"; Harris's *Movements*: "a quarter of a mile").

42. Yeary, *Boys in Gray*, 148; Roche, "Bloody Angle"; *OR* 36(1):1091–92; Harris, *Movements of the Confederate Army*, 27–28; Harris letter to Lewis; Harris letter to Mahone. Harris's own accounts of Rodes's demoralized staffer (others mentioned him too) varied in rancor. His official report, written in December 1864 (*OR* 36[1]:1092), was very harsh and specific; his 1866 letter to Mahone was vague; *Movements* blamed the aide for poor directions but did not mention cowardice; and the undated (but late postwar) *Battle of the Salient* mentioned him not at all.

43. *A Historical Sketch of the Quitman Guards, Company E, Sixteenth Mississippi Regiment* (New Orleans: Isaac T. Hinton, Printer, 1866), 65 (authorship of this item is attributed to "one of the Quitman guards"); Ritchey, "General Lee's Readiness," 546; Harris, *Movements of the Confederate Army*, 28; *OR* 36(1):1092; Holt, *Mississippi Rebel*, 255; Roche, "Bloody Angle." The Harris letter to Mahone (VSL) contains a more lucid explanation of what he should have done, had information been available, than does the later *Movements*.

44. Ott, "Diary of Kirkpatrick"; Holt, *Mississippi Rebel*, 256; Virginia W. Durrett, *From Generation to Generation, the Confederate Cemetery at Spotsylvania Court House* (Spotsylvania, Va.: Privately printed, 1992), 57; Gambrell, "Fighting at Spottsylvania," 225.

45. *Quitman Guards*, 65–66; Yeary, *Boys in Gray*, 148; Durrett, *From Generation to Generation*, 65.

46. Schaub accounts, TCA; undated newspaper clipping in the John J. Hood scrapbook, MDAH; *Quitman Guards*, 67.

47. Harris, *Movements of the Confederate Army*, 28; *OR* 36(1):1092; Roche, "Bloody Angle"; Harris, *Battle of the Salient*, 5; Yeary, *Boys in Gray*, 148–49.

48. Harris, *Movements of the Confederate Army*, 28; Holt, *Mississippi Rebel*, 256; Harris, *Battle of the Salient*, 5; *OR* 36(1):1092.

49. Joseph N. Brown, *The Battle of the Bloody Angle* (Anderson, S.C.: Presses of Oulla Printing & Binding Co., 1910), 4; Hammond letter, USC; Caldwell, "Reminiscences," 829; Caldwell, *McGowan's Brigade*, 141; J. N. Brown, *An Address*, 4. South Carolina sources, including several cited here, use 10:00 A.M. for arrival; most Mississippi accounts say 11:00 A.M.

50. Hemphill, "Gallant Enemies"; V. D. Brown, *A Colonel*, 121; Caldwell, *McGowan's Brigade*, 141–43; James Armstrong, "McGowan's Brigade at Spotsylvania," *Confederate Veteran* 33 (October 1925):376; South Carolina Division, United Daughters of the Confederacy, *Recollections and Reminiscences*, 6 vols. to date (n.p.: South Carolina Division, UDC, 1990–95), 5:478–79, 553. McGowan survived his wound, which was in the right arm. An affecting

last letter written by the mortally wounded Brockman (whose brother also was killed on May 12) is on page 478 of the last source cited.

51. Lancaster (S.C.) *Ledger*, June 7, 1864; "How Calvin Galloway Died," Abbeville (S.C.) *Medium*, March 23, 1905. The story of the 1st's flag is in the Charles E. Whilden Collection, South Carolina Historical Society, Charleston (repository cited hereafter as SCHS). The collection includes war-date letters and clippings and postwar correspondence about the flag dating from 1880 to 1920.

52. Caldwell, *McGowan's Brigade*, 142–43, 146, 149; J. N. Brown, *An Address*, 4–5; V. D. Brown, *A Colonel*, 121–22, 137; Armstrong, "McGowan's Brigade," 377; South Carolina UDC, *Recollections*, 5:177. Two soldiers of the 1st gathered Shooter's "watch, pocket book and other personal effects," but there is no evidence of their survival on record today (Charleston *Courier*, May 28, 1864).

53. *OR* 36(1):1092; Harris letter to Mahone; Harris, *Movements of the Confederate Army*, 28; Harris letter to Lewis; Harris, *Battle of the Salient*, 5; V. D. Brown, *A Colonel*, 276; *Quitman Guards*, 66; Dunbar Rowland, *The Official and Statistical Register of the State of Mississippi* (Nashville, Tenn.: Press of the Brandon Printing Company, 1908), 491–92. The Schaub accounts, TCA, which are the most detailed sources for Ramseur's brigade, claim—with entirely typical battlefield egocentrism—that *neither* Harris nor McGowan accomplished anything to Ramseur's right!

54. Roche, "Bloody Angle"; Yeary, *Boys in Gray*, 149; V. D. Brown, *A Colonel*, 273–75; J. N. Brown, *The Battle*, 4–5; *OR* 36(1):1094.

55. Roche, "Bloody Angle"; Yeary, *Boys in Gray*, 149; Henry Cohen, *A Modern Maccabean* (Baltimore: Press of the Friedenwald Co., 1897), 36.

56. Ott, "Diary of Kirkpatrick"; Yeary, *Boys in Gray*, 149; Harris, *Movements of the Confederate Army*, 28; Holt, *Mississippi Rebel*, 256–57; Roche, "Bloody Angle." The vivid account of hand-to-hand fighting in J. A. Craddock, "Fight at Spotsylvania Drama in Three Acts," Richmond *Times-Dispatch*, October 8, 1916, has little value because its author belonged to the 22nd Virginia Battalion, which was not nearby.

57. The tree cut down by bullets became the much-mooted benchmark for everything that happened on May 12 (and for many Federals as well). Many trees were knocked down by the day's violent metal storm (most of them by artillery rather than musketry), however, and confusion inevitably resulted. The eminently reliable Mississippi accounts by Roche and Holt make clear their presence well toward the right of the Bloody Angle front. Many South Carolina accounts show the center of strength of that brigade around and east of the tree. Tactical identity—and control—was virtually extinct early in the day, to say nothing of the chaos that reigned by dark and through the night.

58. J. N. Brown, *An Address*, 4–5; "Death of Col. Isaac F. Hunt," Abbeville (S.C.) *Medium*, April 17, 1900; V. D. Brown, *A Colonel*, 97, 127, 276; Harris, *Movements of the Confederate Army*, 28. Hunt's obvious and well-founded pride in his performance is apparent in several of the sources cited. Hunt later told Brown emphatically, "I did not see a General or Staff Officer after we re-captured the salient" (V. D. Brown, *A Colonel*, 28).

59. Caldwell, *McGowan's Brigade*, 143; William S. Dunlop, *Lee's Sharpshooters; or, the Forefront of Battle* (Little Rock, Ark.: Tunnah & Pittard, Printers, 1899), 67; Armstrong, "McGowan's Brigade," 377; Jones, "Tree Cut Down," 8.

60. Armstrong, "McGowan's Brigade," 377; Caldwell, *McGowan's Brigade*, 142; Berry

Benson, *Berry Benson's Civil War Book: Memoirs of a Confederate Scout and Sharpshooter* (Athens: University of Georgia Press, 1962), 75; V. D. Brown, *A Colonel*, 136, 253, 258. South Carolinians' estimates of the distance from the works to the east-west ravine range from 20 yards to 70 yards, but it can be easily measured on the ground at exactly 40 yards. The "decline of the hill" quote is from an article by David Holt in the New Orleans *Times-Democrat* in 1900, copy in RG 9, Confederate Records, 16th Mississippi, folder P, vol. 132, MDAH. The clipping has no precise date, and the Holt attribution (which is obvious in any case) is supplied by a handwritten note. This valuable variant on the version in Holt's extremely important book is cited hereafter as "1900 Holt article."

61. The Barlow-Grant dispute is in *PMHSM* 4. The best elucidation of the extent of the Bloody Angle is in V. D. Brown, *A Colonel*, 109, 118–19, 249–51, 256–58. See also J. N. Brown, *The Battle*, 5.

62. *Quitman Guards*, 66; Walter R. Battle to parents, May 14, 1864, "The Civil War Letters of George Boardman Battle and of Walter Raleigh Battle," Wilson County Public Library, Wilson, N.C. (repository cited hereafter as WCPL); Schaub accounts, TCA; G. N. Galloway, "Through the Wilderness," Philadelphia *Weekly Times*, January 8, 1881; Ott, "Diary of Kirkpatrick"; Harris, *Battle of the Salient*, 7; Holt, *Mississippi Rebel*, 256–57. For a South Carolinian's account reminiscent of Holt's, of "mud, blood and brains mingled . . . my head and face were covered or spotted with the horrid paint," see Charleston *Daily Courier*, May 28, 1864. A weather station at Georgetown reported heavy showers during the afternoon "with considerable hail," though no one at Spotsylvania reported any hail but the leaden sort. The temperature at Georgetown at 2:00 P.M. was 75 degrees and at 9:00 P.M. it was 62 ("Weather Journal Recording Observations at . . . Georgetown, D.C., June 1858–May 1866," National Weather Records Center, Asheville, N.C.)

63. Roche, "Bloody Angle."

64. Harris, *Battle of the Salient*, 7; Roche, "Bloody Angle."

65. Yeary, *Boys in Gray*, 149; G. N. Galloway, "Capture of the Salient," Philadelphia *Weekly Times*, November 18, 1882; Holt, *Mississippi Rebel*, 258; *The Medical and Surgical History of the War of the Rebellion*, 6 vols. (Washington: GPO, 1875–1883), 3(2):868; Walter R. Battle, May 14, 1864, WCPL. Private Metzel belonged to Company A, 11th Massachusetts.

66. OR 36(1):1092; Galloway, "Capture of the Salient"; Rowland, *Register of Mississippi*, 492; South Carolina UDC, *Recollections*, 1:211; W. E. Ardrey diary; Owen Edwards to G. N. Galloway, July 15, 1887, George Hay Stuart Collection, LC. An exception to the ineffectiveness of the mortars is described in gory detail by Holt, *Mississippi Rebel*, 260.

67. A. T. Watts, "The Bloody Acute Angle," Galveston *Daily News*, July 15, 1893; *Confederate States Medical and Surgical Journal*, July 1864, 102; *Medical and Surgical History*, 2(1):469, 3(2):6, 360.

68. Benson, *Benson's Book*, 74; Caldwell, *McGowan's Brigade*, 146. J. N. Brown, who was a good bit more gallant about sharing credit than was Harris, in *An Address*, 5, acknowledged that "by night every part of our brigade . . . was intermingled with the brave Mississippians." J. N. Brown, *The Battle*, 12, says: "When our lines . . . became so thinned out by casualties, the right of . . . Harris's closed up with us and assisted us later in the day. They were as brave soldiers as ever went on the field of battle. . . ."

69. Roche, "Bloody Angle"; J. S. McMahon, "From the Army of Northern Virginia," *Daily Southern Guardian* (Columbia, S.C.), May 26, 1864. Examples of Federal accounts of the hand-to-hand fighting are Alfred S. Roe, *The Tenth Regiment Massachusetts Volunteer*

Infantry (Springfield, Mass.: Tenth Regiment Veteran Association, 1909), 266; Mason W. Tyler, *Recollections of the Civil War* (New York: G. P. Putnam's Sons, 1912), 184, 191; Horace Porter, *Campaigning with Grant* (New York: Century, 1897), 110–11; and *Red: White: and Blue Badge Pennsylvania Veteran Volunteers . . . 93rd Regiment* [Harrisburg: Aughinbaugh Press, 1911], 267. In *The Battle*, 10, Col. J. N. Brown acknowledged that his own brigade's line was "so compact, and the line so short that they lost all distinct organization and fought as a unit." That homogeneous unit actually included many Mississippians as well.

70. Holt, *Mississippi Rebel*, 256–59; Gambrell, "Fighting at Spottsylvania."

71. Caldwell, *McGowan's Brigade*, 144–45; Daniel A. Tompkins, *Company K, Fourteenth South Carolina Volunteers* (Charlotte, N.C.: Observer Printing and Publishing House, 1897), 21–22; South Carolina UDC, *Recollections*, 6:425.

72. A thoughtful, if perhaps over-drawn, analysis of these factors by a British analyst is in Atkinson, *Grant's Campaigns*, 302–4.

73. Roche, "Bloody Angle"; Jones, "Tree Cut Down." Caldwell, *McGowan's Brigade*, 143, timed the chaos about "surrender" at "perhaps two hours" after the brigade arrived and Colonel Brown said 2:00 P.M. Other Confederate accounts that use "evening" as a time evidently are employing the southern locution that denominates anything after noon as "evening."

74. Armstrong, "McGowan's Brigade"; V. D. Brown, *A Colonel*, 123; Hemphill, "Gallant Enemies"; Caldwell, *McGowan's Brigade*, 144.

75. South Carolina UDC, *Recollections*, 1:33; Caldwell, *McGowan's Brigade*, 144; Holt, *Mississippi Rebel*, 258; Nathan Church (26th Michigan) letter in Anderson (S.C.) *Daily Mail*, March 10, 1901, printed in V. D. Brown, *A Colonel*, 105n.

76. Benson, *Benson's Book*, 75; Roche, "Bloody Angle"; South Carolina UDC, *Recollections*, 1:33.

77. Roche, "Bloody Angle." A South Carolina account similar to Roche's is McMahon, "From the Army," which speaks of the field "blue with the Yankee dead" and concludes that "Grant does not seem to care what amount of human life he sacrifices."

78. B. F. Brown (1st South Carolina), "The Bloody Angle," unidentified 1895 newspaper clipping, "Clippings" folder, Charles Edgeworth Jones Papers, DU; "Letters from a Private's Portfolio," Abbeville (S.C.) *Medium*, July 19, 1876; Howell, "Didn't Know"; Roche, "Bloody Angle"; Armstrong, "McGowan's Brigade"; V. D. Brown, *A Colonel*, 123; Hemphill, "Gallant Enemies"; Holt, *Mississippi Rebel*, 258; South Carolina UDC, *Recollections*, 1:33; Caldwell, *McGowan's Brigade*, 144–45. Several accounts of Federals shot while returning (some of whom recovered for the customary postwar encounter with a benefactor) can be found in the sources above. The quote in the narrative is from Holt. An episode of Confederate kindness to a wounded Yankee in front of the lines that is confused with the Bloody Angle fighting involved John Moore Nicholls of the 1st South Carolina. Nicholls's regiment, however, was a different 1st, that belonging to Micah Jenkins's brigade, and his deed took place on the Spindle farm west of Brock Road. For that incident, and a poetic tribute to Nicholls by a Federal veteran, see Clement A. Evans, ed., *Confederate Military History*, 12 vols. (Atlanta: Confederate Publishing Company, 1899), 5:776–77; Vivian Minor Fleming, *The Wilderness Campaign* (Richmond: W. C. Hill Printing Company, 1922), 29–31; and V. D. Brown, *A Colonel*, 278n. The 1900 Holt article, MDAH, reports that the man who shot the Federal near him said that "the officer would surely have reported how weak our force was."

79. Roche, "Bloody Angle"; Holt, *Mississippi Rebel*, 260.

80. Caldwell, "Reminiscences," 829.

81. Harris, *Battle of the Salient*, 7; Snakenberg Memoir, 34; Caldwell, *McGowan's Brigade*, 147; *OR* 36(1):1092; *SHSP* 8:107.

82. *The Confederate States Almanac and Depository of Useful Knowledge* (Mobile, Ala.: H. C. Clarke, Publisher, [1863]), sixth unnumbered leaf (6:59 sunset at Richmond); Harris, *Battle of the Salient*, 7; Holt, *Mississippi Rebel*, 259, 261; Benson, *Benson's Book*, 76; Howell, "Didn't Know"; *OR* 36(1):1092; Yeary, *Boys in Gray*, 149–50. Another account of daring ammunition resupply, not used in the narrative, is in Roche, "Bloody Angle." Both Holt and Benson admitted falling asleep.

83. Caldwell, *McGowan's Brigade*, 145–46.

84. Dozens of accounts survive about the memorable tree. The most important follow. Times range from "early in the night" (J. N. Brown, *An Address*, 5) to 10:00 P.M. (Caldwell, *McGowan's Brigade*, 147) to 2:00 A.M. (V. D. Brown, *A Colonel*, 136). Many accounts use the conveniently round witching hour of midnight. For multiple trees, their sizes, and location of the large, famous one, see Allan memoir, SHC; Jones, "Tree Cut Down"; *SHSP* 6:74–75, 33:19; J. N. Brown, *An Address*, 5; Roche, "Bloody Angle" (which is especially good); V. D. Brown, *A Colonel*, 134, 252, 258, 260n.; Dunlop, *Lee's Sharpshooters*, 73; Charleston *Daily Courier*, May 28, 1864; W. R. Tanner, *Reminiscences of the War between the States* (Cowpens, S.C.: Privately printed, 1931), 17th unnumbered leaf; John F. Sale diary, May 31, 1864, copy at Fredericksburg and Spotsylvania National Military Park Library, Fredericksburg, Va. (repository cited hereafter as FSNMP); South Carolina UDC, *Recollections*, 4:43; Cadwallader Jones, "Three [*sic*] Cut Down by Bullets," Columbia (S.C.) *State*, January 18, 1926; and Caldwell, *McGowan's Brigade*, 147. The Tanner work is cited from the true first edition, which has been overlooked or garbled in all bibliographies. One of many examples of the volume of fire that brought down the tree is the report by James L. Bowen of the 37th Massachusetts that that regiment fired more than 400 rounds per man ("General Edwards's Brigade at Spotsylvania," *Century Illustrated Monthly Magazine* 35 [January 1888]:478–79).

85. *SHSP* 33:19; Richmond *Examiner*, June 1, 1864; *The Countryman* (Turnwold, Ga.), August 16, 1864; letter of transfer from the Ordnance Museum to Smithsonian, February 16, 1888, and accession card, in Smithsonian files; unidentified (before 1870) newspaper clipping in the Charles E. Whilden Papers, SCHS; *Quitman Guards*, 68. William D. Matter has written two good summaries of the stump's travels: "The Oak Tree at Spotsylvania," *Blue & Gray Magazine* 1 (June–July 1984):47–48; and Appendix C in his standard campaign study, *If It Takes All Summer*.

86. V. D. Brown, *A Colonel*, 128, 136; Howell, "Didn't Know," 385. There is no evidence that any Confederate died from injuries caused by the tree. Accounts of men hurt, often citing individual names, are Benson, *Benson's Book*, 75; McMahon, "From the Army"; B. M. Powell to wife, November 21, 1907, copy at FSNMP; Hammond letter; V. D. Brown, *A Colonel*, 130, 134; Caldwell, *McGowan's Brigade*, 147; Holt, *Mississippi Rebel*, 257; South Carolina UDC, *Recollections*, 4:43; B. F. Brown to S. A. Cunningham, May 24, 1905, box "Letters 1861–1932 & n.d.," DU. The 1900 Holt article, MDAH, says that men who could see that the tree was doomed made all sorts of suggestions about steering its fall, but the intense fire militated against all of them.

87. South Carolina UDC, *Recollections*, 4:42–43; Hemphill, "Gallant Enemies"; J. N. Brown, *The Battle*, 11; Caldwell, *McGowan's Brigade*, 147; V. D. Brown, *A Colonel*, 128–29.

88. J. N. Brown, *The Battle*, 11; Roche, "Bloody Angle"; V. D. Brown, *A Colonel*, 130; William McWillie Notebooks, MDAH.

89. V. D. Brown, *A Colonel*, 129; Dunlop, *Lee's Sharpshooters*, 471; *OR* 36(1):1094; Caldwell, "Reminiscences"; Howell, "Didn't Know," 384–85; McMahon, "From the Army"; Caldwell, *McGowan's Brigade*, 147; Spencer G. Welch, *A Confederate Surgeon's Letters to His Wife* (New York: Neale Publishing Company, 1911), 96; Hammond letter, USC.

90. V. D. Brown, *A Colonel*, 130, 136; Howell, "Didn't Know", 385; Caldwell, *McGowan's Brigade*, 147; Tyler, *Recollections*, 195; Roe, *Tenth Regiment*, 267.

91. Harris, *Movements of the Confederate Army*, 29; *OR* 36(1):1092; Harris, *Battle of the Salient*, 7; LeGrand J. Wilson, *The Confederate Soldier* (Fayetteville, Ark.: M'Roy Printing Co., 1902), 158–59; Gambrell, "Fighting at Spottsylvania"; Ardrey diary; Schaub accounts, TCA; Watkins memoir; Stikeleather reminiscence, NCDAH; Bryan Grimes to wife, May 14, 1864, Bryan Grimes Papers, SHC; Harris letter to Lewis; Roche, "Bloody Angle"; Ott, "Diary of Kirkpatrick." In the first two accounts cited, Harris said that he *received* the withdrawal order from Rodes at 2:00 A.M., in the third account he said from Ewell at 3:00 A.M. The rest of the sources above report actual execution of the withdrawal by Ramseur's brigade as 2:00 (two sources), 3:00, 3:30, and 4:00 A.M., and that of Harris's as 3:00 (four), 3:30, and 4:00 A.M. (two). Ramseur must have preceded Harris out, but did Brown's end of the line wait until after Harris's left wing? The combination of South Carolinians' emphasis on daybreak rather than dark hours, and their tendency to deprecate Federal reaction, suggests that they went later. It seems likely that Brown's end of the line mostly headed south, rather than southwest down the shoulder of the salient; that probably had more impact on lack of Federal reaction than did the passage of more time. Harris claimed that he ordered both brigades out, but he had only tenuous control over part of his own men and virtually none over Brown's.

92. Holt, *Mississippi Rebel*, 261–62.

93. Yeary, *Boys in Gray*, 150. Regimental losses cumulatively for May 6–12 are reported in Rowland, *Register of Mississippi*, 449, 465, 492, 513. For examples of exorbitant losses within companies, see J. J. Wilson letter, June 12, 1864, MDAH (8 killed); Ott, "Diary of Kirkpatrick" (9 killed); Gambrell, "Fighting at Spottsylvania" (8 killed); *Quitman Guards*, 67 (12 killed); and Franklin L. Riley diary, copy at FSNMP (16 net). In 1881 (Roche, "Bloody Angle"), Harris accurately estimated that he lost one-fourth of his men, although he placed his strength too high. Losses throughout the brigade are reported in detail in the Richmond *Examiner*, May 31, 1864, and in an unidentified newspaper clipping in the J. L. Powers Scrapbook, MDAH—but in each case only for an undifferentiated week. Fortunately, the same scrapbook contains another unidentified but obviously contemporary clipping that supplies *nominal* lists (the only really reliable kind) of casualties for May 12 alone. Those total 73 killed, 162 wounded, and 109 missing for the whole brigade. The nominal list of killed by regiment (which, not surprisingly, totals 15 fewer than the tabular returns) includes 11 of the 12th; 22 of the 16th; 19 of the 19th; and 6 of the 48th Mississippi.

94. *OR* 36(1):1094; Caldwell, *McGowan's Brigade*, 148; *SHSP* 16:21; Belinda and Richard Gergel, *In Pursuit of the Tree of Life, A History of the Early Jews of Columbia*; *Register of Names of Men Buried in the Confederate Cemetery, Spottsylvania C. H., Va.* (n.p.: n.p., [ca. 1910]). For examples of steep company losses, see *Carolina Spartan* (Spartanburg, S.C.), June 9, 1864; South Carolina UDC, *Recollections*, 4:43, 6:457–62; and Lancaster (S.C.) *Ledger*, June 7, 1864.

95. Holt, *Mississippi Rebel*, 263–64; 1900 Holt article, MDAH.

96. Tyler, *Recollections*, 195; Porter, *Campaigning with Grant*, 110–11; *PMHSM* 4:270. For Federal surgeons' accounts of the volume of wounded who inundated the hospital system, see *Medical and Surgical History* 1(1):155, 3(2):867. One horrible effect of slowed treatment was an unprecedented incidence of maggots in wounds.

97. V. D. Brown, *A Colonel*, 135–37, 256–57; Dunlop, *Lee's Sharpshooters*, 73; Armstrong, "McGowan's Brigade," 378; Benson, *Benson's Book*, 77–78.

98. Benson, *Benson's Book*, 77; B. L. Wynn diary, MDAH; J. J. Wilson letter, June 12, 1864, MDAH; 10th Alabama letter in Talladega (Ala.) *Democratic Watchtower*, June 1, 1864; Louis Warlick to "dearest Corrie," May 19, 1864, McGimsey Papers, SHC. Warlick suggested that "Grant is twice as badly whiped now as was Burnside or Hooker but he is so determined he will not acknowledge it."

99. Roe, *Tenth Massachusetts*, 267; Benson, *Benson's Book*, 74; Berkeley, *Four Years*, 75; Hood, "Reference"; Campbell Brown memoir, TSLA; Welch, *Confederate Surgeon's Letters*, 96–97; Cohen, "Modern Maccabean"; Joseph N. Brown to "Order of Loyal Legion . . . Philadelphia," March 6, 1913, copy at FSNMP. Brown's letter expressed frustration because at that late date most people simply could not accept as fact what both Federals and Confederates had done at the Bloody Angle.

100. "Reminiscences of the Civil War between the States," Newberry (S.C.) *Herald and News*, May 3, 1901; Fredericksburg *Ledger*, June 26, 1866.

101. V. D. Brown, *A Colonel*, 252; anonymous 139th Pennsylvania memoir, Harold C. George Papers, LC. There is a detailed report of the earthworks restoration, nicely illustrated, in the files of FSNMP.

102. Holt, *Mississippi Rebel*, 263; McCaleb, *Address*, 11; undated contemporary clipping in the John J. Hood scrapbook, MDAH.

Stuart's Last Ride

A Confederate View of Sheridan's Raid

One way of tracking the waxing and waning fortunes of the Army of Northern Virginia is by studying the many independent operations of its cavalry chief, Maj. Gen. J. E. B. Stuart. His brightest moments often corresponded with those of Robert E. Lee's infantry. Stuart's one controversial expedition over almost three years' time was before Gettysburg, and coincided with his army's only significant defeat during that period. Any prognosticator relying on this theoretical gauge in 1864 must have viewed the advent of the spring campaign with special interest. Brandy Station, Gettysburg, the Buckland Races, and Parker's Store the previous year had showed that neither army's cavalry was dominant. What would the first direct collision of 1864 bring?

The nature of the ground along the Rapidan River kept the horsemen from contributing anything of high visibility during the first week in the Wilderness. Their subsequent actions on May 7–8 proved very significant indeed, yet not until May 9 did Stuart's men receive an opportunity to match strength with their northern foes in open countryside. The ensuing four days tried the Confederate cavalry as never before. The Army of Northern Virginia's horsemen emerged from the ordeal battered and leaderless but by no means broken.

A spat in the Federal high command provided the point of origin for the great cavalry battles of May 9–13. Crusty army commander George G. Meade and his routinely belligerent cavalry leader Philip H. Sheridan exchanged

Major General Philip H. Sheridan.
Robert Underwood Johnson and
Clarence Clough Buel, eds., *Battles
and Leaders of the Civil War*, 4 vols.
(New York: Century, 1887–88), 4:503

heated remarks on May 8 concerning the proper role for Sheridan's men in the campaign. In response, Ulysses S. Grant permitted Sheridan to maneuver with his cavalry unfettered, away from the main army. Dwindling supplies offered another reason for the expedition. With luck the raiders could live off the land for several days and relieve the burdened Union supply apparatus.[1]

Sheridan extracted his entire Cavalry Corps from the woods around Spotsylvania Court House and prepared it for a thrust southward toward Richmond. His three divisions, commanded by Wesley Merritt, David M. Gregg, and James H. Wilson, represented some 12,000 men at peak efficiency. They gathered at Alrich's farm on the Plank Road and struck south early on the 9th. Sheridan's plan, based on orders from Meade, was to "go out and engage the rebel cavalry." By traveling south, the Federal column hoped to threaten Richmond. It also might assist Benjamin F. Butler's Army of the James, at that time menacing the Confederate capital from the southeast.[2]

The destruction of bridges and railroad lines offered additional incentive for a raid. Both the Virginia Central Railroad and the Richmond, Fredericksburg & Potomac Railroad lay in Sheridan's path. The disruption of those two vital supply arteries could greatly embarrass Confederate transportation systems at a crucial time in the campaign. Although those targets attracted Sheridan's attention, events during the raid would illustrate clearly that he sought a decisive battle with Stuart most of all.

As Sheridan's column snaked southward on country roads toward Chilesburg, citizens in its path must have marveled at its size. Union participants placed its length at thirteen miles. Maj. James H. Kidd likely wrote the truth

Major General
James Ewell Brown Stuart.
Francis Trevelyan Miller, ed., *The Photographic History of the Civil War*, 10 vols. (New York: Review of Reviews, 1911), 4:265

when he claimed after the war that Sheridan's corps was "beyond doubt the most superb force of mounted men that ever had been assembled under one leader on this continent." J. E. B. Stuart respected it, writing in a dispatch the next day that if Sheridan's men fought dismounted they would "fight better than the enemy's infantry." This powerful collection of horsemen suffered from two weaknesses. One was inherent in Sheridan's plan: his men would be far from friendly aid in a time of crisis. The three divisions also started their trip with only one half-day's rations of forage. Their horses would have to depend upon central Virginia's farmers for sustenance.[3]

By early afternoon of May 9, Confederates around Spotsylvania Court House had prepared a response. General Stuart dispatched Fitzhugh Lee's two-brigade division to pursue Sheridan. Later that same day, he relieved James B. Gordon's North Carolina cavalry brigade (of W. H. F. Lee's division) from its duties and sent it after Fitzhugh Lee.[4]

Apart from Stuart and Lee, the three primary Confederate figures in the column were brigade commanders Gordon, Williams C. Wickham, and Lunsford L. Lomax, all brigadier generals. Each was a seasoned officer with a long record of successful service in the Army of Northern Virginia. Wickham's four regiments included the 1st Virginia Cavalry, the unit with which Stuart had gained initial fame at First Manassas three years earlier. Lomax commanded

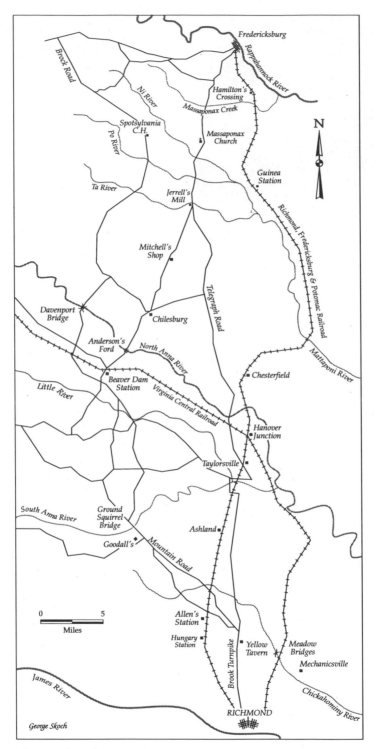

Theater of cavalry operations, May 9–13, 1864

Major General Fitzhugh Lee.
Francis Trevelyan Miller, ed., *The
Photographic History of the Civil War*,
10 vols. (New York: Review of
Reviews, 1911), 4:277

three regiments, less reliable than Wickham's but still efficient. Gordon's three regiments represented the only Tarheel cavalry in the Army of Northern Virginia. They too could point with pride to a solid record in most of the army's biggest battles.[5]

It is interesting to ponder the specifics of these Confederate assignments. The ten regiments sent to chase Sheridan represented less than half of the army's mounted strength. Stuart understood the magnitude of the danger confronting the Confederate rear; instead of remaining with the larger portion of his Cavalry Corps around Spotsylvania, he chose to ride with Fitz Lee on the trail of Sheridan's column. No evidence survives to determine which general decided on the composition of the response, but one can wonder whether Robert E. Lee forced these dispositions on Stuart. Clearly, Lee was anxious never again to suffer the loss of flexibility brought about by the absence of his cavalry. Perhaps on this day he instructed Stuart to leave four brigades behind for duties near Spotsylvania.

Sheridan's first objective was the North Anna River. Only a few bridges and fords afforded access to the river's south bank. The early start on May 9 ensured that the head of the Union advance would reach the river before any Confederates could overtake it. Just as certainly, the tail of the elongated column would be susceptible to a determined pursuit by Stuart. The first serious collision occurred shortly before sunset.[6]

Fitzhugh Lee's two brigades did not leave the lines at Spotsylvania until 1:00 P.M. Hard riding brought them into contact with the rear of Sheridan's formation near Mitchell's Shop, north of Chilesburg. There part of Wickham's brigade fought a typical cavalry engagement. Spying the dangling tip of the Federal column, Wickham aggressively charged along the road with part of the 3rd Virginia Cavalry and briefly managed to arrest the progress of Gregg's division. The fight swirled in a narrow road that funneled the Confederate horsemen into the jaws of a trap. Mounted Yankees defended the road, but dismounted troopers posted among the pine trees on either side proved to be the greatest danger. Capt. George H. Matthews of the 3rd, whom Fitzhugh Lee considered one of the most promising officers in the division, led the ill-fated charge down the country lane in column of fours. Once sucked into the soft center of the Union line, southern horsemen found themselves in danger of being cut off and captured. Injured troopers and horses clogged the road and made it difficult for Wickham to extract his squadrons. Matthews's horse was killed in the melee, but the captain bravely fought on until eventually being surrounded by blue-clad troopers and fatally wounded. The Confederate attack ended in immediate failure, although it harassed Sheridan's rear and induced "considerable temporary confusion" in the ranks of Henry E. Davies's Federal brigade.[7]

As darkness fell and the fighting at Mitchell's Shop dwindled, Stuart arrived on the field. He had stayed behind at Spotsylvania making final arrangements before following Fitzhugh Lee's division. A thrill of recognition swept through the weary Virginians when their leader appeared. Someone yelled out "Hurrah, boys! Here's old Jeb!" This prompted a "long and loud shout" that Stuart had to squelch.[8]

While Wickham struggled at Mitchell's Shop, the van of Sheridan's raiding party forged across the North Anna and pulled into Beaver Dam Station. This vital stop on the Virginia Central Railroad acted as a commissary and quartermaster depot for the Army of Northern Virginia. In and around the station lay 1.5 million rations for Lee's army together with a significant chunk of its reserve medical supplies. George A. Custer's Michigan cavalry brigade rode into the little community at twilight. Its arrival signaled the disruption of direct communications between Richmond and the Shenandoah Valley.[9]

Custer's men liberated between 300 and 400 infantry prisoners who had nearly reached the railroad on their long march to captivity. These lucky fellows gave their saviors a "wild and vociferous welcome." A man in the 44th New York recalled gorging himself on ham garnished with an unlimited number of eggs they found packed in sawdust. The whole scene must have resembled the Confederate cavalry's feast at White House Landing in June 1862, during one of Stuart's happier times.[10]

The Michigan troopers burned what they could not eat, including "a pile of bacon twenty rods long and six or seven feet high." Other than the overwhelmed provost guard accompanying the prisoners, no Confederates immediately came close enough to interfere. Division commander Wesley Merritt complained afterward that Custer's men had been too hasty with their matches, destroying valuable rations that could have been used later in the march. "As it cost nothing in lives or trouble," Merritt admitted, "no one felt like taking serious notice of the gaucherie. . . ." Sheridan went into camp that night with his column strung out on both banks of the North Anna River. A Confederate detachment from the 1st Maryland Cavalry disrupted the scene at midnight by sneaking up on the encampment in what one southern trooper termed a maneuver "of sublime audacity." After much firing and yelling, both sides settled down for the evening around the station. Farther east, Fitz Lee's division rode straight through the night trying to overtake the head of Sheridan's column.[11]

The next morning, Stuart arrived near the smoldering Beaver Dam Station to contemplate the dolorous view. Douglas Southall Freeman has speculated that Stuart felt especially humiliated at the destruction of an army treasure chest that rightly was the responsibility of his cavalry. This led the cavalry commander to renew his effort to catch Sheridan with even more vigor, Freeman theorized. More likely, Stuart realized for the first time at Beaver Dam Station that morning the magnitude of the threat to his capital city. The size, celerity, and direction of Sheridan's advance all suggested more than a circular raid, or even a diversion. Stuart clearly interpreted the evidence as indicating a direct move on Richmond.[12]

This realization prompted a change in his strategy. He left Gordon's North Carolinians to follow in Sheridan's wake and pester his rear. Stuart would hurry with the two Virginia brigades south along the Telegraph Road toward Richmond, enjoying the advantage of interior lines and filling in the hypotenuse of a not quite symmetrical triangle. Diligent riding could place him in Sheridan's path north of Richmond.[13]

The bulk of Confederate literature on Stuart's last days portrays his ultimately successful race with Sheridan as the salvation of Richmond. That comfortable interpretation does not survive scrutiny. On May 10, Sheridan's column marched roughly eighteen miles — a mediocre performance for infantry and positively uninspired for cavalry. A Michigan officer with the column recorded the day's advance as "even more leisurely than on the day before." At least one unit was in camp for the evening by 4:00 P.M. This seems to offer very strong evidence that Sheridan had no plans to enter Richmond. It is more likely that he purposely reined in his men to allow Stuart time to catch up. With his forage problem now solved, the Union general had no immediate goals other than to defeat the Confederate cavalry.[14]

Stuart could not afford to gamble on this. The ride of Wickham's and

Lomax's brigades on May 10 unfolded with a palpable sense of urgency. When one of his officers gloomily suggested that Sheridan could not be overtaken, Stuart (foreshadowing a later comment) retorted: "No, I would rather die than let him go on." Occasionally, the column trampled Federal picket posts in haste, always intent on the larger goal. Their grueling ride took them from Chilesburg that morning to Taylorsville that evening. Sheridan paralleled them to the west, moving obliquely southeastward toward Richmond. He crossed the South Anna River after his leisurely day's march and burned all the bridges behind him.[15]

The two Virginia brigades marched via Trinity Church and Fork Church and arrived at Taylorsville, just north of the South Anna River, around 9:00 P.M. on the 10th. Before making a hasty camp, Stuart inquired of the authorities in Richmond whether the city was in immediate danger. "I am very anxious to give my command a night's rest, if compatible with duty," he wrote. Apparently, he deemed that repose vital, for even Stuart indulged in an intense nap without waiting for a reply from Richmond. One of his staff found it impossible to rouse the sleeping general, even after turning him over. Leiper Robinson rode with the 5th Virginia during the raid, saw Stuart about then, and remembered how he "looked worn out from fatigue." Fitzhugh Lee concurred with the decision to stop, arguing urgently that his command needed a respite of more than just a few minutes. His division had been in the saddle more or less continuously for thirty-two hours. Jaded horses and wearied troopers collapsed in open spaces around Taylorsville. Robert S. Hudgins of the 3rd Virginia probably was not alone when he "slept on the ground with my horse's bridle reins wrapped around one arm."[16]

Now that the contending parties almost had reached the outskirts of Richmond, the tempo of operations increased still more. Both columns arose early to face the dramatic events of May 11. Sheridan's approach to the city by the Mountain Road placed him in excellent circumstances to interdict the Richmond, Fredericksburg & Potomac Railroad. Davies's brigade of Gregg's division got underway by 2:00 A.M. to raid the facilities at Ashland. Others struck south toward Hungary Station. The rest of the column pushed southeastward on the Mountain Road, crossing the railroad at Glen Allen Station. A few miles to the east, Fitzhugh Lee's men resumed their pursuit down the Telegraph Road, toward Ashland, at about 3:00 A.M. During the overnight lull, Stuart had enlarged his artillery support by borrowing a battery from Brig. Gen. Bradley T. Johnson, whose Marylanders guarded Hanover Junction.[17]

The morning's action began at Ashland. Davies set fire to a few buildings and destroyed various pieces of railroad stock. While most of the brigade tore up "quite a section of railroad," the 1st Massachusetts found itself engaged in

Brigadier James Byron Gordon. Francis Trevelyan Miller, ed., *The Photographic History of the Civil War*, 10 vols. (New York: Review of Reviews, 1911), 4:111

a street battle. Col. Thomas T. Munford's dismounted 2nd Virginia surprised Federals who were in the process of setting fire to several buildings. The southerners burst into town and drove off the raiders until a northern counterattack forced the 2nd to defend Ashland in its streets and from its yards and houses. Wat Carson of the 2nd, though slightly wounded, "hobbled out very quick indeed. . . . I did forget I was wounded until the fight was over I tell you I gave them the best I had carbine and pistol." Theodore Garnett of Stuart's staff watched "some heartless wag" pretending that orders required throwing all Yankee prisoners into the flames, but the captives "evidently didn't relish the joke." In some respects, this victory rang hollow. Many miles of railroad track had been damaged together with the exceedingly valuable rolling stock.[18]

The second fight of the morning ignited at the very tail of Sheridan's long line of march. Gordon's North Carolina cavalry brigade had been shadowing the raiders all day on the 10th. Early on the 11th they pushed forward, hoping to harass their foe in some way and perhaps reduce the escalating pressure on Stuart farther east. The South Anna River blocked Gordon's route. No bridges remained intact, and Union picket posts crowned the south bank at all known fords. This seemingly insoluble set of circumstances had no visible impact on Gordon. He merely surveyed several spots along the river, picked the least unlikely looking of them, and "with a mighty plunge" led the way. The banks at this uncharted ford seemed at least fifteen feet high to one participant. "Men were hurt trying to take their horses up that almost impossible bank," remembered a trooper. "Some were seriously hurt," agreed Paul Means of the 5th North Carolina, "but we were out there expecting to get hurt."[19]

Episodes like this, especially in cavalry affairs, often went far in deciding the outcome of actions. Gordon came from the J. E. B. Stuart mold and had a long history of aggressive leadership on the regimental level. A more timid officer would have found the river an insurmountable obstacle and not participated in the May 11 fighting at all. Instead, Gordon shaped events to suit himself. His reward was an exposed Union rear oblivious to its danger. Hindsight shows that Gordon's boldness had no direct influence on the outcome of this particular day's events; nonetheless, a commanding general with enough self-reliant subordinate officers of this type could always make his dispositions with confidence.

Once the Carolinians had crashed across the South Anna River, they struck the rear guard of Sheridan's column, represented by several units from Gregg's division. The resulting fight swirled around Ground Squirrel Church and Mr. Goodall's nearby house and tavern. The 5th North Carolina led the advance dismounted. Soon Gordon brought up the 1st North Carolina, "charging down . . . like so many demons." They struck the left of the Union line near the tavern. This was the 1st Maine Cavalry, caught unprepared for the aggressive Confederates.[20]

After a few volleys, the Maine men broke for the rear, where they scattered members of the 10th New York as they thundered through the New Yorkers' camp. "None of the boys appear to have retained a very clear recollection of just how the thing occurred," admitted the historian of the 10th. "They stood not 'upon the order of their going,'" he wrote. "In point of fact there was not much order to stand upon." This man sagely concluded that in his regiment at least, "It was one of those unaccountable panics which sometimes seize bodies of men without cause."[21]

In time, the Federal cavalry rallied, using artillery to help sort out the situation. The fight then evolved into a partly mounted clash at saber and pistol range. Afterward, soldiers on both sides remembered peculiar and heroic episodes. The Carolinians claimed that the bugler of the 1st North Carolina sounded the charge on his own instrument, galloped into the attack and apprehended his counterpart in the 1st Maine, and then blew the call again on the captured brass. A man in the 10th New York who had been forcibly dismounted reportedly grabbed the tail of a passing horse and allowed himself to be dragged from the field. Saber cuts and powder burns were common wounds that morning. Lt. E. B. Lindsay of the 5th North Carolina slashed at a Yankee color-bearer and reached for the flag but was foiled by his dexterous foe, who weaved and dodged his way to safety. Col. William H. Cheek of the 1st North Carolina wrote after the war that he considered it "the most desperate hand-to-hand conflict I ever witnessed."[22]

The combat finally concentrated around Goodall's Tavern and Ground Squirrel Church. Federal sharpshooters infested the hotel and its outbuildings, located in a piece of open ground. Some of Gordon's men became pinned down trying to carry that strongpoint. Others pushed forward on horseback until they collided with a mounted line of reserve northern troopers and some artillery in a woodline near Ground Squirrel Church. The 1st North Carolina enjoyed moderate success in trying to flank this position on either side of the Mountain Road. More close quarters fighting erupted around the little church. The 5th North Carolina raised a rebel yell and joined the fray. "It was good fighting all around on the 11th," concluded a participant.[23]

The affair near Ground Squirrel Bridge ultimately played itself out later in the morning. Gordon's men relished examining an abandoned encampment that overflowed with preserves, eggs, chicken, geese, and other items stolen from local pantries. A few dead and wounded Yankees sprinkled about the camp confirmed some Carolinians' notions about "immediate retribution." Union troopers correctly maintained that they had successfully protected the rear of Sheridan's column. The Confederates could argue with equal legitimacy that they had fixed the tail of Sheridan's force in place and prevented Gregg's division from participating in the action to the southeast at Yellow Tavern. Gordon's harassing tactics had reduced the pressure on J. E. B. Stuart, then fighting for his life.

Stuart needed that assistance, blended with a large dose of good fortune, to defend Richmond successfully and still emerge with his force intact. Fitzhugh Lee's two brigades had spent a few quiet hours during the night of May 10–11 strung out in makeshift camps between Hanover Junction and Taylorsville. Before dawn, Lee's staff rousted the cavalrymen into their saddles and the race southward continued. Stuart rode through the early morning hours with his chief of staff, Maj. Henry B. McClellan. Writing after the war, McClellan recalled that his ebullient chief was somewhat subdued. "He was more quiet than usual, softer, and more communicative," thought the major. Earlier, Stuart had told A. R. Venable of his staff that he did not expect to survive the war, and did not want to live in a conquered nation anyway. "It seems now," McClellan aptly concluded, "that the shadow of the near future was already upon him."[24]

Lomax's brigade arrived at Yellow Tavern around 8:00 A.M. after galloping much of the distance from Taylorsville. The action at Ashland had detained Stuart, and he did not reach Lomax until after 9:00. The tavern itself bore little importance in the day's operations, but its location at a prominent intersection of roads made it the focal point of all descriptions. The building stood a few hundred yards south of the intersection between the Telegraph and Mountain roads — the two routes traveled by the opposing forces on May 11. The roads united there to become the Brook Turnpike, which then followed a straight course for seven miles into downtown Richmond. The turnpike was "a nice, wide road, in good condition, with a beautiful hedge fifteen or twenty feet high, on either side." Numerous farm roads crisscrossed the area around the tavern. The area thrived on market gardening and produced vast amounts of vegetables and fruit for sale to Richmond's deskbound bureaucrats and their families.[25]

In its glory days, Yellow Tavern had indeed been painted yellow, a garish color for a building in the mid-nineteenth century. The structure stood by the 1830s, and very likely was built earlier than that to serve as a primary stop for stages plying the roads between Richmond and Washington. It rose to a height of three stories, the basement level being brick and the upper two frame. A porch ran the length of the tavern and a bar adorned the inside of the bottom floor. The whole place was about fifty feet long and thirty feet wide. In 1864, a screen of aspen trees stood in front of the building, with a flagstone pavement between the foliage and the structure.

By the time of the battle Yellow Tavern had fallen into disrepair and was abandoned. Soldiers camped nearby (probably in the city's outer defenses) had long ago stripped off many boards and stolen all the doors and window frames for firewood. This unexceptional structure greeted Stuart and his staff on their early morning arrival. Although still scrambling to defend Richmond, Stuart must have felt some small satisfaction at having reached the intersection before his enemy. His little triumph ensured that the Confederate cavalry could mount a defense of the capital on favorable ground away from the city. It also meant the Virginia Central Railroad was safe between Richmond and Hanover Junction, where it could feed into the Richmond, Fredericksburg & Potomac Railroad and connect with Lee's army.[26]

The biggest difficulty Stuart faced lay in sorting out his tactical dispositions. When Sheridan arrived, should the Confederates block his direct route to Richmond, or should they threaten his flank? To narrow the determining factors, Stuart resumed communication with Gen. Braxton Bragg, who served in Richmond as Jefferson Davis's chief military adviser (under Davis's supervision, Bragg was somewhat vaguely responsible for "the conduct of the military operations in the armies of the Confederacy"). Stuart sent a note at 8:00 A.M. explaining his position and dispatched Major McClellan to discuss it all personally. If Bragg had the city defenses well in hand, Stuart felt confident that

Brigadier General
Lunsford Lindsay Lomax.
Francis Trevelyan Miller, ed., *The
Photographic History of the Civil War*,
10 vols. (New York: Review of
Reviews, 1911), 4:111

his cavalry could strike a telling blow on Sheridan's flank as it moved south. Bragg's response would determine the course of action.[27]

While Stuart awaited word from Bragg, he stared westward in the direction whence Sheridan would come. The noise of Gordon's fight with Gregg's rear guard at Ground Squirrel Church wafted across the intervening farms. By mid-morning the advance element of Merritt's division began appearing along the Mountain Road. Stuart sat on horseback near the row of trees in front of Yellow Tavern, where he could see Lomax's skirmishers contesting the open ground to the northwest. Wickham's brigade, slowed by the fight at Ashland, was not yet up. Stuart could delay no longer. He had not heard from Bragg and had to consider the scattered condition of Fitzhugh Lee's division. Under these circumstances there seemed no alternative but to abandon the Yellow Tavern intersection and marshal his forces on Sheridan's flank in hopes of striking an offensive blow.[28]

The new line chosen by Stuart had two almost separate parts. Lomax's three regiments had dismounted and occupied a position in the bed of the Telegraph Road, about one mile north of the tavern and facing west. When Wickham's four regiments arrived they stayed even farther north and faced due south, at right angles to Lomax's line. Thus, the new Confederate position resembled an upside down and backward letter "L," with Wickham project-

Brigadier General
Williams Carter Wickham.
Francis Trevelyan Miller, ed., *The
Photographic History of the Civil War*,
10 vols. (New York: Review of
Reviews, 1911), 10:319

ing west from Lomax's right. Terrain may have played a part in selecting this
new position. The alignment had the advantage of luring the Federal troopers
toward Lomax's visible position where Wickham's veterans could fall on their
left flank. It is likely that Stuart built this trap intentionally and with confidence. He had mentioned in a dispatch to Bragg earlier that morning that
he suspected Sheridan's force numbered 9,000 men — a substantial underesti-
mate. A Virginia cavalryman writing after the war claimed that Lomax's brigade was confident of defeating Sheridan that morning: "We thought we had
him penned and would surely capture his whole command." [29]

The ensuing battle lasted nearly all day. Official reports from the participants do not make this clear, and most historians have lumped together
various memorable moments of the action and treated them as one continuous, fluid experience. In fact, the battle can be broken into three discernible
phases. The first of these pitted Lomax's skirmishers against the spearhead of
Sheridan's column. Gibbs's and Devin's brigades of Merritt's division, moving
dismounted (as virtually everyone did during the battles of Sheridan's raid),
fought a prolonged skirmish with Lomax's men. Initially, they struggled for
possession of a body of woods west of the Telegraph Road. This fight raged for
several hours, with Merritt's men making little progress. Finally, they evicted
Lomax's men from the woodlot and prepared to storm his main line in the
Telegraph Road. To reach it they would have to cross an open field some 500
yards wide. [30]

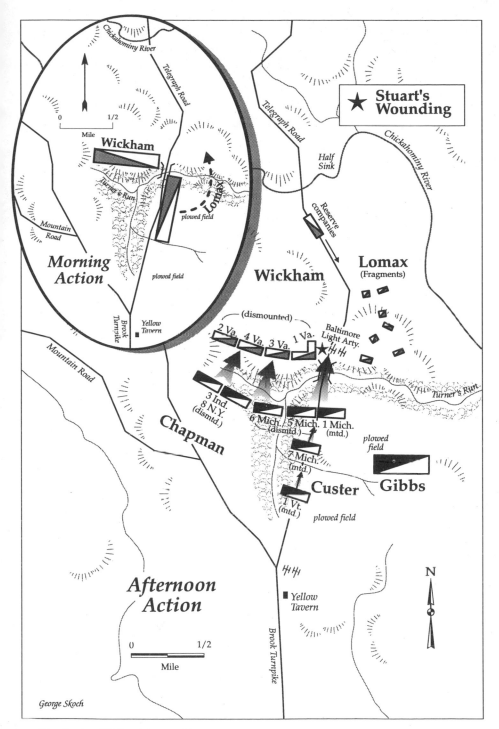

The Battle of Yellow Tavern, May 11, 1864

For some reason not explained in the historical record, General Lomax placed his senior colonel in command of the brigade and rode to a point where he could witness the action. Col. Henry Clay Pate of the 5th Virginia was the man charged with leading the brigade in its defense of the Telegraph Road. The thirty-two-year-old Pate was a fire-eater in the Edmund Ruffin tradition. During the antebellum years, he had edited a newspaper in Petersburg, written two books, and led a proslavery faction in a skirmish with John Brown in Kansas. When the war began he commanded a company in the 5th for a time and eventually became the regiment's colonel. He had been wounded at Aldie the year before. Pate's greatest wartime notoriety came from a bitter dispute with the contentious Gen. Thomas L. Rosser, who court-martialled the colonel. Stuart had supported his protégé Rosser. Pate harbored bitter feelings against them both and reportedly was not even on speaking terms with Stuart.[31]

A lull crept over the battlefield prior to the battle's second phase. During that midday interlude, Stuart initiated a much publicized rapprochement with Pate. A postwar biographical sketch of the colonel reported that Stuart sought out his subordinate during the quiet time and congratulated him on his skillful handling of the skirmish. They clasped hands and Stuart said, "Colonel Pate you have done all that any man could do. How long can you hold this position?" An inspired Pate responded, "Until I die, General." They shook hands again and Stuart rode off.[32]

Stuart's aide-de-camp, Lt. Theodore S. Garnett, recorded a much more realistic account. Writing in 1894, Garnett recalled that he carried a last message from Stuart to Pate: "Go and tell Colonel Pate to hold that position *at all hazards*." Garnett found the colonel dismounted, brandishing his sword and rallying men in the Telegraph Road. Stuart's orders discouraged Pate. "I can see Col. Pate now as he stood," reminisced Garnett, "looking me square in the eye, with his cold grey eyes and pallid face (not from fear for he was habitually pale) but uttering no response, and thinking he had not heard me, I leaned over on my horse closer to him, and spoke louder, repeating the order. . . ." Garnett found that Pate had indeed heard the directive the first time, "and understood my orders in their full significance, as a veritable 'death sentence.' "[33]

The battle resumed as Garnett rode off to rejoin Stuart. Colonel Pate's three regiments occupied a dangerous position. The Telegraph Road offered the only cover in the midst of the giant field they defended. A deep ditch on both sides of the already worn road created a wide piece of low ground. At one point, the road was raised; at another, it ran through a cut. As long as Merritt's men remained out in the field this arrangement benefited Pate, but if they ever broke the Virginians' line, the road suddenly would become a trap. Pate soon found that he had insufficient men to contest every part of the Telegraph Road from Yellow Tavern northward to Wickham's line. Consequently, Union skirmishers, moving from the south, eventually enfiladed the line. Battery D, 2nd United States Horse Artillery set up a section of guns at the tavern and began to pound Pate's left flank. Meanwhile, dismounted Federal cavalry formed in the woods on the western end of the field for their final push toward Pate.

The 9th New York spearheaded the renewed Union effort. Advancing dismounted across the field, they soon struck Pate's own 5th Virginia. The New Yorkers sheltered the left of their line among some farm buildings before enveloping both flanks of the Virginia regiment. "Our fire, protected as we were, did not seem to check their advance in the least," thought Leiper Robinson of the 5th. The gallant Colonel Pate fell dead while waving his hat, shot through the head moments after telling his men, "One more round boys, and then we'll get to the hill." [34]

While the 9th New York advanced across the field, they extended their line, "overreaching the enemy's line and having a flank fire on him." By the time the Federals achieved revolver range, the leaderless Virginians found themselves penned in the worn-down bed of the Telegraph Road, "exposed to deadly volleys from both ends of the cut." "The question was whether to remain in the ditch, where we were safe . . . and surrender," wrote one survivor, "or take the hazard of crossing that newly plowed field right in front of their whole line." [35]

Lomax's brigade, with its namesake apparently watching from afar, disintegrated in the Telegraph Road. Three captains in the 5th Virginia fell dead or mortally wounded. P. J. White of the 5th reflected years later that Yellow Tavern was "the severest and probably the most disastrous fight" in which his unit ever participated. White's comrade Leiper Robinson could hear bullets smacking "like hailstones" the plank fence that bordered the road. Finding that the aged carbine he had borrowed for the occasion was not even functional, Robinson could only watch as the brigade collapsed. Large numbers of his comrades chose to surrender in the Telegraph Road rather than brave the gauntlet, but Robinson joined others sprinting eastward across the far reaches of the open wheatfield. He looked back and saw "the road and ditch-bank, lined with Yankees popping away at us." Several dead and wounded runners lined the route, and Robinson noticed a man nearby clipped by a bullet: "Instead of falling, he yelled out and seemed to double his speed. He left me away behind." More than half the regiment escaped this way; most of the 6th and 15th regiments fled north to the protection of Wickham's brigade on the hill overlooking Turner's Run. [36]

J. E. B. Stuart watched this unfolding disaster from the hill. He sent a staff officer over to Wickham with orders to launch a counterattack into Merritt's flank and perhaps restore the Telegraph Road line. This succeeded in part, forcing Sheridan's men to regroup around Yellow Tavern. For the second time that day, a period of calm fell over the field. Sheridan leisurely reorganized his men before launching a final assault. Apprehensive Confederates viewed the buildup, but Stuart "felt confident of success" and continued to think offensively. Having finally received intelligence that Braxton Bragg had the city's defenders well in hand, Stuart expressed the hope to H. B. McClellan that perhaps the two forces could cooperate and destroy Sheridan. Fitz Lee's division was running short of ammunition, but if infantry could be brought up from below Richmond to attack Sheridan's flank, thought Stuart, "I cannot see how they can escape." He also knew that Gordon continued to shadow the raiders' tail.[37]

As the climactic phase of the battle neared, the irony of the new situation may have impressed some of the more thoughtful soldiers on the field. After an exhausting two-day race in which the Confederates believed they were riding to save Richmond, they had overtaken Sheridan. Now, virtually in sight of the city's spires, they occupied a line of defense that faced due south toward the city. Sheridan's attacks, when they came, would be from the direction of the capital city. Each general had achieved his immediate ambition of bringing the other to battle outside Richmond's defenses.

The mid-afternoon lull dragged on into "a long silence." Stuart posted four guns of the Baltimore Light Artillery adjacent to the Telegraph Road, facing south and southwest from its eastern shoulder. The remnants of Lomax's brigade, little more than a skirmish line, probably stood dismounted east of the road. Wickham's four veteran regiments established their final line west of the road on the edge of the hill, some behind hastily erected rail breastworks and all enjoying the modest cover of a "skirt of timber and a fence." Turner's Run provided an admirable obstacle at the base of the bluff. Maj. James Breathed's battery of horse artillery likely unlimbered somewhere along Wickham's line.[38]

In the distance, Union cavalry formed for a headlong attack with the Baltimore Light Artillery as the point of focus. Devin's and Gibbs's brigades had borne the brunt of the earlier fighting. George Custer's Michigan regiments supplanted them for the final charge. The flamboyant Custer posted three of his units along and west of the Telegraph Road, facing north. The 1st Michigan stayed on horseback, the 5th and 6th fought dismounted, and the 7th stood nearby as a mounted reserve. Slightly westward, Col. George H. Chapman's three regiments deployed to prolong Custer's line. The 1st Vermont would ride into the attack with the Michigan troops; the 3rd Indiana and the 8th New York of the same brigade were to fight Wickham's Virginians on foot.[39]

It was around 4:00 P.M. when Custer's six-regiment strike force moved into Stuart's line of sight. A section of artillery near Yellow Tavern tried to soften the Confederate position. Its shells fell among the Baltimore Light Artillery with both frequency and effect. Shrapnel tore through the battery's horses, eliciting shrieks unnerving enough "to appall the stoutest heart." The shells also sought out humans. A fragment badly smashed Pvt. John F. Hayden's shoulder. The battery surgeon, Dr. John B. Wortham, heroically hoisted Hayden onto his back and staggered off with him into the relative shelter offered by nearby woods, where he managed to stop the bleeding and save Hayden's life. Back at the battery their comrades finally found the range and made Yellow Tavern "a decidedly hot place."[40]

As Custer's men pushed toward Turner's Run, they had five farm fences to negotiate, rendering their advance necessarily slow. Southern skirmishers annoyed them somewhat, but it was the Baltimore Light Artillery, bruised but not suppressed, that obstructed the advance. "The man who thinks they did not succeed in making that part of the neighborhood . . . an uncomfortably hot place, was not there at the time," asserted Maj. James H. Kidd of the 6th Michigan. A trooper in the 1st Vermont agreed, writing that "the enemy threw shell at us without mercy." Once the attackers traversed the field and reached Turner's Run they were in defilade, temporarily secure from the Confederate artillery. They next found that the stream itself interfered with the charge. Custer observed that only three men could cross the little bridge simultaneously, creating a dangerous bottleneck, but these impediments to the Federal advance could only be temporary. Stuart's available reserve to meet this crisis consisted of several mounted companies from the 1st Virginia, two from the 2nd Virginia, and one from the 6th Virginia. The general dispatched couriers and staff officers to hurry forward these reinforcements, who had been posted well to the rear near the Chickahominy River.[41]

The attackers struggled across the creek and up the slope into the Confederate line. The 1st Michigan made for the artillery, which stood only about 200 yards north of the stream. The attackers absorbed a "never ceasing hail of canister" before arriving at the guns. There they rode among their prizes, sabering cannoneers. The Michiganders also captured battery commander Capt. William Hunter Griffin and many of his men. If Griffin ever saw Wesley Merritt's official report, he would have derived grim satisfaction from reading that general's conclusion that the Maryland battery "had been very annoying during the fight."[42]

After capturing the Baltimore Light Artillery, some of the attackers aggressively pushed a short distance north along the Telegraph Road. They soon found themselves confronting the first of Stuart's reserves, Company D (the Clarke Cavalry) of the 6th Virginia, which Lomax led into the attack "like an arrow from a cross bow." Stuart "gave a cheer and waved his sabre" as the tiny force boldly dashed into Custer's men. The Yankees farthest forward hastily began spilling back southward toward their friends. The Virginians partially restored the situation and recaptured Fitzhugh Lee's aide-de-camp, Charles Minnigerode (son of Richmond's famous Episcopalian rector), who "was being rapidly carried off." Stuart and others of Wickham's men concentrated on this bold cluster of men from the 1st Michigan. They lined the fence rail that paralleled the Telegraph Road and fired into passing groups for whom the constricted road offered the only means of escape. A nearby Virginia officer warned Stuart of the danger: "I told him to go away several times . . . but he would [not] go." Instead, Stuart sat astride his horse and emptied his revolver "as coolly as I could fire at a squirrel," thought Cyrus McCormick of the 6th Virginia. When he had fired all his loads, Stuart drew his saber and began yelling "Give it to them! Give it to them! Stand your ground!" B. J. Haden of the 1st Virginia saw one Yankee drop into the road as if shot, then scuttle over into a roadside ditch and feign death. One of Haden's comrades went over to check, found that the man was indeed "playing possum," and shot him. A second installment of reinforcements (Companies B and G of the 1st Virginia under Capt. George Newkirk Hammond) came thundering down the road to add punch to the counterattack. Stuart continued to cheer, yelling, "Boys, don't stop to count fours. Shoot them! Shoot them!" Captain Hammond died leading his men forward, but his squadron of the 1st "completely blockade[d] the road with dead horses and men." [43]

During this stage of the fight, while Stuart sat in the roadside pines anxiously watching the struggle for the artillery, calamity struck. A dismounted Federal trooper making his way to the rear along the road stopped briefly and fired at Stuart. The bullet struck the cavalry chief in the stomach, near the belt line, and exited through his back. He immediately sagged in the saddle, his trademark plumed hat toppling into the dust. Thomas J. Waters of the 1st Virginia saw Stuart and "took off my hat to cheer him" before discovering that his chief was wounded. Confederates around the hilltop position watched in collective horror as Stuart reeled around and grasped the pommel of his saddle to avoid falling off his horse. Men raced to his aid from all quarters. Despite having as many staff officers as any general in the history of the Army of Northern Virginia, none of Stuart's aides was at hand just then. Instead, a large array of men from Company K of the 1st Virginia offered the initial succor. [44]

Capt. Gustavus Warfield Dorsey, the youthful commander of Company K, apparently rescued Stuart from his restive horse and saved the general from toppling to the ground. Pvt. Fred Pitts came up to look at Stuart and "saw that his whole side was soaked with blood." Ignoring Stuart's protests, Dorsey detailed Pvt. Charles Wheatley and Cpl. Robert Bruce, both of Company K, to get him back on a horse and moving toward the rear. Pitts swapped mounts with Stuart, the general's own horse still being too skittish.[45]

This drama unfolded amid chaos in all directions. Courier John Gill remembered "our cavalry having just been driven back to the right, when Stuart was wounded." The 3rd Virginia came up under thirty-one-year-old Lt. Col. William Richard Carter, hoping to reinforce the position at the Telegraph Road. As the men walked toward the vortex of the battle, they first met a courier yelling for a surgeon. A few moments later Stuart himself came by, held onto his saddle by willing hands. William T. Daougherty watched as the general, although unable to speak, "by a motion of hand, urged us forward." Painful spasms wracked Stuart during the trip rearward. T. J. Waters of the rescue party recalled that the general "was suffering such pain that he insisted upon getting off the horse and lying down on the ground." A frantic messenger found Fitzhugh Lee nearby "galloping back and forth behind his line of battle," imploring Wickham's men—some of whom were "running like sheep"—to hold their line against Custer and Chapman. When the courier told Lee that Stuart was wounded and refused to leave the field, Lee galloped to the scene and supervised his commander's removal. The action waxed so fiercely at that point that Lee admitted afterward: "My own time was so much occupied I . . . did not even know the extent of his wound." What Lee did know was that Stuart ceded supervision of the battle to him with confidence. "He called out to me as I rode up to him," remembered Lee after the war, " 'Go ahead, Fitz, old fellow, I know you will do what is right.' "[46]

In time, someone hunted up an ambulance, and Stuart's staff, having reassembled upon hearing of the emergency, escorted the vehicle rearward toward the Chickahominy River. A brief surge by some of Custer's men threatened the ambulance at one point, and someone (probably Maj. James Breathed, himself wounded that day) organized a hasty riposte that allowed Stuart's vehicle to escape. One eyewitness noted that before Stuart left the field he "insisted upon being taken to his wife." John B. Fontaine, chief surgeon of the Cavalry Corps, rode inside the ambulance with Stuart. So did Capt. Walter Quarrier Hullihen of Lomax's staff, but formerly of Stuart's. When the general asked Hullihen about his appearance, the loyal subordinate replied, "General, you are looking right well. You will be all right." This bald prevarication likely did not fool Stuart. A curious cavalryman following "with my horse's head right in the ambulance" observed that Stuart "kept shaking his head with an expression of the deepest disappointment." Soon he "peacefully folded his arms with a look of complete resignation."[47]

Before leaving permanently, Stuart managed one more order. Seeing demoralized and scattered cavalrymen fleeing all around him, Stuart raised himself on an elbow and bellowed out his famous final orders: "Go back! go back! and do your duty, as I have done mine, and our country will be safe. Go back! go back! I had rather die than be whipped." With those spine-tingling final words, Stuart exited his last battlefield. His plea had little influence on his disorganized men that afternoon, but no final defeat could obscure the enormous mark he had left on the landscape of Confederate history.[48]

Back on the hill above Turner's Run, Fitz Lee had little time to relish the compliment from Stuart, or even to stamp the battle with his own leadership. He had inherited an irretrievable situation. Lt. John R. McNulty of the Baltimore Light Artillery escaped with two of the battery's four captured guns in the confusion. Other Confederates managed to patch together a new line several hundred yards closer to the Chickahominy, still along the Telegraph Road. To counter this, Custer sent forward the 7th Michigan in a mounted attack, moving first at a trot, and then at a charge with drawn sabers. The Confederates still had enough cohesion to blast apart this attack. Maj. Henry W. Granger, commanding the 7th, fell riddled at the head of his column. This little victory, gratifying as it must have been, did not significantly alter the complexion of the afternoon's events. A man in Wickham's brigade summed it up accurately when he wrote: "We were pressed back until darkness relieved us." Fitz Lee's men quickly fell back in the twilight across the Chickahominy at Half Sink to reorganize. Word of Stuart's injury spread quickly among his men, one of whom noted: "I never saw such a distressed looking body of men in my life . . . many of them shedding tears."[49]

Sheridan's troopers now controlled the late battlefield. Their largest immediate concern came from James B. Gordon's North Carolinians. During the fighting around Yellow Tavern, Gregg's rearguard division to the west fought continuous skirmishes with Gordon's persistent men, many of whom now were armed with sophisticated Spencer carbines captured that morning at Ground Squirrel Church. At Allen's Station on the Richmond, Fredericksburg & Potomac Railroad, Davies's brigade was forced to stop in the early evening and unlimber a rifled cannon in the Mountain Road. Others deployed along the line of the railroad, facing west. The 2nd North Carolina, with part of the 5th North Carolina in front as skirmishers, charged the cannon just before dusk. A lively fight ensued, with much material damage to houses in the vicinity but few casualties among the participants.[50]

In some ways, the night of May 11–12 impressed itself on the memories of participants more than any other stage of Sheridan's raid. Violent thunderstorms (part of the same weather system that plagued the infantry at the Bloody Angle the next day) swept the region. The unpleasant weather was a clear ally to the Confederates. It made Sheridan's nighttime movements more uncertain and slowed his rate of march. Despite his victory at Yellow Tavern, the Federal commander found himself in a tight corner. Gordon's troopers blocked him from easily doubling back to the west. The Chickahominy River, unfordable and well defended, offered no comfortable escape to the north. To the east, Richmond's outer defenses and the river followed converging courses, at one point running in such juxtaposition that troops could not possibly negotiate the bottleneck without heavy loss. The city of Richmond lay to the south.[51]

No other troops during the Civil War threatened Richmond as seriously as did Sheridan's that night. McClellan's 1862 campaign had greater potential but never accomplished even the necessary steps preliminary to injuring the Confederate capital. Ulric Dahlgren's raid a few months earlier in 1864, frightening as it was, had been small and ill managed. On the night of May 11, Sheridan had the ability and position to take Richmond under fire. Contrary to his boastful claims, he could not have penetrated to the heart of the city, but he probably could have shelled Richmond and cracked its record of impregnability. Already his 6th New York had successfully occupied the outer defenses near Brook Run, whence they could hear ringing bells and whistling locomotives in the city. Sheridan reportedly said after the war that attacking the city was "the greatest temptation of my life." "I could have gone in and burned and killed right and left," he argued, but the city could not have been held indefinitely. All the casualties thus accumulated would have won no lasting advantage. Weighing his options, Sheridan decided to circle Richmond to the north and east in hopes of squeezing by the outer defenses and joining Butler's Army of the James southeast of the city.[52]

The march began in the middle of the night. After traveling south on the Brook Turnpike to Brook Church, Sheridan turned east on a secondary road that skirted Richmond. He shortly began to encounter difficulties. Some enterprising Confederate had planted land mines (called torpedoes in that era) in the road, with dramatic results. Union staff officer George B. Sanford remembered "it was thundering and lightning in the great style overhead, and the torpedoes blowing up under foot. Altogether, I certainly don't expect to see the like again, and don't especially want to." At one point, a handful of troopers dashed through an uninvestigated area only to detonate one of the mines. "The whole set of fours went up into the air," reported Sanford. "It was a very lively night," he dryly concluded.[53]

This irregular method of warfare infuriated Union officers. A large number of prisoners — mostly from the 5th Virginia Cavalry — accompanied the column that night. When the mines became thick, the prisoners were forced to search them out and remove them from the road. S. H. Nowlin of the 5th was given a pick and orders to start digging. Not surprisingly, he found that "This kind of work required a delicate touch and was unpleasantly exciting," though men in the 1st New Jersey Cavalry thought it "a curious and rather entertaining sight." Noisy explosions marked the progress of the column, but casualties were light.[54]

Paranoid cavalrymen marched in unreasoning fear of ambush. Somewhere along the road, McIntosh's brigade of Wilson's division took an incorrect turn, misled by some hapless local impressed into service as a guide. When shots erupted near the head of the column, McIntosh, sensing betrayal from the guide, "blew out his brains with a pistol." In fact, Confederate resistance at this latitude did not exist beyond the anonymous land mines. Nobody claimed any role in impeding Sheridan's overnight advance, and the nearest organized troops would prove their distaste for danger the next morning. The inky darkness, stormy weather, and proximity to Richmond combined to make Sheridan's raiders especially jumpy.[55]

The night remained rainy, but enough light emanated from Richmond's street lamps that soldiers in Chapman's brigade (the lead unit in Wilson's division) could see reflections on the clouds above. After following the Meadow Bridge Road northeast for a time, they secured a guide to lead them southeast to the Mechanicsville Turnpike. Their goal was Fair Oaks Station east of Richmond. Earliest dawn on May 12 revealed Chapman's position to Confederates occupying an intermediate line of city defenses on the turnpike. A cascade of bullets and shells "came mowing through our tired and sleepy ranks" and quickly drove Chapman back to the Virginia Central Railroad, where he faced south and east in conjunction with McIntosh's brigade. Clearly, Sheridan's sidestepping route around Richmond had no future.[56]

This news forced Sheridan into a rapid decision. With Confederate forces of uncertain size on two sides, a contested crossing of the Chickahominy appeared to offer the path of least resistance. He decided to rebuild the partially destroyed crossing at Meadow Bridges and take his chances with whatever forces Fitzhugh Lee could muster on the north bank. A reconnaissance showed that the Chickahominy flood plain was especially swampy there, even by that river's boggy standards. In fact, three crossings loomed before the Union cavalry. The main road first bisected a feeder stream of enough stature to warrant its own bridge. Then two parallel bridges spanned the Chickahominy—one for the road, another for the Virginia Central Railroad. Each probably measured several hundred yards in length. The regular bridge had been entirely destroyed by Confederates, but the railroad crossing apparently remained intact, although not a feasible alternative for horsemen. Everyone agreed that the river was deep and sluggish at Meadow Bridges. The heavy overnight rains (which continued sporadically into the morning of the 12th) had swelled it even more, and steep banks prevented the command's horses from swimming across. While specially detailed men undertook repairs on the road bridge, southern troops tightened the screws of their improvised vise around Sheridan.[57]

Confederate horse artillery on the north bank swept the crossings from a small hill. Until these guns and a swarm of skirmishers were silenced, Union work parties could not rebuild the main bridge. Once again Custer's Michigan brigade drew the dangerous assignment. The 5th and 6th Michigan picked their way across the "perfectly straight" railroad bridge. A few men at a time "tiptoed from tie to tie, watching the chance to make it in the intervals between the shells." This combat crossing was an unusual, perhaps unique, event in Virginia during the war. A staff officer watched the veterans "creeping, crawling—any way to get across. If a man was hit, of course he went into the water, there was nothing to hold on to, and certainly no way to help him."[58]

The first Michiganders arrived on the north bank and began "spreading out like a fan." They still faced several hundred yards of saturated meadow "about waist deep on a man" before reaching Lee's main line of fortifications and the artillery beyond. An especially violent rain shower prevented Merritt's men from even seeing the Confederate position atop the hill in their front. Southern skirmishers yielded ground stubbornly. R. H. Peck of the 2nd Virginia Cavalry offered one of the most bizarre excuses in the annals of military history when he claimed that he and his comrades allowed Custer to establish a bridgehead because they mistook Yankees in the water for large turtles. Confederate source material on the Meadow Bridges fight is deplorably scarce, and it is difficult to determine which units resisted Sheridan's push. Certainly the 2nd and 4th Virginia, and probably the rest of Wickham's brigade, occupied the "heavy breastworks" looking down on the railroad crossing from several hundred yards away. They successfully repulsed several Federal probes during the morning from entrenchments built atop the ridge that parallels the Chickahominy River. The floodplain on the north bank eventually worked against the Confederates. Once Custer controlled it, he was able to fix the defenders in place, allowing the bridge to be rebuilt without enemy harassment. Soon, nearly half of Merritt's division crossed on the railroad bridge and attacked Fitzhugh Lee's position.[59]

The unfortunate death late in the battle of the popular Robert Randolph, commander of the 4th Virginia, stood out as the most memorable feature of the battle for many Confederate survivors. The 2nd Virginia repulsed a few of Merritt's probes, and when the unit ran short of ammunition it launched a charge with swinging sabers. "The fighting was terrific," declared a member of the 2nd a few days later. Troopers from Merritt's expanding bridgehead "by a rather neat flank movement" eventually flushed the 4th Virginia from its

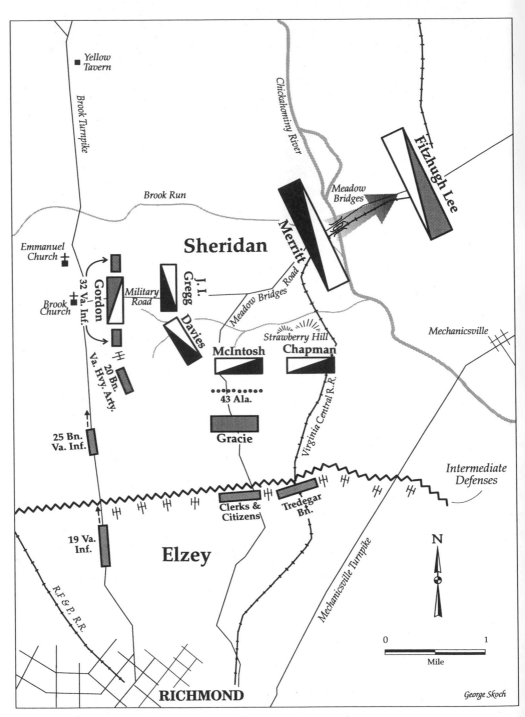

Yellow
Tavern

Brook Turnpike

Chickahominy River

Brook Run

Meadow
Bridges

Fitzhugh Lee

Emmanuel
Church

Sheridan

Merritt

Gordon

32 Va. Inf.

Military
Road

J. J.
Gregg

Davies

Meadow Bridges Road

Brook
Church

20 Bn.
Va. Hvy. Arty.

Strawberry Hill

Mechanicsville

McIntosh

Chapman

•••••••••
43 Ala.

Virginia Central R.R.

25 Bn.
Va. Inf.

Gracie

Intermediate
Defenses

Clerks &
Citizens

Tredegar
Bn.

19 Va.
Inf.

Elzey

N

R.F. & P. R.R.

Mechanicsville Turnpike

0   1
Mile

RICHMOND

George Skoch

Cavalry action north and northeast of Richmond, May 12, 1864 stronghold on the railroad. At that point, Colonel Randolph (in a reprise of Henry Pate's last words the day before) called out " 'Boys, give them one volley before we leave' and as he raised up to get a better view, received a ball through the head which killed him instantly. . . ." Horatio Nelson of the 4th noted in his diary that night: "Our beloved Col. Randolph killed. Tremendous blow to the old 4th. We deeply mourn his death." "I never knew an officer so universally regretted as he is by all classes in his regiment," agreed James Keith of the same unit. Randolph's sister could hear the fight from the house where she was staying. The courier who broke the news to her admitted that the colonel was shot in the head, adding — perhaps to impress the stunned woman — that her brother "fell cheering his men to a charge." Lee's men scattered, leaving the crucial bridgehead in Union hands. Federal cavalry doubling as engineers quickly covered the trestles of the railroad bridge with hewn logs and scavenged boards to allow the rest of the command to cross. Horses and mules had a perilous journey nonetheless. Some animals plummeted over the side or crashed through the feeble bridge and, though still living, "could be seen half sunk . . . by the side of the cause way."[60]

No doubt many causes combined to prompt the collapse of Fitzhugh Lee's men for the second time in as many days. It was uncharacteristic for the best cavalry division in the army to be driven from so powerful a position. Students looking to identify the roots of this collapse should ponder leadership. Between May 7 and 12, four of the seven regiments in the division lost their commanders (three killed). Two other field officers suffered wounds in that time, leaving the units with a shaky command structure. Add to this the death of Stuart and the heavy losses in company officers, especially in the 5th Virginia, and one has the recipe for disaster. Fitz Lee identified this problem as early as May 13, complaining that "many companies are without a commissioned officer and several squadrons are commanded by second lieutenants."[61]

While the bitter fight raged over the Chickahominy crossing, significant action continued on Sheridan's two other fronts. Wilson's division had stumbled into strong Confederate resistance on the Mechanicsville Turnpike and prudently withdrew to Strawberry Hill, a largely wooded area bisected by both the direct road from Richmond to Meadow Bridges and the tracks of the Richmond, Fredericksburg & Potomac Railroad. Heavy guns threatened Wilson from the strong entrenchments of Richmond's intermediate line of defenses. Initially, the only Confederate presence there came from hastily assembled city units such as the Tredegar Battalion (composed of employees from the famous ironworks) and the 3rd Virginia Battalion Local Defense Troops (primarily clerks). Early morning skirmishing on this front gave way to a disorganized

Confederate attack when the first of Braxton Bragg's reinforcements arrived on the field.[62]

Bragg had energetically pulled together frontline units from the battle-fields south of Richmond. The brigade of Brig. Gen. Archibald Gracie arrived first around 9:00 A.M., having slogged through a persistent rain. Marching through the streets of the capital city had inspirited the Alabamians. "We were now cheered on to duty by the beautiful daughters of Richmond, singly and in groups, waiving 'kerchiefs and Confederate flags from window, balcony, or portico," wrote Lewellyn A. Shaver of the 60th Alabama Infantry. "Here and there were . . . wives of those who had fallen in previous battles, dressed in mourning, with streaming eyes . . . pointing us significantly towards the quar-ter whence proceeded the sound of the enemy's cannon." The popular General Gracie marched out the Meadow Bridge Road to its intersection with the inter-mediate line of entrenchments. There he formed his line of battle, with the 43rd Alabama Infantry in front as skirmishers, and moved north toward Wil-son's dismounted Federal cavalry on Strawberry Hill.[63]

The soldiers in Gracie's brigade, recently transferred from the Army of Ten-nessee to Virginia, impressed many observers that morning. Gracie calmly maneuvered his men "as cool as if directing farm operations." The line moved "magnificently" across an open field, trying to ignore shells dropped in on them from Sheridan's horse artillery in the distant woodline. Gracie's mount survived several wounds and its rider reportedly received "one or two slight wounds" as well. Capt. William J. Mims of the 43rd wrote of being "in full view & point blank range of the enemy." A thunderstorm struck while this at-tack pressed forward. "The rain fell in hitting torrents while the heavens above seemed one sheet of continual peal of thunder," recorded John F. Davenport of the 23rd Alabama Battalion Sharpshooters. Worse than the pelting rain, General Gracie found his brigade subjected to an enfilading fire. The position was too exposed for any chance of lasting success, so the Alabamians carefully pulled back to the fortifications. John H. Reagan of the Confederate cabinet thought Gracie's veterans that morning performed "the handsomest and most regular movements I ever saw on a field of battle." This aborted attack ended Confederate operations on the Meadow Bridge Road for May 12.[64]

James B. Gordon's long-standing duel with Sheridan's rear guard continued into May 12 and represented the third distinct front. The Tarheel cavalry had been in constant contact with Gregg's division for about forty-eight hours. Gordon's incessant pressure certainly forced Sheridan's column that morn-ing into an unaccustomedly attenuated and vulnerable formation. Gordon's men launched their attacks from the Brook Turnpike, mostly along the military road followed earlier by Merritt's division. This forced General Gregg to dismount his troopers and face them to the west, with their backs to Meadow Bridges. J. Irvin Gregg's brigade apparently straddled the road while Davies's regiments bent obliquely back from Gregg's left, facing southwest. More of Sheridan's plentiful artillery swept the military road with canister.[65]

Gordon sent the 1st and 2nd North Carolina into action as dismounted skirmishers while he awaited his share of Bragg's reenforcements. When they arrived they proved to be part of Eppa Hunton's Virginia brigade plucked from the defenses below Richmond. The 32nd Virginia Infantry came up first, arriving at about 10:00 A.M. Although its men were by no means grizzled veterans, the unit at least had combat experience with the main army. Gordon took the first four companies that appeared, split them in half, and placed them on either flank of his sturdy skirmish line. The advent of artillery from the city completed his preparations. Before he could get the operation rolling, Gordon discovered that his artillery was useless. Its callow crews could not stand in the face of the canister that swept along the road and clattered among the spokes of the cannon. Without counter-battery fire, Confederate attacks along the military road would be doomed.[66]

The uncooperative performance of the cannoneers ignited Gordon's temper by early afternoon. In a towering rage he "raved and begged. He called it 'Band Box Artillery.' " The veteran Carolinians nearby jeered, laughed, and ridiculed, all to no avail. Finally, "utterly disgusted," Gordon went galloping off to his front, directly along the military road. A Federal bullet soon smashed his left arm. Command of the brigade and its dubious allies fell to Col. Clinton M. Andrews of the 2nd North Carolina. Eventually the 19th Virginia Infantry, 60 cannonless men of the 20th Battalion Virginia Heavy Artillery, and three companies of the 25th Battalion Virginia Infantry ("The City Battalion") all arrived to support the cavalry. The 19th moved to the front "with the usual yell and engaged the enemy furiously, losing twenty men in a very few minutes." The Union defenders had a strong position, enhanced by the erection of modest breastworks made of rocks and logs. The reinforcements behaved well, but without Gordon's decisive leadership the Confederates achieved little along the military road.[67]

It is uncertain who, if anyone, exercised command over the conglomeration of Confederates fighting north of Richmond on May 12. Jefferson Davis appeared frequently along the lines at the Meadow Bridge Road. His propensity for meddling in military operations is well known, but whether he did so on May 12 is not of record. His assistant, Braxton Bragg, had collected the men who did the fighting that day. No one reported seeing him about the field, but it is likely he was there. Finally, Maj. Gen. Arnold Elzey played some role in the day's affairs as commander of the Department of Richmond. He most likely commanded the majority of the units engaged.[68]

The triple-headed fight on the morning of May 12 baffled many of its chroniclers. An interested noncombatant puzzled over its development: "I vainly endeavored to comprehend the situation, or to find in which direction was either front or rear." "It was in fact a field of battle without a rear," he decided.[69]

Confederate sources traditionally have excoriated the reenforcements that achieved so little that May 12 morning. A horseman in the 2nd Virginia Cavalry bitterly wrote immediately after the raid: "We felt perfectly certain that a vigorous attack in their front must result in their capture. . . . We could not," he continued, "by ourselves, fight and capture such an overwhelming force." He concluded darkly: "Whose fault, if anybody's, I shall not discuss. But it wasn't ours." The Richmond *Examiner*, with its customary asperity, charged that the battle "was most timidly managed by our generals. Had they pressed the enemy, instead of standing in their fortifications, they would probably have captured his whole force." "A little more nerve," thought the paper, "and we would have annihilated the enemy." Fitzhugh Lee concurred in 1866, arguing, "Had the troops in the trenches moved upon him whilst he was engaging me, he would have been hemmed in on the Chickahominy, and I confidently believe his destruction would have been the result." Two correspondents in Gordon's brigade were even more direct, blaming Sheridan's escape on the failure of unnamed troops posted to the right of the Carolinians.[70]

These accusations — particularly the official postwar protest of Fitzhugh Lee — demonstrate the Confederates' complete unfamiliarity with the true situation. The local defense troops did in fact attack Sheridan in an effort to divert pressure from Lee's defense of the Meadow Bridges. Hindsight suggests that Fitz Lee and his badly outnumbered colleagues should have rejoiced at Sheridan's departure. The few reliable Confederate soldiers in the vicinity could not have endured the full brunt of Sheridan's three divisions in a pitched battle. That point had been amply illustrated the afternoon before at Yellow Tavern. Far from letting a certain trophy out of their grasp, Braxton Bragg and Fitz Lee had avoided further disaster while courageously defending Richmond.[71]

Once across the Chickahominy, Sheridan's weary troopers fanned out through countryside more conducive to cavalry operations. After a minor skirmish near battle-scarred Mechanicsville, they camped for the night of the 12th near Walnut Grove Church, scene of a historic conference between Robert E. Lee and Stonewall Jackson twenty-three months before. Fitzhugh Lee had insufficient strength to interfere. He could do nothing more than hover to the north, shielding the roads to the Pamunkey River while generally annoying the Union column. During one of these brief flare-ups, a remarkable episode occurred. A British soldier named Charles Cavendish arrived at Fitz Lee's headquarters for volunteer duty as a staff officer. Within "a few moments after he had reported," Cavendish went into a charge with the 6th Virginia, sabered a Union trooper, and had a $3,000 horse killed under him. Such casual heroism, reminiscent of the old J. E. B. Stuart days, likely seemed out of place in the grim new world of 1864 cavalry operations.[72]

On May 14, the Union column arrived without further incident at Haxall's Landing on the James River. There it could communicate with Benjamin Butler's Army of the James and share its supplies in the comforting shadow of the navy's gunboats. The greatest noise associated with the end of the raid predictably came from Sheridan himself. Overwhelmed with his accomplishments, the general boasted to George Meade in a dispatch: "If I could be permitted to cross the James River and go southward I could almost ruin the Confederacy." As it was, he reported, "The country passed through by my command is entirely destitute; there is nothing for man or animals."[73]

Back around Richmond, the greatest harm from Sheridan's raid became evident by May 12. Robert E. Lee's Army of Northern Virginia fought for its life at the Bloody Angle on that day. The havoc wrought at Beaver Dam Station on May 9 affected Lee's men at this crucial time by interrupting their regular chain of supplies. Mangled railroad tracks could be restored; incinerated medical stores could not.[74]

Also on May 12, J. E. B. Stuart died. Following the hair-raising departure from the Yellow Tavern battlefield, his ambulance had carried Stuart into Richmond from the northeast through "thunder, lightning, and pouring torrents of rain," crossing the Chickahominy River twice to sidestep Federals. A friendly bed awaited the general at the home of his wife's brother-in-law on Grace Street. His last day of life is a well-documented, oft-told tale. The nature of Stuart's wound virtually ensured fatal consequences. With serious action flaring on all of Virginia's fronts there was little time for Richmond to grieve. Stuart's remains did draw a sizable crowd when they briefly lay in state on a billiard table, probably at the house where he died.

For the second consecutive May, Lee lost a key component of his army organization. "I have lost my best friend in the army," lamented Maj. Philip Powers of Stuart's staff. "I cannot realize that he is *gone*, that I am to see his gallant figure, nor hear his cheering voice no more. . . ." Former staff officer William W. Blackford echoed those observations after the war: "My own feelings were as if I had lost a brother." Aide-de-camp Theodore S. Garnett's "grief was as great as if my own father was dying." Poor Alexander R. Boteler, a veteran of the staffs of Turner Ashby, Stonewall Jackson, and Stuart, endured the

This wartime engraving of the battle of Yellow Tavern, with its emphasis on cavalrymen crashing together in mounted charges, conveyed a misleading impression of the fighting on May 11. *Frank Leslie's Illustrated Newspaper*, June 11, 1864

death of his third patron in two years. "When I announced his death to the couriers," wrote Boteler in his diary, "those brave men bowed their heads and wept like children. . . ."[75]

The temptation is nearly overwhelming to conclude that Stuart's death represented a benchmark in the declining fortunes of Confederate cavalry in Virginia, but the evidence does not support such a claim. The battle of Haw's Shop, only seventeen days after Yellow Tavern, was one of the most creditable performances in the history of the army's mounted arm. Indeed, the cavalry did well all through the rest of 1864 and into 1865, the only substantial blot on its record being the ragged performance of detachments sent to assist Jubal A. Early in the Shenandoah Valley. In Wade Hampton, General Lee found an acceptable substitute for Stuart. Perhaps the evolving nature of cavalry fighting in 1864 suited Hampton more than it would have Stuart, had the Virginian lived to experience it.

Sheridan's raid also demonstrated that cavalry warfare in central Virginia had reached a new tactical level. Noisy mounted charges no longer sufficed to drive an enemy. Most operations involved larger forces wielded in a mass, often dismounted. The few mounted charges launched during the six days of the May raid invariably failed to achieve decisive results and most often ran afoul of stubborn dismounted resistance.

The expanded role of horse artillery also deserves mention. John Pelham's innovative experiments with "flying artillery" in 1862 served as the prototype, but by May 1864 the guns had come to play a more substantial part in cavalry battles. Pelham and others had used their pieces mainly for harassment. Stuart and Sheridan employed more cannon in 1864 and used them to cement defensive positions or soften up enemy formations prior to attacking. They placed less emphasis on the mobility of horse artillery and assigned more importance to its firepower. This change was in keeping with the adjusted methods of dismounted fighting.

The new style of fighting predictably resulted in higher losses. Sheridan admitted to 580 casualties during the first four days of his expedition. As usual, Confederate casualties are more difficult to determine. Fitzhugh Lee's seven cavalry regiments suffered a total loss of at least 300. The Meadow Bridges fighting on May 12 injured at least 100 men of the infantry reinforcements brought up from Richmond. Casualties in Gordon's North Carolina brigade are not known. About 150 would be a reasonable estimate based on the intensity of the brigade's fighting on May 11–12. This suggests that the casualties for the two forces were almost the same during their dramatic duel.[76]

Confederate veterans always viewed their frantic dash toward Richmond, the two days of intense fighting that followed, and the subsequent death of their beloved leader with great nostalgia. Paul Means of the 5th North Carolina Cavalry pridefully wrote long after the war (when he should have known better): "If Gordon and his North Carolinians had not pressed him as they did, Sheridan would surely have gone into Richmond. . . ." Col. William H. H. Cowles of the 1st North Carolina echoed that conclusion, arguing that but for Gordon's skillful action on May 12 "we would have been overwhelmed . . . and Richmond would have fallen."[77]

In an 1888 ceremony, Stuart's old comrades gathered to dedicate a suitably impressive monument to the famous warrior. They stood on the spot where their chief had fallen twenty-four years earlier and engaged in sentimental reminiscences. They speculated on the potential fate of Richmond had they not overhauled Sheridan's column on May 11. Most of all, they congratulated

The earliest known photograph of the monument to James E. B. Stuart on the battlefield at Yellow Tavern. Looking northwest, it shows an early-twentieth-century automobile on the Telegraph Road in front of the steep embankment that complicated efforts to remove the wounded Stuart from the field.
The Library of Virginia

themselves on having done the best they could under unfavorable circumstances. To them, their duel with Philip Sheridan's cavalry juggernaut somehow marked a turning point in their memories of the war. Thinking of that second week in May 1864, they enjoyed a nostalgic taste of the glory days, of the era when Stuart and his carefree cavaliers routinely performed bold feats that captivated their country. It had been a fitting last ride for J. E. B. Stuart.[78]

NOTES

1. "Two Cavalry Chieftains," in *Southern Historical Society Papers*, ed. J. William Jones and others, 52 vols. (Richmond, Va.: Southern Historical Society, 1876–1959), 16:451 (hereafter cited as *SHSP*); U.S. War Department, *The War of the Rebellion: A Compilation of the Official Records of the Union and Confederate Armies*, 127 vols., index, and atlas (Washington, D.C.: GPO, 1880–1901), ser. 1, 36(1):776–77, 789–90 (hereafter cited as *OR*; all references are to ser. 1). Sheridan reportedly told Meade: "Damn Stuart, I can thrash hell out of him any day."

2. *OR* 36(1):789; 36(2):766.

3. Theodore F. Rodenbough, "Sheridan's Richmond Raid," in *Battles and Leaders of the Civil War*, ed. Robert Underwood Johnson and Clarence Clough Buel, 4 vols. (New York: Century, 1887–88), 4:189 (hereafter cited as *B&L*); J. H. Kidd, *Personal Recollections of a Cavalryman* (1908; reprint, Alexandria, Va.: Time-Life Books, 1983), 290; *OR* 36(1):789, 51(2):912.

4. H. B. McClellan, *I Rode with Jeb Stuart: The Life and Campaigns of Major General J. E. B. Stuart* (1958; reprint, New York: Kraus, 1969), 410; "Report of Major General Fitzhugh Lee of operations of the Cavalry Corps in Virginia, May 1–June 6, 1864," Brockenbrough Library, Museum of the Confederacy, Richmond, Va. (repository hereafter cited as MC). The traditional figure for Stuart's strength during this raid is about 4,000 men. His chief of staff speculated that the entire force totaled between 4,000 and 5,000 troopers. Fitzhugh Lee disputed that, reporting only "about 2,400" men in his two brigades. Only ten regiments accompanied Stuart, so if he really had 4,000 men in his column the regiments must have been unusually strong for that stage of the war, especially after the heavy fighting at Todd's Tavern earlier in the week.

5. W. W. Burgess of the 1st Virginia Cavalry wrote ("Soldier's Story of J. E. B. Stuart's Death," *SHSP* 36:122) that the Confederate cavalry was "well clothed, well fed and well mounted," and "was at that time in the best of condition." He is nearly alone in this claim.

6. "Report of Major General Fitzhugh Lee," MC.

7. Ibid.; William T. Daougherty, "Reminiscences of the Late War," typescript in author's possession; John B. Phillips, "A Desperate Charge," Richmond *Times-Dispatch*, July 26, 1903; Henry R. Pyne, *The History of the First New Jersey Cavalry* (Trenton, N.J.: J. A. Beecher, 1871), 239; "T. M. Fowler's Experiences in the Charge at Mitchell's Shop," MC; McClellan, *J. E. B. Stuart*, 410; "Guy," "Fitz Lee's Cavalry Division," Richmond *Examiner*, May 21, 1864. The rural intersection that witnessed this sharp fight is sometimes incorrectly called Mitchell's Store. It is shown as Mitchell's Shop on the 1864 Campbell map of Caroline County that is in the Jeremy Francis Gilmer Collection, Virginia Historical Society, Richmond (repository hereafter cited as VHS). The site should not be confused with the mid-twentieth-century crossroads known as Mitchell's Store, far to the southeast but still in Caroline County, at the intersection of routes 652 and 725 near Dawn community. For the later Mitchell's Store, see Ralph E. Fall, *People, Postoffices and Communities in Caroline County, Virginia, 1727–1969* (Roswell, Ga.: W. H. Wolfe Associates, 1989), 195.

8. Theodore Stanford Garnett, *Riding with Stuart: Reminiscences of an Aide-de-Camp*, ed. Robert J. Trout (Shippensburg, Pa.: White Mane, 1994), 62.

9. *OR* 36(1):790. For a brief history of Beaver Dam Station, see Arthur H. Taylor III, *Raid on Beaver Dam Depot, May 9th, 1864* (n.p.: n.p, 1989), 3.

10. Accounts of O. L. Munger and Bradford R. Wood in Eugene A. Nash, *A History of the 44th Regiment New York Volunteer Infantry* (Chicago: R. R. Donnelley & Sons, 1911), 256–57, 288.

11. J. B., "Interesting Account," Rutland (Vt.) *Herald*, June 1, 1864; *OR* 36(1):812; W. W. Goldsborough, *The Maryland Line in the Confederate Army* (Baltimore: Press of Guggenheimer, Weil & Co., 1900), 195–96; George W. Booth, *Personal Reminiscences of a Maryland Soldier in the War between the States* (Baltimore: Press of Fleet, McGinley & Co., 1898), 107. The Marylanders were not part of Stuart's force, but operated independently out of Hanover Junction.

12. Douglas Southall Freeman, *Lee's Lieutenants: A Study in Command*, 3 vols. (New York: Charles Scribner's Sons, 1942–44), 3:416. At this time, Stuart briefly spoke with his wife at the nearby home of Edmund Fontaine. The only primary source for this famous last meeting is A. R. Venable to Gov. Fitzhugh Lee, June 7, 1888, VHS.

13. Garnett, *Riding with Stuart*, 63; "Report of Major General Fitzhugh Lee," MC.

14. Kidd, *Personal Recollections*, 294; *History of the First Reg't Pennsylvania Reserve Cav-*

alry (Philadelphia: King & Baird, Printers, 1864), 93. For representative examples of the claims that Stuart saved Richmond, see note 75 below.

15. Garnett, *Riding with Stuart*, 63; B. J. Haden, *Reminiscences of J. E. B. Stuart's Cavalry* (Charlottesville, Va.: Progress Publishing Co., n.d.), 32; Theodore S. Garnett, "The Last Hours of General Stuart," Richmond *Times-Dispatch*, May 21, 1911. The last of these three accounts also appeared in *Confederate Veteran* 19 (December 1911):575. Haden commanded a detachment of prisoners on the night of May 10 and wrote that his collection actually increased overnight as Union stragglers fell in with the marching column of captives.

16. "Report of Major General Fitzhugh Lee," MC; *OR* 51(2):912; Bradley T. Johnson, "A Striking War Incident," *SHSP* 29:228; McClellan, *J. E. B. Stuart*, 411; Leiper Moore Robinson, "Civil War Experiences of Leiper Moore Robinson," 11, March 1896 typescript, VHS; Robert S. Hudgins, *Recollections of an Old Dominion Dragoon*, ed. Garland C. Hudgins and Richard B. Kleese (Orange, Va.: Publisher's Press, 1993), 89.

17. *OR* 36(1):857; "Report of Major General Fitzhugh Lee," MC; Johnson, "A Striking War Incident," *SHSP* 29:227–28. The vital Hanover Junction is now known as Doswell.

18. *OR* 36(1):857; Pyne, *1st New Jersey Cavalry*, 241; "Report of Major General Fitzhugh Lee," MC; "Guy," "Fitz Lee's Cavalry Division," Richmond *Examiner*, May 21, 1864; Joseph Watson Carson to sister, May 19, 1864, typescript in author's possession; Garnett, *Riding with Stuart*, 65.

19. Walter Clark, ed., *Histories of the Several Regiments and Battalions from North Carolina in the Great War, 1861–'65*, 5 vols. (Raleigh, N.C.: E. M. Uzzell, 1901), 3:596–97.

20. Daniel Branson Coltrane, *The Memoirs of . . .* (Raleigh, N.C.: Edwards & Broughton, 1956), 29; "Cavalry Fights around Richmond," Raleigh (N.C.) *Daily Confederate*, May 23, 1864.

21. Edward P. Tobie, *History of the First Maine Cavalry* (Boston: Press of Emery & Hughes, 1887), 261–62; N. D. Preston, *History of the Tenth Regiment of Cavalry* (New York: D. Appleton and Company, 1892), 177–78.

22. "Cavalry Fights around Richmond," Raleigh (N.C.) *Daily Confederate*, May 23, 1864; letter of John P. White in Preston, *History of the Tenth Regiment of Cavalry*, 178–79; D. B. R., "The Raid around Richmond," Richmond *Enquirer*, May 14, 1864; Clark, *Histories of the Several Regiments and Battalions from North Carolina*, 1:465.

23. Clark, *Histories of the Several Regiments and Battalions from North Carolina*, 1:465–66, 3:537; Preston, *History of the Tenth Regiment of Cavalry*, 179.

24. D. B. R., "The Raid around Richmond," Richmond *Enquirer*, May 14, 1864; "Report of Major General Fitzhugh Lee," MC; McClellan, *J. E. B. Stuart*, 411; A. R. Venable to Gov. Fitzhugh Lee, June 7, 1888, VHS. McClellan said that the column resumed the march at 1:00 A.M., but Fitzhugh Lee named 3:00 A.M. as his beginning time. The distance between campsites at Hanover Junction and Taylorsville likely accounts for this discrepancy.

25. *OR* 51(2):918; Johnson, "A Striking War Incident," *SHSP* 29:228–29; Tobie, *History of the First Maine Cavalry*, 266.

26. "The Famous Yellow Tavern," Richmond *Dispatch*, March 3, 1889; Cyrus McCormick, "How Gallant Stuart Met His Death," *Confederate Veteran* 39 (March 1931):98. A shorter, slightly different, unattributed version of McCormick's account appeared as "The Death of General J. E. B. Stuart" in *Southern Bivouac* 3 (September 1884):33–34. According to the *Dispatch*, a Mr. James R. Hawkins used to teach school at the tavern, "and some of the

old residents of the neighborhood will bear testimony to his strength of arm and toughness of his hickory wither." The tavern burned shortly after the war.

27. *OR* 51(2):918; McClellan, *J. E. B. Stuart*, 412.

28. Garnett, *Riding with Stuart*, 66; McCormick, "How Gallant Stuart Met His Death," 98. Garnett postulated with some merit that had Wickham's brigade been closer to Yellow Tavern when the action started, Stuart probably would have blocked the Brook Turnpike with his back to Richmond. With Wickham so distant, Stuart could not adopt that tactic.

29. "Report of Major General Fitzhugh Lee," MC; *OR* 36(2):993; Robinson, "Civil War Experience," 11, VHS. The precise deployment of Stuart's brigades in the battle's initial phase always has been confusing to historians. The difficulty was in reconciling the standard published accounts with the not unreasonable belief that Stuart arranged his force to block the direct path to Richmond. I am indebted to Frank O'Reilly of Guinea Station, Virginia, for pioneering this new interpretation, and to Wilderness/Spotsylvania historian Gordon C. Rhea for both providing me with obscure source material and agreeing with my views on how the battle developed.

30. *OR* 36(1):813; J. Lipscomb Johnson, *The University Memorial: Biographical Sketch of Alumni of the University of Virginia Who Fell in the Confederate War* (Baltimore: Turnbull Bros., 1871), 588–89.

31. J. L. Johnson, *University Memorial*, 588; Robert K. Krick, *Lee's Colonels: A Biographical Register of the Field Officers of the Army of Northern Virginia*, 4th ed. revised (Dayton, Ohio: Morningside, 1992), 299. For details on Pate's court martial, see *Proceedings of the general court martial, in the case of Lieut. Col. H. Clay Pate, 5th Va. Cavalry* (Richmond: n.p., 1863). A death notice in the Richmond *Examiner*, May 17, 1864, calls Pate an acting brigadier general, which is accurate for the May 11 fight but still leaves unsolved the mystery of why Lomax watched from afar.

32. J. L. Johnson, *University Memorial*, 589.

33. Garnett, *Riding with Stuart*, 67. McClellan, *J. E. B. Stuart*, 412, and A. R. Venable to Gov. Fitzhugh Lee, June 7, 1888, VHS, both confirm that Stuart was sincerely impressed by Pate's preliminary defense, and anxious to make up with his gallant colonel.

34. *OR* 36(1):835, 847; Robinson, "Civil War Experiences," 11–12, VHS; "Famous Fight at Yellow Tavern," Richmond *Times-Dispatch*, August 19, 1906; J. L. Johnson, *University Memorial*, 590; Newel Cheney, *History of the Ninth Regiment, New York Volunteer Cavalry* (Poland Center, N.Y.: Martin Merz & Son, 1901), 165. Robinson actually belonged to the 9th Virginia Cavalry, but had attached himself to the 5th during the raid. The buildings used by the 9th New York Cavalry probably belonged to local farmer John S. Mosby—no known relation to the famous Confederate guerrilla. Eight weeks after the battle, two of Mosby's young sons "found an unexploded shell near the Yellow Tavern battlefield and set about opening it. While they were working upon it, it, from some cause, exploded and killed them both" (Richmond *Sentinel*, July 6, 1864).

35. Cheney, *History of the Ninth Regiment*, 165; "Capture and Escape of S. H. Nowlin, Private Fifth Virginia Cavalry," *Southern Bivouac* 2 (October 1883):70; Robinson, "Civil War Experiences," 13–14, VHS.

36. P. J. White, "The Fifth Virginia Cavalry," *Confederate Veteran* 17 (February 1909):73; Robinson, "Civil War Experiences," 12, VHS. J. L. Johnson, *University Memorial*, 590, charges that both the 6th and 15th Virginia Cavalry regiments left the field before the 5th,

allowing that unit to be surrounded. There are too few detailed sources available to render judgment on that claim.

37. McClellan, *J. E. B. Stuart*, 412; Garnett, *Riding with Stuart*, 67–68; "Stuart's Last Dispatch," *SHSP* 9:138–39.

38. Goldsborough, *The Maryland Line in the Confederate Army*, 287; Frank Dorsey, "Battle of Yellow Tavern," Staunton (Va.) *Vindicator*, November 13, 1903; Garnett, "The Last Hours of General Stuart"; McClellan, *J. E. B. Stuart*, 413; *OR* 36(1):828, 879; Kidd, *Personal Recollections*, 303; Daougherty, "Reminiscences of the Late War." Daougherty was a member of the 3rd Virginia Cavalry and complained in his memoir that prematurely exploding Confederate shells irritated his regiment. They probably came from Breathed's battery, or perhaps from Hart's battery, a section of which participated in the battle. McClellan is alone in placing two of the Baltimore Light Artillery's guns actually in the bed of the Telegraph Road.

39. Kidd, *Personal Recollections*, 303–4; *OR* 36(1):817–18, 898.

40. W. W. Goldsborough, *The Maryland Line in the Confederate States Army* (Baltimore: Kelly, Piet & Company, 1869), 319–21; George B. Sanford, *Fighting Rebels and Redskins: Experiences in Army Life of Colonel George B. Sanford, 1861–1892*, ed. E. R. Hagemann (Norman: University of Oklahoma Press, 1969), 233. The Goldsborough book is slightly different in content than his other book, cited elsewhere in this essay.

41. Kidd, *Personal Recollections*, 303–4; J. B., "Interesting Account," Rutland (Vt.) *Herald*, June 1, 1864; *OR* 36(1):818; William B. Poindexter, "A Midnight Charge," Richmond *Times-Dispatch*, May 15, 1904; Joseph Watson Carson to sister. At this point in the events of May 11, an accurate reconstruction of Confederate movements and positions becomes especially difficult. The sequence of events given here represents the author's best effort at sorting out conflicting accounts. An example of this is the 1st Virginia Cavalry, whose veterans (mostly in their dotage) left numerous memoirs of Yellow Tavern. Although nearly all professed to have been near Stuart at the moment of his wounding, they argued heatedly among themselves as to whether the bulk of their regiment was even engaged that day.

42. Goldsborough, *The Maryland Line in the Confederate States Army*, 319–20; *OR* 36(1):813.

43. Thomas D. Gold, *History of Clarke County, Virginia* (Berryville, Va.: Printed by C. R. Hughes, ca. 1914), 284–85; Garnett, *Riding with Stuart*, 70; "Report of Major General Fitzhugh Lee," MC; Joseph Watson Carson to sister; McCormick, "How Gallant Stuart Met His Death," 99; "Famous Fight at Yellow Tavern," Richmond *Times-Dispatch*, August 19, 1906; B. J. Haden, "Stuart's Last Battle," Richmond *Times-Dispatch*, March 14, 1909; Frank Dorsey, "Fatal Shot of 'Jeb' Stuart," *Confederate Veteran* 11 (August 1903):347; N. W. Harris in Frank Dorsey, "General J. E. B. Stuart's Last Battle," *Confederate Veteran* 17 (February 1909):76.

44. "Death of Gen. J. E. B. Stuart," Richmond *Dispatch*, May 13, 1864; T. J. Watson [Waters], "Was with 'Jeb' Stuart When He Was Shot," *Confederate Veteran* 11 (December 1903):553; J. R. Oliver, "J. E. B. Stuart's Fate at Yellow Tavern," *Confederate Veteran* 19 (November 1911):531; Haden, "Stuart's Last Battle"; Hudgins, *Recollections of an Old Dominion Dragoon*, 89; J. R. Gibbons, "Concerning the Death of Gen. J. E. B. Stuart," *Confederate Veteran* 20 (March 1912):120; B. J. Haden, "Stuart's Death Wound," *Confederate Veteran* 22 (August 1914):352. Haden (in the first of the two sources cited) wrote of the "denseness" of the pines where Stuart was shot. He also argued "there is not a man living, or one that has ever lived who could tell who shot General Stuart." Traditionally, Pvt. John Huff of Company E, 5th Michigan Cavalry has been identified as the man who shot Stuart. As a former

member of Berdan's Sharpshooters, Huff may well have been the most accurate marksman on the field that day. However, there are several disturbing discrepancies in this identification. Huff's regiment likely fought a little farther west than the Telegraph Road. More significant, nearly all Confederate sources (with no agenda and nothing at stake in this instance) noted that Stuart was shot by a man who had been unhorsed and who was making a fighting withdrawal with others in a similar plight. The 5th Michigan fought dismounted on May 11. If the Confederate accounts are correct, it would seem more likely that the shooter came from either the 1st or 7th Michigan, as they both fought mounted that day, and were in the Telegraph Road. Finally, and most damning, the only original claim for Huff came from his colonel, Russell A. Alger (OR 36[1]:828). Alger gave an elaborate description of the circumstances that unfortunately bears almost no resemblance to the known facts. I see absolutely no reason to accept the Huff identification, and consider it very likely that whoever shot Stuart did so unwittingly. On the other hand, Stuart reportedly told his doctor that the Yankees, "evidently recognizing his well-known person," purposely shot at him. The doctor's account reported that Stuart returned this fire with all six rounds from his revolver before falling wounded (Dr. Charles Brewer in Richmond Examiner, May 14, 1864; reprinted in SHSP 7:107–10).

45. Krick, Lee's Colonels, 121; Frederick L. Pitts in Winfield Peters, "Stuart's Death, How It Occurred," Richmond Times-Dispatch, September 22, 1907; Frank Dorsey, "Gen. J. E. B. Stuart's Last Battle," Confederate Veteran 17 (February 1909):76; Burgess, "Soldier's Story of J. E. B. Stuart's Death," SHSP 36:123; McClellan, J. E. B. Stuart, 414; "George M. Slater," Confederate Veteran 31 (May 1923):188. Other possible participants in the rescue include Oliver, Waters, Slater, and Holland, all of Company K, 1st Virginia. Capt. Gus Dorsey is on record saying that Stuart's last battlefield words were "Dorsey, leave me here and save your men" ("Fatal Wounding of General J. E. B. Stuart," SHSP 30:237, and "Lieut. Col. G. W. Dorsey," Confederate Veteran 19 [November 1911]:538).

46. Krick, Lee's Colonels, 84; Daougherty, "Reminiscences of the Late War"; "Report of Major General Fitzhugh Lee," MC; Fitz Lee, "Speech of General Fitz. Lee, at A.N.V. Banquet, October 28th, 1875," SHSP 1:102; John Gill, Reminiscences of Four Years as a Private Soldier in the Confederate Army (Baltimore: Sun Printing Office, 1904), 96; McCormick, "How Gallant Stuart Met His Death," 99; Watson [Waters], "Was with 'Jeb' Stuart When He Was Shot," 553; "Stuart's Last Battle," Richmond Times-Dispatch, November 5, 1911. A slightly variant version of Stuart's words to Fitz Lee appears in "Rosencrantz," "How Stuart Fell," Richmond Times-Dispatch, June 12, 1904.

47. McClellan, J. E. B. Stuart, 415; McCormick, "How Gallant Stuart Met His Death," 100; Gill, Reminiscences of Four Years, 97; Pitts in Winfield Peters, "Stuart's Death, How It Occurred"; Watson [Waters], "Was with 'Jeb' Stuart When He Was Shot," 553; A. R. Venable to Gov. Fitzhugh Lee, June 7, 1888, VHS. McCormick told the odd story of how Stuart's ambulance nearly tipped over when negotiating the steep bank of the Telegraph Road. Venable reported having a conversation with Stuart nearly identical to the one Hullihen had.

48. McClellan, J. E. B. Stuart, 415; A. R. Venable to Gov. Fitzhugh Lee, June 7, 1888, VHS. Venable used slightly different words in his account.

49. OR 36(1):818; Goldsborough, The Maryland Line in the Confederate States Army, 320; Daougherty, "Reminiscences of the Late War"; "Report of Major General Fitzhugh Lee," MC; William B. Poindexter, "A Midnight Charge," SHSP 32:121.

50. Preston, History of the Tenth Regiment of Cavalry, 181; "Barringer's N.C. Brigade of

Cavalry," Raleigh (N.C.) *Daily Confederate*, February 22, 1865; Clark, *Histories of Several Regiments and Battalions from North Carolina* 2:100–101, 3:601; "Cavalry Fights around Richmond," Raleigh (N.C.) *Daily Confederate*, May 23, 1864; D. B. R., "The Raid around Richmond," Richmond *Enquirer*, May 14, 1864; "The Raiders That Came to Richmond," Richmond *Times-Dispatch*, May 17, 1864. The author of this last source documented in great detail the damage suffered by the many families in Sheridan's path between Goodall's (where they "stole all Dr. Goodall's clothes save those on his person") and Yellow Tavern. The letter also reported—with a thin veneer of delicacy—on the rape of a servant at Mrs. Allen's house. This crime is not confirmed anywhere else and may be untrue, but one can imagine its reception by an already enraged readership.

51. *OR* 36(1):791.

52. *OR* 36(1):791, 834–35; Philip H. Sheridan quoted in New Orleans *Picayune*, August 12, 1888, and reproduced in *SHSP* 16:452. This second-hand account of Sheridan's views reeks of exaggeration under normal circumstances, but his character and record make it seem more plausible than otherwise.

53. Sanford, *Fighting Rebels and Redskins*, 234–35. Modern Azalea Avenue in Richmond's outskirts approximates the course of the military road used by Sheridan. Gold, *History of Clarke County*, 286, called this the Lafayette Road, an appellation not found anywhere else. The person responsible for planting the mines remains unidentified. Jefferson Davis had proscribed their use two springs earlier on the lower peninsula.

54. S. H. Nowlin, "Capture and Escape," *Southern Bivouac* 2 (October 1883):70; *OR* 36(1):791; Pyne, *History of the First New Jersey Cavalry*, 242. For an outstanding description of the episode with the land mines, see Charles E. Phelps, "Personal Recollections of the Wilderness Campaign," Maryland Historical Society, Baltimore (repository hereafter cited as MHS). I thank Gordon C. Rhea for unearthing and sharing this excellent memoir.

55. Letter of Capt. Field to Theo F. Rodenbough in "Sheridan's Richmond Raid," *B&L* 4:191.

56. *OR* 36(1):898; J. B., "Interesting Account," Rutland (Vt.) *Herald*, June 1, 1864.

57. *OR* 36(1):791; Isaac Dunkelberger Reminiscence, Michael Winey Collection, United States Army Military History Institute, Carlisle Barracks, Pa. (repository hereafter cited as USAMHI); Sanford, *Fighting Rebels and Redskins*, 235. Meadow Bridges is most famous as the spot where Robert E. Lee launched his first operation as commander of the Army of Northern Virginia on June 26, 1862.

58. Kidd, *Personal Recollections*, 310; Sanford, *Fighting Rebels and Redskins*, 236; J. R. Bowen, *Regimental History of the First New York Dragoons* (published by the author, 1900), 163.

59. *OR* 36(1):819; R. H. Peck, *Reminiscences of a Confederate Soldier* (Fincastle, Va.: n.p., 1913), 47; Isaac Dunkelberger Reminiscence, Michael Winey Collection, USAMHI; Pyne, *History of the First New Jersey Cavalry*, 243; John J. Woodall Diary, May 12, 1864, typescript at Fredericksburg and Spotsylvania National Military Park Library, Fredericksburg, Va. (repository hereafter cited as FSNMP). The 2nd Virginia Cavalry occupied entrenchments built that morning, but others apparently fought on grass-covered mounds left from the 1862 battles (Phelps, "Personal Recollections," 144, MHS).

60. "The Second Virginia Cavalry in the Late Fights," Richmond *Sentinel*, May 21, 1864; "4th Virginia Cavalry," Richmond *Sentinel*, May 14, 1864; "The Departure of the Raiders

from around Richmond," Richmond *Dispatch*, May 14, 1864; Horatio Nelson, *If I am killed on this trip, I want my horse kept for my brother*, ed. Harold Howard (Manassas, Va.: Manassas Chapter, United Daughters of the Confederacy, 1980), 12; James Keith to mother, May 19, 1864, Keith Family Papers, section 24, VHS; Phelps, "Personal Recollections," 143–44, MHS; Bowen, *Regimental History of the First New York Dragoons*, 163; Theo. F. Rodenbough, *From Everglades to Canon with the Second Dragoons* (New York: Van Nostrand, 1875), 29; Betty Winston to cousin, May 13, 1864, Ball Family Papers, VHS. The Ball Family Papers also contain a lock of Colonel Randolph's hair cut from his head within hours of the fight.

61. *OR* 51(1):250. The casualties were Major Graves (2nd), Colonel Owen (3rd), Major Wooldridge and Lieutenant Colonel Randolph (4th), Colonel Pate (5th), and Colonel Collins (15th). For biographical details on all these officers, see Krick, *Lee's Colonels*.

62. John H. Reagan, *Memoirs, with Special Reference to Secession and the Civil War* (1906; reprint, Austin, Tex.: Pemberton Press, 1968), 65.

63. Richmond *Sentinel*, May 12, 1864; Lewellyn A. Shaver, *A History of the Sixtieth Alabama Regiment* (Montgomery: Barrett & Brown, 1867), 48; William J. Mims to wife, May 22, 1864, Birmingham Public Library, Birmingham, Ala. (repository hereafter cited as BPL).

64. Reagan, *Memoirs*, 185; *OR* 36(1):887; Richmond *Sentinel*, May 12, 1864; William J. Mims to wife, May 22, 1864, BPL; John F. Davenport to wife, May 27, 1864, typescript at Chickamauga-Chattanooga National Military Park Library, Ft. Oglethorpe, Ga.

65. *OR* 36(1):854; Clark, *Histories of the Several Regiments and Battalions from North Carolina*, 3:602.

66. E. B. Montague, "The Raid around Richmond," Richmond *Enquirer*, May 17, 1864; Clark, *Histories of the Several Regiments and Battalions from North Carolina*, 3:602; "More of Our Casualties," Richmond *Examiner*, May 14, 1864. The only Confederate battery definitely known to have participated is the Caroline Artillery (part of Lt. Col. Charles E. Lightfoot's battalion of reserve artillery). It may have been the battery that came out to assist Gordon that morning.

67. Clark, *Histories of the Several Regiments and Battalions from North Carolina*, 3:602–3; Montague, "The Raid around Richmond"; "Movements during Yesterday," Richmond *Dispatch*, May 13, 1864; "The Losses in the City Battalion," Richmond *Dispatch*, May 14, 1864; J. E. Robertson letter, Richmond *Enquirer*, May 20, 1864; Coltrane, *Memoirs*, 30; Elizabeth Maxwell (Alsop) Wynne Diary, May 20, 1864, VHS. Gordon died of his wounds on May 18 at General Hospital #4. Richmond diarist Wynne mourned his death, calling him "a gallant officer, but I fear, a worldly man." She recorded in her diary that moments before Gordon died he asked a matron "what would my poor Mother say, if she knew I was suffering here?" A casualty list published in the Richmond *Dispatch*, May 13, 1864, suggests that men from Birkett D. Fry's Virginia brigade may have been involved in the Brook Turnpike fighting, too.

68. Shaver, *A History of the Sixtieth Alabama Regiment*, 50; Reagan, *Memoirs*, 184.

69. Phelps, "Personal Recollections," 133, 140, MHS.

70. "The Second Virginia Cavalry in the Late Fights," Richmond *Sentinel*, May 21, 1864; "Report of Major General Fitzhugh Lee," MC; "Barringer's N.C. Brigade of Cavalry," Raleigh (N.C.) *Daily Confederate*, February 22, 1865; "The War News," Richmond *Examiner*, May 14, 1864.

71. Eppa Hunton, *Autobiography* (Richmond: William Byrd Press, 1933), 109. Hunton

makes a fanciful claim that he nearly "captured the whole party," before a bad order from Braxton Bragg saved Sheridan's column from disaster.

72. OR 36(1):791–92; Francis W. Dawson, *Reminiscences of Confederate Service* (1882; reprint, Baton Rouge: Louisiana State University Press, 1985), 134–35; "Report of Major General Fitzhugh Lee," MC; Charles Cavendish Compiled Service Record, M258, microfilm roll 104, National Archives, Washington, D.C. Cavendish's European service was with the 18th Hussars.

73. OR 36(1):778.

74. OR 51(2):918.

75. Garnett, *Riding with Stuart*, 71–72; Philip H. Powers to wife, May 14, 1864, typescript at FSNMP; Alexander R. Boteler Diary, May 13, 1864, William E. Brooks Collection, Perkins Library, Duke University, Durham, N.C.; W. W. Blackford, *War Years with Jeb Stuart* (New York: Charles Scribner's Sons, 1945), 253, 260. Blackford erected a wooden monument to Stuart at Yellow Tavern in the summer of 1864, a memorial that long ago disappeared and is otherwise undocumented. For an account of Stuart's corpse being placed on view in Richmond, see Robert H. Patton, *The Pattons: A Personal History of an American Family* (New York: Crown Publishers, 1994), 56.

76. OR 36(1):184–85. Confederate casualty totals have been cobbled together from various sources. Robert J. Driver, *The 1st Virginia Cavalry* (Lynchburg, Va.: H. E. Howard, 1991), 129, found 168 total casualties in the unit for May. Robert J. Driver, *The 2nd Virginia Cavalry* (Lynchburg, Va.: H. E. Howard, 1995), 179, is more specific for that regiment, listing 44 total casualties between May 9 and 12. Thomas P. Nanzig, *The 3rd Virginia Cavalry* (Lynchburg, Va.: H. E. Howard, 1989), 50, 85, reports 30 casualties during the raid. See also Richmond *Examiner*, May 17, 1864, for 3rd Virginia Cavalry casualties. Losses in the 4th Virginia Cavalry are confusing. The Richmond *Sentinel*, May 14, 1864, tentatively placed the number at 70 men, but the Richmond *Examiner*, May 21, 1864, said 160 total in the 4th Cavalry, all incurred during May 8–13. The 5th Virginia Cavalry lost at least 89 men during the raid, all but three of them in the Telegraph Road disaster of May 11 (Robert J. Driver to author, July 6, 1996). In drastic contrast, one source (J. L. Johnson, *University Memorial*, 590) claimed that the 5th lost 230 of its 350 men engaged on May 11. The 6th Virginia Cavalry reported 107 casualties during May 4–13 (Richmond *Examiner*, May 27, 1864). The 15th Virginia Cavalry is known to have had 3 killed, 17 wounded, and 30 missing at Yellow Tavern (John Fortier, *The 15th Virginia Cavalry* [Lynchburg, Va.: H. E. Howard, 1993], 70). Another source (Richmond *Enquirer*, May 18, 1864) reported 103 casualties out of 200 men engaged between May 6 and 13. Other known Confederate losses are 8 wounded in the 60th Alabama (Shaver, *A History of the Sixtieth Alabama Regiment*, 50); "nearly one-third" of the men in the four companies of the 32nd Virginia Infantry engaged on May 12 (Richmond *Enquirer*, May 17, 1864); and 27 total in the 25th Virginia Battalion's May 12 fight against Gregg's division (Richmond *Dispatch*, May 14, 1864).

77. Clark, *Histories of the Several Regiments and Battalions from North Carolina*, 3:600; W. H. H. Cowles, *The Life and Services of Gen'l James B. Gordon* (Raleigh, N.C.: Edwards, Broughton & Co., 1887), 10.

78. The Confederate Memorial Literary Society, concerned that the Stuart monument was not receiving its proper attention, lobbied in 1922 to have the state highway routed by it. This pointedly illustrates the evolving nature of the preservation agenda. Only seventy-

four years later, the Yellow Tavern battlefield is irrevocably ruined. Two interstate highways bisect the ground, and at the time of this writing the local county (already well known for its indifference toward Civil War sites within its boundaries) is casually developing the last few unturned spadesfull of battlefield soil at Yellow Tavern. See "Confederate Women Fight for Road Route," Richmond *Times-Dispatch*, February 23, 1922.

A Hard Road to Travel

The Impact of Continuous Operations on the Army of the Potomac and the Army of Northern Virginia in May 1864

Many years after the war, a Union veteran from Maine wrote with conviction: "I never expect to be fully believed when I tell what I saw of the horrors of Spottsylvania, because I should be loth to believe it myself, were the case reversed." This emotional assessment cannot be attributed solely to postwar exaggeration. Late in May 1864, after nearly a full month of constant marching, digging, and fighting, Pvt. Joseph Graham of the veteran 140th Pennsylvania had expressed similar sentiments to his family: "We never knew what war was till this spring."[1]

What had transpired in just a few short weeks to inspire these pointed observations from veteran soldiers? Three years of hard war long since had erased any romantic sentimentality about combat. But what did the Army of Northern Virginia and the Army of the Potomac face in May 1864 that the Seven Days, Antietam, and Gettysburg had not prepared them to endure? Simply stated, when they attempted to describe the fighting at the Wilderness and especially Spotsylvania, soldiers set apart May 1864 from all previous campaigns for the seemingly endless quality of its fighting, for its constant reminders of the nearness and randomness of death, and for its relentless physical and emotional stress. Most of the war's great battles to this point had lasted no more than a few days, but in this new kind of constant campaigning that required more than bravery alone, soldiers in both armies needed to develop a hardiness of spirit and endurance to persevere for their respective causes. Nothing in their training or experience readied them for this.

The concept of "military effectiveness" provides some interesting insights into the performances of the Army of Northern Virginia and the Army of the Potomac during this brutal month. An effective army under sound leadership makes maximum use of available political, economic, and military resources, and converts them to fighting power capable of accomplishing its missions. Such key factors as tactical doctrine, the degree to which that doctrine supports strategic goals, stability in force structure and leadership, troop morale, unit cohesion on all levels, organizational flexibility to exploit opportunities and opponent weaknesses, and logistical support all help measure an army's military effectiveness.[2] Applying these concepts to the May 1864 operations of Robert E. Lee's and U. S. Grant's commands, armies so apparently mismatched in size and armament, offers some different perspectives on two of the most famous forces in American military history.

For the Army of Northern Virginia, the spring campaign opened without much fanfare. Under familiar and experienced senior commanders in whom they had great faith, southern soldiers worried mostly about the same things that had concerned them since the war's earliest days. The ranks needed to be filled. In mid-April, on the eve of active operations, Lee counted only 64,000 men under arms ready for duty. Personnel policy provides one marker for evaluating stability in force structure, and the Confederate Congress had just made good on its promise to help alleviate Lee's concerns on this issue. New laws now extended as "voluntary reenlistments" the service of all soldiers already under arms. More new regulations expanded the draft age, terminated the use of substitutes, and eliminated many exemptions from conscription.

All of Richmond's efforts to field and sustain an effective force would be rendered moot, however, if Lee continued to rely on his offensive — and expensive — operational philosophy. Lee's fighting spirit unquestionably had brought many victories, but now, with the pool of potential recruits growing increasingly more shallow, he had to give greater consideration to preserving his fighting power while accomplishing his primary strategic mission in Virginia: the protection of the Confederate capital. That mission compelled him to consider ways to employ his forces defensively when promising offensive opportunities did not appear, even if he felt uncomfortable with the notion intellectually or professionally. His ability to adapt to this reality, translate it into orders and actions on the battlefield as he did at Spotsylvania, and maintain the soldiers' faith in his leadership would provide yet more evidence of the Army of Northern Virginia's military effectiveness before May 1864 ended.[3]

Lee had to find the best way to sustain the kind of fighting spirit that prompted one of his men to write on the eve of the campaign, "[W]e who have suffered most . . . fighting & bleeding on the battle fields, who have suffered and withstood cheerfully the privations of hard marches in all sorts of weather, of cold & short rations & of being kept so long away from home & friends, are not ready nor willing to give up, in short, not whipped."[4]

Numbers alone tell little about military effectiveness. How well, for instance, could the Army of Northern Virginia's supply system meet the soldiers' basic needs? Although the troops could obtain arms and ammunition in acceptable if not plentiful quantities, concerns about quality seemed to be on the rise. Meeting other basic needs proved to be more troublesome, and these logistical concerns easily could have an adverse impact on the battlefield.

By May 1864, Lee's veterans had grown accustomed to doing much with little, but on the eve of another season of active campaigning their hunger pangs simply could not be quieted. Lee himself reported to the secretary of war in January that "Short rations are having a bad effect upon the men, both morally and physically." If conditions did not improve, stated Lee ominously, "I fear the army cannot be kept effective, and probably cannot be kept together." By April, the situation had not improved. A staff officer in Lt. Gen. Richard S. Ewell's Second Corps reported that the "sallow complexions and general appearance of the men indicated that they were insufficiently fed." Military effectiveness, not humanitarianism, drove him to demand an increase in the daily ration: "A soldier fighting for the best of causes should have enough to eat . . . he may put up with frequent irregularities, but if his ration be systematically insufficient for his appetite, his spirits and endurance must surely fail or be greatly impaired."[5] If this officer could have foreseen the continuous operations of May 1864, he might have pressed his case much harder.

Despite their empty stomachs, the spirits of Lee's soldiers remained high that spring. Good morale reflects solid bonds of unit cohesion, a key measure of military effectiveness. The strength of those bonds grows in value during sustained operations, when personal initiative, the ability to absorb and rebound from losses, the will to fight on amid adverse conditions, and the capacity to respond quickly to sudden changes of all kinds become increasingly important.[6] Lee's men still believed in themselves, their leaders, and their cause. As a North Carolina colonel wrote, "Our thinned ranks speak more eloquently than words of what we have suffered and endured," nonetheless "the same spirit that controlled our actions in the beginning of this Struggle *still animates us*."[7]

The same kind of optimism flowed down through the ranks. Lt. John Runzie of the 4th Alabama wrote a friend on May 1 that "the whole command is in fine health & excelent spireits & Ready for the coming strugle perfectly confident of whipping Grant, & that badly — we all believe that this is the last year of the war." In the 45th Georgia, Sgt. Marion Hill Fitzpatrick prepared once more to "buckle on my armour, seize my Enfield, and put forth with energy and devotion to my bleeding country." These men knew war firsthand. Bullets and disease had felled many of their friends in the past three years. Many hoped that General Lee would prevent crippling losses they could no longer afford, but they kept faith with him, come what may. As a Virginia sergeant wrote, "I cannot say with truth that [we] desire a fight but all express a determination to do their utmost when it does come and have confidence in the protection of Providence, leader, and selves."[8]

Naturally, a few discordant notes sounded. New personnel policies had kept some soldiers, including an obviously unhappy North Carolina Sgt. Christopher Hackett, in the ranks unwillingly. "I dont consider myself any deeper inn," he wrote after the new laws passed, and he stated his clear intention to desert: "I intend to get out of this war in some way and there is but the one way that one can make a sure escape." He was captured at Spotsylvania before he made good his threat, but some of his brothers-in-arms made successful departures. In late April, a Union soldier in the 1st Delaware saw southern deserters "a coming over very fast forc they say that they Dread this campaign." His explanation for the influx spoke volumes about the southerners' primary concern about the upcoming campaign: "[T]hey say they will fight behind Breast Works But they will not fight out in the open field for they say we have to Many Men for them."[9]

But those thousands who stayed in the ranks provided Robert E. Lee with a reliable core of veterans. Most seemed to share the sentiments of a Virginian who claimed that "All seem to be in tolerably good spirits and to repose the utmost confidence in Gen. Lee." The new Union commander did not impress this Confederate, nor many of his comrades. U. S. Grant "will be sorry enough to have been put in command where Genl. Lee can get hold of him." Short on numbers, low on food, but high in spirit, the Army of Northern Virginia prepared to face its foe.[10]

On the face of things, the soldiers of the Army of the Potomac shared few of their southern counterparts' concerns. They numbered nearly 125,000 strong, twice the strength of their opponent. Union quartermasters easily met all of the soldiers' basic needs for equipment and supplies. The medical director enforced strict obedience to regulations about "The importance of a proper diet during winter, preparatory of troops for campaign, lifting them above the influence of ordinary depressents (of fatigue, privations, and exposure,) preserving them vigorous" for the spring.[11] In many fundamental ways, the Union army routinely lived a camp life that many Confederates would have considered luxurious.

But not all measures of military effectiveness in the Army of the Potomac registered on the positive side of the scale. In March 1864, its soldiers paraded for yet another new commanding officer, Lt. Gen. U. S. Grant. Like their southern opponents, they did not yet know what to make of this new man from the West. They certainly felt no great trust in him, and they did not know what his plans for them would be. Grant intrigued more than he inspired. After getting his first glimpse of his new general, an artillery officer described him as "stumpy, unmilitary, slouchy, and Western-looking; very ordinary, in fact." A corporal saw only a little more: "Grant if not a good looking officer is a determined looking man."[12] In short, in his soldiers' eyes, he was no Robert E. Lee.

Grant's arrival heralded other disquieting changes as well. In March, the morale of a sizable chunk of the army's veterans absorbed a deep blow when orders consolidated the five corps of the Army of the Potomac into just three. The old First Corps had never made good its severe Gettysburg losses, and its regiments found themselves reassigned to the Fifth Corps. Hardy First Corps veterans had cried when their displaced commander assured them, "Though the corps has lost its distinctive name, history will not be silent upon the magnitude of its services." Two divisions of the Third Corps — veterans of Yorktown and Williamsburg — now became part of Maj. Gen. Winfield S. Hancock's Second Corps. "It was a heavy blow to veterans of the old 3rd Corps to sink their identity into another body," wrote one soldier, but at least he thought the change offered better promise than continuing to serve under their most recent commander, Maj. Gen. William H. "Old Blinky" French, a notorious drunkard, under whom "the corps had a more than even chance of losing whatever reputation it has."[13] Another Third Corps division joined the Sixth Corps. The veterans of disbanded units retained with permission their old corps badges, and several familiar senior officers came to their new commands with them, but this did little to soften the blow to unit pride. Unit cohesion is the glue of armies, and few men believed that these shotgun marriages would forge tight bonds like those that bound the old corps.

Strong ties on the brigade, regimental, and company level might have helped to cushion the blow of reorganization at higher echelons. After all, Civil War soldiers viewed their regiments and companies not merely as military organizations but as links to family, friends, and home. Although legislative enactments had just reinforced those bonds — willingly or not — in Lee's army, great numbers in Grant's force saw their closest bonds breaking.

The problem took several forms. Many of the army's most experienced regiments, first enlisted for three years in the spring of 1861 after Fort Sumter, approached their discharge dates. Some famous units, such as the old 1st Minnesota Infantry, already had left the service by May 1, 1864.[14] Army leaders tried a number of schemes to retain as many of these experienced soldiers as they could. Offers of thirty-day furloughs and appeals to pride and patriotism convinced many individual soldiers to sign up again. If enough soldiers in a tested regiment reenlisted, the War Department promised to keep the unit's name and number on the army's active roll with the new official designation "Veteran Volunteers." A number of blooded regiments did find sufficient numbers to "veteranize" even before the spring campaign opened.

Many regiments originally organized in the spring of 1861 could not muster sufficient numbers to merit this special status. On the eve of active operations, the Army of the Potomac thus included a significant portion of its strength — several dozen regiments — slated for discharge within sixty days. As the start of the spring campaign neared, men in these units debated with great interest the precise date that would deliver them home safely. When the War Department ordered in April that all regiments would stay in line until the three-year anniversary of their muster into *federal* service — a June date for most units — six veterans of the 6th Pennsylvania Reserves protested that they would do no service beyond the April date of their *state* muster. Capt. Benjamin Ashenfelter dutifully took the men to the guard house, but, as he confided to a friend, "I don't think they will be punished very severe as many think their claim is just."[15] Would the presence in the ranks of such significant numbers of men so close to discharge affect the Union army's effectiveness on the battlefield in May 1864?

The Union's manpower problem also wore other faces. Even a successfully veteranized regiment likely contained a sizable number of soldiers who chose not to reenlist and just waited for their personal discharge dates. Would the presence of great numbers of such men in ranks affect how well a unit fought in battle? In yet another twist, every old regiment about to be discharged contained many recruits and draftees who had not yet completed the full term of service for which they had enlisted. The soldiers of the 2nd Vermont, wrote Pvt. Wilbur Fisk, fell into five distinct classes: the initial volunteers of 1861; new recruits in the spring of 1862; additional men from Lincoln's call for 300,000 more volunteers in the late summer of 1862; drafted men and substitutes of late 1863; and newly arrived recruits for the 1864 campaign.[16] All officially belonged to the 2nd Vermont Infantry, but only the 1861 enlistees could be legally discharged if the regiment went home in 1864. The rest would have to stay in the army, most likely transferred to a different regiment to serve with strangers. How might this affect the soldiers and their regiments when called upon in a tight situation on the field of battle?

With the impending departure of so many veteran units, the War Department had approved the raising of new regiments. Some, such as the 57th

Massachusetts, included among its 1,000 men 245 with previous service who claimed the right to call themselves Veteran Volunteers; however, the men in the field did not accept them as such. Capt. Alex Acheson of the 140th Pennsylvania watched as one of these new regiments established its camp in the mud and predicted rightly that their greenness would give them "a full hospital list in a week or two." Officers of these untested units, even those accorded the label of Veteran Volunteers, knew they were not ready for active duty. As one lamented, "give me twenty days and I could make a splendid regiment of this, but man proposes and Grant disposes."[17] Whereas nearly all of Lee's regiments had been blooded on many previous battlefields, Grant's army contained more than a few units yet to prove their battle-worthiness.

Unit cohesion — along with commitment to and confidence in one's cause, comrades, and leaders — all serve as key components in soldier morale and military effectiveness. In the "soldier's battles" of May 1864, these bonds did not seem all that strong in Grant's army. Certainly a spirit of optimism blossomed in Union camps that spring, but northern men seemed more hopeful than confident of victory. "I am in hopes this war may soon be over and I think it will," wrote James L. Rea of the 57th New York at the campaign's start, "but a great many lives have yet to be sacrificed I fear before such will be the case." Questions remained about Grant. Gettysburg had not erased veterans' memories of many previous defeats, and as the army of May 1864 began to look less and less like the victors of July 1863, a pessimistic Pvt. Gideon Mellin of the 93rd Pennsylvania wrote home with some degree of truth, "where we will go I can't tell, but I suppose to some slaughter shop."[18]

Two days of bloody fighting in the Wilderness on May 5–6 merely served as a prelude to greater bloodletting. The death and destruction in the woods appalled everyone, but both armies claimed victory and pressed on to Spotsylvania. Although they could not guess what lay ahead, some soldiers very quickly sensed a change in standard practice. The day of May 7, wrote a New Jersey veteran, "was to behold the inauguration of a new procedure — that of advance after terrible loss." The well-documented initial enthusiasm in Union ranks when Grant turned south to Spotsylvania rather than retreat on Washington quickly gave way to grimness and griping. That very day, Captain Acheson already had begun to complain that the army's supply trains could not keep up with the troops. "We have been on the go for four days," and "I haven't eaten enough to keep a sick kitten alive." He got by "on excitement, coffee, and tobacco."[19] After a winter of regular resupply and little exercise, the Union army felt the strain of active operations after just a few days. How would it perform over the two-week running firefights that lay ahead of them at Spotsylvania?

Both immediately and in later years, Spotsylvania impressed lasting memories, even scars, on the minds of survivors on both sides. They sensed that in these two weeks the war changed somehow, and even worse, that they had paid a high price for those changes. Spotsylvania forced even the toughest veteran to discard many old notions as romantic or outdated. Men on both sides believed that the period May 7–20 tested them most brutally. At the time and later, they filled letters and memoirs with superlatives of the most horrific kinds. Probably because the Union army maneuvered more, attacked more, retreated more, and suffered more casualties, these themes appear far more often and more clearly in the recollections of northern soldiers. Spotsylvania played havoc with the military effectiveness of both armies, however, and neither organization nor the men that composed them survived the fighting unscathed.

Many small elements combined in the soldiers' memories to set Spotsylvania apart as a different kind of war. Consciously or not, a soldier's physical environment rules much of his conduct, and neither private nor general could control many of these intangibles. During May 1864, the weather provided a number of brutal obstacles to effective military operations. Narratives of the march to Spotsylvania and the first few days of fighting feature heat and humidity. Soldiers found little drinkable water. Men in both armies dropped by the wayside, felled by heatstroke. "It was intensely sultry and we had to fall out often," wrote a Maine veteran: "Our suffering from heat and thirst cannot be described on paper."[20] In the battle of May 8, a number of soldiers in both armies, including at least one Union regimental commander, had to be carried off the firing line as heat casualties.[21]

Marching in dry weather on dirt roads, the rival columns kicked up clouds of choking dust. The density of the woods through which they passed, noted the Union army's chief medical officer, prevented "the free circulation of air, or the dissipation of the dense clouds of dust" that almost suffocated the troops. To make matters worse, underbrush caught fire along parts of the marching routes each army followed, and General Ewell himself reported the distressing march of his men "through intense heat and thick dust and smoke from burning woods."[22] For days, smoke and flame from countless brushfires stung their eyes, filled their lungs, singed their uniforms, and, at times, consumed their wounded and dead.

On May 11, the skies opened and rain soaked the soldiers. Union camps, according to the provost marshal general, became "Miserable . . . Wet, sticking, disgusting!" At the bottom of newly dug trenches in the Confederate lines, water pooled inches deep and made the bottom too slippery to walk across easily. Torrents turned the battleground into acres of mud. Six inches became the standard measure. At the end of one march, a soldier wrote, "the mud [was] over our shoes all of the way, in some low places the mud was knee deep." Mud

Combat at the Bloody Angle amid a steady rainfall. Poor weather aggravated the conditions under which soldiers fought at Spotsylvania. Robert Underwood Johnson and Clarence Clough Buel, eds., *Battles and Leaders of the Civil War*, 4 vols. (New York: Century, 1887–88), 4:172

clung to everything. It encased boots so completely that men found it diffi-cult to walk. After a brief skirmish, a Massachusetts soldier noted, "The men's right shoulders were thickly plastered with it from the butts of their muskets." Rain and mud complicated the most basic tasks. Soldiers in the Irish Brigade sparked enough of a fire to boil their nightly coffee, "but no blowing or other inducements could raise sufficient fire to fry the pork or stew the moistened cracker." They finally "sank to sleep in the falling rain, wet to the skin, with their soaked feet to the smouldering embers."[23]

Soldiers understood that weather plagued both armies equally (even as they griped about it), and they recalled even more pointedly those troubles for which some individual could be held accountable. Many men in both armies came out of the Wilderness utterly spent by the two-day fight, yet few were permitted even a brief stop for a cup of coffee or a bite to eat. Instead of the usual break for refitting, their officers marched them into what became a two-week trial of wills for which neither army had much experience or preparation.

The long duration of the campaign reveals itself most clearly in the frequency with which soldiers cited sheer physical exhaustion as one of their most telling memories of Spotsylvania. Sleep deprivation constituted one part of the problem. Lack of sleep destroyed endurance and eroded morale on both sides. As an officer in the 141st Pennsylvania recorded, "many of us passed four and five successive days and nights without an hour's refreshing sleep or rest." He described the men's conduct during this trying period under fire and taking casualties as "more than simply duty; it was heroism." Like many others on both sides, Massachusetts Pvt. Marcus Emmons decided he had two enemies: the army across the lines and his own leaders. For an entire week, he complained, officers tried to defend against surprise attacks by keeping half the regiment awake during the night (Emmons trusted the pickets to do their jobs), but then nobody at all slept because "The Rebs annoyed us some by yelling and firing which would lead us to think that they were advancing when they did not advance a step." Some members of the 2nd Vermont became so exhausted, wrote Private Fisk, that they "began to exhibit a state of mind the fartherest removed from patience or obedient resignation." Even during the height of the musketry near the "Bloody Angle" on May 12, soldiers in the 24th Michigan grew so weary that some lay down in the mud "and slept soundly amid the thunders of battle." Just across the lines, a South Carolinian reported that, "worn out from two days and nights without rest of sleep, I did an incredible thing—I fell asleep. Just when I don't know; but fall asleep I did, and I suppose I was taken for dead, for nobody waked me." Even today, a reader senses the glee of Pvt. Maurus Oesterreich as he wrote in his diary on May 15 that the previous night "We even had a good night's sleep, the first in the last 10 days."[24]

If the soldiers blamed their officers for lack of sleep that contributed to physical exhaustion, they hated even more the constant maneuvering that also sapped their energies. As the two armies sought the advantage of position during this two-week period, they marched back and forth across acres and acres of ground. This wore especially hard on the Union army, which lacked the security of interior lines that would facilitate such moves. Imagine the condition of the 141st Pennsylvania after spending much of the period May 9–11 "chiefly in marching and countermarching with the brigade, with [only] some unimportant skirmishing." Col. William S. Tilton's brigade on May 13 waded through

Soldiers of the Union Second Corps rest behind just-completed works at Spotsylvania while comrades clear a field of fire in front of the position.
Frank Leslie's Illustrated Newspaper, June 4, 1864

nine miles of mud and water from the right of the army to the extreme left. Although they marched in response to an emergency call, they arrived at the crucial point with fewer than half their men and well after the crisis had passed. Making it worse, many of these cross-country moves took place at night, when darkness and lightning often added a special eeriness to the endeavor. Weary soldiers blamed their officers, as exemplified by a member of the 17th Maine harboring a healthy hate for a captain who "dragged us in and through all the mire he could find within the radius of a mile." Nearly the entire Second Corps likely would have agreed when, after six more days of marching and maneuvering, this man wrote: "Mighty sure are we that General Hancock will never be accused of that masterly inactivity that has been charged to McClellan." [25]

What did officers demand of the men once they stopped marching? On both sides, orders came down to dig. "How we dig," wrote Pennsylvania Capt. John Willoughby: "Talk of McClellan digging; we lay him in the shade. Both armies after an hour's halt are entrenched." The first trenches the armies dug at Spotsylvania were fairly simple affairs, much like those they had used at the Wilderness. One southern gunner described them as just "a single line of earth, about four feet high, and three to five feet thick. It had no ditch or obstructions in front." He saw "no physical difficulty in men walking right over that bank! I did it often myself, saw many others do it, and twice, saw a line of Federal troops walk over it, and then saw them walk *back* over it, with the greatest ease, at the rate of forty miles an hour." [26]

The terrain around Spotsylvania featured more open ground than did that in the Wilderness. Troops or artillery could be maneuvered into flanking positions more easily there, and the rippled nature of the landscape no longer lent itself to the use of relatively straight, single trench lines. The works had to be stronger, deeper, more complex, and supported by still more defenses. In front of the line, soldiers used felled trees and brush to form an abatis that slowed attackers. All of this hard labor fell to the soldiers themselves, and the work continued both day and night. After several days of concentrated efforts in a single location, Confederate defenses near what became known as the Bloody Angle appeared far more imposing than those first thin lines each army had built. After digging an entrenchment about four feet deep, the southerners had added traverses at intervals to protect against flanking fire. They reminded a Wisconsin officer who saw them later of "a row of cellars without drainage." Some called those cellars "horse-stalls" or "pig pens." In time, water filled the pens and turned them into pools. In some places, Confederates put headlogs in place to protect their upper bodies as they fired. These were impressive works then and remain so today. The soldiers never before had built such an extensive system of trenches. Even though he had covered very little distance, a soldier from Mississippi recalled his most exhausting three-day span of the battle this way: "We moved back and dug rifle pits. Sunday, we finished digging, then moved forward 100 yards to the right, where we dug more pits! . . . Monday, about 10, Longstreet's corps moved back from the left, forming a line in our front. Gratefully we moved back—and started digging again!" [27]

All this marching and digging in dust or rain or mud inevitably tested the men's endurance in other fundamental ways. Reliable logistical support in active campaigning measures an army's effectiveness, and during the Spotsylvania campaign both forces found their supply efforts wanting. The Union army probably suffered greater discomfort in this regard. As the troops moved actively from place to place, its supply trains simply could not keep up. Moreover, after enjoying the plenty of camp life, northern soldiers felt the want in the field more than Confederates, who had become more inured to shortages of food and other basics.

Trains of wagons carrying food, coffee, and other necessities bogged down in the mud or lost contact with rapidly moving commands. Food still remained scant in southern ranks. During the first marches of the campaign one gunner referred to dinner as "Cracker nibbling on the fly." As a Texan recalled, "Flour became a luxury, corn-bread the staff of life. Hunger — incessant, never-satisfied hunger — prevailed." As the campaign dragged on, delivery of rations became increasingly irregular for both armies. The commander of the 69th Pennsylvania halted his men in place without orders at dark on May 10 because they fell "exhausted from fatigue and want of food." An opportunity to brew coffee made such an impact on men that it could find its way into official reports; the 40th New York regiment fought near the Bloody Angle "all day and night without cessation, until the morning of the 13th, when the firing ceased and the command was allowed to make coffee, [their first] opportunity in thirty-six hours." The Union army's chief medical officer made it clear that such seemingly trivial matters had produced an adverse effect on military effectiveness. After the clash on May 12, he reported that "The amount of shock and depression of vital power was noticed to be comparatively much greater in the wounded of this battle than in any preceding one of the campaign, and more especially so in those of the Second Corps who went into action without having had the usual morning cup of coffee." [28]

When the army could not supply their needs, soldiers simply fended for themselves, sometimes in exceptional ways. The southern lines had hardly stabilized after the repulse of Col. Emory Upton's attack on May 10 when soldiers in the 44th Virginia jumped over the works and "got some knapsacks off of dead Yankee bucks" to search for food. A Tennessee private stumbled in the dark over what he thought was a log, "but it proved to be a dead man whose haversack was well filled with bacon and hardtack." He, too, expressed no qualms about retrieving what he called "his treasure." Even as they freely scavenged for necessities, however, they disapproved of out-and-out robbery. One Tennessee soldier munching on food he had scrounged watched on appalled as "a notorious coward" in his unit showed off $182 in United States money and a Union officer's field glass, "which he sold for [$50]." Draft animals suffered alongside the soldiers. A Union artilleryman noted that his teams were down to half-rations of "five pounds of grain a day and nothing else." [29]

Personal cleanliness also affected soldier morale. Even if the men could muster the energy and inclination to tend to hygiene, they found opportunities limited. Officers and privates endured similar discomfort in this regard. One Rhode Island officer reported that neither he nor his men took off their boots for two weeks. Col. William H. Penrose, whose 15th New Jersey tested experimental infantry equipment during the campaign, proclaimed the trial a success when he heard no complaints about sore muscles from soldiers who had been able to take off the new accoutrements only once in fourteen days. By May 17, a Maine man quipped that "a little *ablution* would be worth more than all the *absolution* of all the priests in Christendom."[30] Maybe it is not so strange that a dirty Confederate, while in battle under intense fire, could complain about his need for new underclothing, open up a Yankee knapsack, extract the needed items, strip down completely, don the clean garments, put his muddy uniform back on, and resume firing.

Only one thing could make the marching and digging and starving and stinking even worse. Too often at the end of a hard march or in mid-dig, fighting broke out. Imagine the exhaustion of the men of the 155th Pennsylvania who, after building trenches in the rain and a "disagreeable and toilsome" all-night march, received orders to deploy as skirmishers at the front line for the next thirty-two hours. No wonder, perhaps, that by May 14 one Union division commander insisted that his troops were so completely exhausted by continual exertion that "it would have been utterly impossible to charge the enemy, even if they had not (as was the case) been found in strong force and strongly entrenched." Grant had informed Abraham Lincoln on May 11 that he intended to "fight it out on this line if it took all summer," but he needed an army of sufficient size, endurance, and resilience to accomplish that mission. After the first week of fighting at Spotsylvania, some elements of his army may have reached the limit beyond which they could not be counted on to carry out the strategic designs of their commander. In this all-important measure of military effectiveness, at least in the short term, Grant's plans may have required more of the Army of the Potomac than it could deliver.[31]

At Spotsylvania, Grant meant to fight, and by many accounts, both armies fought harder than they ever had before. "It was the hottest place ever we was in yet," wrote one of the first veteran Pennsylvanians to enter the Bloody Angle on May 12. He added simply, "I never want to see another charge."[32] Old soldiers spoke with new authority, and greener men considered their assessments seriously. "It was one of the bloodiest battles, the old soldiers say, that ever the army had," reported a northern private. A Confederate courier wrote the same sentiment: "Some old soldiers said yesterday's fight was the hottest they ever was in."[33] Coming so shortly after the horrors of the Wilderness, such commentaries compel belief.

Physical exertion and exhaustion weighed heavily on all the soldiers, but combat brought its own unique stresses. "[T]he mental suspense is terrible," wrote Confederate Maj. Eugene Blackford. The historian of the 105th Pennsylvania concurred in summing up the unit's Spotsylvania experience on May 12: "There were days when they lost more men and did harder fighting, but on this day they were sleepy, tired, hungry and wet," yet were forced to march into a battle that became "one horrid saturnalia of sound that might well have been copied from Dante's inferno."[34]

Even the most tested combat veterans recalled the fighting at Spotsylvania as the worst combination of emotionally wringing experiences they ever had endured. Of May 12, a New Jersey man wrote, "Combine the horrors of many battlefields, bring them into a single day and night of twenty four hours, and the one of May 12th includes them all." The rain and the mud that seemed so bothersome on the march and in the trenches now magnified the special horrors of battle. The works in the Bloody Angle, a Mississippian recalled, "were slippery with blood and rain." A Union soldier fighting there saw a wounded Confederate completely covered in mud, "part of the mud, actually," gasping for air while screaming in pain. After a full day of firing, the 24th Michigan's rifles had become so completely fouled with mud that some of its men had to be detailed to clean weapons while their comrades fought on. A Massachusetts soldier wrote home from a frontline trench just before the worst of this fighting: "I just live, father, and that is about all; I have been lying in a rifle pit for 24 hours, during a continued rain, and with the severe cold, enemy's bullets, and the deep mud and water." No wonder he considered this "9th day of uninterrupted fighting, the most fearful and protracted that has ever taken place on this continent, no doubt."[35]

Most firefights in the Civil War were brief affairs. Thus, whether they considered a single long day on the firing line or the sustained combat of the entire campaign, soldiers could not forget the unceasing nature of the fighting at Spotsylvania. Those who participated in the all-day fight on May 12 at the Bloody Angle recalled that clash in particular as a monumental test of human endurance. Pvt. Henry Keiser could not remember how long he fought that day, but as darkness fell he found his right arm "almost useless tonight from the rebound [recoil] of my rifle." Gen. Samuel McGowan officially reported "a storm of balls which did not intermit one instant of time for 18 hours." A North Carolinian remembered the "sad requiem, which those minie balls sung over the dead and dying for twenty-two hours."[36]

The fight at the Bloody Angle lasted for just one day, but not a single day in fourteen passed without some kind of exchange of hostilities. Soldiers in both armies who found time to write home at nearly any point during this fight invariably commented on its unceasing nature. A Georgia sergeant told his family not to wait for the end of the battle to write him, "for there is no telling when it will end." Even as the armies moved away from Spotsylvania, soldiers looked back and marveled at their constant activity. Some variation of the message the 1st Delaware's Maj. William Smith sent home on May 30 went out to thousands of northern and southern homes alike: "We have been Continually on the go ever Since the Night of May 3rd and have been under fire every day excepting one Since that time."[37]

The seemingly unending combat of Spotsylvania can be explained in part by a key change in the way the armies now fought. The days of maneuver battles in the open field, such as Antietam or Gettysburg, had ended. Spotsylvania showed just how completely soldiers and generals alike embraced a new combat philosophy that relied upon the utility of earthworks. Lee had been forced to incorporate them into his thinking as a cost-effective way to husband his fighting power against a numerically superior foe. Grant's army, as the maneuvering force, needed to build them to protect its advances, to defend against surprise southern advances, and, unconsciously perhaps, to shelter thousands of soldiers who now harbored doubts about surviving until their approaching discharge dates.

This great reliance on trenches at Spotsylvania instilled in soldiers of both armies a new respect for the randomness of death, a fear deepened by the reality that it might come at any time. A sharpshooter mystique maintains a firm grasp on memories of Spotsylvania. Organized units of marksmen had applied their skills in both armies since the war began and not every soldier who fired off a few rounds at the enemy lines in this battle belonged to one of them, but now both targets and opportunities beckoned with a frequency never before experienced. As the snipers plied their trade, soldiers quickly learned to keep down. A careless moment could mean death. As Pvt. Charles Brown of the 57th Massachusetts walked along the Fredericksburg Road looking for his regiment after a hospital stay, a Confederate sharpshooter "drew a bead on him and ended his luck forever." Rank provided no special protection from the sniper's bullet. A North Carolinian wrote, "There was no one too nice . . . to drop himself behind the breastworks" to avoid being hit. "Brigadiers and colonels lay as low in the trench and water as the men." Soldiers on both sides quickly attributed to a sharpshooter's bullet the battle's most senior casualty, Union Sixth Corps commander John Sedgwick, killed on May 9. Sgt. Luther Furst of the Sixth Corps signal detachment recalled the general's last words as "they couldn't hit a mountain" rather than the more familiar "they couldn't hit an elephant," but he concurred with one of Sedgwick's Vermonters that the general "died with his armor on, and we cherish his memory, emulate his bravery so that, though dead, he still lives with us."[38]

Very quickly, the taking of earthworks from the enemy, or the defense of one's own entrenched positions, became the key to victory. To capture such a line meant physically wresting it away from its occupants, most often by frontal assault and by far more close-range fighting than that to which most

Entrenchments at Spotsylvania with sharpened tree limbs in front (engraving from a wartime photograph). Earthworks such as these, which sheltered Confederates at Laurel Hill, greatly influenced the fighting around Spotsylvania Court House. Robert Underwood Johnson and Clarence Clough Buel, eds., *Battles and Leaders of the Civil War*, 4 vols. (New York: Century, 1887–88), 4:133

Civil War soldiers had become accustomed. A veteran Vermont captain explained that combat at Spotsylvania "resembled a hand-to-hand fight rather than a modern battle with long range weapons. The men clubbed their muskets, and repelled [the enemy] by mere physical force." [39]

Both armies rediscovered the bayonet at Spotsylvania, the perfect weapon for close-range fighting. As a Pennsylvanian asserted with some hyperbole, "there have been plenty of what are called bayonet charges," but Spotsylvania "was the first time the bayonet was ever *used* in all the battles of the Army of the Potomac." Likewise, a Georgian saw "several of our men wounded with the bayonet, which is the first of the kind that has come under my observation since I have been in the army." The men of the 1st Texas long since had discarded their bayonets as cumbersome and useless, but at Spotsylvania "they 'saw the point' that such weapons were good things to have." In short order, the Texans possessed new bayonets, some taken from Yankee dead and some "borrowed" — unbeknownst to their owners — from an Alabama brigade in another division. They would need them; as one Texan wrote of May 10, "The Federals and us were *closer to each other* today than since the war commenced.'" A South Carolina chaplain who saw one of his soldiers "with a bayonet wound in his back and a corresponding one in the breast in front, both made by the same bayonet," marveled to learn that the man had survived. Veterans of Upton's attack on a salient in the Confederate line on May 10 recalled that troops on both sides used bayonets freely; officers even used their swords as more than symbols of authority. When the 41st Virginia's Lt. Charles DeNoon saw a Union soldier aim at him, he used his blade to whack the man into submission.[40]

In this kind of combat, especially in green units and in veteran Union units close to mustering out, officers had to lead by personal example. In taking or defending trench lines, moreover, they often had to lead from the front, an especially nasty shock for experienced officers who had grown accustomed to directing fire from behind the regimental battle line. "This engagement developed more clearly the courage and ability of most of the line officers," a New York captain reported, with considerable truth. The list of experienced senior regimental officers on the casualty lists of both armies attested to that. By the end of the battle, the 2nd Vermont had to be consolidated from ten companies into four, wrote Private Fisk, and "even then we have hardly officers enough to keep it going." Three companies in the 15th New Jersey came out of the battle under the command of corporals. Southern officers more likely to be leading defensive efforts than grand charges found no greater safety in their roles. Many a junior Confederate officer suddenly found himself in the same position as did Capt. John Webb of the 9th Georgia: "My field officers have all been wounded and I am commanding the Regiment."[41]

Spotsylvania tested the mettle of officers of all ranks in both armies in ways unknown in their previous experience. As they gave in to mental and physical exhaustion, they made mistakes and irresponsible decisions for which their soldiers all too often paid with their lives. Union survivors' narratives report with considerable frequency that enlisted men began to lose faith in their leaders, an erosion in command relationships that marks another clear sign of a decline in tactical military effectiveness.[42]

"It seems to me it must require an extraordinary military genius to comprehend the reasons for all the movements that we make, and their results," a sarcastic Private Fisk wrote of his senior commanders toward the end of the battle. Far worse, some men watched their officers leave the field, some even offering elaborate pretexts for going to hospitals in the rear. A gunner saw a colonel hide behind a tree, open up a cartridge, and smear gunpowder on his face, transforming himself from "a trembling coward" to a "blond bewhiskered brave." He dreamed that night of "comic plays and extravagant burlesques," but he could not match "the actual one I saw in the forest." The provost guard rounded up a number of these weak-willed officers. Some considered redeemable went to a unique squad called Company Q, attached on May 13 to the 150th Pennsylvania. Shorn of all rank and privileges and handed a private's rifle, the former officers were given an opportunity to "share the fortunes of the regiment and refurbish, if possible, their tarnished reputations."[43] Most of them eventually did so.

But the armies lacked time for such officers to work out their personal weaknesses. They faced immediate problems of leadership. Veteran troops knew a bad spot when they saw it, and they wondered why their leaders did not work actively to prevent their slaughter. After the 20th Maine was assigned temporarily to the supervision of Brig. Gen. Samuel W. Crawford, Major Spear complained that on May 8 he did not "see or hear from Crawford, or any of his staff, and no pains were taken by them to ascertain where we were, to rally us if we had gone back, or to give us orders if we had remained." When a soldier in the 83rd Pennsylvania went into that same attack, he believed the regiment had been ordered in "without any display of skill or foresight on the part of their commanding generals. [We] met with severe loss and gained nothing except that [we] fully sustained [our] old reputation for bravery." Instructed to attack strengthened southern positions at the same place two days later, this soldier confessed that he still "had some misgivings as to the judgment of the commanding general who had ordered or advised this charge" and believed that "every man in the ranks saw the folly of the attempt." Elsewhere along the line, another Pennsylvanian decried "an approach to the ridiculous in the manner of [an order's] communication." Generals ordered assaults without bothering to examine the approaches to the Confederate lines, and "the whole expression of the person who brought the message seemed to say 'The General commanding is doubtful of your success.'"[44] Not surprisingly, such lapses in leadership proved horribly destructive to Union morale. As a New Jersey man recalled, "The terrible losses we sustained, and the continual checks we met, combined with the effects of this marching and counter-marching, from right to left, and left to right again, produced a feeling of listlessness and discouragement, which extended throughout the army. The men felt that they were doomed to slaughter." A soldier from Maine recalled that "the inner voice of the army was, 'How long, O Lord, how long!' "[45]

At Spotsylvania, the bond of authority between officers and their men broke down on several occasions in a particularly spectacular way. They had no name for it then, but the Vietnam generation gave it one: combat refusal. The Union army's short-timers seemed most prone to commit this serious infraction. It first occurred in the Wilderness on the road to Spotsylvania, when some veteran Second Corps troops who "had no intention of dying when they knew that home was just a matter of days away" ignored orders to advance. Although officers yelled themselves hoarse, the men refused to move forward, one reporting that "They had done all that they were going to do . . . and that was final." Just a few days later, on May 10, when a bullying staff officer ordered forward a Maine regiment, one man recalled that "we refused to move another step." The officer "didn't move us a hair. . . . We firmly refused to sign our death warrants or be driven or bullied any further by him or any other drunken pimp." On a later occasion, the veteran 35th Massachusetts, just returned from home and determined to see it again, watched the green 56th Massachusetts advance through a killing crossfire. Although officers ordered them to double-time to their fellow Bay Staters' support, the veterans simply about-faced and moved to a place of safety.[46]

The intensity of the fighting brought many Union soldiers to the limits of their endurance. A provost marshal detachment close behind the front lines stopped individuals and demanded to see blood before allowing them to proceed to the rear. They sent unwounded soldiers back to the front or arrested them, but still could not stem the increasing flow of men seeking the protection of the hospitals. One particularly telling sign of severe demoralization in the Union ranks appeared all too frequently at Spotsylvania. Pvt. William Andrews of the 57th Massachusetts shot himself with his own rifle rather than advance against the Confederate works. Beyond this individual case, the army's chief medical officer reported officially that he saw thousands of soldiers hit in the hands and arms, with skin so black with gunpowder "as to prove that the injury was self-inflicted either by design or accident." In Fredericksburg, he saw many men "sick and slightly wounded, many of the latter self-mutilated."[47]

Spotsylvania's most lasting impressions centered on the grand scale and high degree of its brutality, butchery, and intensity. Even if northerners did not always exhibit great enthusiasm for frontal assaults on earthworks, Confederate defenders accorded them new respect for attempting the challenge under trying circumstances. A survivor from Cobb's Legion wrote, "The fighting during this series of battles has been more stubborn than at any time heretofore, by *both* parties," even admitting, "The Yankees have fought well and only for our superior Generalship they would have whipped us long ago." [48]

Indeed, southerners looked for answers to explain just why the Union soldiers now fought so much more fiercely. One rumor that gained considerable currency attributed Yankee bravery to intoxication. Major Blackford reported that Grant gave his soldiers "whiskey before every fight and then sends them out to meet their death in a furious state of intoxification." A North Carolinian similarly wrote that the Yankees would come "over the brest works drunk with out any guns[.] the men who fought them say they were all drunk [and] I think so myself." Confederate soldiers found it difficult to "think of having our best men butchered up by a set of drunkards," as they perceived the Yankees to be. Far worse, though, rumors swept through the Confederate line that Grant had offered each of his men who charged the rebel line a $50 bounty. An appalled Major Blackford marveled, "Can you conceive of the avarice of a people who will receive money to undertake such work in such a cause?" [49]

Even for soldiers who fought for so many days on so many different parts of the field, no phase of the Spotsylvania campaign matched the special horrors of the Bloody Angle. For many, the carnage of this one day sufficiently summed up the two-week experience. A survivor from Maine called it "a seething, bubbling, roaring hell of hate and murder." A North Carolinian remembered the different sounds the bullets made, including in his catalogue, among other noises, the "humming of bees" and "cats in the depth of the night." A South Carolinian could not wax quite so eloquently: "I was splashed over with brains and blood. In stooping down or squatting to load, the mud, blood and brains mingled, would reach up to my waist, and my head and face were covered or spotted with the horrid paint." A Pennsylvania private recalled a Confederate captain and twelve of his men all covered in mud and blood who ran into the northern lines crying, "The Devil couldn't stand it in there." [50]

Union artillery played an especially gruesome role in this phase of what became primarily an infantry battle. Projectiles fired on a flat trajectory failed to penetrate the log and soil embankments. One frustrated Union gunner later commented that, up to this point at least, "The artillery was pleasantly employed in burying good iron in Confederate earthworks," resulting "in the remarkable discovery that three-inch percussion shells could not be relied upon to perform the work of a steam shovel." Northern gunners next began to employ coehorn mortars that could arch shells high into the air to explode in and above southern trenches near the Bloody Angle. The men of the 1st New Jersey brigade watched with interest the paths of the mortar shells and made bets "whether an arm or a foot or a head would be thrown into the air" when the projectiles struck home. A Wisconsin officer described the effects of a shell from just such a mortar: "I saw the body of a rebel sitting in the corner of [the trench line] in a position of apparent ease, with the head entirely gone, and the flesh burned from the bones of the neck and shoulders."[51]

Grant added to the battlefield's grisly nature by prohibiting the use of flags of truce to collect the dead and wounded of both armies caught between the lines. Days and nights filled with the groaning of the injured seared into the memories of northerners and southerners alike. A Confederate gunner incensed at what he considered evidence of northern inhumanity demanded that "someone must answer for the unnecessary waste of life." Just as often, however, southern troops fired on Union soldiers trying to help the wounded. A Maine soldier complained: "This chivalrous conduct on the part of our Southern 'gentlemen' is unbelievable. They call us 'vulgar Yankees' yet I never knew a Yankee so vulgar as to fire on wounded men."[52]

If the fighting at the Angle was in itself horrible, visual images of the harvest of dead that remained afterward sealed in memory forever scenes of nearly indescribable carnage. Private Keiser saw Union dead "swollen and bloated so that they could scarcely be recognized." When two of his officers could not agree on the identity of one of his regiment's dead, Keiser was ordered to search the slain soldier's pockets for identification. He found a carving knife in one, but when he reached into the other, "I got the full length of my fingers into a pile of maggots." Rain had washed off the surface blood, but Keiser had dipped into a pocket right over the fatal wound where the larvae feasted on pooled blood that had not been rinsed away. New Jersey Pvt. Thomas Capern wrote his mother three days after his fight, "I have seen men perfectly riddled with bullets and mashed to a jelly. What do you think of that?" Survivors of the 24th Michigan saw Confederate dead used as breastworks to protect the living. Even worse, they noted, burial parties did not bother to remove southern corpses from the trenches at the Bloody Angle, "but turned the breastworks over upon them for a covering—thus they actually died in their graves."[53]

Spotsylvania touched all the senses. Beyond the awful visual images, a northern private noted that after a few days the heat turned corpses "so rotten that it was impossible for any person to stand it for the smell." On May 18, as the Second Corps formed for yet another attack, one that would carry them over unburied dead killed on May 12, one man noted that "the stench which arose from them was so sickening and terrible that many of the men and officers became deathly sick from it." One Confederate went so far as to attribute Lee's next move to this same cause: "[T]he battle field smelt so bad general Lee has fell back to hanover junction on the north Anner [North Anna] river and fortified himself there."[54]

In the midst of all this death, the timely arrival of reinforcements might be

Confederate dead from the fighting at the Harris farm on May 19 awaiting burial. The sight of large numbers of bodies, many of them decomposing as they lay vulnerable to the elements, added a grisly element to the experience of soldiers at Spotsylvania. Francis Trevelyan Miller, ed., *The Photographic History of the Civil War*, 10 vols. (New York: Review of Reviews, 1911), 3:61

expected to make a positive impact on an army's combat effectiveness. Only the Union army enjoyed the addition of substantial numbers of new troops while the contest dragged on, but these newcomers received an odd reception. At first, Private Fisk was glad to see the 11th Vermont march into line to strengthen the remaining fragments of the Vermont Brigade's five battered regiments, noting that "it contains more men than all the rest of the brigade." He admired the newcomers' admirable "determination to acquit themselves." When green men and officers posted in front of the veteran troops began to send back excited warnings against firing into their rear, however, Fisk soon joined his comrades in chiding the untested soldiers, drolly commenting that, after all, "Vermonters generally understand their duty after being told of it upwards of a dozen times." [55]

Many of the Union reinforcements belonged to heavy artillery regiments fresh from the defenses of Washington and now converted to infantry. To Grant and other senior Union leaders, the decision to use these garrison soldiers in active campaigning may have seemed an effective use of available resources. But the battle-weary veterans seldom greeted these garrison soldiers as worthy comrades. Even in the midst of the Spotsylvania fighting, they doubted both the ability and the willingness of the "heavies" to fight at all. A Pennsylvania captain believed that "Thousands were induced to enlist in this branch because they would escape the draft, get the bounty, and run no risk." Thus, many veterans toyed with them. Several of the more lightly wounded took special pleasure at showing impressionable heavies the corpses of horribly maimed soldiers.[56]

The heavies displayed their greenness in an initial encounter with Confederates at the Harris farm on May 19. The 1st Massachusetts and 1st Maine Heavy Artillery regiments fought as if they were on the drill field. As one of their captains explained, "they had not yet fully learned the habit of the old troops in digging themselves into a hole in the ground the minute they stopped in the presence of the enemy." Indeed, they found themselves thrown into action knowing nothing of the reality of battle other than the tactics learned on the drill field. They stood shoulder-to-shoulder in straight ranks and died in droves. Some fell immediately, pierced by southern bullets. Others died from gangrene that set in after they misapplied tourniquets to minor wounds. Veterans praised the heavies publicly for their work that day but privately wondered how much their generals valued veteran lives if they could simply summon more heavies to make good on losses. For one jaundiced Maine infantryman, the arrival of the heavies and the high losses they quickly absorbed meant little more to him than an opportunity to "replenish our wardrobes" from the new men's unguarded knapsacks.[57]

When the armies finally broke contact on May 20 for the first moves toward the North Anna River, both armies showed serious signs of organizational dysfunction. Each had lost the services of one infantry corps commander (Sedgwick, killed in action, for the North; Ewell, relieved of command at the end of the fighting at Spotsylvania, for the South), and Lee had lost his great cavalry leader J. E. B. Stuart to a mortal wound at Yellow Tavern the day before the fight at the Bloody Angle. Dozens of division, brigade, and regimental officers on both sides had fallen; thousands of their men had followed them to the death. Medical facilities could not accommodate all the wounded. In addition, each army sent thousands of captured soldiers to their increasingly deadly systems of prison camps. The human cost exacted by the fighting at Spotsylvania appalled both sides.

Despite all they saw, smelled, and endured, however, so long as survivors on both sides continued to believe that so much death and destruction held meaning, they would try to find ways to deal with it. The speed with which each side's fighting spirit recovered from the battering of Spotsylvania suggests much about the way soldiers assessed the performance of the armies and their leaders and the effectiveness of each force.

Many in the Army of the Potomac struggled to justify the high cost of Spotsylvania as a necessary part of Grant's intention to maintain constant pressure on Lee's army. A Massachusetts soldier admitted that he and his comrades were "tired sleepy and worn out" but still looked for some hopeful sign: "[I]f we could believe that everything was working out all right we should be satisfied." Plenty of men tried hard to remain optimistic. "Grant is a fighter and bound to win," wrote a Rhode Islander as the campaign came to an end. Many more, however, tempered their hopes with nagging doubts. As a Pennsylvania sergeant commented, "Grant does his work slow but I think sure," adding wistfully, "At least I hope so." [58]

Many other Union soldiers freely voiced serious criticisms of their new commander. Veterans in the Vermont Brigade began to refer to Grant as "Old Useless." A Michigander later mused, "What would [be] the cry against our old commander, Little Mac, if he lost so many men in such a short time. The cry would be long before this, perhaps, to hang him for incapacity." " 'The Army of the Potomac has always longed for a fighting general — one who would fight, and fight, and fight — and now it has got him,' " one Union combatant quoted a wounded comrade as saying. "But," he added, "he does not seem to know that Lee's veteran infantry cannot be driven out of skilfully constructed earthworks by direct assault." The injured man had concluded that "The enlisted men have been sacrificed." An onlooker to this scene recorded, "This was the first complaint I heard about Grant. I heard plenty [more] before the campaign closed." [59]

In some ways, Spotsylvania made veteran northern soldiers reconsider the possibility of death in battle. Private Fisk wrote, "I have sometimes hoped, that if I must die while I am a soldier, I should prefer to die on the battle-field." But after Spotsylvania he concluded, "one cannot help turning away and saying, Any death but that." A certain bitterness crept into the letters of the usually optimistic Private Oesterreich, who had lost his best friend on May 10 when he and his comrades "did what they were ordered to do and went into a deadly hail of bullets." Superiors had failed to send up sufficient support, and "all was wasted. The many killed and wounded had done their duty for nothing." [60]

Perhaps the most lamentable deaths were those that some believed should not have happened at all. In the veteran 102nd Pennsylvania, Pvt. Lewis White mourned the loss of his cousin in the 11th Pennsylvania Reserves, who fell "after his time [in service] had expired." In an entirely different kind of death, even before the armies left Spotsylvania, a private in the 19th Massachusetts was shot by a firing squad for displaying cowardice on May 10. Although soldiers of the 19th Maine who witnessed the execution understood it to be "an example of military severity," they wondered if it really had served any useful purpose to kill this one man for giving in to fears they nearly all had experienced in recent days. For a few, the death and destruction simply reached the point beyond which they could comprehend it. One veteran Union private's diary at the end of the Spotsylvania campaign reads simply: "I have seen so much that I can't nor will put it in this book. I will seal this in my memory by myself. God have mercy on those who started this cruel war." [61]

Yet even after all it had endured, the Union army showed marked resilience. Rest assuredly helped the men continue. The wagon trains caught up with them, and most of the soldiers enjoyed their first real food in two weeks. Between May 18 and 20, much of the army welcomed their first mail call since breaking camp early that month. A Vermont private gratefully received a letter from home with the admission that "it seems as if I had lived an age" since he last heard from family and friends. A Wisconsin officer rejoiced to receive five letters: "I will not try to write how burdens are lightened and how life comes back." [62]

But not all the changes augured well for the future of the Army of the Potomac. The number of personnel lost to end-of-tour discharge continued unabated, even speeded up. In later years, survivors of the famous 14th Brooklyn recalled May 22, 1864, as a special memory. Fresh from the carnage of Spotsylvania, they got an answer to their "dreams in camp and prayers on bloody battlefields for three long years. . . . They were going home!" [63] They were not alone. Within just a few weeks, the sad remnants of more than two dozen veteran Union regiments left Virginia for discharge and home. The Union army never developed an effective answer to this ongoing drain of manpower.

In Lee's army, troop morale did not require the same degree of rebuilding as that needed in Grant's force. Like their northern counterparts, southern soldiers did need food, sleep, and a chance to clean up, read their mail, and write home. A South Carolinian complained, "we are running day and night. I never was so near worn out in my life." But because they prevented Grant from getting around them and capturing Richmond, Confederate soldiers tended to make a more clear-cut claim to victory at Spotsylvania, a luxury denied northern combatants. "The valor of our army by the Grace of God has repulsed one of the grandest and most desperate efforts that was ever made at a people's subjugation," wrote a Virginia lieutenant right after the battle: "Should we not feel encouraged and thankful?" [64]

Southerners certainly recognized the growing pressure of northern resources. A North Carolinian feared that "they have so many men they doant mind loosing a hundred thousand no more than we do too or three regiments." Some southerners also blanched at the cost of the Spotsylvania fighting. A veteran of the famed Stonewall Brigade, most of which was captured on May 12, explained his comrades' fate and told his brother, "My shattered nerves will not allow of my writing more." A North Carolinian had grown "heartily sick of blood & the sound of artillery & small arms & the ghastly, pale face of death and all the horrible sights and sounds of war." Southerner James F. Bryant, upon learning on May 25 that his mother had given birth to his new baby sister, greeted the news with joy but also felt that "So great has been the losses to the male portion of our population" recently "that I should have preferred having another brother." Even though they received no substantial reinforcement, most soldiers' confidence in the war's final outcome remained strong. As one Georgian boasted, "Ewells Bull dogs is barking pretty finely again, and old Grants Bulldogs is barking at Ewell, but Lee has dogs enough for all the dogs Grant can bring up." [65]

Indeed, the few signs of gloom in Confederate ranks seemed to dissipate quickly. A South Carolinian who visited the trenches near the Bloody Angle a few days after the fighting recalled, "If a man wants to see hell upon earth, let him come and look into this black, bloody hole." This soldier wondered "how a man can look upon such a scene and still take pleasure in war." Nonetheless, he believed "the revulsion of feeling is only temporary," and in a few days he and his comrades were "spoiling for a fight." The southern army's fighting spirit largely survived Spotsylvania—though many of its soldiers did not. While home on leave the previous winter, a North Carolina cavalryman had argued with one of his father's friends who said that Lee's army could not fight much longer. Just days before he died of wounds on May 17, he reminded his father of the exchange: "I told him then that if they were called upon that they would do some of the best fighting they had ever done and it has so turned out. Better fighting has never been done since the war. . . . I wonder what Abraham thinks! I guess he will lay Grant on the shelf and give up Richmond as a hard road to travel." [66]

Faith in Lee remained strong. Although unaccustomed to fighting from prepared earthworks, the men greatly respected the general who successfully had adjusted his tactics to fit his army, his resources, and his strategic obligations. He had not thrown away his soldiers' lives as they believed Grant had done with Union troops. Edward E. Sill of South Carolina wrote home after the battle that "Every thing is confident of our ability to check Grant in any movement he may make." To stop Grant's force, which he estimated as

185,000 strong, Sill applauded that "Gen. Lee acted altogether on the defensive." As the armies moved south from Spotsylvania, Lee's chief engineer, Maj. Gen. Martin L. Smith, praised his commander's defensive prowess. "Grant's crab movements have sidled both his & our army half way across the State and b[r]ought him to a position which he could have taken at first without the loss of a man by simply landing from his transports and marching a few miles," observed Smith. Because of Lee's stout resistance, however, "the Yankees have lost all their boldness and dash which characterized their first movements and are now proceeding with extreme caution." [67]

The events of mid-May helped to clarify in the soldiers' minds that they indeed did face a different kind of war. They agreed with Joseph Graham that they had not known war before the spring of 1864. This new kind of war proved more brutal, less compromising, less forgiving, seemingly unending. The soldiers who fought had to be physically and mentally tough, disciplined, and entirely committed to victory. Officers had to lead responsibly and by example to retain the confidence of the soldiers while seeking to accomplish their costly missions. Richmond and Washington had to provide all possible manpower and logistical support to their respective armies. At least in May, the Army of Northern Virginia seemed to enjoy a slight edge in many of these areas. That would not remain the case for much longer, but for now, in terms of military effectiveness, the Confederacy had done the better job of employing its fighting power.

In late May, a Mississippian accurately summed up the changing face of war. "Every time we stop we dig another hole," he wrote. "From Orange Court House to Richmond, from a soldier's point of view, the country is made up of holes, each dug by hand (laboriously), sometimes with shovels but usually with bayonets or sharpened sticks and flattened canteens. We seldom charge 'gloriously' as we did 3 years ago. Instead we build fortifications and try to flank the enemy. The enemy does the same." Indeed, beginning with Spotsylvania for both armies, "Fighting has become an every day business. It is no longer an occasional affair from which we can relax into peaceful camp life. Now we have become hardened to it as our normal condition." [68] It is perhaps well that Spotsylvania helped to harden them. For those who survived, Cold Harbor and Petersburg lay ahead.

NOTES

1. Thomas W. Hyde, *Following the Greek Cross, or, Memories of the Sixth Corps* (Boston: Houghton Mifflin, 1895), 201; J. S. Graham to Ellen Lee, June 8, 1864, in *Aunt and the Soldier Boys from Cross Creek Village, Pennsylvania, 1856–1866*, ed. Janice Bartlett Reeder McFadden (Santa Cruz, Cal.: Moore's Graphic Arts, n.d.), 136.

2. For the fullest explanation of this concept, see Allan R. Millet, Williamson Murray,

and Kenneth H. Watman, "The Effectiveness of Military Organizations," in *Military Effectiveness, Vol. 1: The First World War*, ed. Allan R. Millett and Williamson Murray (Boston: Allen & Unwin, 1988), 1–30 (quotation is from p. 2).

3. Ibid., 22.

4. Asbury Hall Jackson to sister, February 11, 1864, Harden Family Papers, William R. Perkins Library, Duke University, Durham, N.C. (repository hereafter cited as DU).

5. Robert E. Lee to James A. Seddon, January 22, 1864, in U.S. War Department, *The War of the Rebellion: A Compilation of the Official Records of the Union and Confederate Armies*, 127 vols., index, and atlas (Washington: GPO, 1880–1901), ser. 1, 33(1):1114 (hereafter cited as *OR*; all references are to series 1); McHenry Howard, *Recollections of a Maryland Confederate Staff Officer* (1914; reprint, Dayton, Ohio: Morningside, 1975), 252.

6. Millett, Murray, and Watman, "Military Effectiveness," 23.

7. William Ruffin Cox, in sketch of the 2nd North Carolina State Troops, February 2, 1864, George Holland Collection, North Carolina State Archives, Raleigh, N.C.

8. Lt. John L. Runzie to "Bill," May 1, 1864, vol. 35, no. 2, Lewis Leigh Collection, U.S. Army Military History Institute, Carlisle Barracks, Pa. (repository hereafter cited as USAMHI); Marion Hill Fitzpatrick to wife, April 29, 1864, in Marion Hill Fitzpatrick, *Letters to Amanda from Sergeant Major Marion Hill Fitzpatrick, Company K, 45th Georgia Regiment, Thomas' Brigade, Wilcox Division, Hill's Corps, CSA to his wife Amanda Olive Elizabeth White Fitzpatrick 1862–1865*, ed. Henry Mansell Hammock (Culloden, Ga.: n.p., 1976), 132–33; John F. Sale to aunt, April 22, 1864, John F. Sale Papers, Virginia State Library, Richmond.

9. Christopher Hackett to parents, February 25, March 26, 1864, John C. Hackett Papers, DU; Cpl. Thomas D. Grover Smith to mother, April 25, 1864, in Smith Brothers Papers, vol. 35A, Lewis Leigh Collection, USAMHI.

10. William M. Parsley to sister, April 12, 1864, Eliza Hall Parsley Papers, Southern Historical Collection, Wilson Library, University of North Carolina, Chapel Hill. On morale in Lee's army at the beginning of the Overland campaign, see Gary W. Gallagher, "Our Hearts Are Full of Hope: The Army of Northern Virginia in the Spring of 1864," in *The Wilderness Campaign*, ed. Gary W. Gallagher (Chapel Hill: University of North Carolina Press, 1997).

11. *OR* 36(1):211.

12. Charles S. Wainwright, *A Diary of Battle: The Personal Journals of Colonel Charles S. Wainwright, 1861–1865*, ed. Allan Nevins (1962; reprint, Gettysburg, Pa.: Stan Clark Military Books, 1993), 338; Frederick Pettit, *Infantryman Pettit: The Civil War Letters of Corporal Frederick Pettit*, ed. William Gilfillan Gavin (New York: Avon Books, 1990), 132.

13. General John Newton's comments are quoted in O. B. Curtis, *History of the Twenty-Fourth Michigan of the Iron Brigade, Known as the Detroit and Wayne County Regiment* (1891; reprint, Gaithersburg, Md.: Olde Soldier Books, 1988), 225; John W. Haley, *The Rebel Yell & the Yankee Hurrah: The Civil War Journal of a Maine Volunteer*, ed. Ruth L. Silliker (Camden, Me.: Down East Books, 1985), 139.

14. The 1st Minnesota's last parade was held at Fort Snelling on April 28, 1864. A small contingent of recruits and reenlisted veterans returned to Virginia in June 1864 to continue the organization's name on the army's order of battle, but altered to the 1st Minnesota Battalion Infantry Volunteers. See Richard Moe, *The Last Full Measure: The Life and Death of the First Minnesota Volunteers* (New York: Henry Holt and Company, 1993), 300–303.

15. Benjamin Ashenfelter to "Father Churchman," April 23, 1864, in Harrisburg Civil War Round Table Collection, USAMHI.

16. Wilbur Fisk, *Hard Marching Every Day: The Civil War Letters of Private Wilbur Fisk, 1861–1865*, ed. Emil and Ruth Rosenblatt (Lawrence: University Press of Kansas, 1992), 208.

17. A. W. Acheson to mother, April 5, 1864, in James M. Fulcher, ed., *Family Letters in a Civil War Century* (Avella, Pa.: n.p., 1986), unpaginated; Warren Wilkinson, *Mother, May You Never See the Sights I Have Seen: The 57th Massachusetts Veteran Volunteers* (New York: Harper & Row, 1990), 12, 70.

18. James L. Rea to unknown, May 1, 1864, bound vol. 146, Fredericksburg and Spotsylvania National Military Park Library, Fredericksburg, Va. (repository hereafter cited as FSNMP); Gideon Mellin to sister, April 27, 1864, Pennsylvania Save the Flags Collection, USAMHI.

19. Alanson A. Haines, *History of the Fifteenth Regiment New Jersey Volunteers* (New York: Jenkins & Thomas, 1883), 155; A. W. Acheson to mother, May 7, 1864, in Fulcher, *Family Letters in a Civil War Century*, unpaginated.

20. Haley, *Rebel Yell & Yankee Hurrah*, 148.

21. See, for example, Margaret Greenleaf, ed., *Letters to Eliza from a Union Soldier, 1862–1865* (Chicago: Follett Publishing, [1970]), 89; Arthur A. Kent, ed., *Three Years with Company K* (Rutherford, N.J.: Fairleigh Dickinson University Press, 1976), 262, 264.

22. *OR* 36(1):226, 1071.

23. Marsena Rudolph Patrick, *Inside Lincoln's Army: The Diary of Marsena Rudolph Patrick, Provost Marshal General, Army of the Potomac*, ed. David S. Sparks (New York: Thomas Yoseloff, 1964), 371; Greenleaf, *Letters to Eliza from a Union Soldier*, 90; Ernest L. Waitt, *History of the Nineteenth Regiment Massachusetts Volunteer Infantry, 1861–1865* (Salem, Mass.: Salem Press, 1906), 309; St. Clair A. Mulholland, *The Story of the 116th Regiment, Pennsylvania Infantry* (1903; reprint, Gaithersburg, Md.: Olde Soldier Books, 1990), 194.

24. *OR* 36(1):478; Marcus A. Emmons to "Friend Henry," May 21, 1864, vol. 5, no. 18, Lewis Leigh Collection, USAMHI; Fisk, *Hard Marching Every Day*, 220; Curtis, *History of the Twenty-Fourth Michigan*, 243; Berry Benson, *Berry Benson's Civil War Book: Memoirs of a Confederate Scout and Sharpshooter*, ed. Susan Williams Benson (Athens: University of Georgia Press, 1962), 76; Maurus Oesterreich diary, Harrisburg Civil War Round Table Collection, USAMHI (entry for ca. May 15, 1864; there is clear evidence of much emendation and the addition of material at a later time in this "diary").

25. *OR* 36(1):477, 652; Haley, *Rebel Yell & Yankee Hurrah*, 147, 158.

26. Capt. John Willoughby to Simpson, May 13, 1864, Corporal James Randolph Simpson and Sergeant George Simpson Papers, Civil War Miscellaneous Collection, USAMHI; William Meade Dame, *From the Rapidan to Richmond and the Spotsylvania Campaign* (1920; reprint, Richmond, Va.: Owens Publishing Co., 1987), 140–41.

27. Rufus R. Dawes, *Service with the Sixth Wisconsin Volunteers* (1890; reprint, Dayton, Ohio: Morningside, 1991), 268; Austin C. Dobbins, ed., *Grandfather's Journal: Company B, Sixteenth Mississippi Infantry Volunteers, Harris' Brigade, Mahone's Division, Hill's Corps, A.N.V.* (Dayton, Ohio: Morningside, 1988), 196 (entry for May 14–16, 1864).

28. Dame, *From the Rapidan to Richmond*, 98; J. B. Polley, *Hood's Texas Brigade* (1910; reprint, Dayton, Ohio: Morningside, 1976), 237; *OR* 36(1):445, 474, 231.

29. Benjamin A. Jones memoir, *Civil War Times Illustrated* Collection, USAMHI; William A. Clendening memoir, *Civil War Times Illustrated* Collection, USAMHI; Wainwright, *A Diary of Battle*, 373.

30. Elisha Hunt Rhodes, *All for the Union: The Civil War Diary and Letters of Elisha*

Hunt Rhodes, ed. Robert Hunt Rhodes (New York: Orion Books, 1985), 153; Col. William H. Penrose to Lt. John R. Edie, July 7, 1864, in "Official Report on Colonel Mann's *Improved Infantry Accoutrements*, Made to the Chief of Ordnance by Colonel Penrose, an Officer of the Old Regular Army, of Great Experience . . . ," vol. 24, no. 25, Lewis Leigh Collection, USAMHI; Haley, *Rebel Yell & Yankee Hurrah*, 159.

31. *OR* 36(1):558, 612; Millett, Murray, and Watman, "Military Effectiveness," 24.

32. J. S. Graham to James Lee, May 19, 1864, in McFadden, *Aunt and the Soldier Boys*, 135 (copy in Graham Family Papers, Civil War Miscellaneous Papers, USAMHI).

33. Gideon Mellin to sister, May 15, 1864, Pennsylvania Save the Flags Collection, USAMHI; "Bobbie" to "Aunt," May 11, 1864, vol. 19, no. 31, Lewis Leigh Collection, USAMHI.

34. Maj. Eugene Blackford to sister, May 14, 1864, vol. 33, Lewis Leigh Collection, USAMHI; Kate M. Scott, *History of the One Hundred and Fifth Regiment of Pennsylvania Volunteers* (Philadelphia: New-World Publishing Co., 1877), 102.

35. Haines, *History of the Fifteenth Regiment*, 172; Dobbins, ed., *Grandfather's Journal*, 194 (entry for May 12–13, 1864); Charles Harvey Brewster, *When This Cruel War Is Over: The Civil War Letters of Charles Harvey Brewster*, ed. David W. Blight (Amherst: University of Massachusetts Press, 1992), 296; Curtis, *History of the Twenty-Fourth Michigan*, 243; Robert Goldthwaite Carter, *Four Brothers in Blue, or, Sunshine and Shadows of the War of the Rebellion* (1913; reprint, Austin: University of Texas Press, 1978), 397.

36. Henry Keiser diary, Harrisburg Civil War Round Table Collection, USAMHI (entry for May 12, 1864); *OR* 36(1):1094; Walter Raleigh Battle to parents, May 14, 1864, in *Forget-Me-Nots of the Civil War: A Romance, Containing Reminiscences and Original Letters of Two Confederate Soldiers*, ed. Laura Elizabeth Lee (St. Louis, Mo.: A. R. Fleming Printing Company, 1909), 116.

37. Marion Hill Fitzpatrick to wife, May 19, 1864, in Fitzpatrick, *Letters to Amanda*, 137; Maj. William F. Smith to mother, May 30, 1864, Smith Brothers Papers, vol. 35A, Lewis Leigh Collection, USAMHI.

38. Wilkinson, *Mother, May You Never See the Sights I Have Seen*, 116; Walter Raleigh Battle to parents, May 14, 1864, in Lee, *Forget-Me-Nots of the Civil War*, 116; Luther C. Furst diary, Harrisburg Civil War Round Table Collection, USAMHI (entry for May 9, 1864); Fisk, *Hard Marching Every Day*, 219.

39. *OR* 36(1):716.

40. Amos M. Judson, *History of the Eighty-Third Regiment Pennsylvania Volunteers* (1865; reprint, Dayton, Ohio: Morningside, 1986), 200; Atlanta *Constitution*, May 25, 1864; Polley, *Hood's Texas Brigade*, 238–39; Thomas L. McCarty diary, Thomas L. McCarty Papers, University of Texas, Austin (entry for May 10, 1864); William Porcher DuBose reminiscences, copy in bound vol. 134, FSNMP; C. E. DeNoon to "Father and Mother," May 15, 1864, in Charles E. DeNoon, *Charlie's Letters: The Correspondence of Charles E. DeNoon*, ed. Richard T. Couture (Collingswood, N.J.: C.W. Historicals, 1989), 220.

41. *OR* 36(1):404; Fisk, *Hard Marching Every Day*, 219; Haines, *History of the Fifteenth Regiment*, 178; John G. Webb to father, May 11, 1864, vol. 32, no. 3, Lewis Leigh Collection, USAMHI.

42. Millett, Murray, and Watman, "Military Effectiveness," 23.

43. Fisk, *Hard Marching Every Day*, 234; Frank Wilkeson, *Recollections of a Private Sol-*

dier in the Army of the Potomac (New York: G. P. Putnam's Sons, 1887), 95; Thomas Chamberlin, *A History of the One Hundred and Fiftieth Regiment Pennsylvania Volunteers, Second Regiment, Bucktail Brigade* (Philadelphia: F. McManus Jr. and Co., 1905), 239.

44. Ellis Spear to unknown, circa May 8, 1864, bound vol. 145, FSNMP; Judson, *History of the Eighty-Third Regiment*, 199–200; John Day Smith, *The History of the Nineteenth Regiment of Maine Volunteer Infantry, 1862–1865* (Minneapolis, Minn.: Great Western Printing Co., 1909), 151.

45. Haines, *History of the Fifteenth Regiment*, 183; Hyde, *Following the Greek Cross*, 204.

46. Wilkinson, *Mother, May You Never See the Sights I Have Seen*, 72, 118; Haley, *Rebel Yell & Yankee Hurrah*, 151.

47. Wilkinson, *Mother, May You Never See the Sights I Have Seen*, 113; OR 36(1):235.

48. Both quotations in Atlanta *Constitution*, May 25, 1864.

49. Maj. Eugene Blackford to sister, May 14, 1864, vol. 33, Lewis Leigh Collection, USAMHI; F. B. Ward to sister, May 26, 1864, vol. 19, no. 65, Lewis Leigh Collection, USAMHI; Joseph F. Shaner to parents, May 17, 1864, FSNMP.

50. Haley, *Rebel Yell & Yankee Hurrah*, 157; Walter Raleigh Battle to parents, May 14, 1864, in Lee, *Forget-Me-Nots of the Civil War*, 116; Charleston *Courier*, May 28, 1864; Henry Keiser diary, Harrisburg Civil War Round Table Collection, USAMHI (entry for May 12, 1864).

51. Wilkeson, *Recollections of a Private Soldier*, 89, 92; Camille Baquet, *History of the First Brigade, New Jersey Volunteers from 1861 to 1865, Compiled under the Authorization of Kearny's First New Jersey Brigade Society* (Trenton, N.J.: MacCrellish and Quigley, 1910), 125; Dawes, *Service with the Sixth Wisconsin Volunteers*, 269.

52. Dame, *From the Rapidan to Richmond*, 174; Haley, *Rebel Yell & Yankee Hurrah*, 152.

53. Henry Keiser diary, Harrisburg Civil War Round Table Collection, USAMHI (entry for May 13, 1864); Thomas H. Capern to mother, May 15, 1864, vol. 4, no. 39, Lewis Leigh Collection, USAMHI; Curtis, *History of the Twenty-Fourth Michigan*, 244.

54. Gideon Mellin to sister, May 15, 1864, Pennsylvania Save the Flags Collection, USAMHI; OR 36(1):361; F. B. Ward to sister, May 26, 1864, vol. 19, no. 65, Lewis Leigh Collection, USAMHI.

55. Fisk, *Hard Marching Every Day*, 220.

56. A. W. Acheson to mother, June 5, 1864, Pennsylvania Save the Flags Collection, USAMHI; Wilkeson, *Recollections of a Private Soldier*, 85.

57. OR 36(1):232; Haley, *Rebel Yell & Yankee Hurrah*, 160.

58. Brewster, *When This Cruel War Is Over*, 298; Rhodes, *All for the Union*, 153; Sgt. Jacob Siebert to father, May 20, 1864, in Siebert Family Letters, Harrisburg Civil War Round Table Collection, USAMHI.

59. Fisk, *Hard Marching Every Day*, 225; D. G. Crotty, *Four Years Campaigning in the Army of the Potomac* (Grand Rapids, Mich.: Dygert Brothers and Co., 1874), 134; Wilkeson, *Recollections of a Private Soldier*, 88.

60. Fisk, *Hard Marching Every Day*, 221; Maurus Oesterreich diary, Harrisburg Civil War Round Table Collection, USAMHI (entries for ca. May 10, 13, 1864).

61. Lewis C. White memoir, 102nd Pennsylvania, Pennsylvania Save the Flags Collection, USAMHI; J. D. Smith, *History of the Nineteenth Regiment*, 172–73.

62. Jerome Cutler to "My dear Emily," May 19, 1864, in Jerome Cutler, *Letters of Jerome Cutler[,] Waterville, Vermont[,] during His Enlistment in the Union Army 2nd Regiment Ver-*

mont Volunteers 1861–1864 (Bennington, Vt.: Privately printed, 1990), not paginated; Dawes, *Service with the Sixth Wisconsin Volunteers*, 258.

63. C. V. Tevis, *The History of the Fighting Fourteenth* (1911 [?]; reprint, Baltimore, Md.: Butternut and Blue, 1994), 126.

64. E. E. Ross to sister, May 21, 1864, bound vol. 130, FSNMP; Lt. Overton Steger to "Miss Cordelia," May 16, 1864, vol. 19, no. 37, Lewis Leigh Collection, USAMHI.

65. F. B. Ward to sister, May 26, 1864, vol. 19, no. 65, Lewis Leigh Collection, USAMHI; Alfred D. Kelly to brother, May 25, 1864, Williamson Kelly Papers, DU; Benjamin Wesley Justice to wife, May 20, 1864, Benjamin Wesley Justice Papers, Emory University, Atlanta, Ga.; James F. Bryant to father, June 5, 1864, in *Three Rebels Write Home*, ed. Edgar Jackson (Franklin, Va.: News Publishing Company, 1955), 65; James Wesley Williams to wife, May 18, 1864, James Wesley Williams Papers, Emory University, Atlanta, Ga.

66. Benson, *Berry Benson's Book*, 77; W. L. Barrier to "Dear Father," May 8, 1864, in *"Dear Father": Confederate Letters Never Before Published*, ed. Beverly Barrier Troxler and Billy Dawn Barrier Auciello (North Billerica, Mass.: Autumn Printing Corporation, 1989), 122.

67. E. E. Sill to mother, May 16, 1864, bound vol. 130, FSNMP; Martin L. Smith to "Sarah," May 29, 1864, bound vol. 139, FSNMP.

68. Dobbins, ed., *Grandfather's Journal*, 196 (entry for May 17–19, 1864).

We Respect a *Good* Soldier,
No Matter What Flag He Fought Under
The 15th New Jersey Remembers Spotsylvania

U nder a furious rain, the 15th New Jersey charged across a narrow field toward the famous "Bloody Angle." Just fifty yards from the enemy's works, a Confederate volley ripped through the regiment's right flank. In less than thirty minutes, 151 New Jerseyans had fallen, more than half of the unit present that morning. The regiment's chaplain and first historian, Alanson Haines, believed that "no experience during the whole time the Fifteenth was in the service was more destructive than the half hour, from ten o'clock to half-past ten, of the morning of May 12th." Four days earlier, the 15th had lost 121 men at Laurel Hill in the opening battle of the Spotsylvania campaign. Among all Union regiments, only the 148th Pennsylvania surpassed the New Jerseyans' losses of 272 killed, wounded, and missing at Spotsylvania.[1]

These grim statistics, though a testament to the regiment's horrifying experience at Spotsylvania, fail to convey the battle's psychological impact on the unit's survivors. The ghastly scenes of combat, the intense suffering of the wounded, and the striking loss of human life left those in the ranks feeling dazed, numb, and gloomy about the future. At Laurel Hill and the Bloody Angle, the regiment had been handled roughly by its officers. Some New Jerseyans even blamed poor leadership for the 15th's long casualty list. A few days after the battle, a regimental officer captured the dark mood of his unit in observing that "the men are listless and feel down." Another soldier described the horror of the battle in a letter to a New Jersey newspaper: "[Y]ou cannot imagine what carnage there has been.—Waterloo and Gettysburg were skir-mishes." This man predicted that "another such . . . fight, and the country will be a vast hospital."[2] Spotsylvania not only depleted the ranks of the 15th New Jersey, but it also assaulted the men's most basic assumptions about soldier-ing. Some doubted the value of extreme courage in the face of entrenchments; others must have questioned whether saving the Union should exact such a heavy human toll.

Although the 15th New Jersey's experience at Spotsylvania disillusioned some and embittered others, the unit's veterans returned to the Bloody Angle in 1909 to unveil a regimental monument. What compelled these New Jersey-ans to commemorate an event wrought with painful memories and ambiguous meanings? The immediate shock of battle had prevented them from prop-erly mourning dead comrades. Indeed, most of these men had undergone a hardening process as part of the transition to becoming veteran soldiers be-fore they even reached Spotsylvania.[3] Such a defense mechanism emotionally insulated them from the dehumanizing slaughter of Ulysses S. Grant's Over-land campaign. As the men adapted to civilian life during the postwar years, they gradually lost this callous perspective. Time enabled them to confront the terror, sadness, and confusion of combat. Paying homage to lost friends on hallowed ground enabled the 15th's veterans to come to terms with their wartime experience. They considered the "pilgrimages" to the Bloody Angle a sacred duty, the last act they would perform as soldiers.

In trips to Spotsylvania in 1906 and 1909, members of the 15th New Jersey Association were not content simply to honor the dead. They used these op-portunities to articulate a brand of nationalism based upon heroic action and militarism.[4] The result was a nostalgic view of soldiering that diminished the horrors of combat while expressing admiration for their former opponents. During the 1909 dedication at Spotsylvania, the 15th's veterans emphasized the valor of Union and Confederate soldiers to remind Americans of the terrific sacrifices made on both sides. In this way, they advanced the theme of national conciliation without delving into controversial political or social issues. Union veterans and northern and southern politicians praised the courage of the New Jerseyans and their Confederate foes to argue that the martial spirit dis-played on the fields of Spotsylvania reflected a distinctive, superior American character. A central part of this message was the implicit theme that future generations might have to tap these aggressive masculine traits to defend the nation against an outside threat.

The 15th New Jersey's collective memory of Spotsylvania illuminates the meaning of veteranhood while also providing insights into the process by which soldiers became their own historians and struggled to explain their experiences to outsiders. The 15th typified the makeup of most northern regiments. Farmers and laborers, intermixed with some miners, storekeepers, and craftsmen, filled the ranks.[5] During July and August 1862, the regiment drew recruits from the rural counties of Sussex, Warren, Hunterdon, Morris, and Somerset in the northwestern portion of the state. A modest local bounty, a Federal bounty of $100, and an advance of $25 from the state lured a number of men to the regiment's camp of instruction at the Flemington Fair Grounds. Despite the allure of these various bounties, regimental historian Haines understandably argued that most of the men were "animated by ardent patriotism" and the earnest desire to preserve the Union.[6]

On August 25, the 15th New Jersey was mustered into service with 925 officers and men. Two days later, they left for the Washington defenses, remaining there until assigned in September to the Army of the Potomac's First Brigade of the First Division of the Sixth Army Corps, an association the unit would maintain for the remainder of the war. On December 13, the unit saw limited action at Fredericksburg near the center of the Union line. A few months later at Chancellorsville it faced an initial test of serious combat near Salem Church. When a portion of the Union line collapsed in the men's initial real battle, the Jerseymen held their ground at a cost of more than 150 casualties. Filled with confidence after their defiant stand at Salem Church, the 15th completed an impressive thirty-five-mile forced march to Gettysburg in early July, only to spend most of the battle in a reserve position north of Little Round Top.[7] The regiment also missed much of the fighting at the Wilderness; however, its calm response to the collapse of the Union right flank on the evening of May 6 earned high praise from the demanding Emory Upton, who wrote in his official report that the 15th "behaved under all circumstances with a steadiness indicative of the highest state of discipline."[8]

Spotsylvania introduced the Jerseymen to Grant's aggressive style of warfare. After the Confederates checked the Federal advance on May 8 at Laurel Hill, the Union high command planned a combined attack by Gouverneur K. Warren's Fifth Corps and John Sedgwick's Sixth Corps. This final assault was scheduled for 1:00 P.M. against the Confederate position astride the Brock Road. A lack of cooperation between Warren and Sedgwick and the exhausted state of the troops, who had completed a fatiguing march from the Wilderness, delayed the attack until 6:30.[9] An hour before launching the main assault, an exasperated General Warren approached Lt. Edmund D. Halsey of the 15th and demanded to know who commanded the brigade. A staff officer answered Col. Henry W. Brown. "And where is Colonel Brown," asked Warren. The staff

Line officers of the 15th New Jersey and friends, March 12, 1864. Front row, left to right: Captain Cornelius C. Shimer, Company A; Captain William T. Cornish, Company H; Captain James Walker, Company D; Captain Lewis Van Blarcom, Company C; Captain Ellis Hamilton, Company F. Back row, left to right: First Lieutenant Lowe Emerson, Quartermaster; Captain James S. McDanolds, Company B; Lieutenant James Northrop, 2nd New Jersey Infantry; First Lieutenant Ebenezer Davis, Company I; First Lieutenant William J. Cooke, Quartermaster, 4th New Jersey Infantry; First Lieutenant William Van Voy, Company C; Samuel Young, Sutler; First Lieutenant Nehemiah Tunis, Company B; First Lieutenant John P. Crater, Company E; First Lieutenant Edmund D. Halsey, Adjutant; First Lieutenant William W. Penrose, Company F. Shimer and Walker were killed at Spotsylvania; Van Blarcom lost a leg and was captured by the Confederates.
Hunterdon County Historical Society, Flemington, New Jersey

officer pointed to the rear of the brigade. Outraged that Brown did not lead by personal example, Warren decided to take command of the Jersey Brigade and moved it to a gap between the two corps, just east of the Brock Road.[10]

The irascible Warren was not finished with the Jerseymen. Just before dusk the men were preparing to make a reconnaissance-in-force when Warren rode up to the brigade and shouted: "Where is the commander of this Brigade, I ordered it into action an hour ago." Warren then directed Col. William H. Penrose of the 15th New Jersey to form the brigade and charge the hill (because he had upset Warren, Colonel Brown would lose command of the brigade the next day). Penrose quickly deployed the 3rd New Jersey as skirmishers, with the 15th following close behind in lines of battle. After sloshing through some marshland, the Jerseymen moved across a field and advanced to within fifty yards of the enemy's light works when Confederate volleys slashed into both flanks of the regiment. The men persevered, surged over the first line of trenches, and engaged the southerners in some brief hand-to-hand fighting. Without proper support, the 15th found itself isolated, in the open, and exposed to fire from three directions. The unit abandoned its foothold and scurried to the rear. Survivors collapsed in the tall grass at the base of the hill until darkness covered the field and permitted a safe return to their lines. The regiment sustained 101 casualties and captured one enemy soldier in a mission that likely seemed pointless to the men.[11] The main Union attack that followed later that evening also failed.

The next two days brought considerable activity but no heavy fighting for the 15th. Sniper fire greeted the Jersey Brigade on the morning of May 9, killing a color sergeant and wounding another noncommissioned officer. As he rode along the front, Gen. John Sedgwick noticed the exposed position of the Jerseymen and ordered them to retire. The general failed to show the same concern a few minutes later when he chided some artillerists for dodging sharpshooter fire. Such contempt for southern marksmanship soon cost the Jerseyans' their beloved corps commander when "Uncle John" fell with a mortal wound to the head. That afternoon, the 15th and 1st New Jersey tried to find the elusive Ninth Corps. It was an exhausting mission, requiring the Jerseyans to cross some rugged terrain while continually skirmishing with the Confederates. Near dusk, both regiments halted on the extreme left flank of the Sixth Corps without connecting with Burnside's troops. When Gershom Mott's Second Corps division plugged the hole in the Union line on May 10, the 15th and 1st regiments were temporarily assigned to his command. Both units guarded the right flank of Mott's force, which had been ordered to support Emory Upton's attack against the western face of the Confederate "Mule Shoe" salient. Mott's failure to assist Upton shielded the 15th from heavy casualties but generated considerable controversy in the army.[12]

The Jerseyans rejoined their brigade on May 11, a day in which they enjoyed a much needed respite from fighting. While the 15th recovered from the rigors of active campaigning, Grant selected Hancock's Second Corps to spearhead a major attack against the Confederate salient the next day. An early morning fog screened the Federal advance. Before the southerners detected the Union movement, Hancock's men swarmed across the Confederate works and bagged thousands of prisoners. Hancock's lines disintegrated, however, as the Federal units mingled together and lost their sense of purpose. A lack of strong leadership prevented the Unionists from delivering a decisive blow against Lee's army. The most successful attack in the history of the Army of the Potomac stalled at the moment when a crushing victory seemed to be within its grasp. Instead of pressing forward, Hancock withdrew his corps to the original point of the breakthrough and waited for reinforcements. Emory Upton hurried to the scene with the lead elements of the Sixth Corps. He relieved some of Hancock's men who were pinned down by enemy fire along a depression paralleling the west angle of the salient, across from a section of Confederate works later known as the Bloody Angle. A severe enfilading fire blistered Upton's right flank. More troops were needed if Upton were to hold his ground; the 15th and the rest of the Jersey Brigade rushed to the scene.[13]

High spirits predominated among the Jerseyans when they received their call to the front at 10:00 A.M. A proclamation announcing Hancock's initial success had cheered the men earlier in the morning. Patriotic airs from the brigade band inspired the 15th as it embarked on what would be its severest test of the war. The regiment marched into a woodlot of scrub pines and cedar trees before halting at the edge of a field, a few hundred yards southwest of the West Angle and not far from the scene of Upton's famous charge on May 10. Penrose deployed his regiments into the line of battle with the 15th anchoring the brigade's extreme right. Strict orders prohibited the men from firing until they reached the enemy's trenches.[14] Blasts of Confederate musketry greeted the Jerseyans as soon as they left the shelter of the woods. Charging at the left oblique toward the West Angle exposed the 15th's right flank to Stephen Dodson Ramseur's North Carolina brigade, which devoured the inviting target with one crushing volley. "It seemed to me as if the right wing was swept away in an instant," recorded Edmund Halsey of the 15th. A survivor of the charge wrote after the war that "we got a volley that killed or wounded half of the 15th."[15]

The companies on the regiment's left as well as the rest of the brigade forged ahead, striking the enemy's works at the juncture of Nathaniel H. Harris's Mississippi brigade and Ramseur's North Carolinians. Hand-to-hand fighting erupted across the log and dirt embankments as the Jerseymen shot or bayoneted any Confederate who tried to escape. Few were able to surrender. In this confused melee, Lt. George C. Justice mounted the works, waved his sword, and shouted encouraging words to his company. A skulking southern prisoner lunged for a musket and shot the lieutenant in the back, then quickly fell victim himself to the bayonet thrust of a New Jersey private. The regiment's chaplain complained that a number of southerners "lifted their hands in token surrender, and lay crouching in the ditch," only to grab "their weapons when their captors were more hardly pressed."[16]

Confederates on both sides of the 15th turned their muskets on the Jerseymen's flanks. Penrose quickly determined that his regiment could not hold

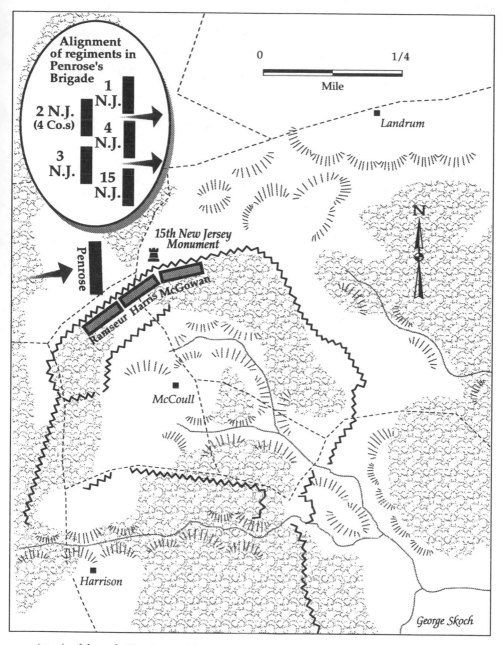

Alignment of regiments in Penrose's Brigade

1 N.J.

2 N.J. (4 Co.s)

4 N.J.

3 N.J.

15 N.J.

0   1/4

Mile

Landrum

15th New Jersey Monument

N

Penrose

Ramseur Harris McGowan

McCoull

Harrison

George Skoch

Attack of the 15th New Jersey, May 12, 1864

First Sergeant Paul Kuhl of Company A was among the members of the 15th New Jersey who died in action on May 12. John Kuhl collection

the captured works and accordingly ordered his men to retire. The regiment's wounded and dead remained in the hands of the enemy, including the popular Sgt. Paul Kuhl, who had been shot in the leg. Kuhl had improvised a tourniquet by tying a handkerchief to his ramrod to stop the bleeding. The following day his lifeless form, riddled by hundreds of bullets, was found near the Confederate works. Another member of the 15th grimly noted that "64 of my regiment lay dead inside their lines." Between fifty and seventy-five men miraculously escaped the slaughter, carrying with them a handful of southern prisoners and one captured Confederate battle flag. Together with the rest of the brigade, the 15th's survivors rallied in some woods not far from the attack's starting point. They remained in reserve for the remainder of the evening. In just thirty minutes the regiment had sustained approximately 150 casualties, including 7 line officers and every member of the color guard except one. Diarist Edmund Halsey sadly confided: "It was a grievous day for the 15th."[17]

The following day, Chaplain Haines organized volunteers from the 15th to bury the regiment's dead. Some forty bodies could be identified by comrades who expressed a desire to give every fallen soldier a proper funeral. Unfortunately, there was no time to mourn. Only eleven men had been buried in hastily dug graves before the 15th received orders to move. The strange hands of paid grave diggers placed the rest of the unit's dead in an unmarked mass grave. Filling the vacant positions in the color guard became a priority for Halsey. Exemption from tiresome fatigue duties always had made these posts of honor particularly attractive, but after Spotsylvania no noncommissioned officers stepped forward to volunteer. The charge near the Bloody Angle had demonstrated that certain death awaited those standing near the regiment's battle flags. Prudence thus dictated that the noncommissioned officers remain in the ranks of their own companies. Only when Halsey promised some privates quick promotion to corporal did he secure the necessary volunteers.[18]

As the 15th New Jersey marched away from the scene of its destruction toward the North Anna River, the survivors could not erase images of comrades mutilated by enemy fire or escape the overwhelming loss of so many departed friends. Some turned bitter, others appeared lost, almost disconnected from the world. Shortly after the battle, the regiment coldly greeted an official proclamation that exhorted them to redouble their efforts against the enemy as a tribute to their fallen comrades. It appears that some soldiers even felt betrayed by their officers. James Maguire, who was hit by five bullets on May 12, believed his regimental or brigade superiors rather than anyone more senior in the army's command might have been responsible for the debacle at the West Angle. Two years after the war he wondered why the 15th had not been supported properly. He suggested that the charge might have been "unauthorised from Head Quarters" but "never could learn" for certain. Descriptions of courageous acts do not appear in the few surviving postbattle letters of the 15th. A month after the Bloody Angle, Joseph Sullivan, who was badly wounded on May 12, tried to capture the battle's tragedy in cold numbers. He had counted eighty-eight men in his company before the fatal charge; only eleven remained when the fighting subsided. "You see," Sullivan concluded with considerable understatement, "we had a hard time of it. . . . [O]ur Regiment is very Small now," he added, and "moast of our officers has bin killed."[19]

The Jerseyans made their first Bloody Angle pilgrimage shortly after Lee's surrender at Appomattox. When the 15th marched through Spotsylvania Court House on its way to Washington for the Grand Review, Chaplain Haines and some others made a quick sidetrip to the salient to pay their respects to comrades who had fallen on May 12. Once at the site of the 15th's charge, images of the conflict readily came to mind. Writing about this episode later, Haines could not bring himself to divulge its details, nor did he describe the battle as a heroic event in the 15th's history. The tremendous loss of life preoccupied his thoughts, just as it had overwhelmed the survivors of the 15th immediately after the battle. He was awed by "the many heaps and the long, low mounds" of ditches of Union and Confederate dead. When they located the graves of the 15th, Haines was thankful to find that "those whom we had buried were undisturbed" and "the head-boards remained as we left them."[20]

As Haines surveyed the field, he realized that a traumatic chapter in his life had come to a close. The serenity of nature and its powers of restoration conveyed cause for hope that he and his comrades would experience their own healing process once they reentered the civilian world. Haines wrote that "the grass was growing green and rank on the ground once pressed with the tread of many feet, in charge and counter-charge." The soothing peacefulness of the Bloody Angle impressed him the most, "in contrast with all the sounds of deadly conflict with which it was associated." It appeared to Haines that "nature was putting forth her most luxuriant vegetation as though she would cover the scars of war."[21] Just as nature had rehabilitated the battered landscape of Spotsylvania, Haines believed that over time new layers of memories would cover the painful recollections of Spotsylvania. His desire to disconnect himself from the past, to bury the discordant memories of the war, and to move forward with his life must have been shared by most of the 15th's veterans.

When the Jerseymen were mustered out of service, they discovered that friends and family also wanted to distance themselves from the war. Remembering the conflict only reminded them of loved ones killed in the army, political dissension in their communities, and painful sacrifices at home. They took pride in the preservation of the Union, but the job was finished and they wanted to tackle new challenges. Northern civilians craved a return to the way of life they had known before 1861. Although a desire to honor the memory of soldiers who had given their lives spontaneously appeared across the North in 1866 and 1867, resulting in the national holiday of Memorial Day, civilians displayed lukewarm interest in commemorating the war. They focused instead on careers, recreation, and other activities in the immediate postwar years.[22]

The memory of the war receded in the northern consciousness until the 1880s, when the Grand Army of the Republic, largest of the Union veteran organizations, experienced a fraternal revival that broke with the group's rigid hierarchy and its political agenda. Membership soared in this egalitarian environment as ex-soldiers saw themselves as comrades bound together by the shared experience of combat. Defending the memories of the dead united them in purpose and action. The formation of regimental veteran organizations and yearly reunions accompanied the resurgence of the GAR.[23] The 15th New Jersey Volunteers Veteran Association held its first regimental reunion in 1880 and continued the practice annually until 1929.[24] As the years passed and the association's ranks thinned, the veterans' interest in returning to the Virginia battlefields heightened. At the annual reunion in 1905, the aging soldiers decided to make a pilgrimage the following year to the regiment's old campground at White Oak Church near Fredericksburg.[25]

On May 22, 1906, eighty members of the 15th's association boarded trains for Virginia, stopping briefly in Washington, D.C., before arriving in Fredericksburg at 6:30 that evening. At the depot, they received a warm welcome from the town's mayor and other prominent citizens who escorted the veterans and their thirty-five guests to the Exchange Hotel. Early the next morning the Jerseymen left the town in a wagon caravan. They passed by the Fredericksburg battlefield and the ruins of Burnside's headquarters before stopping at White Oak Church. At their old campgrounds, the men took a special interest in pointing out the baking ovens of the Jersey Brigade, the parade grounds, and the church where they attended the services of Chaplain Haines. One man recalled that it was his duty as orderly sergeant to gather all the men who did not attend church. To encourage these godless soldiers to respect the Sabbath in the future, he read the articles of war while the chaplain gave his sermon to more pious members of the unit. He believed his tactics had awakened the religious sensibilities of more soldiers than had the chaplain.[26]

It is significant that the 15th's survivors held their formal ceremony at their winter quarters of 1862–63 instead of paying tribute to the regiment's service on the battlefield. The old camp coincided with the veterans' sentimental view of soldiering. This tranquil setting provided a perfect backdrop for them to evoke images of brotherly camaraderie, shared sacrifice, and Christian duty. Although one soldier admitted that sickness had taken the lives of many Jerseymen, nostalgia and excessive nationalism shaped the veterans' recollections of the war. Members of the 15th who spoke in front of the crowd at White Oak Church remained silent about their ambiguous response to the human carnage of battle. They appealed to northerners and southerners to remember the brave acts of both sides as a means to instill love of nation. "When we consider that we were brothers," proclaimed Theodore F. Swayze, "that you were bone of our bone and flesh of our flesh, it is not so wonderful that the fighting was fierce. To-day we say, without fear of contradiction, that you were as brave in war as we were." Like many of his comrades, Swayze considered manliness the defining characteristic of national identity. He reminded the audience that "nations are made up of men, and no nation can be better than its men." True manhood, in his mind, transcended regional differences. Because northern and southern soldiers had showed themselves superior fighters, he concluded that Americans on both sides of the Mason-Dixon still possessed those same traits that the rest of the world respected and feared.[27]

The second day of the pilgrimage tested the endurance of the aging veterans. They covered a forty-mile route across the battlefields of Chancellorsville, the Wilderness, and Spotsylvania. After a brief stop at Salem Church, which the congregation had opened to the veterans, the men stopped at the ruins of the second Chancellorsville house. The urge to gather souvenirs prompted some of the ex-Union soldiers to carry off pieces of wood from the ruins (although these relics were not from the building that had stood at the time of the battle of Chancellorsville). Once the party turned onto the Brock Road, passed Todd's Tavern, and drew near to Spotsylvania, one member of the association noticed that the old soldiers became visibly excited. Before reaching their destination, one carriage plunged into a creek because the bridge lacked guard rails. All five occupants were tossed into the stream, and Christopher Ehni was sent to Martha Washington Hospital with severe injuries. Ironically, Ehni served as chairman of the Committee on Bridges of Somerset County, New Jersey, where he enforced building codes that required bridges to have protective iron rails. The historian of the association, J. Frank Lindsley, hoped that the accident would be "a lesson here."[28]

An elaborate lunch awaited the 15th at the monument to John Sedgwick. After paying respects to their former corps commander, a few men walked across Laurel Hill looking for bullets before rejoining the group for its final stop at the Bloody Angle. Once they reached the venerated ground, the veterans seemed to stay to themselves, gathering in small groups, locating "well remembered" spots, and, according to one observer, speaking "with awed voices" about "that awful time of carnage." Veteran Albert Whitehead pinpointed the area where the 15th's right flank had been destroyed in that fatal charge and suggested that a marker should be erected there. The association was already discussing the possibility of dedicating a monument at Salem Church. During the trip home, the Jerseymen reached a tentative agreement that at the next annual reunion a resolution would be adopted asking the New Jersey state legislature to appropriate funds to erect monuments at Spotsylvania and Salem Church.[29]

The regimental association energetically pursued this project. In less than a year, the group purchased small plots of land at Salem Church and Spotsylvania and petitioned the legislature for funds. The lower and upper houses passed the measure, granting an appropriation of $6,500, but Gov. Edward C. Stokes vetoed the bill, killing the project for the remainder of the year. In the winter of 1907, the legislature revived the bill and newly elected governor J. Franklin Fort signed it into law, granting a civilian commission $6,500 for the erection and dedication of a monument at Salem Church and a "tablet" at Spotsylvania. A private donation of $2,000 covered the expenses of every veteran of the 15th who would attend the dedications. Ceremonies were planned for May 12, 1909, the 45th anniversary of the Bloody Angle fighting.[30]

A special eight-car train heading from New Jersey carried 350 veterans, dignitaries, and other guests to Fredericksburg on the afternoon of May 11. More than a hundred local residents welcomed their northern visitors, including some Confederate veterans who cordially greeted their old adversaries. The Jerseymen could not find adequate accommodations at the Exchange Hotel —

except for Governor Fort, who found a spacious room awaiting him. "If there has been any time in our life more than another that we felt a burning desire to be Governor of a State," observed one veteran, "it was right then." Generous townspeople took many of the Jerseyans into their homes, rescuing the Exchange Hotel from an embarrassing situation.

That evening, the Maury Camp of the Sons of Confederate Veterans held a public reception at the courthouse. The speakers, Judge John T. Goolrick of Fredericksburg and Governor Fort, pleaded for sectional reconciliation by turning the gathering into a virtual lovefest between North and South. Both men barely mentioned the actions of the 15th New Jersey. They also refrained from discussing the destruction of Fredericksburg by Union troops in 1862 or the bitter fighting and staggering losses that occurred on both sides. They used this opportunity to promote greater loyalty to the nation without delving into the divisive issues of the past. Goolrick asserted at the close of his address that "in our Union is strength. Whom God hath joined together no power can burst asunder." Fort reiterated a similar theme in his glowing tribute to Robert E. Lee. He reminded the audience that New Jersey and Virginia had stood together during the American Revolution, then asked the crowd to give three cheers for Virginia's veterans, a plea that elicited an enthusiastic response. After the group sang the "Star Spangled Banner" and "America," the meeting adjourned amid a spirit of sectional harmony that set the tone for the 15th's dedication ceremony.[31]

The next day a wide variety of buggies, wagons, and carriages waited for the pilgrims outside the Exchange Hotel. To accommodate the 350 people for the thirty-mile ride to Spotsylvania and Salem Church, "every available rig for ten miles around had to be pressed into service," one observer believed. Mules pulled many of the vehicles, which sparked amusement among the Jerseyans. Treacherous roads made the twelve-mile journey to Spotsylvania a difficult undertaking. One New Jerseyan remarked that a road overseer in his state "would be quickly indicted for maintaining roads half so bad as the roads in that section of Virginia." After about two uncomfortable hours, the pilgrims reached the battlefield. The old members of the 15th soon discovered that they could not pinpoint the regiment's exact position. The terrain had changed considerably since the war, and a bystander remarked that it took the veterans some time to find their "bearings." They argued among themselves about the location of the regiment's disastrous charge but eventually reached agreement about the site and began relating personal anecdotes associated with the battle.[32]

The sound of reveille brought the assembly together at 11:00. The sponsors purposefully orchestrated an event that emphasized the nationalistic themes of

The 15th New Jersey monument opposite the Confederate lines at the Bloody Angle. National Park Service

sectional harmony and loyalty to the Union.[33] This was not a ceremony devoted exclusively to the 15th New Jersey or the state's contribution to ending the rebellion. Northern organizers made sure that the opinions of ex-Confederates were respected and represented during the service. After a short prayer and the singing of "America," the lieutenant governor of Virginia gave the welcome address. Next came the unveiling of the tablet by four young women, two from Virginia and two from New Jersey. A series of brief speeches followed from Governor Fort, two veterans of the 15th, and a New Jersey congressman. The speakers stood near an oversized U.S. flag draped over the monument. The final display of sectional brotherhood occurred with the dramatic return of the 14th Georgia Infantry's flag, which had been captured on May 12. Although the Jerseymen insisted that it belonged to the Georgia unit, the latter's survivors claimed they never lost it and refused to send any representative to the event. Nevertheless, the 15th handed it over to some southerners who promised to pass it along to the rightful owners. As the banner changed hands, an elderly Virginia woman asked to touch it. She kissed the flag and told the audience that her husband and three sons had been killed fighting under the Confederate emblem.[34]

The nationalistic imagery of the monument's unveiling, with its inclusion of southern representatives and symbols, provided the perfect backdrop for the common message of the northern speakers. Whether a politician or veteran stood behind the podium, each agreed that the war had accomplished the critical mission of reuniting the nation. No one mentioned the divisive issue of slavery, the war's devastation of the South, or the failures of Reconstruction. They celebrated reunion as an inevitable outcome of progress and implored the audience to display greater loyalty to the nation. Governor Fort best captured this theme when he bluntly told the audience that the state's duty was "to perpetuate the memory of its illustrious dead" as a means to secure the allegiance of the nation's citizens. Although he acknowledged the special contributions of the Jerseymen, he reminded the audience that "all who fought here are now canonized as heroes." "Our lesson," Fort concluded, "is greater devotion to the country for which they gave so much." [35]

Although northern and southern civilian speakers focused almost exclusively on nationalistic themes and political goals, the 1909 dedication served a more spiritual and didactic purpose for the veterans. At last they were able to pay homage to those who had been lost in battle. The demands of active campaigning and a hardened view of war prevented these men from coming to terms with the painful emotions associated with battle. The 15th's two speakers, Theodore F. Swayze and Albert Whitehead, also honored their departed friends by imparting a moral lesson to future generations. According to both men, their comrades killed at Spotsylvania embodied true manhood with their unwavering sense of duty, honor, and patriotism. They hoped this memorial would inspire Americans to follow the courageous example of those who had given their lives to preserve the Union. Swayze believed the monument would encourage the sons of the 15th's veterans to hand down the memory of the regiment's services to future generations.[36]

In memorializing their comrades at the Bloody Angle, Swayze and Whitehead did not dwell on the butchery of May 12. They offered a more palatable version of war that ignored the conflicting dilemmas of combat. Swayze acknowledged that the regiment was nearly destroyed on May 12, but stressed that the men's fierce determination had earned them immortal fame deserving of memorialization. Weariness over Grant's costly tactics, doubts about whether the Union was worth the human sacrifice, and the bitterness of losing so many comrades in a seemingly mismanaged charge were issues that had confronted Jerseymen after Spotsylvania and probably weakened their morale. But these troubling questions did not surface in any of the presentations in 1909. Disillusionment and confusion gave way to a heroic vision of combat that sanctified courage as the defining trait of American identity. The courageous example of the 15th mirrored the "history of many another regiment," Swayze believed. He had asked himself "many times" whether the wholesale loss of life was worth it. But when he considered "our condition today as a world power," Swayze realized that "it was worth the fearful sacrifice." By honoring Civil War soldiers, suggested the speakers that day, future generations would always be in touch with the aggressive masculine traits that had enabled northern soldiers to save the Union and position the United States to rise as a world power after the Spanish American War.[37]

In avoiding the chilling descriptions of combat provided by writers such as Ambrose Bierce, Swayze and Whitehead reassured their audience with a nostalgic, sentimental description of Spotsylvania. The speakers conveyed no hint of the agony of leaving wounded in the hands of the enemy or of finding a comrade's lifeless body shredded by bullets almost beyond recognition. Nothing in the postwar remembrances of the Jersey veterans approached the simple description of Charles R. Paul, a member of 15th serving on the brigade staff, who wrote in his diary on May 13, 1864: "I have passed over many a battlefield since the war commenced, but I never before, and I hope I never shall again witness such a sight. The dead were piled in places three and four deep, wounded and dead together, in all manner of positions. Some with muskets clasped in their hands[,] others with hands clasped together in the agony of death." [38]

Swayze and Whitehead also ignored questions surrounding the regiment's leadership at Spotsylvania. The charge at Laurel Hill had lacked proper support, and the attack against the Angle had exposed the 15th to enfilading fire. Between the two cases, the Jerseymen had accomplished little for their high casualty lists. Curiously, the new monument stood at the Bloody Angle, near the site of the famous oak tree, even though the regiment had struck the Confederate lines a good two hundred yards to the south. Perhaps the regimental association believed such a prominent location would cast New Jersey in a more favorable light as a faithful supporter of the Union cause. During and after the war the state could not escape an undeserved reputation as a wartime haven for Copperheads and other disloyal elements.[39]

Glossing over the vicious acts committed at the Bloody Angle enabled northern speakers more easily to express empathy for former Confederates. Recalling images of Union soldiers bludgeoning southerners with muskets would have dampened the conciliatory mood at the unveiling, to say the least. Speakers maintained strict neutrality in extolling the bravery of all combatants. The spirit of revenge and hatred that motivated soldiers in 1864 found no place at the Bloody Angle in 1909. No one mentioned the southern prisoner who shot Lieutenant Justice in the back. No one even hinted at the fact that both sides were reluctant to show quarter when the Jerseymen temporarily broke the Confederate lines. The desire for reconciliation demanded a type of selective amnesia that filtered out old rancor and highlighted common courage. When returning the 14th Georgia's flag, for example, Whitehead remarked that the fighting at Spotsylvania "demonstrated to the world that no braver nor better soldiers ever lived than those produced" in the Union and Confederate armies. "We respect a *good* soldier," he added, "no matter what flag he fought under." [40]

Like most northern veterans, the Jerseymen did not believe their tribute to Confederate valor threatened the picture of the Union cause as a virtuous crusade led by selfless men. But their admiration for southern soldiers might have reflected a degree of dissatisfaction and alienation with fellow northerners. By talking with ex-Confederates and reuniting with old comrades at Spotsylvania, the Jerseyans found familiarity and understanding in the shared experience of soldiering. Returning to the battlefield also gave them an opportunity to shape how the Civil War would be understood in popular culture. Future generations who visited Spotsylvania, saw the monument, and reflected on what happened at the Bloody Angle might remember that Civil War soldiers personified the ideal of American manhood.

Their message proved enduring and influential. Fifty-five years after the 1909 pilgrimage to Spotsylvania, another crowd gathered on the same ground to rededicate the 15th New Jersey's monument. On this occasion, John P. Read of New Jersey proclaimed: "We rededicate these Monuments to the North and the South—because in this ceremony we see the symbols of our unity, our love of country, of our cry that we are all Americans, cherishing and protecting the same ideals conceived by our forefathers." On the southern side, Virginia historian Virgil Carrington Jones noted that both of his grandfathers fought under Lee and "came out of the experience without bitterness or hatred." "They were Americans," asserted Jones, "and so were the New Jersey soldiers who fought here on this field a century ago." [41]

The 15th's veterans would have approved of these conciliatory sentiments in 1909, but in 1864 they would have rejected such warm feelings for Confederates. The surge in nationalism after the Spanish American War altered how many Jerseymen and other northern veterans interpreted the past. Their collective memory suddenly embraced ex-Confederates as a worthy foe who, like all true Americans, fought in defense of their homes. Unlike civilians who could not appreciate the sacrifices and values of Civil War soldiers, the enemy had become a comrade in arms who understood the importance of courage and the test of combat.

Perhaps more than anything else, returning to the Bloody Angle fulfilled a deep emotional need for the 15th New Jersey's veterans. The trauma of battle and the demands of active campaigning had prevented them from properly mourning their dead comrades at the time. With the passage of time, the history of the Bloody Angle did not seem so awful, so unbearable. At the 1909 monument dedication, these veterans stepped simultaneously out of the past and into the past, by connecting with the memory of their comrades who had given their lives at Spotsylvania.

ACKNOWLEDGMENTS
The author would like to acknowledge the invaluable assistance of Joseph G. Bilby, John W. Kuhl, and Tim Nist, all historians of the 15th and residents of New Jersey.

NOTES
1. Alanson A. Haines, *History of the Fifteenth Regiment New Jersey Volunteers* (New York: Jenkins & Thomas, Printers, 1883), 178; Joseph G. Bilby, *Three Rousing Cheers: A History of the Fifteenth New Jersey from Flemington to Appomattox* (Hightstown, N.J.: Longstreet House, 1993), 149.

2. Edmund D. Halsey diary, May 15, 1864, Halsey Collection, U.S. Army Military History Institute, Carlisle Barracks, Pa. (repository hereafter cited as USAMHI); "From the 15th Regiment," Hunterdon (N.J.) *Republican*, May 20, 1864.

3. On the process of civilian-soldiers adopting a veteran perspective to the realities of war, see Gerald F. Linderman, *Embattled Courage: The Experience of Combat in the American Civil War* (New York: The Free Press, 1987), 156–215.

4. For a discussion of the nationalistic symbolism of Civil War veteran ceremonies, see John Pettegrew, " 'The Soldier's Faith': Turn-of-the-Century Memory of the Civil War and the Emergence of Modern American Nationalism," *Journal of Contemporary History* 31 (January 1996):49–73.

5. For a detailed history of the 15th New Jersey, see Bilby, *Three Rousing Cheers*. See also Haines, *History of the Fifteenth Regiment*, and Camille Baquet, *History of the First Brigade, New Jersey Volunteers from 1861 to 1865, Compiled under the Authorization of Kearny's First New Jersey Brigade Society* (Trenton, N.J.: MacCrellish & Quigley, State Printers, 1910).

6. Haines, *History of the Fifteenth Regiment*, 7.

7. For a summary of the 15th's military actions, see Bilby, *Three Rousing Cheers*.

8. U.S. War Department, *The War of the Rebellion: A Compilation of the Official Records of the Union and Confederate Armies*, 127 vols., index, and atlas (Washington, D.C.: GPO, 1880–1901), ser. 1, 36(1):666 (hereafter cited as *OR*; all references are to ser. 1).

9. For good treatments of the action at Laurel Hill, see William D. Matter, *If It Takes All Summer: The Battle of Spotsylvania* (Chapel Hill: University of North Carolina Press, 1988), and Gordon C. Rhea, *The Battles for Spotsylvania Court House and the Road to Yellow Tavern: May 7–12, 1864* (Baton Rouge: Louisiana State University Press, 1997).

10. Halsey diary, May 8, 1864, Halsey Collection, USAMHI.

11. Ibid.; Haines, *History of the Fifteenth Regiment*, 158.

12. Haines, *History of the Fifteenth Regiment*, 161; Bilby, *Three Rousing Cheers*, 138–42. On Mott's controversial actions, see Matter, *If It Takes All Summer*, 156–61.

13. On Hancock's assault against the salient and the response of the Union Sixth Corps, see Matter's *If It Takes All Summer* and Rhea's *Battles for Spotsylvania*.

14. A more thorough examination of the 15th's role on May 12 can be found in Bilby, *Three Rousing Cheers*, 142–46.

15. Halsey diary, May 12, 1864, Halsey Collection, USAMHI; James Maguire Narrative, June 4, 1867, William Orlando Bourne Collection, Library of Congress, Washington, D.C. (repository hereafter cited as LC).

16. Haines, *History of the Fifteenth Regiment*, 175.

17. Ibid., 178–79; James Maguire Narrative, June 4, 1867, William Orlando Bourne Collection, LC; Halsey diary, May 12, 1864, Halsey Collection, USAMHI.

18. Haines, *History of the Fifteenth Regiment*, 182; Halsey Diary, May 13, 1864, Halsey Collection, USAMHI.

19. James Maguire Narrative, June 4, 1867, William Orlando Bourne Collection, LC; Joseph E. Sullivan to Mary Ewing, June 27, 1864, Mary Ewing Rutger Papers, Special Collections, Rutgers University Library, Trenton, N.J. (repository hereafter cited as RUL). Only a few Spotsylvania letters and diary entries survive from members of the 15th New Jersey. See Charles R. Paul diary, May 8–18, 1864, Murray J. Smith Collection, USAMHI (by the time of Spotsylvania, Paul had left the 15th and served on the staff of the 1st Jersey Brigade); Halsey diary, May 8–18, Halsey Collection, USAMHI; "From the Fifteenth Regiment," May 20, 1864, Hunterdon (N.J.) *Republican*; "From the Fifteenth Regiment," May 27, 1864, Sussex (N.J.) *Register*.

20. Haines, *History of the Fifteenth Regiment*, 314–15.

21. Ibid., 315.

22. Linderman, *Embattled Courage*, 271–75.

23. Stuart McConnell, *Glorious Contentment: The Grand Army of the Republic, 1865–1900* (Chapel Hill: University of North Carolina Press, 1992), 167–70.

24. Bilby, *Three Rousing Cheers*, 249. For descriptions of some of the 15th's reunions, see "The 15th at Newton," Washington *Star*, September 27, 1883; "The Fifteenth's Reunion," Washington *Star*, September 27, 1900; "Veteran Association Reunion," Hunterdon (N.J.) *Republican*, June 19, 1907.

25. *Pilgrimage of the Fifteenth New Jersey Volunteers' Veteran Association to White Oak Church Camp Ground and Battlefields of Fredericksburg, Va. and Vicinity May 22 to 26, 1906* (Newark, N.J.: Madison & Co., 1906), 7–8.

26. Ibid., 9–11, 19. For another account of the 15th's first trip to Fredericksburg, see "On the Old Battle-Fields," Sussex (N.J.) *Register*, May 31, 1906.

27. *Pilgrimage of the Fifteenth New Jersey*, 13, 16. In the same pamphlet, see also the speeches of Col. E. W. Davis and A. W. Whitehead of the 15th (pp. 19, 21–22).

28. Ibid., 27–28, 61–62.

29. Ibid., 32, 58.

30. Donald C. Pfanz, "History Through Eyes of Stone: A Survey of the Monuments in Fredericksburg National Military Park," 38–39, photocopy, Fredericksburg and Spotsylvania National Military Park Library, Fredericksburg, Va.; *Fourth Annual Pilgrimage of the Fifteenth Regiment New Jersey Volunteers' Veteran Association, May 11th to Fifteenth, 1909, Fredericksburg, Washington, and Gettysburg* (Washington, N.J.: Washington *Star* Printery, 1909), 11–12; *Journal of the Sixty-Sixth Senate of the State of New Jersey being the One Hundred and Thirty-fourth Session of the Legislature* (Trenton, N.J.: MacCrellish & Quigley, 1910), 74–76 (entry for January 25, 1910).

31. *Fourth Annual Pilgrimage of the Fifteenth Regiment*, 47, 49; "Inspiring Occasion," *Evening Journal* (Fredericksburg, Va.), May 12, 1909; *Fourth Annual Pilgrimage of the Fifteenth Regiment*, 50–53.

32. *Fourth Annual Pilgrimage of the Fifteenth Regiment*, 54–56.

33. The most complete account of the 1909 ceremony can be found in ibid. See also "Dedication of Monuments: Order of Exercises," in the private possession of John W. Kuhl; "Memorials to Men Who Fell at Spotsylvania," Richmond *Times-Dispatch*, May 13, 1909; "The Fifteenth's Monuments," Sussex (N.J.) *Register*, May 20, 1909; "Honor Jersey Heroes," Hunterdon (N.J.) *Republican*, May 19, 1909.

34. Although survivors of the 15th insisted they captured the flag of the 14th Georgia, that unit was not in the vicinity of the Bloody Angle. The banner probably came from one of Ramseur's North Carolina units, which engaged in hand-to-hand fighting with the Jersey-men. The only member of the 15th who wrote about this incident immediately after the battle did not identify the flag's owners. He concisely reported: "Our regiment captured a battle-flag from the rebels. We took it off their breastworks." But wartime newspaper coverage indicated that the 15th took a flag from an unidentified Tarheel regiment ("The New Jersey Troops," Sussex [N.J.] *Register*, May 20, 1864, and "From the Fifteenth Regiment," Sussex [N.J.] *Register*, May 27, 1864).

35. *Fourth Annual Pilgrimage of the Fifteenth Regiment*, 12–13.

36. Ibid., 13–16.

37. Ibid. The speeches of Governor Fort and Congressman R. Wayne Parker did not contain graphic accounts of the slaughter at Spotsylvania. They pointed to the heroism of both sides as proof that Americans were one people. See *Fourth Annual Pilgrimage of the Fifteenth Regiment*, 12–13, 19.

38. Charles R. Paul diary, May 12, 1864, Murray J. Smith Collection, USAMHI.

39. By carefully distinguishing between the minority of Democrats who opposed the war and the majority who supported it, William Gillette demonstrated that a commitment to unionism prevailed in New Jersey. See his *Jersey Blue: Civil War Politics in New Jersey, 1854–1865* (New Brunswick, N.J.: Rutgers University Press, 1995). For a less analytical treatment, see Charles M. Knapp, *New Jersey's Politics during the Period of the Civil War and Reconstruction* (Geneva, N.Y.: Humphrey, 1924).

40. *Fourth Annual Pilgrimage of the Fifteenth Regiment*, 17.

41. Photocopy of "Proceeding of Rededication Program: Honoring the Memory of the Gallant New Jersey Men Who Fought in the Battles of Salem Church, the Wilderness and Spotsylvania, May 16, 1964," 7, 9, RUL.

Grant's Second Civil War
The Battle for Historical Memory

lysses S. Grant fought Confederates twice in his life: once to save the Union and a second time to salvage his military reputation. In the former battle, Grant directed the Federal armies; in the latter, he commanded pencil and paper to compose his *Personal Memoirs*. He left behind a document richly praised over the past century for its fairness and style. Mark Twain exalted it as the best military memoir since Caesar's *Commentaries*. Sherwood Anderson, Gertrude Stein, and critic Edmund Wilson also extolled the prose and its creator. More recently, scholars John Keegan and James M. McPherson have reminded us about the historical treasures that the volumes contain. Although Grant's prose deserves credit for its understatement and military commentary, the tragic circumstances surrounding the composition of the memoirs and the spare style have masked the author's biases, which were similar to those of his opponents in the battle of memoirs.[1]

The campaign by architects of the Lost Cause to write the southern version of the war shaped the Union leader's reminiscences in noticeable ways. When Grant wrote in 1885, former Confederates had spent the better part of fifteen years portraying him as a man of limited intelligence and as a general inferior to Robert E. Lee. Although using restraint, Grant engaged in a literary contest with these critics, attempting to show why he deserved to be remembered as more than a hammerer who had bludgeoned his foe into submission. In doing so, he overstated the size of the enemy's army and diminished Robert E. Lee as a lucky commander lacking in audacity who chose to stay behind entrenchments.

Battles such as Spotsylvania during the Overland campaign of 1864 provided the focal point for this war of historical memory. Confederate officers who formed a Lee cult targeted the period from Grant's crossing the Rapidan to the siege of Petersburg as evidence that the Union commander was a dull-witted, slogging general who simply employed the overwhelming numbers at his disposal to maul Lee's army. Although outnumbered by roughly 3 to 1, Lee outgeneraled Grant in repulsing all assaults instead of retreating. By portraying Lee as the aggressor at Spotsylvania and elsewhere even though the Confederacy fought on the defensive, this interpretation denied that Grant dictated the action. As evidence, Confederate writers argued that Lee's army bloodied the Federal troops so much that Grant had to change the base of his operations four times during the campaign. Ultimately, claimed these writers, the Confederacy lost because the Army of Northern Virginia was worn down rather than defeated by a better general. John Warwick Daniel, a U.S. senator from Virginia and former Confederate officer, captured the essence of this logic when he proclaimed in a speech that the Federal general knew that "he who had the most heads could butt the longest."[2]

These and similar assaults on the Union commander required a regional myopia that ignored the Western Theater of war and Grant's responsibility for all Federal movements, not just those in Virginia. Former Confederates concentrated on the contest between the Army of the Potomac and the Army of Northern Virginia to fashion Lee into a national hero and hurt Grant's reputation for the better part of a century.[3]

As he composed his memoirs, Grant knew about the opinions of the Confederate officers and their impact on his military reputation. The controversy absorbed more than American interests. European writers also explored Lee's character and generalship. Without the fuss typical of many military authors, Grant nonetheless challenged the glorification of Lee. The Wilderness and Spotsylvania provide an example. Grant claimed that the northern and southern public credited the Virginian with superhuman capacities when in truth luck and terrain played greater roles in the fighting. Grant also asserted that the Confederate army was so disrupted after the Wilderness fighting that its officers prevented collapse only by keeping the men entrenched. Had it not been for the choking woods, Union soldiers would have seen the confusion in Confederate ranks on May 5. Good fortune—rather than sound planning by Lee—also positioned the southern army at Spotsylvania at the critical moment. And when the Army of the Potomac withdrew from its position at Spotsylvania Court House to move toward the North Anna River, Lee not only failed to exploit its vulnerability but also chose to remain behind entrenchments. More to the point, Lee appeared to operate in a fog, unable to fathom where the Union general was heading. "He seemed really to be misled as to my designs," Grant wrote about his opponent, answering Confederate critics who had pronounced him guilty of lacking the skill to outmaneuver Lee.[4]

For the campaign as a whole, Grant countered the claim that he had wasted his own army in a war of attrition by arguing that his opponent enjoyed advantages of terrain and public support that negated any Union edge in manpower. Confederate accounts by the late 1870s consistently portrayed the Army of the Potomac by the first week of May 1864 as having 141,000 troops versus the Army of Northern Virginia's fewer than 50,000. Historians today place the same troop strengths at 120,000 and 64,000 respectively. The Union leader correctly noted that the Wilderness's second-growth forest, streams, and other natural obstacles favored an army fighting on the defensive. Confederates, he pointed out, also were on their own terrain, benefiting from people familiar with the area for directions and having no need to guard rear areas and supply trains against guerrillas or a hostile public. All of this was true and has become an acknowledged part of current analysis about Confederate chances to achieve victory. The postwar battle with Confederates, however, caused Grant to go too far in his defense. He estimated that the Army of Northern Virginia contained roughly 80,000 soldiers — at least 16,000 more than current scholarship suggests — and alleged that North and South essentially fought on equal terms. "I deem it safe to say," Grant concluded in his memoirs, "that there were no large engagements where the National numbers compensated for the advantage of position and intrenchment occupied by the enemy."[5]

Grant had not always needed to fight for his reputation. Immediately after the war he enjoyed the unabashed acclaim of the northern public, which celebrated him as the Civil War's greatest military figure. The handful of biographies that existed, if they truly can be called such, praised Grant as the hero of the republic and as the quintessential American — the plain son of a tanner who entered the military reluctantly and carried himself in a simple, unpretentious way. His tendency to stick with a task until completed was regarded then as a positive trait rather than — as southerners later alleged — an indication of a man of limited intelligence who only used troops as a bludgeon. Grant initially served as the model for how persistence could conquer any obstacle. Writers referred to this man who remained of the people as perhaps the first great military leader of modern republican institutions. For the most part, Grant sailed

Ulysses S. Grant composing his memoirs.
Library of Congress

through the 1860s respected by a majority of the northern public and even by some southerners grateful for the lenient surrender terms he extended to the Army of Northern Virginia.[6]

The mood changed noticeably in the 1870s as southerners exerted new historical muscle and politics buffeted President Grant. One of Lee's chief wartime lieutenants, Jubal A. Early, emerged to lead the Southern Historical Society. The organization's journal, published in Richmond, would provide the main vehicle for Confederate survivors to disseminate their version of the war and counter what they believed were egregious errors in northern histories. Early had a unique blend of characteristics that made him a formidable figure in the construction of Confederate memory of the Civil War. When Lee died in 1870, Early was the third highest ranking surviving officer from the Army of Northern Virginia. A lawyer before the war, "Old Jube" never backed down from controversy, especially to defend whomever he deemed to be powerless. He was motivated to write the southern version of history partly because his own military reputation had suffered unfairly in the Shenandoah Valley campaigns of 1864. As president of the Southern Historical Society, he held the right position to review material before publication in the Society's papers. The slightest deviation from Early's perceptions of battles or leaders brought down a forest of paper—tedious letters of often more than ten legal-sized pages crammed with a tight, pointed scrawl that looked like a modern electrocardiogram and probably quickened a few hearts upon receipt. He spared no one in this effort, Confederate or Federal, continuing the paper onslaught until the original author changed his account or the public tired of the debate. Even then he might not yield.[7]

Early also constituted a natural postwar opponent because the conflict had placed him against Maj. Gen. Philip H. Sheridan, a favorite of Grant's who had earned fame partly at the expense of Old Jube. In the Shenandoah Valley during 1864, Sheridan's Union forces defeated troops commanded by Early in three decisive battles. A fourth disaster for Early, against part of Sheridan's old army at Waynesboro, Virginia, in March 1865, finally caused Lee to relieve him from command. Not surprisingly, when Early took up the pen to write about his wartime experience he concentrated first on the final year of the war to show how badly Sheridan's force had outnumbered Confederates in the Valley—a circumstance that was largely true. The thrust of Early's critique was remarkably similar to the criticism he would mount against Grant. Sheridan won the Shenandoah Valley contests of late 1864 by bringing greater numbers to bear rather than through adroit strategy and tactics. Yet after the war, Sheridan gained accolades from military writers who at the same time denigrated his opponent's abilities. This rankled Early, who also held a grudge against the

Jubal Anderson Early in 1869.
Library of Congress

Union military for its destruction of the Valley. Beginning around October 6, 1864 — at the instigation of Ulysses S. Grant — Sheridan had systematically destroyed crops, agricultural equipment, and livestock to prevent this fertile region from supplying goods to the army. Early never stopped holding Grant and Sheridan accountable.[8]

Politics represented a final dimension of this battle of memoirs, a point historians have begun to appreciate more recently about the Lost Cause in general.[9] The struggle to define the memory of the war identified who took which side in the postwar conflicts over Reconstruction. The past could justify the contemporary political climate, even if indirectly. Rebels, believed many northerners, deserved to be punished and should not easily win back power in the nation. The cause of the war itself would justify how southerners would be perceived in the postwar world. Northern histories featured southerners as fighting to protect slavery, in effect to deny freedom. How Lee was presented offered one lens through which to filter the contemporary political context. For instance, if the general were, as one writer indicated, "a fitting representative of a cause, originating in treason, based on the enslavement of a race," then the outcry of southerners against the expansion of black rights under Radical Reconstruction could be dismissed or at least exposed as an attempt to retain power over those same individuals.[10] At the least, "traitors" deserved what they got no matter how radical the change. This meant that a battle over how to define the southern cause, played out through the use of history, could have enormous consequences. Treason might be made odious, as Andrew Johnson once proclaimed, but a forgivable attempt to protect state sovereignty might allow for reunion.

Grant himself came to the presidency in 1869 during a critical juncture in postwar politics, which put him on a collision course with the ultraconservatives who dominated southern historical writing in the 1870s. Although not a radical by nature, the new president had come to share the goal of black suffrage and owed his election as president partly to the Reconstruction Acts of 1867 that had turned most of the southern states into military districts in which Federal troops registered black voters.[11] Jubal Early's primary nemesis, Sheridan, also had served as a military commander of Louisiana and Texas, helping to establish the Republican Party there while using his authority to purge former Confederates from political office. When Confederates opened their war of history against Grant in 1870, the general who had saved the Union led a United States that had just ratified the Fifteenth Amendment to guarantee African American suffrage. Conservative southerners cried foul at the revolution coerced by Federal troops. All of this provided Grant and Sheridan with extra cachet as enemies to the conservative cause.

To Jubal Early, endorsing the northern version of history not only diminished the southern war effort but also validated the conduct of the enemy in Reconstruction. Early hinted at the political context of this battle of memoirs in the final paragraph of a clarification of southern manpower in the Overland campaign. When Early wrote in November 1870, Lee had been dead for a little more than a month and Virginia—through a deal struck with Grant by a committee of nine representing what became the Conservative Party—had avoided experiencing the full effect of Radical Reconstruction.[12] Old Jube regretted that Lee had died before seeing the heel of military power lifted from his people's necks, although he still found much to criticize in the legacy of Reconstruction. "We have just witnessed," he wrote, "the elections throughout several states of this 'Free Republic,' some of which are called 'loyal states,' superintended by armed agents of the United States Government, backed by U.S. troops, for the purpose of perpetuating the power of the ruling faction, through the instrumentality of the ballot in the hands of an ignorant and inferior race." Early could not conceive that the men who submitted to this indignity were descendants of the same people who had resisted British oppression during the Revolution: "We look on in amazement at the spectacle . . . and aware of the fact that we are now powerless and helpless—our only earthly consolation being that derived from a sense of duty performed and the conviction that the world will yet learn to do justice to our acts and motives."[13]

Privately, Early and his colleagues were more direct about connecting memory to politics. One of the sticking points concerned the surrender at Appomattox, for which Grant had earned a reputation as a generous victor by pardoning all who swore loyalty to the Union and stopping a celebratory salute by the Union artillery. Grant's refusal to humiliate defeated Confederates prevented southern accounts from dismissing him entirely; indeed, many felt compelled to acknowledge the general's "magnanimity" — an adjective that became a cliché when describing the northern leader's gestures at Appomattox. But Early and company would not concede even this attribute to Grant. Early cited the actions against civilians by Sheridan and his mentor in the Shenandoah Valley as more indicative of the true nature of the opposition. He also believed that the president's political activity exposed this harsher character. Early specifically mentioned opposition to President Andrew Johnson during Reconstruction and the later appointment of Sheridan to command the District of Louisiana as proof that Grant did not act very magnanimously.[14]

Early did not take it for granted that "the world will yet learn to do justice to our acts and motives" without a nudge in that direction. To that end, southerners worked diligently to get their message across to the international community. The Virginian corresponded heavily with overseas writers, hoping to influence their interpretations of the war. One target in particular was Francis Lawley, who had written an article about Lee in *Blackwood's Edinburgh Magazine* in 1872 that praised the general but elected not to rank him with the top commanders in world history. Lawley placed such European figures as Frederick the Great on a higher plane for one obvious reason: they had won, and Lee had lost. Although Early could not persuade Lawley to amend this view, the two struck up an amiable exchange that had an impact on the Englishman. Early convinced Lawley that politics lay behind northern accounts of the war, distorting its true nature, the character of the chief combatants, and the overwhelming nature of northern advantages of men and material. Lawley admitted to Old Jube in 1872 that he grew more amazed as he understood the odds that Confederates faced on battlefields in the Virginia theater. "Politics," he agreed, "have been imported into the scale with a view to obscuring the true history of your war & to elevating Grant, Sheridan & a dozen more to a pinnacle wh[ich] they will not always hold."[15] Thus, the campaign over "history" meshed with the struggles over who would rule in a reconstituted Union.

Knocking Grant from his pinnacle formed part of the motivation behind a dispute between Early and Adam Badeau, with Europe again providing the venue. A former newspaper correspondent who had become part of the general's staff during the war, Badeau in 1868 had published the first volume of his *Military History of Ulysses S. Grant*. Written with the approval of its subject, the book represented — as John Y. Simon has noted — about as close to an au-

Adam Badeau (standing at far left) together with Grant (seated at far left) in the field.
Library of Congress

thorized biography as existed at the time. It was not Badeau's *Military History*,
however, but a letter written by him to the London *Standard* that escalated
Early's war on Grant in 1870. In his letter, Badeau tried to head off growing
claims by former Confederates that Lee was outnumbered 3 to 1 in the Overland campaign. Badeau argued that the opposing armies in the Wilderness
and Spotsylvania were more evenly matched, indicating that Lee commanded
72,000 men as Grant began his errand into the Wilderness with 98,000. He accused Confederate apologists of counting all of the Union's available forces —
whether absent from sickness, detailed to duties other than fighting, or stationed far from the main area of conflict — while acknowledging only those
present for duty in their own ranks.[16]

   Early refuted Badeau in a long letter to the same London *Standard* where
the controversy had begun. Records of troop strengths remain frustratingly
inaccurate; in the 1870s, southern writers had no benefit of the *Official Records*

and little documentation on which to rest their claims. The government also denied southerners access to Confederate records. Historians and former officers alike leaned on a variety of sources that included the memories of participants, whatever could be scrounged from the files of combatants, newspaper reports, and documents published by the Federal government. In this case, Early turned to a report by Secretary of War Edwin M. Stanton dated May 1, 1864, that placed strength in the Army of the Potomac at 120,380 aggregate and in the Ninth Corps (which joined in the Overland campaign) at 20,780. From this, Early estimated that Grant had no fewer than 141,000 soldiers at his immediate disposal. Significantly, when it came to composing the numbers for the Army of Northern Virginia, the former general had no hard data on which to draw. He instead supported his memory that the army numbered fewer than 50,000 by noting that Lee had endorsed that figure in a private letter in late 1865. Cronies such as William Preston Johnston praised Early for the "annihilation of Badeau," adding, "The Yankees are manufacturing history at a great rate; and most Southern bookmakers are doing nearly as much mischief. What we want is facts."[17] During the next decade, Early's numbers became the "facts" that Confederate apologists cited.

The careful combing of records in a tedious numbers game can numb the mind against the simple mission behind the effort: to prove that Grant demonstrated no skill in beating the South and that Lee, even in defeat, was the better general. In fact, carried to its extreme, the logic dictated that the Army of Northern Virginia was not beaten at all but had fallen apart because of scarcer resources. The southern campaign to preserve the gap between the two armies as nearly 3 to 1 provided the main evidence for portraying the Union leader as an inferior foe — a general as common as his clothing.

W. Gordon McCabe's account of the Overland campaign demonstrates the elements of the Confederate critique that had coalesced in the 1870s. Published in 1876 as an analysis of the Petersburg siege, the article included the trilogy of engagements on which southerners focused to diminish Grant: the Wilderness, Spotsylvania, and Cold Harbor. McCabe used Jubal Early's figures for the strengths of both armies, placing Grant's at 141,000 and Lee's at "a bare 50,000." Despite the odds, he asserted, Lee fought so vigorously that he forced his opponent to change his line of operation four times. A frustrated Grant, goaded by the needs of the Republican Party, eventually lashed out at Cold Harbor and failed abysmally, even though he had been reinforced by 30,000 men after Spotsylvania. The debacle left the Army of the Potomac shattered and unwilling to obey its high command. McCabe went into these and other details so deeply "because the truth in regard to the matter, will alone enable those who come after us to understand how such a handful, ill-appointed and

THE RELATIVE STRENGTH OF THE ARMIES

OF

GEN'LS LEE AND GRANT.

Reply of Gen. Early to the Letter of Gen. Badeau to the London Standard.

TO THE EDITOR OF THE LONDON STANDARD.

To a people overpowered and crushed in a struggle for their rights, there is still left one resource on earth for the vindication of their conduct and character: that adopted by England's great Philosopher—an appeal to "foreign nations on to the next age." A persistent and systematic effort to falsify the truth of history has been made, since the close of the late war in this country, by the adherents of the United States Government in that conflict; and such a generous desire to vindicate the truth as that evinced by your recent articles upon the death of General Lee, has awakened a deep sense of gratitude in the hearts of all true Confederates. Presuming upon the kind sentiments manifested in your columns, I venture to ask the privilege of correcting, through the same medium, some of the gross errors contained in the letter of General Badeau, the late " military and private secretary to General Grant," which has been extensively copied from your journal into American journals.

In reference to the campaign of 1864 from the Rapidan to James River, General Badeau makes this remarkable statement:

" The calculation that Grant had three times as many men as Lee has been obtained by omitting Longstreet's corps altogether from the estimate, and by giving only Lee's force present for duty on the Rapidan; while in reckoning Grant's numbers, not only the present for duty are counted, but those constituting what, in military parlance, is called the total, which includes the sick, the extra-duty men, and various others, invariably amounting, in any large army, to many thousands. Manifestly, either Lee's total should be compared with Grant's total, or Grant's present for duty with Lee's present for duty. But besides this, in order to make out Grant's army three times as large as Lee's, Grant's two forces in the Valley of Virginia and on the James River (each at least one hundred miles from the Wilderness) are included in the estimate of his strength; while the troops which Lee had in front of these separate forces of Grant are left out of the calculation altogether. I repeat that in the battle of the Wilderness Lee had about 72,000 engaged, while Grant had 98,000 present for duty — according to the confidential field returns made at the time by each General to his own government, when no General would intentionally misstate or mislead."

That officers of Grant's army, after witnessing the terrible havoc made in their ranks by the small force opposed to them at the Wilderness, at Spotsylvania C. H., and at Cold Harbor, should over estimate the strength of that force, is not to be wondered at, but when the report of Mr. Edwin M. Stanton, the United States Secretary of War, made at the opening session of Congress for the years 1865-6, is critically examined, it will be regarded as most surprising that Gen. Badeau should have committed such gross blunders in regard to the strength of Grant's army. In order to expose those blunders, and to enable you to verify the extracts which I shall make from Mr. Stanton's report, I send you an official copy of that report printed under the authority of the United States Congress.

On page 3rd of his report, Mr. Stanton says:—

" The national forces engaged in the Spring campaign of 1864 were organized as armies or distributed in military departments as follows —

" The Army of the Potomac, commanded by Major-General Meade, whose headquarters were on the north side of the Rapidan. This army was confronted by the rebel army of Northern Virginia, stationed on the south side of the Rapidan, under General Robert E. Lee.

" The 9th corps, under Major-General Burnside, was, at the opening of the campaign, a distinct organization, but on the 24th of May, 1864, it was incorporated into the Army of the Potomac.

The first page of Early's published response to Adam Badeau.
Editor's collection

ill-fed, maintained for so long a time against overwhelming odds the fiercest defence of modern times." [18] Others added another component to the criticism of the Union's hero: that he conducted a blundering campaign by land when he could have gone by sea and taken Richmond with fewer losses by marching up the Peninsula as McClellan had done. In the end, this analysis argued, Ulysses S. Grant wore his own army down for no reason.

The theory that Grant should have conducted a water-based campaign originated not in a southern critique but in one of the earliest northern histories of the Army of the Potomac. Written by William Swinton, a journalist whom Grant had banned from the army in 1864, this book recognized the Union leader as a capable general, especially when maneuvering around his opponent. Swinton, however, handed the South ammunition in their battle to prove Lee the better general. Confederate apologists cited his statistics about Federal troop strengths and losses, especially to show that Grant should have moved his force by sea to prevent the staggering losses from the overland route, which Swinton placed at more than 60,000 but which would balloon in southern hands to 100,000. No one mentioned that McClellan had failed in such a strategy in 1862, that Grant had multiple targets in mind, or that he preferred to damage Lee's army before it could fall behind the well-engineered defenses of Richmond. Still, Grant felt compelled to respond in his memoirs, not by disputing numbers but by impugning Swinton's character. He recalled that during the war Swinton misrepresented himself as a "literary figure" rather than a newspaper correspondent to gain access to the army. In Grant's memoir, Swinton exists as a shadowy figure lurking around the high command to eavesdrop on conversations. Grant eventually exiled the journalist from camp. This anecdote appeared solely as a means to discredit Swinton's history by portraying the journalist as holding a grudge against the general. But it was not Grant's style to be so obvious. He cut from the manuscript the final sentence that provided the reason for the story: "These circumstances may account for the animus of the book which he has since written." However readers might understand Grant's treatment of Swinton when the memoirs appeared in 1885, the notion that the Union commander should have considered a seagoing campaign had become a part of the southern interpretation.[19]

As with all such debates, more moderate voices existed, but in the South even these tended to give Grant grudging accolades while portraying him as a rather blunt instrument. Dabney H. Maury, for example, tried to offer a more gracious assessment in an article published in 1878. Maury listed among Grant's attributes courage, the ability to select good subordinates, tenacity, and careful planning. He also appreciated the Union general's dignity and respect for the South at Appomattox. Yet even Maury claimed that the general's abilities had been overestimated. Ultimately, Maury followed the party line by saying that Grant "soon found he could only defeat our armies by overwhelming them with much greater armies, and he had the force of will to compel his government to furnish him with such armaments as modern war has never seen."[20] Even a supporter such as Lt. Gen. James Longstreet—who married a cousin of Grant's wife and typically praised his former enemy—could not avoid this historiographical rut. When Longstreet published his memoirs well after Grant's death, he claimed that attrition "became a prominent feature during this part of the campaign, and showed that the enemy put his faith in numbers more than in superior skill and generalship."[21]

Ironically, Grant had handed his adversaries the metaphor with which to characterize his leadership. Confederate critics seized upon key phrases in the general's final report of the Richmond campaign, encompassing activity from March 1864 through May 1865. Near the beginning of this report—widely distributed at the time—he mentioned that no peace would come until the Union forces smashed the military power of the rebellion. Consequently, he decided to use all the power of the United States to prevent the enemy from shifting supplies and manpower between or within theaters of war. Then he employed the description that would haunt him. According to Grant, his goal in the forthcoming campaign was "to hammer continuously against the armed force of the enemy and his resources until, by mere attrition, if no other way, there should be nothing left to him but an equal submission with the loyal section of our common country to the constitution and laws of the land." Swinton had repeated the metaphor of a hammer when he grouped Grant among "the class of generals who have been named Thor-strikers," with the grisly results of Spotsylvania and Cold Harbor proving the futility of the approach.[22] Later critics dutifully quoted the general's words as evidence that he had judged himself as a person unable to win a war of maneuver against the resourceful Lee and consequently had simply hammered at the Army of Northern Virginia.

That Grant waited so long to answer his critics—and then in such a muted fashion—was typical of how he handled such situations throughout his life. He rarely acknowledged criticism whether of military prowess or presidential decisions, observing that responses merely provided recognition for the accusers. He had been a taciturn man who shunned public controversy and resisted revealing his private side to the outside world. When his father published a letter about him during the Mexican War, it caused Grant to become even more guarded about the persona he presented to the public. In a letter to his wife, Grant noted: "I intend to be careful not to give them any news worth publishing." Grant's success at this habit led to the quip later in his life that he could be silent in several languages. If inclined to dispute an allegation, he usually worked through other people, with Badeau serving as the public guardian of his military reputation. For most of his life Grant refused to comment on or write about his military career, dismissing such requests with: "It's all in Badeau."[23]

And indeed, most of the interpretations of strategy and personalities that appeared in the memoir were expressed by Badeau in his three-volume work. This should be no surprise in light of the fact that the two kept in close contact with each other over the project. When the controversy arose in the London *Standard* in 1870, Badeau requested a copy of Early's response from Grant "so that I can answer it (without seeming to do so) in Vol. 2" of the *Military History*. Later in the decade, the general reviewed subsequent volumes before publication and pronounced himself more than satisfied. He especially enjoyed how Badeau had handled the Valley campaign between Early and Sheridan, pronouncing it one of the better chapters in the book and in the process acknowledging the impact of Old Jube. "It shows Early in an unpleasant light," Grant observed, adding that it also "shows the Southern character — for lying — as it should be shown."[24]

One time Grant exposed his feelings about Lee to the public, providing insight into how the *Personal Memoirs* should be viewed. The incident came after he had left an embattled presidency. Scandal plagued his administration, with several controversies implicating subordinates and even a family relation in corrupt practices. The president emerged without personal blemish, in that few believed he had either participated in or condoned the activities. Yet his reputation suffered as critics came up with a new name for corruption, "Grantism." A fall in military reputation followed — not only in the southern historical press but also in northern media that welcomed reminiscences from Confederates in a new spirit of sectional reconciliation. The Philadelphia *Weekly Times* began running a series of wartime reminiscences in the 1870s designed to present both sides of the story. Some of these articles were collected into a book published as *The Annals of the War* in 1879. In it appeared the usual praise of Grant from a northern writer characterizing the general as "a plain business man of the republic" who exhibited little sentiment as he concentrated on the task at hand. But the collection also contained an account titled "Lee and Grant in the Wilderness" by Cadmus M. Wilcox, a former Confederate general who had fought in the campaign. His article featured the typical southern estimates of troop strengths — 141,000 for Grant and fewer than 50,000 for Lee — and the quotation from the Union general's report that he would hammer against the armed force of the enemy. Although crediting Grant with knowing how to direct his overwhelming resources, Wilcox called the Wilderness a Confederate victory because Lee's men had bloodied the northerners and forced the army to change its path, leaving behind the field with its unburied dead. The southern argument against the general had migrated into northern journals.[25]

In this climate, the president shared opinions about a number of military figures with a journalist. John Russell Young of the *New York Herald* accompanied Grant on the world tour the president took upon leaving office. While traveling the two spoke about the war. Published first in 1878 as conversations with Grant and later as part of a compilation in book form, the resulting article indicated that the general could not understand the fuss over Robert E. Lee. Grant believed that his opponent had been vastly overrated and was not nearly as much of a threat as Joseph E. Johnston. According to Grant, the Confederate general had everything in his favor: unanimous support of the South, support from Copperheads in the North, and sympathy from the outside world. "Everything he did was right," Grant said, indicating that the press helped create the image of Lee as invincible. "He was treated like a demi-god. Our generals had a hostile press, lukewarm friends and a public opinion outside." The president showed a sensitivity to his critics when in the next breath he said: "The cry was in the air that the North only won by brute force; that the generalship and valor were with the South. This has gone into history, with as many other illusions that are historical." Grant then added the somewhat gratuitous observation that "Lee was of a slow, conservative, cautious nature, without imagination or humor, always the same, with grave dignity. I never could see in his achievements what justifies his reputation."[26] It is likely that Grant spoke from the heart when relating these impressions of Lee, even though they fly against the accepted wisdom of the southern general whom most credit with an overabundance of audacity. Whatever the motivations behind Grant's characterization, the statements would become the basis for his interpretation of Lee in the *Personal Memoirs*.

Grant claimed to recognize the impropriety of publishing these comments, yet he regretted only the casualty figures that the account contained—numbers that were far lower than southern estimates. In a letter to Badeau, the general indicated that the remarks were not intended for publication, but had slipped out over the course of the long travel time shared with the reporter. Yet Young had given Grant a copy of the manuscript to review before printing and the president had few quibbles with the article's accuracy, feeding the likelihood that the normally guarded Grant purposefully had let his observations slip. The only exception concerned Grant's statements that the Army of the Potomac during the movement from the Rapidan to the James lost about 40,000 men, much lower than Swinton's estimates of more than 60,000 or southern claims of 100,000. Grant knew it would be easy to find numbers that contradicted his, but dismissed this by noting that officers typically reported the highest possible casualties at the time. The general apparently could not resist blurting out figures that would counter the assault on his record. In the letter to Badeau, he referred to recent accounts by former secretary of the navy Gideon Welles and former Confederate general Richard Taylor in the *New York Herald* that "would soon have it pass into history that we had 100,000 men killed in getting to the James river, when we could have gone by boat, without loss, and ignoring the fact that Lee sustained any loss whatever."[27] This exchange again shows that criticism of his campaigns had an impact, causing the general to play the numbers game as loosely as the Confederates. As significantly, Grant had no concern about the public's knowing his assessment of Union or Confederate generals, especially his sentiments about Robert E. Lee.

At the time, Grant's reputation was enjoying a comeback. The tour of the world renewed interest in his military accomplishments. England treated citizen Grant with the protocol of a head of state, allowing royalty to fete him. Banquet invitations, menus, and toasts by royalty still litter his personal papers at the Library of Congress. One clipping in a scrapbook indicates that the battle for his reputation could yet be won. In 1879, a newspaper previewed the laudatory biographical entry on Grant that would appear in the forthcoming *Encyclopaedia Britannica*. This account favored Grant's view of troop strengths, crediting him with 110,000 soldiers and Lee 75,000 at the start of the Overland campaign. Battles such as Spotsylvania were among the hardest fought in the war, yet despite stiff rebel resistance, after each contest Grant "advanced and Lee withdrew. They [the battles] cost the national commander dear, but they inflicted losses on Lee from which he never recovered, and thus accomplished the object at which Grant was aiming."[28]

Nearly all the ingredients that would influence the writing of Grant's memoirs had come together. Information about most of his military activities during the Civil War would come out of his reports, especially the one involving the Richmond campaign that had been published in the summer of 1865. This contained the strategic view from which he would not deviate. Badeau's *Military History* provided further insight into the general's thinking about his military operations. According to Badeau, Grant recognized that he needed to conduct a "people's war" to conquer the will of southern civilians as well as to defeat Confederate armies. He thus targeted the slaves, livestock, and supplies of the enemy. Badeau also echoed the general's assessment of Lee, calling him "stubborn, valiant, arrogant," and proclaiming that the Confederate leader "lacked sustained audacity. He never, at least after Grant commanded in his front, succeeded in anything that required that trait. He thought more boldly than he acted."[29] Grant also had reason to answer his critics. The numbers game played by both sides for nearly two decades after the war would dictate how he presented troop strengths and how he dealt with Spotsylvania and the Overland campaign.

Only one thing more was needed: something to motivate Grant to reveal himself to the world. Unfortunately, it took another round of bad fortune to overcome his natural reticence. Between his trip around the world that had renewed interest in his military achievements and the writing of his memoirs, his finances turned sour. The general was embarrassed, both personally and financially, by the collapse of the banking firm Grant & Ward. The bank had been established by the general and his son in partnership with Ferdinand Ward, who ran the operation. As during his presidency, Grant trusted the wrong man. When the bank collapsed in 1884, Ward admitted to a grand jury that he had doctored the books. He also had encouraged the erroneous impression that the firm benefited from government contracts because of the president's former connections. Grant remained ignorant of the practices but found himself bankrupt and under investigation, with some angry creditors calling for his arrest. Newspapers fed the spectacle, questioning whether the president had been guilty of misrepresentation. Ward went to prison and Grant was cleared of wrongdoing; however, the incident left his family in precarious straits and Grant the subject of public pity.[30]

Under these circumstances, Grant became receptive to writing his way out of his difficulties. He began with articles for *Century Magazine* on Shiloh and Vicksburg and was surprised at their warm reception and at the money they returned. By 1885 he had settled into writing the more extended memoirs, but with a more formidable enemy threatening the project's completion. In the summer of 1884, Grant noticed pain when swallowing a peach but put off examination until the fall. It soon became clear that he suffered from throat cancer. The news inevitably became public and added a tragic interest as the general raced death to complete the memoirs. He thus had a number of priorities facing him in this effort: saving his family financially, restoring his own good name, and handling the Confederate assault on his record. In his final months on earth, Grant prepared the literary monument that addressed the Confederate argument point by point.

One of the first clues that Grant attempted to correct Confederate histories comes in the portion of the reminiscences dealing with the Mexican War. Near the end of that section he mused over how the Mexicans still celebrated the battles of that war in a way that turned defeat into victory. The battles of Chapultepec and El Molino del Rey had become national holidays, with leaders commemorating the resistance to the United States and the large sum of money the Americans paid after the conflict. The parallel with how Confederates turned defeat into victory proved too strong for Grant to resist. "With us, now twenty years after the most stupendous war ever known," the general observed, "we have writers—who profess devotion to the nation—engaged in trying to prove that the Union forces were not victorious; practically, they say, we were slashed around from Donelson to Vicksburg and to Chattanooga; and in the East from Gettysburg to Appomattox, when the physical rebellion gave out from sheer exhaustion." Perhaps only Jubal Early could have presented the southern case better and certainly not as succinctly. Grant then concluded about the Mexican and southern memories: "There is no difference in the amount of romance about the two stories." Sensitive to humiliating a defeated opponent, the general did not want to declare national holidays to celebrate the Union victories, but he did want "to see truthful histories written." [31]

Analysis of the original manuscript underscores that Grant had no second thoughts about this statement. He had softened two other comments bracketing the one about the southern memory of the war. In his first draft, the general had claimed that the Mexicans turned every battle into a victory through orators who proclaimed that they had "whipped us from place to place until at last they drew us in to a cul de sac—the City of Mexico" before compelling the U.S. to pay $15 million. Upon consultation with Matias Romero, a minister from Mexico who became a friend, the author qualified his comments, narrowing them to the two battles and removing the more inflammatory statements about oratory. In talking about the southerners, he retained a passage linking slavery with the war: "As time passes, people, even of the South, will begin to wonder how it was possible that their ancestors ever fought for or justified institutions which acknowledged the right of property in man." What he eliminated, however, showed the passion that he felt about the peculiar institution. Grant cut a statement about slavery as authorizing the buying and selling of human beings, "when man and wife, mother and child, kindred were separated without their consent like cattle." [32] As this indicates, he tried to limit obvious, inflammatory statements throughout his memoir, except when he believed the criticism was deserved. Significantly, the comments about "historians" remained without amendment.

That the author felt strongly about his subject can be seen in other parts of the memoir, especially those devoted to the Overland campaign in which he argued that the Union army never enjoyed any significant advantage in numbers. He listed the troops that crossed the Rapidan in May 1864 at about 116,000—approximately what most scholars accept today. Exaggeration appeared when Grant alleged that Lee commanded at least 80,000 soldiers. He neither described how he derived these figures nor cited reports to bolster his statement. To Grant, though, a few thousand troops either way mattered little.

He firmly believed the Confederates had numerous advantages by fighting on their own turf and virtually repeated the analysis that had appeared in his conversations with John Russell Young in 1878. Southern generals like Lee had less to worry about because they operated in friendly territory and had the support of the public and the press. Operating on the enemy's ground created difficulties for the North. Coupled with the normal absences to leaves and infirmity, the need to guard supply trains gobbled Union manpower. When all was said and done, the general believed, the Union held no advantage in numbers for any battle during the Overland campaign or elsewhere in the war. He answered the charge that he should have moved his troops by sea to conduct a campaign up the Peninsula by saying that the maneuver only would have caused the further reinforcement of Richmond as Lee moved his troops to support the city. "It was better to fight him outside of his stronghold than in it," Grant wrote, stressing that the Army of Northern Virginia — and not Richmond — remained the primary target.[33]

Grant again expounded on the numbers debate in a section that compared northern and southern society. As before, he stressed that the disparity between the two sides in manpower was less important than the advantages held by the South. He sternly dismissed the notion that the Confederacy deserved praise for a splendid fight of 12 million people against 20 million (the populations actually were about 9 million and 22 million, respectively). Grant claimed, with considerable truth, that the Confederacy resembled an armed military camp that mobilized most of its population for either military service or war-related production. To accomplish this, the South leaned on its population of 4 million slaves to keep the army fed. Consequently, Grant explained, "All the troops in service could be brought to the front to contest every inch of ground threatened with invasion." This military effort was made all the more formidable because the southern populace supported the war: "The cause was popular, and was enthusiastically supported by the young men."[34] Special circumstances thus allowed Confederate troops to be deployed at the front. Meanwhile, northern generals had to protect supply lines in rear areas while also facing opposition to the war by Copperheads on the northern home front. Lee had none of the discord at home that complicated military decisions. Grant created in his memoirs a Confederate leader who could concentrate purely on military affairs without worrying about politics, while enjoying consistent adulation from the southern press.[35]

In taking these positions, Grant offered reasonable arguments, many of them militarily sound. But he misrepresented the extent of political tensions within the South, the ease with which the Confederacy rallied to produce goods and field an army, and even the extent of criticism against Lee. Each state had its problems with malcontents. A peace movement had taken root in North Carolina by 1863. The following year, the same state featured a gubernatorial contest in which the opponent to the incumbent promised to secede from the Confederacy. Throughout the Confederacy, deserter communities took root in isolated regions. The government in Richmond received numerous protests from citizens and government officials against conscription, impressment of goods, and favoritism shown to rich men who could buy their way out of the war through hiring substitutes. In 1863, bread riots occurred in at least seven cities. Grant was correct in noticing that the southern press generally supported its army and even at times censored itself concerning problems at home. But the Davis government came under withering attacks in that same press, and even Lee was so criticized after Gettysburg that he offered his resignation to Jefferson Davis to stem anger against the government.[36]

The interpretation in the *Personal Memoirs* likely reveals Grant's own sense of political pressures during the war, something that his friend William Tecumseh Sherman noticed in the Vicksburg campaign. At the time, Sherman said that Grant "trembles at the approaching thunders of popular criticism and must risk anything." Military historians have used this as an indication that public sentiment also affected the general's campaign against Lee.[37] From Grant's perspective, the criticism from his own section undoubtedly felt stronger than what he saw levied against Lee and the Confederate government in the southern press.

Perhaps the more interesting subtext within the *Personal Memoirs* concerns the lack of respect the author demonstrated for the South's leading military figure. Grant largely dismisses Lee, portraying him as a person scarcely worthy of concern. He begins to knock Lee from his pedestal in volume one, just after dealing with the Mexican War. According to the author, the experience in Mexico gave him an appreciation for the characteristics of certain military leaders who became prominent in the Civil War, including Lee. "The natural disposition of most people," Grant wrote, "is to clothe a commander of a large army whom they do not know with almost superhuman abilities. A large part of the National army, for instance, and most of the press of the country, clothed General Lee with just such qualities; but I had known him personally, and knew that he was mortal; and it was just as well that I felt this."[38] For Grant, Lee's reputation was partly a fabrication of the southern press, helped by willing northern traitors who wanted to stop the war.

Grant waited until discussing the campaign from the Rapidan to the James before revealing why Lee was a mere mortal of less concern than Gen. Joe Johnston. In the *Personal Memoirs*, Lee refuses to come out from behind his entrenchments to fight and is largely befuddled by the Union army's flanking maneuvers. His army escapes disaster at the Wilderness and Spotsylvania largely because of luck: at the former because the terrain obscured how badly the enemy was hurt and at the latter because burning woods forced troops under Maj. Gen. Richard H. Anderson to push on toward a critical intersection at night rather than bed down. Had it not been for this "accident," the Army of the Potomac would have seized the critical intersection that placed it between the southern army and Richmond. Grant portrays himself as the man of action, willing to risk the offensive in an attempt to entice a timid Lee into a decisive engagement. "It was my plan then," wrote the general about the Wilderness, "as it was on all other occasions, to take the initiative whenever the enemy could be drawn from his intrenchments if we were not intrenched ourselves." [39] But Lee never exposed himself, even as the army withdrew from Spotsylvania and Grant believed his troops were vulnerable. When the army crossed the North Anna, it precariously straddled the water, splitting the force in two with Lee's whole army on the south side. Although Grant claimed Lee was by this time reinforced with 15,000 troops, the Confederate general "did not try to drive us from the field." [40]

Grant employs similar reasoning in a subtle way to defend the tragic assault at Cold Harbor, focusing on the aftermath to prove Lee's timid nature and on a dispute over tending the wounded to highlight his adversary's mean spirit. Reviewers of the work typically have noted the general's frank admission of regret that he ordered the charge of his troops on June 3 that cost between 7,000 and 8,000 men in the matter of an hour. Relatively unnoticed has been how Grant quickly followed his regret with reasons why the slaughter mattered so little. First, despite the shattering Union repulse, the enemy did not attempt to exploit any weakness in the army. Lee sat still behind his defensive works, rejecting a counterattack. "In fact," Grant added, "nowhere after the battle of the Wilderness did Lee show any disposition to leave his defenses far behind him." [41] The general next dismissed charges by Confederates that the assault helped wreck his army by rendering the men unwilling to obey commands. According to the memoirs, when the soldiers arrived at the James River "all effects of the battle of Cold Harbor seemed to have disappeared." This flies in the face of current analysis that shows the Army of the Potomac infected by a "Cold Harbor syndrome" that thwarted a wonderful opportunity in June to capture Petersburg and perhaps reduce the time needed to bring the war in the East to a close. Although poor coordination by officers contributed to the problems, by the time the Union army arrived at the James River many of its veteran soldiers had lost their willingness to attack entrenched positions. Some refused direct orders to assault and encouraged their comrades to lie down rather than charge. [42]

Concerning the wounded after Cold Harbor, the *Personal Memoirs* reproduces correspondence between the two commanders, presumably to show how Lee's pettiness cost the lives of hundreds of men. This was not one of Lee's better moments. Grant had requested that unarmed stretcher bearers be allowed to collect the wounded whenever the opposing forces were not engaged. An agreement was necessary because Confederate sharpshooters repelled efforts to aid the wounded. Lee rejected the plan as potentially confusing. He had the luxury of considering protocol because most of the wounded were Federal soldiers. Grant countered with another plan, which Lee also rejected. It finally became clear that Lee insisted on having the Union commander officially ask for a flag of truce, which in military custom reflected an admission of defeat. Grant finally did so. By the time the two reached agreement it was June 7, and, after nearly four days under the brutal Virginia sun, most of the wounded had died.[43] Lee's most influential biographer later asserted that Grant had allowed his own men to die rather than admit defeat to Lee. As usual, Grant himself supplied no commentary on his perceptions of Lee's behavior. Badeau, however, offers a clue into his hero's sentiments. The *Military History* portrays the Virginian as allowing men to die to satisfy a fixation with etiquette, adding: "Whether his military reputation gained sufficiently to compensate for the sufferings he deliberately and unnecessarily prolonged, is questionable."[44]

The *Personal Memoirs*, then, elaborated on Grant's analysis in his published conversations with Young. The general could not understand in 1878 why Lee's achievements deserved note, and nothing had changed in seven years. He repeated the characterization of Lee as an aloof man, conservative in nature, and unapproachable to subordinates. More to the point, the Confederate general did nothing to live up to his vaunted reputation for audacity, proving more of a frustration because he would not leave his defenses even when an opportunity allowed. Grant may or may not have questioned Lee's manhood in this reasoning, but he clearly wanted to assure readers that the Confederate leader had caused him little alarm during the Overland campaign. According to the memoirs, the southern press manufactured the reputation of Lee. A portion of the northern press—driven by Copperhead opposition to the conflict—participated in the charade by exaggerating the size of the Union army and making the southern force smaller. The publicity campaign had a telling effect not only on the public but also on officers in the Army of the Potomac who seemed obsessed with Lee. Grant often heard that officers in the eastern army remarked: "'Well, Grant has never met Bobby Lee yet.'"[45] The general added that there were officers from the army who still believed that the Army of Northern Virginia was superior to the Union one, which Grant denied. One of the missions behind his memoirs consisted of restoring northern pride in the National army, as he called it, which involved exorcising the ghost of Robert E. Lee.

Grant also protected his principal lieutenants, especially Sheridan. Spotsylvania provides an excellent example of this tendency. The issue involved who should bear responsibility for the Federal army's losing the chance to seize the bridge over the Po River on May 8, a key position that would have placed the Union force between Richmond and the Confederate army. Meade and Sheridan stood at the center of the controversy. For a while, Sheridan won the battle of postwar accounts. His 1866 report blamed Meade for allegedly changing orders late on May 7; if left alone, the original orders would have placed the cavalry in the right spot to contest the Confederate advance. According to Sheridan, Meade's instructions put cavalry ahead of infantry on the Brock Road, which in turn choked traffic, delayed the arrival of Federal soldiers at the bridge, and allowed Confederates to hold the area. Grant presented virtually the same account in the *Personal Memoirs*, observing that Meade unfortunately changed orders at the wrong time. A recent historian of the battle labeled Sheridan's story "patently untrue." William D. Matter also believed that Grant erred in accepting the story, adding, "It is a sobering experience to be obliged to dispute the accuracy of even a minute portion of what was once considered by some to be the greatest military writing since Caesar's *Commentaries*." [46]

Inexplicably, Grant ignored published accounts at odds with Sheridan's — not only southern ones, but especially a book by Andrew A. Humphreys, a former chief of staff and corps commander in the Army of the Potomac. Humphreys's *The Virginia Campaign of '64 and '65* was recognized as one of the better early histories of the conflict and retains a valued place in Civil War military literature. Humphreys committed the sin of contesting Badeau's interpretations of the war and, by extension, challenging Grant. Confederate historians widely quoted from Humphreys as more unbiased than the typical northern study. As to Spotsylvania, *The Virginia Campaign of '64 and '65* openly supported Meade against Sheridan in the dispute over culpability for the loss of the bridge over the Po River. Published two years before Grant began writing his memoirs, the book receives no mention in the *Personal Memoirs*. Yet evidence suggests that Grant considered challenging some of Humphreys's conclusions. Handwritten notes in his personal papers posed the question: "Is Humphrey correct in orders Meade gave Merritt. P. 67–68 when H. differs from Badeau"; this section of *The Virginia Campaign of '64 and '65* expressly covers the controversy between Meade and Sheridan. Grant then argued that Humphreys, when estimating manpower, committed the same error as Confederate historians by counting all soldiers, whether absent or noncombatants. For whatever reason, Grant thought better of this and did not include the analysis in the published account. He simply ignored Humphreys's critique of Sheridan.[47]

The general's writing style makes it easy to miss his biases. He did not embellish comments or dwell at length on controversy. This in itself was a remarkable (and welcome) departure from the usual military memoir that puffed up the writer at the expense of rivals. *Personal Memoirs* features a simple prose style, understated and efficient. It lacks the emphasis on personalities typical of the genre. But the comments are present, if not as blatant. Grant's true sentiments about individuals such as Robert E. Lee can be formed into a composite picture only by gathering bits and pieces from various portions of the memoir. Such was the general's nature: make a statement and move on. He wrote the way he interacted with acquaintances. Badeau himself warned the public against being deceived that Grant's prose reflected a calm, dispassionate man. "I sometimes wondered," he wrote, "whether he was conscious of his own emotions, they were so completely under control; but they were all there, all alive, all active, only enveloped in a cloak of obstinate reserve and majestic silence which only at the rarest intervals was torn aside by misfortune or lifted for a moment to a friend."[48]

When the memoirs were published, few reviewers or readers noticed that the general had stepped into controversial areas with debatable information. Acclaim generally greeted the book, which became a raging best-seller and achieved Grant's top priority of restoring his family's finances. Most reviews agreed that the prose style distinguished the memoir. Columnists also appreciated the insight provided into the general's mind. As an example, they invariably cited the clear, calm way in which Grant ignored the chaos around him to focus on just the right place to apply pressure against his enemy.

Muted in the northern reviews was recognition that the author had not quite gotten all the facts straight. In a look at the first volume, *The Nation* indicated that historians would still need to consult "the great storehouse of the official records for the full correction of the history of the time," adding that if Grant had "lived to see his memoirs published, there can be no doubt that he would have recast some important passages."[49] Another reviewer cautioned readers against being misled by the dispassionate style: "The book is so moderate in tone that the severity of some of its criticisms may not be at once appreciated." The same writer called volume one, which ended with the capture of Vicksburg, "the most damaging commentary upon the management of our military affairs at the West that has ever been published" and marveled at the "precision with which its keen shafts are aimed."[50]

Southerners predictably considered the book less exemplary, although a number of factors prevented public criticism from becoming too harsh. For one thing, the country was moving toward greater reconciliation between the sections. For another, Grant had written the memoirs while facing cancer and then died before seeing the project published. He also had proven gracious at Appomattox and had kept, as the reviewer for the *Southern Historical Society Papers* noted, "a very kindly tone" in his memoirs. Before the memoirs were published, Charles Colcock Jones Jr., a former Confederate officer, referred to the general's fight against cancer and his actions at Appomattox as reasons to tender Grant "assurances of our sincere and profound sympathy in this the season of his direful extremity." Under the circumstances, an outcry would appear to be poor etiquette to say the least, although it did not stop Jubal Early from privately seething over sympathy shown by southerners that sometimes included praising Grant's military abilities. "I begin to believe," he wrote a crony, "that history is nothing but a 'lying bitch.' " [51]

Yet the memoirs did not escape criticism. The reviewer for the Southern Historical Society left little doubt that the book contained problems. Calling it "full of blunders and flat contradictions of the official reports," this critic warned that future historians who accepted the content of the memoir would be "led very far astray from the real truth." The depiction of Lee versus Grant in the Overland campaign caused concern, especially Grant's assertions that Lee never came out of entrenchments and that the morale of the Army of the Potomac remained high. According to the reviewer, published accounts already presented a different story—including the study by Humphreys. It was Lee who attacked Grant more consistently, causing the Union forces to entrench more often than the Confederates and enticing the Union general into the siege at Petersburg. Grant's interpretation thus remained "the veriest romance that was ever attempted to be palmed off as history" and invited a critical study comparing it with the official record. [52]

Oddly enough, such a study appeared relatively quickly from the pen of a northerner with quite a different agenda in mind. Carswell McClellan published *The Personal Memoirs and Military History of Ulysses S. Grant versus the Record of the Army of the Potomac* roughly a year after Grant's volumes had come out. As the title suggests, it challenged the memoirs, but less to help Confederates than to elevate Meade and other eastern officers in the army. A Pennsylvanian and West Point graduate, McClellan had served in the Army of the Potomac in various capacities, including as a special aide to General Humphreys. Clearly a supporter of Meade, McClellan portrayed Grant as a western usurper who capitalized on the efforts of generals who had forged the army into a fighting machine able to take on Lee. He criticized Grant for establishing his headquarters with the Army of the Potomac for more than its impact on Meade. As general-in-chief, McClellan argued, Grant belonged in Washington.

By being in the field, the general delayed communications — and thus coopera-tion among all of the armies — by requiring orders to pass through Halleck in Washington. McClellan also sided with Humphreys's history of the campaign, especially where it conflicted with Badeau's *Military History*. Underlying the criticism was a sectional jealousy between East and West that had created ten-sions within the army during the war. Westerners had emphasized that their armies always won, whereas the Army of the Potomac habitually lost until Grant went to Virginia. McClellan's book, which offers an interesting counter-point to the general's memoirs, barely disguises that some within the army resented Grant as an outsider who overshadowed the accomplishments of the true commander of the Army of the Potomac.[53]

Perhaps the most important admission that *Personal Memoirs* contained problems came from Frederick Dent Grant, the president's son and editorial assistant in the final stages of the project. In an edition of the memoirs pub-lished a decade after his father's death, Fred Grant printed if not an apology at least a concession that the general's disease had affected the latter portions of the reminiscences. He insisted that the advancing cancer had forced Grant to rush through the section beginning with the spring campaigns of 1864. By this point, conceded the hero's son, "the decline in General Grant's strength became clearly manifest, and it was found necessary to bring his task to a close as soon and as easily as possible." The general pressed on without consulting notes as he had for the earlier sections of the manuscript. The son, however, did not specify what would have changed had time been more gracious to the father. It is unclear if Fred Grant referred to numbers, interpretations, or overall approach. He left the matter ambiguous, declaring only that his father wanted to treat the last campaigns as "a panorama of one vast campaign directed by the central power — the Lieutenant-General of the Army of the United States."[54]

Critics continued to chisel at the general's reputation, succeeding to the ex-tent that by the turn of the century Lee had become a national hero and the object of greater public interest, even among northerners. Perhaps it is accu-rate to say that Grant's image did not decline so much as Lee's soared above it, for the Union leader never lacked a following. The *Personal Memoirs* had sold so well that, as Edmund Wilson later wrote, it maintained a constant presence on the shelves in pro-Union homes until sometime in the twentieth cen-tury. However, the public's preoccupation with Lee grew, helped by Douglas Southall Freeman's *R. E. Lee*, which earned its author a Pulitzer Prize in the 1930s. For various reasons, Lee offered a more attractive figure to a nation that had undergone a sometimes painful transition to industrialization. The Vir-ginian struck a nostalgic chord as a dignified aristocrat who viewed the war as his tragic, reluctant duty to preserve an agrarian life that seemed simpler and purer — especially when historians and the white public divorced the war from its roots in slavery. Lee's popularity had been part of the bargain for reuniting the white South with the North.[55] Grant waited in a dark antechamber of the nation's memory until military historians rediscovered him and the public followed suit in the 1960s as the Civil War's centennial brought a new appreciation for his talents. The *Personal Memoirs* aided in this revival, leading a new generation back to the mind of the man who had helped save the Union.[56]

And now we chisel at that edifice as well, revealing that it had a few underlying cracks all along. But this critique of the memoirs should not be construed as dismissing the work or the man. Grant's memoirs remain a valuable source and a good, if imperfect, narrative. The military analysis offers a useful starting point for anyone interested in studying the war, especially if trying to figure out how the North won. As contemporary reviewers suggested, the writing — despite its reserve — offers insights into the personality of Grant. If anything, the recognition of biases in the *Personal Memoirs* increases Grant's humanity: he wrestled with life's pettiness, like most people, although he usually suppressed this fact from the public, unlike most generals. That Grant also felt public pressures to the extent that Lee's difficulties seemed as nothing in comparison demonstrates the political cauldron in which he operated and helps explain the tragic decision at Cold Harbor.

We can debate the degree of manipulation behind Grant's reconstruction of southern troop strengths and his assessment of Lee, but at least two factors suggest rejecting a conscious effort to lie. First is the cancer that ate at the general, causing him to hurry through the final portions of the project while taking cocaine. This leaves room for doubt about the origins of factual errors. The second is that the interpretations of the Overland campaign in the memoirs is consistent with Grant's report in 1865, which suggests both undoubtedly represent the truth as he understood it. Whatever the case, we might follow his own example with the South and be magnanimous in our assessment of him.

We should not, however, treat the reminiscences as more than what they are: the remembrances of a human being who told the story as he knew it, who told it well but not without prejudice. Henry Adams wrote about his own autobiography in words that describe what every human being attempts when capturing a life with pen and paper. "The volume," he told Henry James, "is a mere shield of protection in the grave. I advise you to take your own life in the same way, in order to prevent biographers from taking it in theirs."[57] *Personal Memoirs* serves as Grant's own shield from the grave.

1. Edmund Wilson, *Patriotic Gore: Studies in the Literature of the American Civil War* (New York: Oxford University Press, 1962), 131–73; John Keegan, *The Mask of Command* (New York: Viking, 1987), 202; James M. McPherson, "Grant's Final Victory," in *Drawn with the Sword: Reflections on the American Civil War* (New York: Oxford University Press, 1996), 159–73. For an assertion that the memoirs have become surrounded by a "romantic gauze," see William S. McFeely, *Grant: A Biography* (New York: W. W. Norton, 1981), 493, and also his summary of critical acclaim on pp. 501, 513.

2. "Address of Major John W. Daniel, L.L.D.," in *Southern Historical Society Papers*, ed. J. William Jones and others, 52 vols. (1876–1959; reprint, with 3-vol. index, Wilmington, N.C.: Broadfoot, 1990–92), 11:355 (hereafter cited as *SHSP*). The Lee cult is identified in Thomas L. Connelly, *The Marble Man: Robert E. Lee and His Image in American Society* (New York: Alfred A. Knopf, 1977).

3. For the creation of Lee as a national hero and its impact on Grant, see Connelly, *Marble Man*, esp. chap. 4, and McFeely, *Grant*, 522.

4. Ulysses S. Grant, *Personal Memoirs of U. S. Grant*, 2 vols. (1885; later printing, New York: Charles L. Webster & Company, 1892), 2:211–12, 226, 244 (quotation).

5. Ibid., 2:291, 505 (quotation). For current estimates of troops and strategic discussion, see James M. McPherson, *Battle Cry of Freedom: The Civil War Era* (New York: Oxford University Press, 1988), 724; Herman Hattaway and Archer Jones, *How the North Won: A Military History of the Civil War* (Urbana: University of Illinois Press, 1983), 538–40; Archer Jones, "Military Means, Political Ends: Strategy," in *Why the Confederacy Lost*, ed. Gabor S. Boritt (New York: Oxford University Press, 1992), 45–77.

6. For an excellent discussion of Grant's postwar image, see the essay by John Y. Simon in James G. Barber and Simon, *U. S. Grant: The Man and the Image* (Washington: National Portrait Gallery, Smithsonian, and Carbondale, Ill.: Southern Illinois University Press, 1985), 13–26 (this title is an exhibition catalogue). For a reference that demonstrates the persistence of Grant as the product of a republican government, see "Grant's Memoirs: Second Volume," *Atlantic Monthly* 58 (September 1886):419–20.

7. For Early's impact on the Lost Cause, see Connelly, *Marble Man*, 47–61, 73–78; Gary W. Gallagher, *Jubal A. Early, The Lost Cause, and Civil War History: A Persistent Legacy*, Frank L. Klement Lecture, No. 4 (Milwaukee: Marquette University Press, 1995); Gaines M. Foster, *Ghosts of the Confederacy: Defeat, the Lost Cause, and the Emergence of the New South* (New York: Oxford University Press, 1987), 50–62.

8. Gallagher, *Jubal A. Early*, 12–14; Jubal A. Early, *A Memoir of the Last Year of the War for Independence, in the Confederate States of America* (Toronto: Lovell & Gibson, 1866); J. A. Early to J. Randolph Tucker, February 22, 1866, Tucker Family Papers, Southern Historical Collection, Wilson Library, University of North Carolina, Chapel Hill.

9. For examples of linking memory of the war to political struggles, see Jeffrey J. Crow, "Thomas Settle Jr., Reconstruction, and the Memory of the Civil War," *Journal of Southern History* 47 (November 1996):689–726; David W. Blight, " 'For Something beyond the Battlefield': Frederick Douglass and the Struggle for the Memory of the Civil War," *Journal of American History* 75 (March 1989), 1156–1178; Foster, *Ghosts of the Confederacy*, 142, 194–96.

10. Adam Badeau, *Military Memoirs of Ulysses S. Grant*, 3 vols. (New York: D. Appleton, 1868–1882), 3:652.

11. For Grant's journey to the radical position, see his *Personal Memoirs*, 2:511–12.

12. For Virginia's political context and the rise of the Conservative Party, see Richard Lowe, *Republicans and Reconstruction in Virginia, 1865–70* (Charlottesville: University Press of Virginia, 1991), and Jack P. Maddex Jr., *The Virginia Conservatives, 1867–1879: A Study in Reconstruction Politics* (Chapel Hill: University of North Carolina Press, 1970).

13. Lynchburg *Virginian*, November 24, 25, 1870.

14. J. A. Early to Jefferson Davis, April 20, 1885, Jefferson Davis Papers, Howard-Tilton Library, Tulane University, New Orleans, La. For the persistence of Grant's image in this regard, see attempts to contradict the depiction in "General Grant's 'Magnanimity' at Appomattox," *Confederate Veteran* 17 (December 1909):596, and "Grant the Magnanimous," *Confederate Veteran* 34 (October 1926):365–66.

15. F. Lawley to Jubal A. Early, August 16, 1872, Jubal A. Early Papers, Library of Congress, Washington, D.C. (repository hereafter cited as LC). For a reprint of Lawley's article, see Gary W. Gallagher, ed., *Lee the Soldier* (Lincoln: University of Nebraska Press, 1996), 75–94.

16. Simon, *U. S. Grant: The Man and the Image*, 20–21; "Reply of Early to Letter of Badeau to London Standard," *SHSP* 2:6–21.

17. *SHSP* 2:7–9; William Preston Johnston to Jubal A. Early, March 2, 1871, Early Papers, LC.

18. *SHSP* 2:260–63.

19. William Swinton, *Campaigns of the Army of the Potomac: A Critical History of Operations in Virginia, Maryland and Pennsylvania from the Commencement to the Close of the War, 1861–5* (1866; new ed., New York: University Publishing Company, 1871), 406–8, 489–96; Grant, *Personal Memoirs*, 2:143–45; U. S. Grant, "Personal Memoirs," handwritten manuscript, microfilm reel 5, 1001, Ulysses S. Grant Papers, LC. To see the extensive use of Swinton in the battle of numbers, see McCabe's "Defence of Petersburg," *SHSP* 2: 256–306. For Grant's wartime inquiries about Swinton and the orders to exclude him, see U.S. War Department, *The War of the Rebellion: A Compilation of the Official Records of the Union and Confederate Armies* , 127 vols., index, and atlas (Washington, D.C.: GPO, 1880–1901), ser. 1, 40(2):559–60, 582 (hereafter cited as *OR*). For the assessment that Swinton "is not considered a friendly historian to Grant," see Edward Porter Alexander, *Fighting for the Confederacy: The Personal Recollections of General Edward Porter Alexander*, ed. Gary W. Gallagher (Chapel Hill: University of North Carolina Press, 1989), 407.

20. *SHSP* 5:227–39, 230 (quotation).

21. James Longstreet, *From Manassas to Appomattox: Memoirs of the Civil War in America* (1896; reprint, New York: Da Capo Press, 1983), 551.

22. *OR* 46(1):11; Swinton, *Campaigns of the Army of the Potomac*, 494.

23. U. S. Grant to Julia Dent, November 7, 1846, in Ulysses S. Grant, *The Papers of Ulysses S. Grant*, ed. John Y. Simon, 20 vols. to date (Carbondale: Southern Illinois University Press, 1967–), 1:117; language quip in Hattaway and Jones, *How the North Won*, 539; Badeau reference in Thomas M. Pitkin, *The Captain Departs: Ulysses S. Grant's Last Campaign* (Carbondale: Southern Illinois University Press, 1973), 10.

24. Grant, *Papers*, 20:320; Ulysses S. Grant to Adam Badeau, June 22, 1879, in Adam Badeau, *Grant in Peace: From Appomattox to Mount McGregor, a Personal Memoir* (Hartford, Conn.: S. S. Scranton & Co., 1887), 515. For an example of how Grant borrowed from Badeau's history the figures for the armies from Belmont through Chattanooga, see his handwritten note in the draft of the *Personal Memoirs* in the Grant Papers, reel 5, LC.

25. [A. K. McClure], ed., *The Annals of the War: Written by Leading Participants North and South* (Philadelphia: Times Publishing Company, 1879), 342–56, 484–501.

26. "Heroes of the War," republished in Philadelphia *Weekly Times*, August 3, 1878. Also see John Russell Young, *Around the World with General Grant* (New York: American News Company, 1879).

27. U. S. Grant to Adam Badeau, August 22, 1878, in Badeau, *Grant in Peace*, 504–5. For a current estimate on casualties that shows Swinton as being close to the mark, see McPherson, *Battle Cry of Freedom*, 741–42.

28. McFeely, *Grant*, 450–77; unidentified newspaper clipping dated February 14, 1879, microfilm reel 2, Grant Papers, LC.

29. Badeau, *Military History*, 3:651–52.

30. Pitkin, *The Captain Departs*, 1–7.

31. Grant, *Personal Memoirs*, 1:169–70.

32. Ibid., 132; Grant, "Personal Memoirs," handwritten manuscript, microfilm reel 5, 240–41, Grant Papers, LC.

33. Grant, *Personal Memoirs*, 2:289–91, 125–27, 178–80, 140–41 (quotation).

34. Ibid., 2:500–504, 502 (first quotation), 503 (second quotation).

35. For the claim that the Copperhead press served as "an auxiliary to the Confederate army," see ibid., 2:503.

36. For Lee's offer to resign, see R. E. Lee to Jefferson Davis, August 8, 1863, in R. E. Lee, *The Wartime Papers of R. E. Lee*, ed. Clifford Dowdey and Louis H. Manarin (Boston: Little, Brown, 1961), 589.

37. For the Sherman quotation and the assessment of politics on the Overland campaign, see Hattaway and Jones, *How the North Won*, 583 n. 75.

38. Grant, *Personal Memoirs*, 1:192.

39. Ibid., 2:197, 211–12, 193 (quotation).

40. Ibid., 2:244, 249–50.

41. Ibid., 2:271–72.

42. Ibid., 2:277. For the "Cold Harbor syndrome," see McPherson, *Battle Cry of Freedom*, 271.

43. Grant, *Personal Memoirs*, 2:273–76; McFeely, *Grant*, 171–73; Bruce Catton, *Grant Takes Command* (Boston: Little, Brown, 1968), 270–72.

44. Douglas Southall Freeman, *R. E. Lee: A Biography*, 4 vols. (New York: Charles Scribner's Sons, 1934–35), 3:392; Badeau, *Military History*, 2:310.

45. Grant, *Personal Memoirs*, 2:292.

46. William D. Matter, *If It Takes All Summer: The Battle of Spotsylvania* (Chapel Hill: University of North Carolina Press, 1988), 369–70. For Grant's account, see *Personal Memoirs*, 2:212–13.

47. Andrew A. Humphreys, *The Virginia Campaign of '64 and '65: The Army of the Potomac and the Army of the James* (1883; reprint, Wilmington, N.C.: Broadfoot, 1989), 67–70; Grant, *Personal Memoirs*, 2:385.

48. Badeau, *Grant in Peace*, 459–60.

49. *The Nation* 42 (February 25, 1886):174.

50. *New York Daily Tribune*, December 2, 1885.

51. *SHSP* 14:575, 13:359–60; J. A. Early to General Wm. H. Payne, August 4, 1885, Mss1 H9267a 5–10, Virginia Historical Society, Richmond.

52. *SHSP* 14:575–76.

53. Carswell McClellan, *The Personal Memoirs and Military History of U. S. Grant versus the Record of the Army of the Potomac* (Boston: Houghton Mifflin Company, 1887).

54. Ulysses S. Grant, *Personal Memoirs of Ulysses S. Grant*, 2 vols. (2nd ed., New York: Century, 1895), 2:71.

55. Wilson, *Patriotic Gore*, 132–33; Connelly, *Marble Man*, chap. 4; Nina Silber, *The Romance of Reunion: Northerners and the South, 1865–1900* (Chapel Hill: University of North Carolina Press, 1993), 108–9, 181–82.

56. For an early resurrection of Grant, see J. F. C. Fuller, *Grant and Lee: A Study of Personality and Generalship* (New York: Charles Scribner's Sons, 1933). The true renaissance began in the 1950s with studies such as Kenneth P. Williams, *Lincoln Finds a General: A Military Study of the Civil War*, 5 vols. (New York: Macmillan, 1949–52); Lloyd Lewis, *Captain Sam Grant* (Boston: Little, Brown, 1950); T. Harry Williams, *Lincoln and His Generals* (New York: Alfred Knopf, 1952). Finally, the 1960s saw Grant gaining greater recognition and emerging from Lincoln's shadow in such works as Wilson's *Patriotic Gore* and Bruce Catton's *Grant Moves South* (Boston: Little, Brown, 1960) and *Grant Takes Command*. Today, Grant has become prominent even in social histories of the war, described most recently as "Everyman" or the quintessential American in Phillip Shaw Paludan's *A People's Contest: The Union and Civil War, 1861–1865* (New York: Harper & Row, 1988), chap. 12.

57. Henry Adams to Henry James, May 6, 1908, in Henry Adams, *The Education of Henry Adams*, ed. Ernest Samuels (1918; reprint, Boston: Houghton Mifflin, 1973), 512–13.

Bibliographic Essay

Spotsylvania has received considerably less attention from historians and participant authors than battles such as Antietam or Chancellorsville (not to mention Gettysburg), but readers hoping to pursue the campaign in detail nevertheless will find many worthy titles. For a good sampling of published material, they should consult the notes accompanying these essays, wherein the authors cite, and sometimes evaluate, a wide range of titles.

The best source for printed primary material on Spotsylvania and the rest of the Overland campaign is U.S. War Department, *The War of the Rebellion: The Official Records of the Union and Confederate Armies*, 127 vols., index, and atlas (Washington: GPO, 1880–1901), ser. 1, vol. 36, pts. 1–3. Coverage of the respective armies regrettably is very unbalanced, however, as more than 90 percent of the reports, correspondence, and other documents in these volumes relate to the Federal army. Volume 6 of *Supplement to the Official Records of the Union and Confederate Armies*, ed. Janet B. Hewett and others, 42 of a projected 100 vols. published to date (Wilmington, N.C.: Broadfoot, 1994–), contains additional material about both armies, including a number of official reports from important Confederate officers.

Invaluable Confederate testimony about Spotsylvania is in J. William Jones and others, eds., *Southern Historical Society Papers*, 52 vols. (1876–1959; reprint, with 3-vol. index, Wilmington, N.C.: Broadfoot, 1990–92); *Confederate Veteran*, 40 vols. (1893–1932; reprint, with 3-vol. index, Wilmington, N.C.: Broadfoot, 1984–86), and Walter Clark, ed., *Histories of the Several Regiments and Battalions from North Carolina in the Great War 1861–'65*, 5 vols. (Raleigh: E. M. Uzzell, Printer and Binder, 1901). For comparable Union material, readers should consult the *Papers* of the Military Order of the Loyal Legion of the United States, 66 vols. and 3-vol. index (Wilmington, N.C.: Broadfoot, 1991–96). Read before the state commanderies of the MOLLUS, many of these papers shed light on Spotsylvania. Additional useful testimony from former Federals and Confederates is in vol. 4 of *Papers of the Military Historical Society of Massachusetts*, 14 vols. (1895–1918; reprint in 15 vols. with a general index, Wilmington, N.C.: Broadfoot, 1989–90), and vol. 4 of *Battles and Leaders of the Civil War*, ed. Robert Underwood Johnson and Clarence Clough Buel, 4 vols. (New York: Century, 1887).

The best scholarly treatments of Spotsylvania are William D. Matter's *If It Takes All Summer: The Battle of Spotsylvania* (Chapel Hill: University of North Carolina Press, 1989), which is especially thorough on the Federal side, and Gordon C. Rhea's *The Battles for Spotsylvania Court House and the Road to Yellow Tavern: May 7–12, 1864* (Baton Rouge: Louisiana State University Press, 1997), which covers the period May 7–12 and accords approximately equal attention to Confederates and Federals. A projected second volume will extend Rhea's treatment through the end of the campaign. A pair of more general titles containing long sections on Spotsylvania are Noah Andre Trudeau's unannotated but impressively researched *Bloody Roads South: The Wilderness to Cold Harbor, May–June 1864* (Boston: Little, Brown, 1989) and Clifford Dowdey's compellingly written and unabashedly pro-Confederate *Lee's*

Last Campaign: The Story of Lee and His Men against Grant—1864 (Boston: Little, Brown, 1960). Andrew A. Humphreys's *The Virginia Campaign of '64 and '65: The Army of the Potomac and the Army of the James* (New York: Charles Scribner's Sons, 1883) stands out among narratives by participants. Humphreys approached his task with the instincts of a scholar, using records from the War Department as well as correspondence with officers from both sides who had been at Spotsylvania to produce a book of lasting significance.

For the Union high command at Spotsylvania, vol. 10 of *The Papers of Ulysses S. Grant*, ed. John Y. Simon (Carbondale: Southern Illinois University Press, 1982), includes letters and telegrams that illuminate the general-in-chief's decisions and actions. Grant's *Personal Memoirs of U. S. Grant*, 2 vols. (New York: Charles L. Webster, 1885), include his essential and entertaining, but scarcely even-handed, postwar interpretations. George Gordon Meade Jr., *The Life and Letters of George Gordon Meade*, 2 vols. (New York: Charles Scribner's Sons, 1913), sheds considerable light on Meade's accommodation to his reduced role as Grant took increasing control of the Army of the Potomac during the Overland campaign. Philip H. Sheridan's *Personal Memoirs of P. H. Sheridan*, 2 vols. (New York: Charles L. Webster, 1888), by turns bombastic and revealing, almost perfectly reflects the character of its author.

Robert E. Lee never wrote his memoirs, but letters and other documents relating to Spotsylvania are in *The Wartime Papers of R. E. Lee*, ed. Clifford Dowdey and Louis H. Manarin (Boston: Little, Brown, 1961). For Lee's pointed postwar comments about Richard S. Ewell's generalship, see William Allan, "Memoranda of Conversations with General Robert E. Lee," in *Lee the Soldier*, ed. Gary W. Gallagher (Lincoln: University of Nebraska Press, 1996). Walter Taylor, *Lee's Adjutant: The Wartime Letters of Colonel Walter Herron Taylor, 1862–1865*, ed. R. Lockwood Taylor (Columbia: University of South Carolina Press, 1995), offers an excellent perspective through the eyes of a member of Lee's staff. Of the Confederate corps commanders at Spotsylvania, only Jubal Early wrote about the campaign. His *Lieutenant General Jubal Anderson Early, C.S.A.: Autobiographical Sketch and Narrative of the War between the States* (Philadelphia: Lippincott, 1912) is a straightforward, useful account.

Only a handful of the myriad biographical studies pertinent to Spotsylvania can be mentioned. The respective army commanders are best explored through a pair of venerable, and sympathetic, titles: Bruce Catton's *Grant Takes Command* (Boston: Little, Brown, 1969) and Douglas Southall Freeman's *R. E. Lee: A Biography*, 4 vols. (New York: Charles Scribner's Sons, 1934–35). Although somewhat thinly researched, Freeman Cleaves, *Meade of Gettysburg* (Norman: University of Oklahoma Press, 1960), remains the standard life of Grant's principal lieutenant at Spotsylvania. Other worthwhile biographies include Emory M. Thomas's *Bold Dragoon: The Life of J. E. B. Stuart* (New York: Harper & Row, 1986); Donald Pfanz's massively researched *Richard S. Ewell: A Soldier's Life* (Chapel Hill: University of North Carolina Press, 1998); William Marvel's revisionist *Burnside* (Chapel Hill: University of North Carolina Press, 1991); David M. Jordan's *Winfield Scott Hancock: A Soldier's Life* (Bloomington: Indiana University Press, 1988); Roy Morris Jr.'s *Sheridan: The Life and Wars of General Phil Sheridan* (New York: Crown, 1992); and Emerson Gifford Taylor's *Gouverneur Kemble Warren: The Life and Letters of an American Soldier, 1830–1882* (Boston: Houghton Mifflin, 1932).

As with all Civil War operations, some of the most valuable published material on Spotsylvania is in the form of letters, diaries, and reminiscences. Among the best Union sources are artillerist Charles S. Wainwright's *A Diary of Battle: The Personal Journals of Colonel Charles S. Wainwright, 1861–1865*, ed. Allan Nevins (New York: Harcourt, Brace & World,

1962), and Theodore Lyman's *Meade's Headquarters 1863–1865: Letters of Colonel Theodore Lyman from the Wilderness to Appomattox*, ed. George R. Agassiz (Boston: Atlantic Monthly Press, 1922). For the common soldier's point of view about the campaign, Wilbur Fisk's *Hard Marching Every Day: The Civil War Letters of Private Wilbur Fisk, 1861–1865*, ed. Emil and Ruth Rosenblatt (Lawrence: University Press of Kansas, 1992 [originally published privately as *Anti-Rebel: The Civil War Letters of Wilbur Fisk*]), is exceptional. Also noteworthy is John W. Haley's *The Rebel Yell & the Yankee Hurrah: The Civil War Journal of a Maine Volunteer*, ed. Ruth L. Silliker (Camden, Me.: Down East Books, 1985).

Among Confederate accounts, Edward Porter Alexander's *Military Memoirs of a Confederate: A Critical Narrative* (New York: Charles Scribner's Sons, 1907) and *Fighting for the Confederacy: The Personal Recollections of General Edward Porter Alexander*, ed. Gary W. Gallagher (Chapel Hill: University of North Carolina Press, 1989), are unexcelled in terms of dispassionate analysis. One of the most riveting personal accounts of the fighting at the Bloody Angle is David Holt, *A Mississippi Rebel in the Army of Northern Virginia: The Civil War Memoirs of Private David Holt*, ed. Thomas D. Cockrell and Michael B. Ballard (Baton Rouge: Louisiana State University Press, 1995). J. Tracy Powers's *Lee's Miserables: Life in the Army of Northern Virginia from the Wilderness to Appomattox* (Chapel Hill: University of North Carolina Press, 1998) draws on, and quotes liberally from, a mass of unpublished manuscript evidence to explore in great detail the actions and attitudes of Confederate soldiers.

For photographs relating to Spotsylvania, readers should consult William A. Frassanito, *Grant and Lee: The Virginia Campaigns, 1864–1865* (New York: Charles Scribner's Sons, 1983). As with his earlier books on Gettysburg and Antietam, Frassanito placed modern photographs alongside period views of numerous sites and provided a useful analytical text. Other illustrative material may be found in Gregory Jaynes and the Editors of Time-Life Books, *The Killing Ground: Wilderness to Cold Harbor* (Alexandria, Va.: Time-Life Books, 1986).

Finally, three general works deserve the attention of anyone interested in Spotsylvania. Herman Hattaway and Archer Jones, *How the North Won: A Military History of the Civil War* (Urbana: University of Illinois Press, 1983), places the battle within the larger strategic picture of the Overland campaign and the war in the Eastern Theater. The third volume of Douglas Southall Freeman, *Lee's Lieutenants: A Study in Command*, 3 vols. (New York: Charles Scribner's Sons, 1942–44), describes and analyzes Confederate leadership in memorable prose, and Bruce Catton's *A Stillness at Appomattox* (Garden City, N.Y.: Doubleday, 1953) employs comparably distinguished writing to cover the Army of the Potomac's activities.

Contributors

William A. Blair is a member of the Department of History at the University of North Carolina at Greensboro. His publications include *A Politician Goes to War: The Civil War Letters of John White Geary*, a forthcoming study of the Virginia home front during the Civil War, and several articles and essays on Civil War–era subjects.

Peter S. Carmichael is a member of the Department of History at Western Carolina University. The author of *Lee's Young Artillerist: William R. J. Pegram*, as well as several essays and articles in popular and scholarly journals, he is completing a study of Virginia slaveholders' sons and the formation of southern identity in the late antebellum years.

Gary W. Gallagher is a member of the Department of History at Pennsylvania State University and editor of the Civil War America series at the University of North Carolina Press. He has edited *The Third Day at Gettysburg and Beyond*; *The Fredericksburg Campaign: Decision on the Rappahannock*; *Chancellorsville: The Battle and Its Aftermath*; and *The Wilderness Campaign*, four previous titles in the Military Campaigns of the Civil War series.

Robert E. L. Krick, a Richmond-based historian, was reared on the Chancellorsville battlefield. The author of *The Fortieth Virginia Infantry* and a number of essays and articles, he is completing a biographical register of the staff officers of the Army of Northern Virginia.

Robert K. Krick grew up in California but has lived and worked on the Virginia battlefields for more than twenty years. He has written dozens of articles and ten books, the most recent being *Stonewall Jackson at Cedar Mountain* and *Conquering the Valley: Stonewall Jackson at Port Republic*.

William D. Matter is a retired U.S. Air Force pilot who lives in Harrisburg, Pennsylvania. His publications include *If It Takes All Summer: The Battle of Spotsylvania* and several articles on Civil War military topics.

Carol Reardon is the military historian at Pennsylvania State University and a former holder of the Harold Keith Johnson Visiting Professorship in Military History at the U.S. Army Military History Institute and U.S. Army War College. She is the author of *Soldiers and Scholars: The U.S. Army and the Uses of Military History, 1865–1920*; *Pickett's Charge in History and Memory*, and numerous essays in the fields of Civil War and military history.

Gordon C. Rhea is an attorney who resides in Mt. Pleasant, South Carolina. He is the author of *The Battle of the Wilderness: May 5–6, 1864*; *The Battles for Spotsylvania Court House and the Road to Yellow Tavern: May 7–12, 1864*; and several essays on Civil War military history.

Index

Belle Plain, Va., 47

Bennet, Newton L., 110

Berdan's Sharpshooters, 164 (n. 44)

Bierce, Ambrose, 218

Birney, David B., 48, 50

Blackford, Eugene, 183

Blackford, William W., 157, 168 (n. 75), 190

Black Hills, 62

Blackwood's Edinburgh Magazine, 230

Blair, William A., xiv

"Bloody Angle," x, xi, xii, xiii, 51, 52, 73, 80–126, 148, 157, 179, 181, 182, 183, 184, 203, 208, 211, 212, 214; as a focal point of fighting at Spotsylvania, x, xi, 190, 191; memorialized by veterans, 214–19, 222 (n. 34); oak tree at, 101, 102, 106, 109, 110, 121 (n. 57), 124 (nn. 84–86)

"Bloody Lane," 80

"The Bonnie Blue Flag" (song), 91

Boteler, Alexander R., 157, 158

Bragg, Braxton, 138–40, 144, 154–56

Brandy Station, 127

Bratton, John, 111

Breathed, James, 144, 147

Bristoe Station, 9, 62, 93

Brockman, Benjamin T., 99, 120 (n. 50)

Brock Road, 36, 38, 40, 45, 46, 52, 55, 57, 67, 69, 71, 81, 123 (n. 78), 205, 206, 214, 245

Brook Church, 149

Brook Run, 149

Brook Turnpike, 138, 149, 154, 163 (n. 28), 167 (n. 67)

Brown, Benjamin F., 118 (n. 29)

Brown, Charles, 185

Brown, G. Campbell, 18, 89, 115 (n. 7)

Brown, Henry W., 205, 206

Brown, John, 142

Brown, Joseph N., 102, 107, 110, 111, 113, 115 (n. 5), 122 (n. 68), 123 (n. 69), 126 (n. 99)

Brown, Varina, 115 (n. 5)

Brown house, 38, 42, 45, 46, 48, 50

Bruce, Robert, 146

Bryant, James F., 196

"Buckland Races," 127

Burgess, W. W., 161 (n. 5)

Burnside, Ambrose E., xi, 29, 31, 37–39, 43–48, 51–54, 56–58, 73, 80

Butler, Benjamin F., 128, 149, 157

Caesar, Julius: *Commentaries*, 223, 245

Camden, Edward D., 86

Carmichael, Peter S., xiii, xiv

Carson, Wat, 135

Carter, Thomas H., 81, 114

Carter, William R., 147

Cavalry tactics, xii, xiii, 31, 158, 159

Cavendish, Charles, 157, 168 (n. 72)

Cemetery Hill, 14, 57

Cemetery Ridge, 57

Century Magazine, 239

Chancellorsville campaign, ix, 8, 13, 22, 27 (n. 33), 205, 213

Chapman, George H., 144, 147

Chapman's cavalry brigade (Army of the Potomac), 144, 150

Chapultepec, battle of, 239

Chase, Emily. *See* Warren, Emily Chase

Chattanooga, Tenn., 240

Cheek, William H., 137

Chickahominy River, 145, 147, 148–51, 153, 156, 157

Chilesburg, Va., 128, 131, 134

Civil War centennial, 249

"Clarke Cavalry" (Company D, 6th Virginia Cavalry), 145

Clyburn, Thomas F., 107

Coehorn mortars, 105

Cold Harbor, Va., ix, 67, 197, 232, 235, 249; Federal losses at, 243; Grant's postwar statements about, 243, 244

Cold Spring, N.Y., 61

Columbia Hebrew Benevolent Society Cemetery, 112

"Combat refusal," 189

Comstock, Cyrus B., 47, 48, 51

Confederacy: internal dissension, 242; mobilization of manpower, 241; support for among white populace, 241

Confederate Congress, 8

Conservative Party, 229

36, 38, 42, 43, 45, 46, 54, 55, 57, 64, 66, 67, 70, 73, 75, 174, 185, 205, 207, 208

Skoch, George, xiv

Sleep deprivation, 179

Smith, Martin L., 6, 81, 114 (n. 2), 197

Smith, William, 184

Somerset County, N.J., 205, 214

Sorrel, Moxley, 20

South Anna River, 134, 135, 136

South Carolina troops: 1st Infantry, 95, 99, 100, 112, 121 (n. 51), 123 (n. 78); 12th Infantry, 95, 99, 100, 112; 13th Infantry, 95, 99, 102, 110; 14th Infantry, 95, 99, 102, 106, 110, 113; Hart's Battery, 164; Orr's Rifles, 95, 99

Southern Historical Society, 227, 247

Spanish American War, 218, 219

Spear, Ellis, 188

Spencer carbines, 148

Spindle farm, 68, 69, 74, 123

Spotsylvania campaign, ix, x, xi, 5, 8, 11, 15, 20, 22, 23, 55, 176–97; overall casualties, ix, x, xiv, xv, 237; postwar remembrances of, xiii, 204, 211–20, 224, 225, 232, 235, 243, 245; results of, ix, 56, 58; terrain of, 6, 7

Spotsylvania Court House, ix, 16, 31, 33, 37, 38, 43, 47, 55, 58, 67, 69, 76, 80, 81, 95, 128, 129, 131, 132, 211, 213–15, 225

Stafford, Leroy, 19, 86

Stafford's Louisiana brigade, 19, 86, 87

Stanton, Edwin M., 232

Stepp, Tisdale, 91

Steuart, George H., 86, 87

Steuart's Virginia and North Carolina brigade, 86, 116 (n. 16)

Stevens, Walter H., 81, 114 (n. 2)

Stockett, Peter, 101

Stokes, Edward C., 214

Stonewall Brigade, 84, 85, 87, 196

Strawberry Hill, 153, 154

Stuart, J. E. B., xii, 19, 32, 33, 127, 129, 131–40, 142–48, 153, 159, 161 (n. 4); death of, 157–59, 164 (nn. 41, 44), 165 (nn. 45, 47), 168 (n. 75), 193; monument to at Yellow Tavern, 159, 160, 168 (n. 78)

Sumner, J. B., 98

Sussex County, N.J., 205

Swan, William W., 67

Swayze, Theodore F., 213, 217, 218

Swinton, William, x, 234

Swittenberg, A. M., 98

Taylor, Richard, 238

Taylor, Walter, 8; comments on Lee's generalship, 20, 21

Taylorsville, Va., 134, 137

Telegraph Road, 133, 134, 138–40, 142–45, 147, 148, 160, 164 (n. 38), 165 (nn. 44, 47)

Terry, William, 84

Texas Brigade, 96

Texas troops: 1st Infantry, 187

Third Corps (Army of Northern Virginia), 5, 8, 9, 11, 17, 19, 20, 24, 37, 66

Third Corps (Army of the Potomac), 174

Third Division, Cavalry Corps (Army of the Potomac), 33

Third Division, Second Corps (Army of the Potomac), 48

Tiller, George W., 86

Tilton's Brigade (Army of the Potomac), 179

Todd's Tavern, 31, 33, 36, 38, 46, 67, 68, 214

Traveller (Lee's horse), 95, 96

Tredegar Battalion, 153

Trinity Church, 134

Tunis, Nehemiah, 206

Turner's Run, 143, 144, 145, 148

U.S. Army Corps of Topographical Engineers, 62

U.S. Colored Troops, 33

U.S. Engineers, 6, 40, 41

U.S. Horse Artillery, 2nd: Battery D, 143

U.S. Regular Army, 56

U.S. Senate, 45

Upton, Emory, 41–43, 45, 205, 208

Upton's attack, 41–43, 45, 81, 182, 207

Valley campaign of 1862, 13

Van Blarcom, Lewis, 206

Van Voy, William, 206

Wright's brigade (Army of Northern Virginia), 12, 26

Yellowstone River, 62
Yellow Tavern, xii, 19, 136–39, 144, 145, 148, 162; battle at, 140–48, 156, 157, 158, 163

(n. 28), 166 (n. 50), 193; development of battlefield, 169 (n. 78)
Yorktown, Va., 174
Young, John R., 237, 241, 244
Young, Samuel, 206